Marcelle
Merry Christmas
Happy fresh cooking
Enjoy, Love Robin & Michelle

ENJOY COOKING

west coast
seafood !

west coast seafood

THE COMPLETE COOKBOOK

JAY HARLOW

SASQUATCH BOOKS
SEATTLE

Text copyright ©1999 by Jay Harlow
Photographs copyright ©1999 by Angie Norwood Browne
All rights reserved. No portion of this book may be reproduced or utilized in any form, or by any electronic, mechanical, or other means without the prior written permission of the publisher.

Printed in the United States of America.
Distributed in Canada by Raincoast Books Ltd.
03 02 01 00 99   5 4 3 2 1

Cover and interior design: Kate Basart
Cover and interior photographs: Angie Norwood Browne
Interior illustrations: Dan McClain

Library of Congress Cataloging in Publication Data
Harlow, Jay, 1953–
        West Coast seafood : the complete cookbook / Jay Harlow.
                p.   cm.
        ISBN 1-57061-170-X
        1. Cookery (Seafood) 2. Seafood—Pacific Coast (U.S.) I. Title.
        TX747.H347   1999
        641.6'92—dc21   99-27058

SASQUATCH BOOKS
615 Second Avenue
Seattle, Washington 98104
(206) 467-4300
books@SasquatchBooks.com
www.SasquatchBooks.com

contents

full-flavored fish

sturgeon, catfish, shad & other freshwater fish

shellfish, part I:
crab, shrimp & lobster

shellfish, part II:
oysters, mussels, clams, scallops, abalone & squid

sauces

recipes

salmon & trout

halibut, sole & other flatfish

lean, mild & white fish

sturgeon, catfish, shad & other freshwater fish

shellfish, part I: crab, shrimp & lobster

shellfish, part II:
oysters, mussels, clams, scallops, abalone & squid

sauces

Acknowledgments

This book draws on nearly two decades of cooking with and writing about seafood, and to thank everyone who contributed in one way or another to my understanding of the subject would mean either adding a lot of pages or cutting several recipes. The list of people who have provided information and/or inspiration would easily run into the hundreds, probably thousands. So if I haven't mentioned your name, I hope you will recognize yourself among one of the following groups.

First, the fishermen (of both genders; forgive me if I can't quite get used to the term fishers) and aquaculturists who provide us with the delicious raw materials, often at great personal or financial risk. Without their work there would be no point to a seafood cookbook. Zeke Grader of the Pacific Coast Federation of Fishermens' Associations, Diane Pleschner of the California Seafood Council, and Barbara Belknap of the Alaska Seafood Marketing Institute have been especially helpful through the years.

Second, those seafood wholesalers and retailers who work so hard to provide a reliable supply of seafood in a most unpredictable business, and still manage to maintain their standards of quality. In particular, thanks to Paul Johnson, Tom Worthington, Kim Steele, and all the staff of Monterey Fish; Ted Iijima of Berkeley Bowl Seafood; shellfish maven Bill Marinelli; and Jon Rowley, who has worked in many aspects of the business and is always ready to share his knowledge of seafood.

Third, the public servants in the various state, provincial, and federal agencies concerned with our seafood supply. No matter what they do, someone will be unhappy, but I have to believe that we are all interested in the same goals: sustainable fisheries and scientifically sound processes that supply safe, high-quality seafood now and into the future. Special thanks to Lily Dong and Dr. Susan Loscutoff of the California Department of Health Services, and to Bob Price and Pamela Tom of the U.C. Davis Sea Grant program.

Fourth, the chefs who work with seafood day in and day out, balancing tradition and innovation, preserving and reinterpreting the classics while creating and refining new ones. Despite the old cliche of the chef shielding the pot from view while adding the secret seasonings, I have found most chefs very generous in sharing recipes, tips, and sources of ingredients. Your influence is felt far beyond your own dining rooms.

Fifth, my fellow cooking teachers and food writers. No cook works in a vacuum. When new ingredients, ideas, and cooking methods are introduced, experimented with, tossed around, used (and misused), and eventually understood, they become part of our common cooking vocabulary, and we are all richer for it. My hat is off particularly to those who have the ability to travel, to immerse themselves in other cultures and learn about their cuisines in context, then share the results with the rest of us. My own cooking style has definitely benefitted from the work of Paula Wolfert on Moroccan and other Mediterranean cuisines; Diana Kennedy and Rick Bayless on Mexican cooking; Mark Miller on chiles; and Barbara Tropp on Chinese food. And to Harold McGee, who helps all of us understand the science behind the art of cooking.

Thanks also to the newspaper and magazine editors who have provided me with a platform to share what I have learned through the years, and helped me express it: Jo Mancuso, Michael Bauer, Mary Ann Mariner, Cynthia Nims, Martha Holmberg, and Sally Bernstein.

At Sasquatch Books, thanks to my editor Gary Luke and to Kate Basart, Sarah Smith, Kim Foster, Justine Matthies, and Aley Mills. Also to photographer Angie Norwood Browne, food stylist Patty Wittmann, and illustrator Dan McClain.

And finally, to my wife, Elaine, loving and supportive partner in everything important in my life. Elaine has eaten far more seafood than she might have chosen over the years, and never hesitates to give me her honest opinion, up or down. And to our daughter, Rebecca, who loved squid the first time she tried it but as of this writing still doesn't like asparagus. She'll come around in time.

Introduction:

Seafood, West Coast Style

As recently as the mid-1970s, shopping for salmon in a West Coast fish market was fairly simple. Fresh salmon were available from late spring to early fall, mostly chinooks or "kings" early in the season, and later cohos and perhaps some "silverbright" chums toward the end. From late October until the next spring, your main choice in salmon was between frozen and canned. A lot has changed since then. By the early 1980s, Norwegian salmon, raised on farms and available fresh in the winter, effectively ended the concept of a fresh salmon season. Today many wild salmon stocks on the Pacific Coast have plummeted and qualify for endangered-species protection, while others are robust and support record catches. Alaska salmon processors who used to sell most of their catch to Japan are increasingly looking to consumers in the Lower 48, but they have to compete with inexpensive farmed salmon, either locally grown or imported from as far away as Chile.

While salmon is a fitting symbol of the fishing industry on the Pacific Coast, it's only one of many fisheries that are undergoing dramatic changes. From snow crab in Alaska to farmed mussels in Puget Sound to sardines in Southern California, West Coast seafood is in a state of flux, with the supply of some species on the way up as others become scarce.

The main focus of this book is the commercially available fish and shellfish of the Pacific Coast from Alaska to Baja California, including fish caught commercially in rivers draining into the Pacific and farmed in the same region. Most of the region, from Alaska to central California, is characterized by cold ocean waters; typical seafoods of this zone include salmon, crab, halibut, herring, and oysters. The warmer waters off Southern California and Mexico (roughly south of Point Conception, near Santa Barbara) are home to other species, including tuna, swordfish, sardines, spiny lobster, and squid. The boundary between the zones changes from year to year with subtle changes in ocean temperature. Swordfish routinely migrate up and down the coast from Mexico to Washington, and in El Niño years subtropical fish like barracuda may show up off San Francisco.

Also covered in this book are some fish from Hawaii and other Pacific islands, which send a lot of fish to our area, as well as imports from other places that are widely available and firmly established in the cuisine of the region: yellowfin tuna, warmwater shrimp, Atlantic lobster, southern catfish, and Chilean sea bass.

Since the first Ice Age humans arrived from Asia over the Bering land bridge, the Pacific Coast of North America has absorbed wave after wave of immigrants, and their food traditions. Prehistoric shellmounds in many coastal areas testify to the importance of oysters and other shellfish to the earliest inhabitants. Native Americans smoked, salted, and dried salmon and other fish, a technique that survives in the traditional beach bake (split salmon spread on a wood frame to cook in front of a fire) and its modern descendant, planked fish. The area's rich natural resources attracted Europeans, including many from Scandinavia and the British Isles who became the first commercial fishermen. Later they were joined by immigrants from Portugal, Sicily, Yugoslavia, and other Mediterranean countries, with their traditions of charcoal-grilled fish and tomato-based fish soups. Asian immigrants, first from China, then Japan and the Philippines, brought soy sauce and ginger into the American mainstream via the Pacific Coast, and later waves from Indochina and Thailand are doing the same with lemongrass and Thai basil, now widely available in farmers' markets, if not in your supermarket. Migrant farm workers were spreading Mexican foods and flavors throughout the West long before there were national taco chains. Migrant and wartime workers from other parts of America, especially the Deep South, have made it easy to find Memphis-style barbecue and Louisiana gumbo in any city in the region.

The Pacific Coast is rich in many food resources beyond seafood. Much of the region enjoys a Mediterranean climate, with dry summers and rainy, cool but not frigid winters. Coastal and inland valleys provide microclimates and soil types needed to produce nearly every kind of fruit, vegetable, and grain, from citrus and avocados in Southern California to apples from the vast orchards of inland

Washington and British Columbia. European grape varieties produce world-class wines, and a new generation of brewers make abundant use of Northwestern hops in their beers and ales.

In the increasingly multicultural world of the West Coast, we are all growing more familiar with each other's food traditions. Many people with no Mediterranean ancestry are leaning toward the "Mediterranean diet," with its emphasis on vegetables, fruits, grains, and olive oil (and more seafood than red meat). Latin American foods have grown steadily in popularity, and not just among Hispanics; in the 1990s salsa passed ketchup as America's favorite condiment. Young Asian-Americans happily devour pizza and quesadillas, while Anglo-Saxon chefs travel to Japan, China, and Thailand to learn more about Asian ingredients and techniques.

Labels like "East-West," "Pacific Rim cuisine," and "fusion cuisine" are attempts to capture the essence of this ongoing evolution of West Coast foodways. The old image of the melting pot is giving way to a tossed salad, or an international buffet: In typically American fashion, we incorporate something from here, something from there into our cooking style, sometimes with great respect for tradition and sometimes in total disregard of the old rules. The results are not always successful, but sometimes brilliant, and rarely boring.

Seafood is often at the center of this culinary evolution, and today's changing seafood market offers the home cook both new challenges and new opportunities. The challenge includes knowing how best to cook fish that look and sound similar but differ widely in flavor and fat content. Increased variety means learning about new and unfamiliar species of fish and shellfish, but it also gives the informed cook many more ways to prepare delicious, healthful seafood meals.

I feel fortunate to be living here and now, and for the opportunity to work with all these wonderful ingredients, learn from other cooks and other cultures, and develop my own favorites. And I am delighted to be able to share what I have learned with you, in the recipes and information in this book. I hope you find it helpful in your own exploration of seafood, West Coast style.

seafood
cookery basics

Shopping for Seafood

Seafood is available in lots of places: specialty fish markets, supermarkets (either from a service seafood counter or cut and wrapped in the self-serve case), small independent markets, farmers' markets, and sometimes directly from the producers. Wherever you buy, you can learn to use your own senses to get the best each source has to offer.

The first cues are visual. While experienced fish buyers know how to spot a few particular keys to quality (some of which are described below and in the recipe chapters), it doesn't take a practiced eye to see the difference between a moist, glistening fresh fish and a dull, dry, tired-looking one, or between the bright surface of freshly cut fillets and steaks and the flat, browning appearance of those that have been sitting around for days.

Before you even look at the seafood, take a look around the store. Are the surfaces clean? Is the seafood well chilled, either with ice or refrigeration or both? Is the fish protected from sunlight, flies, dust? Do the other fresh foods (meats, produce) look fresh and inviting? Is the store busy, so it turns over its stock rapidly?

Touch is another sense you can use in judging fish, at least some of the time. Where whole fish are laid out on tables, a gentle push with a fingertip can tell you a lot about the condition of a fish; some fish are naturally firmer than others, but any fresh fish should feel resilient rather than mushy. Fillets and steaks are another matter; you probably won't get the chance to handle them except through the package.

Follow your nose as well, from the time you walk into the fish market or seafood section of the supermarket. If there is a strong fishy smell in the air, it is coming from either fish that is too old or equipment and surfaces that are not cleaned well enough or often enough. That's not to say there is no good seafood to be found here, but be on your guard.

When in any doubt about freshness, sniff the seafood itself. If this seems inappropriate, there are various surreptitious ways to go about it. If the fish is being weighed on a countertop scale, stand as close as possible to the scale; in a market with fish laid out on open-topped tables of ice, you can bend over the fish a bit as you inspect it. Either way, you should be able to get your nose close enough to the fish to spot a bad one without being too obvious. If you are too shy to do any of these, but still have suspicions, or if you are buying prepackaged seafood from a self-service case, open the package right outside the market, and if it doesn't smell right, march back inside for a replacement or a refund.

Get to know the specialties of different markets. A box of iced mackerel on the floor of a little ethnic market may turn out to be the freshest mackerel in town, and chances are it will all be gone by midafternoon.

If you shop regularly in the same markets, get in the habit of cruising by the seafood counter every time you shop, even when you aren't specifically shopping for seafood. Look to see how the selection changes from week to week. If the same items appear all the time, chances are the seafood buyer is not very knowledgeable or adventurous. A constantly changing selection indicates a buyer who is at least trying to keep up with the day-to-day variations in the wholesale market.

When you find a retailer you like, make yourself known as a customer. Don't be afraid to ask questions: "Where is this fish from?" "I've never tried _____ before; how should I cook it? How does it compare to _____ ?" "Have you tasted these oysters lately?" "I'm looking for something to grill/bake/poach/steam—what would you recommend?" Of course, you have to be willing to try their recommendations at least some of the time. And be sure to give your fishmonger feedback: "I really loved that sockeye salmon you had last week—will you be getting any more?" "The yellowtail was a little strong for my family's taste; next time I'd like something milder." Share your recipe ideas, what works and what doesn't. Make your preferences known: If you want more local fish, more fresh fish, more frozen fish, if you prefer white shrimp to tiger, if you wish they would cut their swordfish steaks thicker or thinner, their portions larger or smaller, speak up!

The following is a rundown of the commonly available forms of fish and shellfish, and how to shop for each.

LIVE FISH One of the distinguishing features of a Chinese fish market is a large aquarium-style tank (usually several tanks) of water containing live fish and shellfish. To the Chinese trade, and to a lesser extent in some other ethnic markets, live fish and shellfish are the standard of freshness, and everything else is seen as a lesser alternative. This attitude has been slower to take hold in Western fish markets, where typically only lobster and crab are kept in live tanks, but it may become more common in the future.

The principle of live shipment and storage is simple: As long as the animal is alive, its own immune system is at work defending it from the bacteria inside and all around it. Once it dies, the process of decay begins, although it can be minimized by prompt chilling and holding the fish at low temperatures. In a good live market, any fish that die in the tanks are promptly removed and iced, to be sold at a lower price.

Most farmed freshwater fish can be shipped live to market and held in tanks: catfish, trout, tilapia, carp, striped and black bass, even small sturgeon. Wild-caught rockfish, lingcod, and similar species delivered alive are becoming more and more common in Asian markets. In some cases, local or state fish and game laws prevent live shipment of certain species that would become pests if accidentally or intentionally released into the wild.

When buying live fish, first look at the condition of the tanks and the water inside. The less crowding, and the cleaner and more aerated the water, the better. The fish should be active rather than sluggish. Avoid fish with open wounds or skin lesions, and certainly any floating listlessly or upside down.

Once you have chosen your fish in the tank, or at least a group of similar fish any of which will do, the fishmonger should retrieve it from the tank with a net and kill and clean it for you.

First he or she will stun the fish with a quick blow to the head, then weigh it and calculate the price (prices are always based on the live weight). Cleaning in a Chinese market usually consists of scaling (except scaleless varieties like catfish) and gutting only. Some fishmongers trim the fins of fish, but the head is usually left on because most customers want it. (If you don't want the head, you might as well have them remove it. If it is big enough, they will likely sell it to another customer for soup—better all around than having it go in the trash.)

LIVE SHELLFISH Bivalve shellfish (clams, mussels, oysters) and abalone are typically sold alive. Here, the issue is one of safety as well as aesthetics. In as little as a few hours, depending on the temperature, bacteria inside the shell of a dead oyster or mussel can multiply to dangerous levels. Live bivalves should be tightly closed, or close when handled; see Storing Seafood, page 8, for how to maintain them in a live state.

Crabs and lobsters are the most commonly sold live crustaceans, but saltwater tanks of live shrimp, a common sight in Hong Kong and other Asian cities, have begun to appear in better Chinese restaurants and markets in this country. Crayfish are also sold alive in season, though usually not in tanks; they can live for several days refrigerated in mesh bags. With any live crustaceans, choose lively, feisty ones over listless ones.

ROUND FISH In seafood terms, "round" (or sometimes "in the round") describes an intact fish just as it came out of the water. Some fish can be stored this way for a few days without suffering in quality, but others, especially the more predatory varieties such as salmon and trout, need to be gutted soon after killing to keep them in good condition. Within hours after death, the powerful stomach acids and digestive enzymes of these fish, which were kept under control by chemical buffers while the fish was alive, begin to attack the fish's own tissues, eventually reaching the surrounding meat. (See **DRESSED FISH** below.)

In any fish, the uncontrolled growth of bacteria in the gut will eventually cause spoilage of flavor, aroma, and texture. Ironically, many fish are sold round as a guarantee of freshness: As long as the bellies are firm, the fish is fresh; too-old specimens will be given away by bloated or soft bellies.

Some of the criteria for judging round fish have been discussed above. Look for a glistening appearance and bright eyes. Lift the gill cover (or ask the fishmonger to do it for you) to inspect the gills; they should be red or bright pink, not pale or brownish. Bellies should show no swelling, and the aroma of the fish should be clean and pleasant. Depending on the market, cleaning and other cutting may or may not be included in the price. To do it yourself, see page 10.

If you buy round fish at a Chinese market, cleaning and scaling are generally included. However, they don't always do the most thorough job, so plan on doing some final inspection and cleaning yourself. There are likely to be scales remaining around the fins and head; remove them as described on page 10. Inspect the cavity well for remaining bits of blood and organs. Pay special attention to the kidneys, two strips of blood-rich tissue lying near the backbone, under a clear membrane. Cutting open this membrane and washing away all the bloody parts will give a much cleaner taste to the fish. Give everything a rinse inside and out, pat it dry, and you are ready to proceed.

DRESSED FISH Dressed fish has various meanings. It always indicates that the fish has been gutted, although the gills may or may not have been removed. "Whole" salmon and trout are in fact dressed. The basic purpose of dressing is to extend the shelf life by removing the easily spoiled entrails. Further dressing has to do with making the cook's job easier, by removing other unneeded parts. **PAN-DRESSED** fish are usually minus heads, fins, and scales if necessary (or in the case of farmed catfish, fully skinned)—basically reduced to two fillets attached to the central bone.

Quality indicators for dressed fish are the same as for a round fish, although the gills may not be present. Look for fish with most of their scales intact. A lot of missing scales, especially in vertical marks that come from the fish being caught in gillnets, are signs that the fish may be bruised. Look inside the belly cavity for any breaks in the inner lining of the cavity or, worse still, a corroded appearance ("belly burn") caused by late or careless cleaning.

FILLETS The meat on one side of a fish, removed in one piece, is called a fillet. Fillets are one of the most convenient forms of fish for the cook, and are among the most common market forms for all sorts of fish.

Fillets should be stored on, but not under, ice. Choose fillets with a bright, moist surface and even color. Pale patches in a darker fish like salmon are a sign of direct contact with water or melting ice, which can result in waterlogged

meat and lost flavor. The fatter meat near the skin should be pink, not brown.

Most fillets are sold skinless, but some varieties, like trout and the small rockfish known as "ocean perch," are usually sold with the skin still attached. This usually means that the fish is easier to cook and/or more flavorful if cooked with the skin on, but if you want to remove it, see page 13. Skin-on portions should be stacked with the skin sides together rather than skin against meat. Except in the case of fish with edible tiny scales (trout and char, most mackerels, smaller flatfish, and a few others), the fish should have been scaled before cutting.

While cutting fillets separates the meat from the main bones of the fish, fillets are not necessarily boneless. Most species have a row of "pin bones" perpendicular to the ribs which remain in the fillet after cutting. Some fillets also contain clusters of small bones supporting the various fins, or include the fins themselves. To remove these bones and fins, see page 11.

STEAKS Many fish markets routinely cut salmon, halibut, and other medium-size fish crosswise into steaks, each containing a cross section of the whole fish—two fillet sections attached to the central bones, with the skin intact. Larger fish like tuna, swordfish, and the larger sharks are generally divided first into half fillets or "loins," then cut crosswise into quarter-round steaks.

A steak thickness of ¾ inch to 1 inch is ideal for most cooking methods and species. Sometimes, depending on the size of the fish, this may turn out to be an awkward quantity, too large for a single serving and too small to serve two.

With salmon and similarly sized fish, where you have a choice of steaks or fillets, steaks are perhaps more convenient for the cook. Their compact shape allows you to cook more per square foot of grill or pan, and the skin and bones help hold the meat together. Also, both sides of a steak look equally nice, so if you mess up one side you can present the other side up. However, steaks mean more work for the diners, who have to deal with the skin and bones. Fillets are simpler to eat, especially if you remove the pin bones before cooking, but they may require a little more skill on the part of the cook to get them off the fire in one attractive piece.

Choose steaks by the same guidelines as fillets. Look especially at the fat layer just under the skin; red to pink indicates fresher fish, browner means older. As fish steaks are meant to be cooked as is, it should go without saying that the fish was scaled before cutting. Yet I am amazed at the number of supermarkets, even the upscale stores with "full-service" fish counters, that sell salmon steaks with the scales still attached. If this happens to you, complain!

MISCELLANEOUS FORMS Beyond the basic cuts, there are a variety of forms processed for further convenience. Trout is especially rich in these "value-added" products, including boned "butterfly" whole fish (central bones removed, with out without the head) and "guaranteed boneless" fillet cuts (with all pin bones and traces of fins removed). At least one brand-name farmed salmon is available in uniformly sized boneless portions, although these go mainly to the restaurant and hotel trade. Several big Southern catfish processors sell marinated fillets in flavors like lemon-pepper and Cajun spice.

"FRESH" VERSUS FROZEN All things being equal, fresh seafood is preferable to frozen—but all things are seldom equal.

First, a problem with definitions. English being an imprecise language, "fresh" has various meanings even within the narrow context of seafood. In one sense, the opposite of fresh is frozen; in another sense, the opposite of fresh is stale, spoiled, or rotten. To some people "fresh" in the sense of never frozen carries a connotation of higher quality, but freezing seafood at the source and keeping it frozen through the distribution system can actually be a better way of delivering it in a fresh (unspoiled) condition. Frozen food marketers sometimes use terms like "fresh frozen" or "fresher than fresh" to emphasize this image of food preserved in its just-harvested state.

In this book, the meaning of "fresh" depends on context. Where the subject is product forms, fresh means never having been frozen. In a discussion of the condition, quality, and wholesomeness of a given piece of seafood, fresh means without signs of spoilage, as it would be applied to, say, lettuce or flowers.

With most seafoods, a combination of factors—the fishing or farming site, market demands, production and harvest cycles, to name a few—tend to determine whether the preferred form is frozen or fresh. Some fish, like Alaska pollock, are caught hundreds of miles at sea, on trips that can take a week or more, so these fish are usually frozen at sea. Shrimp farms are often located in remote coastal areas, making frequent fresh shipments less practical than it might be for a catfish farm near a major highway. Shrimp also tend to be harvested in large quantities, a whole pond at a time. For these reasons, and because frozen shrimp enjoys a high market reputation, most farmed shrimp is frozen at or near the farm.

Salmon farming, on the other hand, grew up largely as a result of restaurant and hotel chefs demanding fresh salmon on a year-round basis. A salmon farmer can pull ten fish or a thousand out of a net pen according to demand and market conditions. Many other intensively cultured fin-

fish, from trout and catfish to tilapia and hybrid bass, are also geared primarily to the fresh market. With established distribution systems ready to handle fresh shipments on a regular basis, there is little need for freezing these products.

Other than shrimp and squid, which are often frozen in blocks, the most common form of frozen seafood is IQF, or individually quick frozen. Individual pieces (fillets, scallops, peeled shrimp, or whatever) are positioned on freezing

Seasonal Specialties

With the steady year-round availability of many farmed fish and shellfish, and some staple varieties like rockfish and flatfish that can show up any time of year, it's easy to forget that many seafoods have a prime season, that time of the year when they are at their best, or most abundant, or cheapest (often all three). The following are some of the seasonal highlights in the Pacific Coast seafood market.

SPRING Oysters still in prime shape for half-shell eating. Pacific halibut begins mid-March. Some troll Alaska salmon in early spring; West Coast ocean king salmon mostly after May 1. Copper River kings in late May to early June. Good prices on Atlantic lobster in May and June. Hawaiian swordfish peaks April to July; bycatch includes opah, escolar. Mackerel, sardines, anchovies pick up off California. Southern California barracuda. Oregon pink shrimp. East Coast shad April to May, Columbia shad in June.

SUMMER Rockfish, small flatfish, sablefish in best supply. Halibut, king salmon still plentiful. Peak sockeye runs in Copper River, Bristol Bay in July; Alaska and Canada cohos late July and August. White seabass, yellowtail. Fresh squid from Monterey. Albacore off California and Oregon in late summer. Oysters for barbecuing. Mediterranean mussels growing bigger, meatier.

FALL Atlantic lobster prices dip after Labor Day. Lingcod landings peak. Chum salmon. Columbia sturgeon. Rockfish, flatfish landings stay high, weather permitting. Albacore, swordfish, thresher shark peak in October. Act fast for spiny lobsters in early November. First Dungeness crabs in time for Thanksgiving.

WINTER Dungeness crab peaks in December and January in California. Oysters return to prime half-shell quality; blue mussels replace Mediterranean. San Pedro squid. Columbia steelhead, some sturgeon. First king salmon run in February.

pans or conveyer belts so they do not touch each other; once frozen solid, they can be packed loose into bags or boxes. The advantage of IQF products is that the cook can thaw just what is needed, rather than a whole package.

Frozen seafood is often sold thawed and ready to use, along with the fresh seafood in the display case. It should carry a label like "previously frozen" or the less obvious "thawed for your convenience." Unless you plan to use it right away, it's better to buy frozen seafood frozen, and thaw it yourself when needed. All frozen seafood should be solidly frozen; any partial thawing and refreezing will cause loss of moisture and quality. Look for IQF packages with a minimum of ice crystals. The pieces should not be frozen together in clumps.

CANNED, SMOKED, ETC. A few recipes in this book call for canned, smoked, and otherwise prepared seafood. Canned seafood is fully cooked in the canning process, and should be ready to eat. The same goes for smoked and cured products, whether fully cooked (like hot-smoked fish) or cured in a raw state (lox, gravlax). In any case, read labels carefully and follow their instructions when it comes to storing and using these products. Be especially careful with any seafood product in a pouch. At first glance, two packages of smoked salmon, one vacuum-sealed in plastic and the other in a foil-like pouch, look similar; but while the latter is basically a soft can, designed for storage at room temperature, the vacuum-packed product is perishable and must be kept refrigerated.

Storing Seafood

Home cooks should follow the same rules that commercial seafood processors live by: keep it clean, keep it cold, and keep it moving. The first is mainly a matter of safety (see page 35); the latter two have largely to do with quality. (For home cooks, "keep it moving" means cooking and eating seafood as soon as possible after buying it.)

The biggest single factor in maintaining seafood quality, from the time it leaves the water to the time it goes into the pot, is temperature. Near-freezing temperatures dramatically slow down, but do not stop, the growth of spoilage bacteria. These bacteria can grow quickly at temperatures that seem cold to us. The closer you can keep seafood to the ideal storage temperature of 29°–32°F, the longer it will keep in prime condition; the farther you get from this ideal, in the store or at home, the shorter the shelf life. According to seafood specialist Robert Price of the University of California at Davis, every 10°F increase above 32°F reduces the shelf life by half.

FRESH The ideal way to store fresh fish and shellfish is in contact with ice, either natural or artificial. You can simply lay one or two wrapped packages of fish on top of a layer of ice in a bowl or roasting pan and place it in the refrigerator. Whole fish require a larger pan.

Reusable gel ice packs that you store in the freezer are handy and less messy than real ice; ask your fish market if they have any to spare. Fillets and steaks of lean white fish generally will not suffer from sitting in direct contact with ice. (Drain off the melt-water periodically so the fish does not sit in water.) Darker-fleshed fish like salmon and tuna will get water-spotted and are better separated from the ice by at least a layer of plastic wrap. Store fish in the bottom or back of the refrigerator, which generally stay colder than the top shelf and door.

Don't ignore temperature control when shopping. If possible, make the place you buy seafood (along with other meats and frozen foods) the last stop on a shopping trip, and seafood the last item you pick up in the market. If the weather is warm or you have a long way to get home, consider bringing an insulated cooler with you and packing the seafood with artificial ice or with frozen foods bought at the same time. Most fish markets will pack your purchase with some crushed ice if you ask.

Even under ideal temperature, seafood has a limited shelf life. Two or three days is the usual limit, but trust your nose. If fish is just starting to smell a little stale, rinse it well with cold water and smell again; if a fishy smell persists, it is too far gone.

LIVE Live shellfish should be kept cold, but not as cold as fish, shucked shellfish, and other fresh seafood. At least as important as temperature is moisture; live crustaceans and mollusks need protection from the drying air of a refrigerator. Store live crabs, lobsters, or crayfish loosely enclosed in a paper or plastic bag, but not airtight. Bivalves (clams, mussels, oysters) keep best when covered with a damp cloth or several thicknesses of damp newspaper. Be sure oysters are layered in the bowl or box with their deeper shell halves down rather than tossed every which way. Do not store any salt-water shellfish in fresh water or they will die.

FROZEN For long-term storage, frozen seafood should be held below 0°F, which is colder than the "freezer" of a typical home refrigerator. Think of your freezer as a storage place for a matter of weeks, not months. If you have a separate freezer chest, you should be able to keep frozen foods longer.

Freezing seafood at home is mainly a stop-gap measure, a way of dealing with more than you can use fresh. Home freezers do not freeze as quickly or as deeply as commercial equipment. Try to make the decision to freeze on the first day, not a couple of days down the road when the fish is already half spoiled, and plan to use it sooner rather than later.

For best quality and safety, thaw frozen seafood in the refrigerator. A handful of IQF shrimp may thaw in a matter of minutes with a quick rinse, but a block of frozen shrimp or a whole frozen salmon can take up to two days to thaw under refrigeration. If you are in a hurry, you can thaw block shrimp and similar items in cool water, either running water (slightly quicker, but wasteful) or changing the water every quarter hour or so. Avoid the temptation to thaw under warm water or out of the refrigerator; this can lead to the outside getting quite warm and beginning to spoil while the inside is still solidly frozen.

Cutting It Up

Most of the time, you should be able to buy fish already cut into fillets, steaks, or other forms, but from time to time you may need to do it yourself, so here's how. But first, a little terminology, to orient you in the instructions that follow.

Dorsal refers to the upper or "back" side of the fish—think of the dorsal fin of a shark at the water's surface.

Opposite that side is the *ventral* (belly) side, so called because it includes the *vent* (anus).

Behind the vent on the ventral side is the *anal fin*. In front of it is a pair of *pelvic fins*, and forward and above those (usually well up on the sides of the fish) are the *pectoral fins*.

In front of the pectoral fins is the *collarbone*. In front of that are the *gills*, covered by a bony flap of the head called the *opercle*, or less formally the *gill cover*.

All the following techniques can be performed with two knives, an ordinary boning knife and a heavier, stiffer knife, either a chef's knife or a Chinese cleaver. A fillet knife, basically a boning knife with a longer, more flexible blade, makes some jobs easier. Whatever the knife, it has to be sharp, so start with a well-ground edge and learn how to use the sharpening steel to maintain it.

All these cutting techniques take some practice, so don't be dismayed if you mangle the first few fillets you try; I certainly did. Just take your time, study the bone structure of the fish as you go along (and after you are done, for future reference), and try to make your cuts as long, smooth, and few as possible. When filleting, try to resist the temptation to peel back the flesh all the time to see how you are doing; this makes lots of breaks in the fillet. With experience, you can do most of it by feel, without even seeing where the knife is.

Laying several sheets of newspaper on your cutting board for the early steps makes cleanup easier. As you finish each step, you can simply wrap up the trash from that stage (entrails, skin, etc.) and throw it away.

DRESSING First decide if the fish needs to be scaled. If the fillets will be skinned before cooking, there is no need to scale the fish, and the scales may make it easier to deal with by giving stiffness to the skin. To scale, use either a specialized tool or the back of a stiff knife (I use

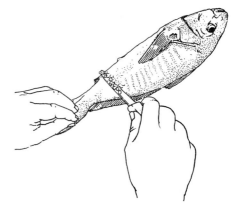

the cutting edge of a clam knife) and scrape from the tail toward the head. To keep scales from flying all over the kitchen, try scaling the fish inside the bag you brought it home in, or with newspaper flopped over the top, or even under water. Watch out for sharp and sometimes venomous spines on the fins of many species, which can inflict painful puncture wounds.

After scaling, lay the fish on a cutting board. Insert the tip of the boning knife in the vent, and cutting outward with as shallow a cut as possible, slit the belly open all the way to the point under the chin where the collarbones come together. Lift the gill cover and look at the gills; they are anchored at the top and bottom to both the head and the collarbone. Cut them free at both ends. Pin the gills down to the board with the tip of the knife and pull the fish away; the entrails should come free with the gills, but they may need to be cut free here and there with the knife. The belly cavity should now be nearly empty, but you're not done yet. Slit open the membrane near the backbone to expose the kidneys, and scrape them away with the knife tip or a metal spoon, and you are ready to rinse out the cavity.

While a dressed fish is ready to cook as is, you can make it quite a bit easier to serve and eat with a few additional cuts. The most troublesome bones in a fish are not the big central bone and its extensions, but the smaller bones that support the fins. Removing them before cooking makes carving at the table much simpler, while still preserving the appearance and advantages of fish cooked on the bone.

First, lift up the pectoral fin and cut the base and the attached bones away from the surrounding meat, then lift out the bone and pectoral fin. Next, remove the pelvic fins by cutting away the thin belly flesh where the ribs end. (Depending on how the fish was cleaned, these may already have been removed.)

Next, make a shallow cut inward on top of

the anal fin, about ½ inch toward the center bone; lift the flap of fillet and you should see

the small bones at the base of the fin. Rotate the fish and make a similar shallow cut along the

full length of the dorsal fin. Turn the fish over and repeat these last two cuts to expose the

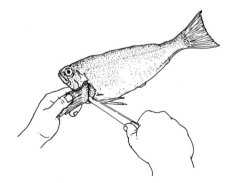

other side of the anal and dorsal fins. You should now be able to pull away the entire dorsal and anal fins and their short supporting bones. Remove the pectoral fin as on the other side. You are now left with the two fillets attached to the central bone, head, and tail, an easy package for both cooking and serving.

PAN-DRESSED fish have the heads removed as well. It's a technique I use mainly for small flatfish like sanddabs or rex sole, as follows: Place the fish on a cutting board, with the head toward your cutting hand and the belly side away from you. Feel where the meat ends and the belly cavity begins, and imagine a diagonal line from just behind the head to just behind the belly cavity. With a heavy, sharp knife, cut along this line to separate the head and belly from the fillets. If you cut at just the right point, you will remove the entrails without spilling a drop, leaving only a small pocket of kidneys to dig out with a fingertip. To remove the long dorsal and anal fins and their supporting bones, which is optional, rotate the fish so the base of the fin is under the tip of the knife and slide the knife forward, trapping the fish between the curved cutting edge and the board. Trim off the tail or leave it attached as you like.

STEAKING With the heavy knife, cut the dressed fish crosswise to the desired thickness. You need some power behind the knife to cut through the backbone. Some cooks use a plastic or rubber mallet to pound on the back of the blade. At the head end of the fish, you have to decide if you want to continue cutting into steaks and lose the triangular portion next to the head, or leave a relatively large section that will produce one fillet portion on each side. When the taper of the tail section makes

it too small for steaks, leave the rest in one piece to be filleted or cooked whole.

FILLETING Fish with a strong bone structure like rockfish do not need to be dressed before filleting; the ribs that surround the belly cavity allow you to remove the whole fillets without cutting into the entrails. (If the fish is already dressed, see below.)

With the fish lying on its side, feel with your fingertips for where the meat meets the collarbone, which curves well forward on the dorsal

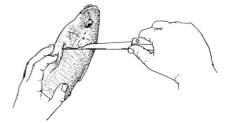

side. Starting on top of the head, trace the collarbone with the tip of the boning knife, cutting in at a diagonal so the knife rides along the collarbone and you get all the possible meat. Stop when the knife reaches the midpoint of the fish, to avoid cutting into the cavity.

Return the tip of the knife to the top of the head. Hold the blade horizontally, parallel to

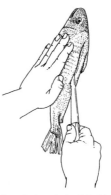

the length of the fish. Holding the skin taut with your other hand, cut just above the dorsal fin back toward the tail, cutting in about an inch until you can see the ends of the long extensions of the backbone. Repeat this cut, keeping the knife against the bones, until you hit the thick part of the backbone. The upper half of the fillet is now free, the ventral side still attached.

Starting at the point on the backbone just above the vent, ride the tip of the knife up over the bone, then cut outward toward the anal fin as you cut toward the tail; again, keep the knife as close as possible to the bone to get as much meat as possible.

Last, return to the head end and cut up over the backbone, cutting through the tiny pin bones that stick out into the fillet perpendicular

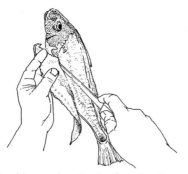

to the backbone; let the knife ride along the ribs until you reach the ends of the ribs near the belly. Cut through the thin flap of belly meat and skin and the fillet should come away.

Turn the fish over and repeat the process. You may find it easier to make certain cuts with a backhand motion on the second side. Some cutters make dorsal cuts on both sides of the fish before cutting the first fillet away.

Filleting flatfish like sole, flounder, and halibut is essentially the same process, although the distance from the dorsal fin to the backbone is greater and the fillets are thinner. Also, the belly cavity on most flatfish is quite small,

with the vent as little as 10 percent of the way back from the head to the tail.

There is another, slightly easier method of filleting dressed fish, especially those with fairly thin ribs, like salmon and trout. Following the diagonal of the gill cover, cut the head

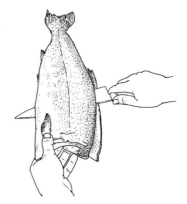

off, leaving as much as possible of the collarbone intact. Cut through the first couple of ribs where they meet the backbone, then insert the knife into this notch, crosswise to the fish. Using the collarbone as a handle for the fillet, and pressing the knife blade down against the backbone and the bones on the dorsal side, cut down the length of the fish, severing the ribs as you go. Flip the fillet over on the skin side, slide the knife in under the ribs, and cut them free from the fillet, all at once if your knife is long enough, or in a couple of groups. While this technique doesn't remove every last gram of meat from the bones, it gives a very good yield and a nice smooth surface to the fillet.

To skin a fillet, lay it skin side down on the cutting board, close to one edge, and pin down the near end with a fingertip. Holding the knife at a 15° to 20° angle from horizontal—think of shaving with a straight razor, or sharpening the knife on a stone—scrape against the tightly held skin (don't worry about the meat, it can flop around all it wants) with a long backhand cut. You should be left with little or no meat attached to the skin. If you cut through the skin, you are holding the knife at too steep an angle. If you hold it too flat, the blade will ride up as you cut, leaving meat attached to the skin. Trim off any ragged edges or especially thin flaps of meat and rinse the fillets. Clean up any scales, skin slime, and other debris from the cutting board before proceeding.

The final step is to remove the pin bones, anywhere from six or seven to thirty depending on the species, that run diagonally out through

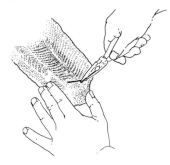

the meat to near the skin at the head end. You don't have to remove them; when the fish cooks the muscle shrinks, so the pin bones protrude slightly and are very easy to pull out at the table. However, if the fish will be presented enclosed in pastry, leaf wrappings, or anything else that covers the fillet, it's better to provide a completely boneless portion.

To remove pin bones from a raw fillet, grasp the end of each with clean needle-nose pliers or special tweezers made for this purpose and pull it up and toward the head end. It's also possible to remove pin bones by cutting very close on either side of the row and pulling out a thin strip of meat with the bones in it, leaving a

notch in the head end of the fillet.

DIAGONAL SLICING Many recipes in this book call for diagonal slices, a cut that is not always easy to find in the market. When faced with a fish in the range of 4 to 10 pounds (salmon, white seabass, yellowtail, and many of the other "summer fish" described on page 165), a lot of fishmongers simply cut the long, thick fillets straight across into half-pound pieces, as if they were cutting a beef tenderloin into châteaubriand, filets mignons, and tournedos. Trouble is, when you apply this technique to fish fillets in the neighborhood of 1 inch thick, you get clunky-looking blocks that are not quite steaks and not quite fillets. It's a cut that is neither very attractive nor the easiest to cook, although it is suitable for the skillet-roasting method discussed on page 18.

I much prefer to slice thick fillets diagonally, yielding pieces no more than ¾ inch thick. It's a technique I learned twenty years ago on one of my first restaurant jobs, and one I suggest you learn if you ever have occasion to cut up a whole fillet of salmon or similarly shaped fish.

Depending on the size of the fillet and the angle of the cut, a diagonal slice may appear half again as large on the plate as the equivalent weight in a rectangular block. More important, it cooks more quickly and evenly, and the finished result looks better to my eye. Given the natural elasticity of the meat, when a diagonal slice is laid bone side down on a pan or grill, the diagonal face and the bone side become one flat surface, providing the maximum area for browning and grill marks. And because the thickness is reduced, the heat penetrates to the center faster, making it easier to cook with high heat, which maximizes browning and the flavor it brings.

It's easiest to visualize this cut when you have a whole fillet: If the fillet was cut for maximum yield, the surface of the head end where

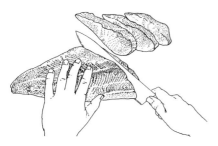

it was cut away from the collarbone will not be perpendicular to either the cutting board or the length of the fillet, but diagonal to both. Slice off a portion with a cut roughly parallel to this surface, and you get a piece whose cross section is a parallelogram (remember your high-school geometry?) rather than a rectangle. Continue cutting this way, adjusting the distance between the cuts if you want to maintain consistent weight per portion. As you get nearer the tail, the cuts will get farther apart, and the final portion will be a good-sized triangle of tail. With really thick fillets, cut closer to vertical to maintain a reasonable thickness.

I wish more fish markets would offer this cut. If your fishmonger doesn't, ask for it. Take in this book or a photocopy of this page if you have trouble describing it.

BUTTERFLY CUT One way to cope with the square-cut blocks described above is to reduce their thickness by half with a butterfly cut. Lay the skin side down against the cutting board (this works best with skinless portions, but it is possible with the skin intact; just make sure the fish has been scaled). Cut down the middle of

the portion, almost but not quite through the meat. You should then be able to lift up the middle and fold the two halves back, making two symmetrical pieces (like butterfly wings) joined by a thin seam in the middle. It will look a little like a salmon steak, but with no bone in the middle or skin around the outside. If the butterflied piece doesn't lie flat, you have not made the cut deep enough.

"Butterfly" is sometimes used in a slightly different sense, for whole trout or similarly shaped fish that have been split lengthwise almost all the way through and the backbone removed, leaving the two fillets attached by back or belly skin.

Miscellaneous Techniques

SALTING The most common culinary use of salt is to enhance the natural flavor of food. With fish, part of its role is also negative; it has a way of drawing out and neutralizing "fishy" flavors. This is a quality that has perhaps been best explored in Japanese cooking, which uses several different techniques for salting different kinds of fish. In his authoritative book *Japanese Cooking: A Simple Art,* Shizuo Tsuji outlines four separate salting techniques for fish: sprinkling on the salt by hand, soaking in salted water, covering with a heavy layer of salt and then rinsing, and salting through absorbent paper laid on top of the fish. The first technique is further defined by the type of fish. The lightest dose of salt is used on fish to be served raw, an average amount on lean white fish, and a heavier hand on fatty fish. Time is another variable, with lean and mild-flavored fish being salted just before cooking, and oilier, stronger fish often being salted a half hour or more ahead of time.

In all of these methods, the salt draws out some of the moisture from the fish, and with it seems to come some of the "fishy" flavor and odor as well. Some salt soaks into the fish, of course, but not as much as you might expect.

In addition to altering flavor, salt has an effect (sometimes dramatic) on the texture of seafood. Salting a soft, bland fish for twenty to thirty minutes before cooking (particularly using the heavy salt and rinse method) can make it noticeably firmer as well as more tasty, without making it salty. Shrimp, especially frozen shrimp, are much improved by a preliminary salting (see page 232). I have indicated a salting step in certain recipes where I consider it essential, but you may find that it improves other dishes as well. When in doubt, salt sooner rather than later.

DRUGSTORE WRAP A few recipes call for wrapping food (in aluminum foil, banana leaves, or whatever) using the "drugstore wrap." Here's how it's done: Place the food in the center of a large rectangular sheet, then fold the long sides up over the food, matching the edges. Fold the doubled edge halfway down and crease, then fold this seam down flat against the package, trapping the open edges. How you seal the ends of the resulting tube depends on the material; foil can be rolled up, or twisted like a sausage casing, while banana leaves are typically just folded inward once and secured with a skewer.

Cooking Techniques

The purposes of cooking seafood are basically two: to alter its flavor and texture to make it more palatable (although some fish are perfectly delicious raw or partly cooked), and to kill any bacteria or parasites that might be present and might lead to illness. If safety were the only consideration, the advice would be simple: cook all fish and shellfish to an internal temperature of 145°F. Unfortunately, seafood protein begins to turn firm and opaque at a lower temperature than other meats, around 105°F versus 120° to 140°F in terrestrial meats. The temperature at which it is fully cooked, meaning the muscle proteins have shrunk all they can and in the process squeezed out a good deal of their moisture, is also much lower than in other meats. The microbiologically safe temperature is dangerously close to overcooked from a culinary standpoint. The art of the seafood cook is to provide a dish that is both safe and a pleasure to eat. Knowing when it is "done" is a major part of this challenge.

Unless parasites are a major concern, the ideal range of internal temperature in cooked fish is somewhere between 125° and 140°F, when the fish is firmer than raw but still slightly translucent in the center. The most accurate way to judge this in any piece of fish more than an inch thick is with an instant-reading thermometer. (A less scientific method is to insert a toothpick into the center for a few seconds, then remove it and immediately touch it to your lips. If it's hot, the fish is cooked through.) Bear in mind that fish may continue to cook for a minute or more after it comes off the fire, as heat on the surface continues to penetrate to the center, and may rise five degrees or more in the center. So even if you want fully cooked fish, remove it from the fire when it reaches 135°F in the center.

Another way to test fish for doneness, mentioned in many of the recipes, is the skewer test. When you poke a thin skewer or toothpick into a piece of raw fish, you can feel it cutting its way through the layers of connective tissue (myocommata) between the layers of muscle. The myocommata turns to gelatin and melts away by the time the fish is fully cooked, which is why fish comes apart into flakes. At this stage the skewer will slip in and out with little resistance. Using the skewer as a probe, you can feel for the point at which it still grabs a little in the center of the thickest part of the almost-cooked fish. It's hard to describe exactly, but if you get in the habit of skewer-testing fish as it cooks, your muscle memory will eventually tell you what a perfectly cooked piece of fish feels like.

A widely quoted "rule" for cooking fish is to measure the thickness of the fish and calculate 10 minutes per inch—thus, 5 minutes for a ½-inch-thick fillet, 7½ minutes for a ¾-inch steak, and 20 minutes for a whole fish that is 2 inches thick at its thickest point when laid on its side. While this is useful for estimating cooking times, there are too many variables in heat, cookware, density and temperature of the uncooked fish, and other factors for me to recommend it as a rule. It will put you in the ballpark, but I still recommend a thermometer or the skewer test for the final determination.

SAUTÉING AND ITS VARIATIONS Sautéing, pan-frying, stir-frying, and searing are all names for related methods of cooking food in a shallow pan with a small amount of oil. Most of the heat is conducted into the food directly from the hot surface of the pan, rather than being carried by the hot oil as in true frying (a form of convection). In its most basic form, the cook heats a skillet with a thin layer of oil (sometimes a nonstick skillet without oil) over fairly high heat, seasons a fish fillet or other relatively thin piece and perhaps dusts it with flour or another crusting ingredient, and lays it in the pan to cook until browned on the first side. The fish is turned once to brown the other side, then lifted out of the pan with a spatula to the plate. The browned drippings in the pan may then be incorporated into a sauce.

Use bigger pieces of fish and enough oil to come up around the sides, and the process becomes pan-frying. Chinese stir-frying is related, but the pieces are cut rather small (or are naturally discrete units like shrimp), and

Grilling in the Great Outdoors . . .

Grilling is the archetypal outdoor cooking, even if the outdoors is only a city park. However, grilling fish can be a tricky proposition with the facilities available in most public picnic areas. A rusty grill with huge warped bars, encrusted with barbecue sauce from countless previous users, is not a good bet for producing perfectly grilled salmon steaks. If you can't take along the home barbecue, you might still want to bring the removable grill part, and lay it over whatever surface is available. Or you can use a long-handled wire folding grill, the kind with two flat grills joined by a hinge or else a shallow basket shape with a removable top. Either one will also work in improvised settings like a driftwood fire on the beach. Don't forget the wire brush, for cleaning the grill before and immediately after cooking.

Whether you are cooking in a public park or in your own back yard, give your neighbors a break and don't use lighter fluid or "instant-lighting" briquets. A chimney starter and a couple of sheets of newspaper do the job easily and with no petroleum smell.

they are tossed or stirred as they cook to brown them on all sides.

Skillet-roasting is my term for another variation, a favorite method of restaurant cooks that can be useful for home cooks as well. A lot of the dishes described on menus as "sautéed," "roasted," "pan-roasted," or "seared" are cooked by a combination of sautéing and roasting. The cook heats a skillet to near smoking on top of the stove, adds oil and a piece of fish (or chicken or meat), and cooks it briefly, perhaps turning it once, before sliding the skillet into a 500°F oven. For restaurant cooks, it's partly a matter of convenience; a sauté cook has only so many burners within easy reach, and getting a pan off the stove and into the oven frees up a burner for the next entree. Even if you have plenty of room on the stovetop, this technique is unmatched for producing a crisp browned surface, not to mention that most of the oil splattering takes place in the oven rather than right under your face. Just make sure your skillet has a heatproof handle.

SKILLET-ROASTING works best with steaks and fillet portions ¾ to 1 inch thick, which can be cooked without turning. With fillets of lean and moderately oily fish, I prefer to leave the skin on (after scaling, of course). To keep the skin from shrinking too much and distorting the meat, score the skin with shallow cuts ½ inch or so apart, cutting about ⅛ inch into the meat.

Whichever side goes down in the pan will get the maximum browning and crisping, and should be served facing up on the plate. If you roast a piece of skin-on fillet with the skin down, the skin side becomes flat and crisp, and when you invert it onto the plate, the effect is striking—a crisp flat top and a curved underside. If the fillet has been skinned, however, I think it looks better with the bone side showing, so that's the side that should go face down in the skillet.

. . . and in the Great Indoors

When either weather or space constraints make outdoor grilling impossible, there are still ways you can enjoy grilled seafood. Cookware manufacturers have come up with numerous stovetop "grills," each with its advantages and drawbacks. One popular design is a modern version of the dome-shaped Mongolian grill, with ridges and grooves to carry away the drippings (and a water moat to catch those drippings). Others simply add parallel ridges to a flat surface, which may be cast iron or nonstick or anodized aluminum. These grills come in round, square, and rectangular shapes, some reversible to a flat griddle on the other side.

My favorite grilling pan is a 9-inch cast iron skillet with ridges in the bottom. Not only is this the cheapest option, but the height and spacing of the ridges (a full ¼ inch high and ¾ inch apart) give the best simulation of real grilling, with minimal metal in contact with the food and most of the heat radiating from the metal underneath. The size is a slight disadvantage, as it's only big enough for two good-sized steaks, but it's so much cheaper than the alternatives that you can probably afford two! The skillet type needs to be treated like any cast iron, and is harder than some grills to clean thoroughly; rubbing it with a squeezed-out lemon half during cleanup helps, but it still tends to smell of fish the next time you heat it up.

For the true flavor of grilled food, there is nothing like cooking over real hot coals. If you have a working fireplace, there is no insurmountable reason why you can't cook in it at least occasionally. The key to fireplace grilling is a hardwood fire that has burned down to glowing coals, rather than the classic stack of blazing logs. This means starting the fire two to three hours or more before you are ready to cook, and adding the last log at least an hour before. Specially designed fireplace grills are available from some catalogs and specialty stores, with adjustable height to match the height of your fire grate. I just borrow the grill from my kettle barbecue, with an assortment of bricks to hold it at the appropriate height.

Rather than heat up the oven just for this dish, consider other uses for the oven at the same time—baked potatoes, a mixture of roasted vegetables, or a savory flat bread baked on a pizza stone. While you're at it, you can use the heat of the oven to preheat the skillet.

BROILING AND GRILLING are related cooking methods, both of which rely mainly on intense radiant heat to cook food quickly and give a nicely browned appearance.

The typical home broiler, located in or underneath the oven, uses either an electric coil or a gas burner as the heat source, but in either case the heat also radiates from the surrounding metal, especially when the broiler is preheated. In broilers inside an oven, there is some convection heat as well, as heating the broiler heats up the air inside the oven considerably.

To broil fish, adjust the oven shelf (bearing in mind the combined height of the broiling pan and rack) to position the fish 2 to 4 inches from the heat source, and preheat the broiler. Except for very thin portions like trout fillets, which can cook on only one side, plan to turn the fish once during cooking. Start with the better-looking side of the fish down, then finish with the good side facing the heat, and serve face up.

Grilling is similar to broiling, except that the heat comes from underneath. Also, the grill itself transfers some heat to the food, providing the characteristic grill marks. More than any other cooking method, grilling requires you to get to know your cooking equipment. The design of the grill and the fuel (charcoal, gas, or electric) determine the intensity of the heat at the grill surface, which governs how quickly the food cooks, how much smoky flavor it takes on, and all the other variables that make grilling an art as much as a science.

Whatever your heat source, the grill surface itself should have bars spaced not more than about ¾ inch apart, with a surface that can be scoured clean with a wire brush before, after, and whenever possible during cooking. Rubbing the grill with a little vegetable oil on a rag and preheating the grill thoroughly before adding the fish will help keep the fish from sticking. Fish is almost guaranteed to stick to a cold grill.

The right degree of heat depends on the type and size of fish to be cooked. In general, thinner pieces can cook more quickly over a hotter fire; thicker pieces, such as whole fish and "roasts," need a somewhat slower fire to keep them from burning on the outside before

the inside is done. To test the hotness of the fire, try to hold your hand an inch or two above the cooking surface. In the recipes, a "moderate" fire means you can keep it there 4 to 5 seconds; "hot," 2 to 3 seconds; and "very hot" a second or less.

Most of the problems in grilling fish have to do with getting it off the grill at the right moment and in one piece. Assuming the heat is right and the grill is clean, this is mostly a matter of planning and timing. First, be sure to position each piece of fish so its longest dimension is across the grill bars rather than parallel to them, to minimize the amount of fish in contact with the metal. A long-bladed spatula and a pair of long cooking tongs are the best tools for turning grilled fish. Use the spatula sideways and slide the long edge of the blade under the whole piece at once, rather than trying to work it under the fish from one end to the other. I usually keep the tongs in the other hand to loosen, nudge, and otherwise guide the fish onto the spatula.

Every time you move the fish on the grill is one more chance for it to stick, so plan to turn fish only once, a little more than halfway through the cooking time. The result will be a clear, single set of grill marks and a minimum of sticking. If the fish is sticking, wait a bit; often it will release more easily after another half-minute or so of cooking. Cook on the second side just long enough to brown the outside, and remove the fish from the grill when slightly underdone, as the heat on the surface will continue cooking the fish for another minute or two. The side that goes against the fire first will get the better browning and grill marks, so start cooking on the side you want to present. To my eye, the bone side of a fillet is more attractive than the skin side, so it goes toward the fire first.

For additional flavor, "perfume" the fire by adding fresh or dried herbs just before cooking the fish. Try rosemary with swordfish, oregano with tuna, wild fennel stalks with salmon, or thyme with just about anything.

Basting with oil or marinade is often suggested in grilling recipes, but it is not really necessary if the fire is hot enough and the fish cooks quickly enough. If the grill surface is clean and hot, the fish will release when it has cooked sufficiently; if it's not, oil probably won't make the difference. Besides, the oil may drip off the fish into the fire and burn, giving a charred flavor.

Likewise, don't rely on oil in a marinade to replace the natural moisture in the fish. Once fish has cooked to the point that it loses its juices, no amount of oil will make the individual flakes of fish moist again, although it may mask their fundamental dryness. Better to keep the moisture in the fish in the first place by not overcooking (this applies equally to broiling, and in fact to all cooking methods).

OVEN COOKING Most "baked" fish is not baked in the same sense as bread is. In true **BAKING**, the food is exposed directly to radiant heat from the walls of the oven and heat transferred by the air in the oven (convection). When applied to meats and poultry, this form of baking is usually called **ROASTING**. It's a fine technique for whole fish and certain large cuts, but most fish dishes we refer to as baked are enclosed in some way. Whether you use a baking dish with a lid, a sheet of aluminum foil, or an edible wrapper such as pastry or grape leaves, the effect is similar: The fish is separated from the dry air of the oven, cooking instead in a moist, steamy environment.

Baking fish in a tightly covered casserole is called **BRAISING** or pot-roasting, or sometimes bake-poaching or oven-steaming. Whatever you call it, it involves a small amount of liquid, which may be elaborated into a sauce or simply spooned over the fish at the table. You can get a similar effect on top of the stove, if your cookware is heavy enough to diffuse the heat from underneath.

While simply cooking fish in an enclosed container will generate some steam (the water cooking out of the fish itself), it's typical to add some liquid for a combination of moisture and flavor. The liquid may be stock, milk, wine, tomato sauce, or even that old pantry standby, canned soup. Onions, tomatoes, celery, carrots, or other vegetables are often included, and they also release moisture as well as flavor into the baking dish.

Keep the overall amount of liquid in the baking pan small, however; the fish should be surrounded by steam as it bakes, not completely immersed in liquid (remember, this is baking, not poaching). As a general rule, the liquid should come no more than a third of the way up the sides of the fish. The ideal situation is for the fish to sit on top of a layer of vegetables that form a natural cooking rack, holding it above the liquid.

Maintaining a moist cooking environment is no substitute for careful timing; no amount of liquid can rescue an overcooked piece of fish. Once the fish has had its natural moisture content cooked out of it, it can be swimming in liquid and still taste dry. Judge doneness either by the skewer test (see page 17) or with a thermometer.

One of the simplest and most adaptable ways to bake fish is to seal individual portions

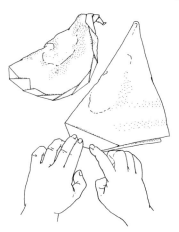

in parchment packages—in French, en papillote—where they bake quickly at a relatively high temperature. Because the paper transmits the heat from the oven quickly, and there is no heavy baking dish to heat up, this technique takes very little time. You can also use aluminum foil, but foil is not as aesthetically pleasing as a browned, puffy package of paper that almost looks like it's made of filo dough or the thinnest puff pastry. For an example of this technique and the method of folding the packages, see Salmon, Wild Rice, and Mushrooms en Papillote, page 70.

To fully experience the appeal of parchment baking, plan to serve each portion in its package, to be opened at the table. As each diner slashes open the package with a steak knife, it releases all the aromas of the fish and seasonings, which would otherwise be left behind in the kitchen. In an informal setting,

it's fine to cut the package open on the top, peel back the edges, and eat the fish right out of the paper. If you prefer a little neater look, show each diner how to slit the packages open along the edge and slide the contents out onto the plate. Then pass around a plate to collect all the papers and remove them from the table.

The typical parchment sold in grocery stores and cookware shops comes in 15-inch rolls; a square piece is adequate for most single servings of fish. Better and far more economical are the large sheets of silicone-treated baking pan liners used by restaurants and commercial bakeries. The only drawback to this paper is the way it's packaged: Commercial restaurant-supply and paper-supply houses stock it in boxes of 1,000 sheets. If a full box seems like a lifetime supply (I'm actually on my second or third box), you might look for a way to buy it in smaller quantities. Ask if your local bakery will sell you some, or get some cooking and baking friends together and go in on a whole box.

POACHING, simmering in a flavored liquid, is one of the most fundamental cooking methods for fish. A properly poached piece of fish comes out moist and tender, with all its natural flavor and moisture intact, ready to be served hot or cold. Once you master the basic poaching technique, you can apply it to anything from a single steak or fillet to a whole fish, depending on your cookware.

It's important to remember that poaching is not boiling. When the liquid is at a slow simmer, it cooks the fish evenly and gently. A rolling boil is a much more violent form of cooking, and the result is often an overcooked and tough piece of fish. At a proper simmer, there should be just a few bubbles breaking the surface of the liquid around the edges.

The poaching liquid is another key to success in poaching. Even with the best technique, there is some transfer of flavor from the fish to the liquid, so it should be compensated for by a similar transfer of flavor from the liquid to the fish. At the very least, water flavored with a little salt plus a small amount of wine or an even smaller amount of vinegar is preferable to plain water. A better choice is court-bouillon, (page 329), which adds herbs and aromatic vegetables to the wine and water mixture.

The basic poaching procedure is the same whether you are poaching a whole fish or a few portions. First, prepare the court-bouillon and strain it. Use a pan large enough to hold the fish in a single layer and deep enough for the liquid to cover the fish. If you are not sure how much liquid to use, measure the capacity of the pan with the fish in it with cold water, and use that much court-bouillon. Bring the liquid to a simmer, then carefully lower the fish into the pan. (If you don't have a pan deep enough for the liquid to cover the fish entirely, lay a piece of buttered waxed paper or foil loosely over the exposed parts of the fish.)

An alternate method, especially useful with rolled fillets or other fragile pieces, is to place the fish in the cold pan first, then carefully pour the hot court-bouillon over and around it. In practice, this can be part of the straining step; just prepare the court-bouillon, lay the fish in the poaching pan, and when the liquid is ready, strain it over the fish.

Adjust the heat under the pan so the liquid just simmers. Poaching time will vary according to the type of fish and the thickness. Fillets of thin fish such as sole may be done in as little as 2 or 3 minutes, while thick salmon or halibut steaks could take up to 10 minutes. For whole fish, use the "10 minutes per inch" rule as a guideline, but use a thermometer or the skewer test to tell for sure.

Depending on the size and cut of fish you use, you can poach fish in anything from a deep skillet to a specialized oblong fish poacher. A fish poacher is not absolutely necessary even for whole fish. In *The L. L. Bean Game and Fish Cookbook*, Angus Cameron writes of poaching salmon of 6 to 7 pounds in an old enameled refrigerator vegetable crisper. A large oval or rectangular roasting pan is another possibility for fish up to about 16 inches long. In fact, any flameproof pan at least 3 inches deep can function as a poacher for a small to medium-size whole fish.

Individual pieces of fish are easily retrieved from the poaching pan with a slotted spatula. Larger pieces or whole fish can sometimes be handled with two spatulas, but the removable rack in most poaching pans makes the job easier. If you don't have a poaching rack, wrapping the fish in a single layer of cheesecloth before cooking makes it easier to retrieve.

The fish gives some of its flavor to the poaching liquid, so don't let it go to waste. Many a classic fish dish uses the reduced poaching liquid as a base for the sauce for the fish. Or strain and freeze the court-bouillon (you might want to boil it down to save freezer space) and use it as the base for the next batch. It will get richer with each use. Add a little more onion and a splash of wine each time you reheat it to refresh the flavors, and taste for the balance of other ingredients.

STEAMING If you want to taste fish in its purest and simplest form, try steaming it. This cooking method, especially associated with Asian cooking but equally adaptable to Western meals, is one of the best ways to preserve the flavor and texture of the most delicate fish. It's a technique suitable for most kinds of fish, in any form from a single steak to a whole fish to serve at a banquet.

The basic principle of steaming is to hold the fish above boiling water in a covered pan so it is surrounded by hot steam. Water vapor is capable of carrying more energy than boiling water, so this can be a faster method than cooking directly in the water.

The steaming pan itself can be any covered pan deep and wide enough to hold a plate of fish under the cover. A Chinese wok, with its dome-shaped lid, is frequently suggested as a steaming pan, and most wok sets come with some sort of steaming rack. Unfortunately, steaming is rough on the minute layer of hardened oil that makes up the smooth, food-releasing surface of a "seasoned" steel wok. Many cooks reserve their best wok for stir-frying and use a cheaper one, often made out of another material, for steaming.

My recommendation for a steaming pan is an inexpensive wok, or the modified version called a "stir-fry pan," at least 12 inches in diameter. Some are made of stainless steel, others have a nonstick cooking surface, but all the cheaper versions share a thin metal construction that makes for poor heat distribution, rendering them next to worthless for stir-frying.

When the pan is full of water, however, the hot and cold spots are irrelevant. Before you buy a new one, check around at garage sales and flea markets, where most of these pans wind up before long. Several years ago I picked up a large, flimsy stainless steel flat-bottomed wok at a garage sale—best dollar I ever spent—and I use it all the time now for steaming.

Other possible steaming pots include an oblong fish poacher, at least for fish of appropriate size and shape; a covered oval "turkey roaster" (to my mind, useless for roasting turkey, but ideal for steaming a whole fish); or any large covered pot. I have even used a large stainless steel mixing bowl, set right on the stove burner and covered with a wok lid.

In Asian-style steaming, the fish is usually set on a plate or in a shallow bowl, which collects the juices released by the fish and other ingredients, whether they will be served or not. The plate usually goes straight from the steamer to the table, avoiding any problems of the cooked fish falling apart when it is transferred to a serving dish.

To support the plate, you will need some sort of rack or basket to hold it a couple of inches above the boiling water. Wok sets usually include some kind of steaming rack that fits inside the wok, and Chinese stores sell various designs that stand on the bottom of the wok or rest against the sides. Stacking bamboo steamer baskets allow you to steam more than one type of food at once over the same pot of water, but they reduce the size of plate you can fit over a pan of a given size. A 12-inch basket is about right for a couple of salmon steaks, but it won't hold a whole fish of much size, and two tiers will likely be necessary for four servings.

If you use a roasting pan or other large pan, you will need to improvise a steaming rack. A nifty solution suggested by Barbara Tropp in *The Modern Art of Chinese Cooking* is to set the plate on several empty tin cans with both ends removed. Two tuna or water chestnut cans will work for an oval platter, but three make a more stable platform for a round platter.

Whatever your steaming setup, be sure it will hold enough water to cook the fish without boiling dry. Also make sure the steaming rack holds the plate high enough above the water surface that the water does not boil into the plate, washing away the seasonings. To avoid burning yourself, be sure to open the steamer lid away from you and let the steam dissipate for a few seconds before removing the lid. Chinese markets sell a cheap but ingenious gadget for retrieving the plate from the steamer, with three arms that spread wide and then hook onto the edges of the plate so it can be lifted out with one hand.

Lean, delicate fish like sole and flounder are ideal for steaming, as are most white-fleshed ocean fish, including rockfish, lingcod, cod and its relatives, snappers, and the various fish known as sea bass. Given the choice, a Chinese cook will usually steam fish on the bone. A whole fish is ideal if of a suitable size, but larger fish in Chinese markets are often cut into thick crosscuts of a pound or more to cook as a chunk. Freshwater fish like trout, catfish, and bass are also suited to steaming, usually whole. Fatter, more flavorful fish with a tender texture, like salmon, sablefish, butterfish, and pompano, really get to show off their silky richness when steamed.

About the only category of fish that does not take well to steaming is dense, meaty types like swordfish and tuna. These seem to me to need the direct dry heat of grilling, broiling, or sautéing to bring out the best in their flavor and texture (think of the difference between grilled and boiled beef).

While it is possible to steam fish without any added flavorings, most Chinese and Japanese cooks include at least a bit of ginger and green onion on the plate. Both these ingredients are thought to enhance the flavor of fish, as well as counteract any undesirable "fishy" flavors. A little rice wine or dry sherry is also a frequent addition, again intended to enhance rather than overpower the flavor of the fish.

FRYING Frying is messy, somewhat tricky, and potentially dangerous, but when it's done right, the reward is a crisp, tasty, and altogether appealing piece of fish. I can't remember in whose cookbook I once read that "people either fry or they don't," with the implication that those who do already know how and there's no point in giving instructions to the rest. This stance is tempting, but it's a cop-out. Even if you fry foods at home only once in a blue moon, it's important to know how to do it well and safely.

The keys to frying (sometimes but redundantly called deep-frying) are simple: Use good oil, in ample quantity, at the proper temperature, and fry in small batches. The first is a matter of flavor; the last three are mostly about the texture and oil content of the finished food.

Other than coming out burned or raw, the worst thing that can happen to fried food is a coating that is soggy with oil rather than crisp and dry. Most often, the culprit is oil that is not hot enough. Even if you start with oil of the proper temperature, 350° to 375°F, frying too much food at once can bring down the temperature drastically. It can take several minutes to recover, by which time the damage is done.

Other than a thermostatically controlled electric fryer, the best frying setup for home cooks consists of a special pan that looks like a deep saucepan and a frying basket of approximately ¼-inch mesh wire. A bar sticking up on the side of the pan opposite the handle serves as a rest for the basket. After frying the food, you hang the basket over the pan for a few seconds to let the oil drain back into the pan. The smallest size, with a capacity of 5½ quarts (enough for a little less than a gallon of oil) sells for around $40 at restaurant supply houses. If you do a lot of frying, you might find it a good investment. The basket alone sells for about half as much and can be used in any large pot.

If you fry only occasionally, a standard steel wok will do fine, with a large Chinese skimmer to retrieve the fried foods. Use a wok ring for stability, even with a flat-bottomed wok—tipping over a wok filled with a quart or more of hot oil is just too frightening to contemplate. Some wok sets include a crescent-shaped rack that clips to the edge of the pan, for draining fried foods over the oil. Whatever pan you use, fill it no more than two-thirds full of oil to avoid spills and boilovers.

Ultimately, frying becomes an exercise in observing and adjusting. Clip a frying thermometer to the side of the pan, and let the oil heat to slightly higher than your target frying temperature before adding the first batch of food. Watch how far and fast the temperature drops, and how long it takes to recover, and adjust the size of the batches and the heat under the oil to keep it in the optimal frying range.

For the best fried foods, invest a few dollars in a gallon can of peanut oil. If carefully filtered after each use through several layers of cheesecloth, the oil can be reused five or six times. (Coffee filters are too slow—half the oil will still be in the funnel in the morning.) If your frying sessions are months apart, it's probably better to use the once-used frying oil for other uses such as stir-frying. Discard frying oil when it has darkened noticeably or begins to smell burnt; if your oil can has a plastic spout and cap, save them to allow you to seal the used oil back in the can for the neatest disposal.

PRESERVING Long before there were refrigerators, cooks all over the world had devised ways to preserve fresh fish and shellfish beyond the day it was caught. Many of these preserving methods, including salting, drying, smoking, and pickling, remain popular today simply because they make fish taste good.

SALTING may be a complete preserving method or a preliminary curing step in other methods. As the fish sits in a strong brine or with a surface coating of dry salt, for anywhere from a few minutes to many hours depending on the size and density of the fish, a two-way exchange takes place, with some moisture drawn out of the fish and some salt soaking in. (Sugar acts in much the same way, and sometimes replaces part of the salt in the cure.) This combination of reduced moisture and salt inhibits the growth of spoilage bacteria, thus preserving the meat. Salt-cured fish can range from a moist and luscious Gravlax (page 74) to rock-hard salt cod that will keep for years.

Another way to dry-cure fish is with smoke, which adds a nice flavor if it is done right. Most modern fish **SMOKING** does not dry the fish enough to preserve it at room temperature, but it's still a fine way to extend the refrigerator life of fish (see Hot-Smoked Fish, page 175).

PICKLING in all its various forms relies on acid as well as salt to inhibit bacterial growth. Some pickled fruits and vegetables use acids produced naturally in the pickling process, but with seafood, the acid usually comes from vinegar or citrus juice. The simplest form is *ceviche*, raw fish marinated in lemon or lime juice. A related treatment for cooked fish, and probably related linguistically as well, is *escabeche*.

In most versions of *escabeche* small whole fish or chunks of larger fish are cooked in oil, then covered with a hot vinegar mixture and allowed to cool in the marinade, where they will rest several hours to a couple of days before being served cold or at room temperature. See Sierra en Escabeche, page 177, and Pesce in Saor, page 184, for Latin American and Italian variations on this technique.

Equipment

Nothing very fancy is required to prepare most of the recipes in this book. Basic cookware needs are a good-sized skillet or sauté pan (nonstick is nice) for sautéing and poaching; an assortment of saucepans, at least one with a nonreactive (i.e., not uncoated aluminum) surface for reducing acid sauces; and a big pot for stocks and boiling whole crabs or pasta. In skillets and saucepans, look for a heavy base of aluminum or another metal with good heat-conducting properties. A wok is handy not only for stir-frying but also for the occasional deep-frying; it also makes a perfect extra-large sauté pan, with enough capacity to toss four servings of pasta in a sauce. For specialized equipment for steaming fish, see page 24; for grilling, see page 19; for smoking fish, page 174.

The three basic cook's knives—a short paring knife, a longer, heavier chef's knife (or a Chinese vegetable knife), and a boning knife—will handle all the cutting chores. If you expect to do a lot of cutting up of your own fish, you should have a fillet knife, basically a boning knife with a longer, more flexible blade. I have been using the same 9-inch, wooden handled, rustable carbon steel fillet knife (Russell model 2333-9) for almost 20 years, and I wouldn't want to be without it. You may have to go to a commercial restaurant supply (or a fishermen's supply store, if you live near a fishing port) to find one that long.

A few hand tools that make life easier for the seafood cook are an offset spatula with a long blade, for lifting whole fish fillets out of the pan and off the grill; spring-loaded tongs, for everything from turning shrimp in a sauté pan to lifting swordfish brochettes off the grill; a skimmer, preferably the Chinese woven wire type with a bamboo handle, for lifting foods out of boiling water or hot oil; and an instant-reading thermometer, to check the internal temperature of fish cooked by any method. An oyster knife is essential for opening raw oysters (see page 263). A clam knife (the two are not interchangeable) is necessary only if you have occasion to open raw clams. I've never bothered to buy a special tool for scaling fish. I use my clam knife for this job far more often than for opening clams. A shrimp deveining tool is handy but not essential.

FOOD PROCESSOR, BLENDER, AND FOOD MILL
A food processor is useful for chopping mousse-like mixtures, but a blender often does a better job on more liquid ingredients, such as the marinade for Jerk Fish (page 98), and on grinding dried mushrooms to a powder for the halibut dish on page 100. Some blenders come with smaller jars especially for blending tiny amounts of food, and at least one major brand is designed so that a half-pint or pint mason jar will screw into the base that attaches the blade to the jar; the mixture can then be stored in the same jar with a lid. This setup will even work as a spice grinder, if you have a sufficient quantity to grind.

A hand-cranked food mill is one of the most underappreciated kitchen tools in America. No food processor or blender can do what it does so simply and so well, simultaneously puréeing and straining. I consider mine indispensable for certain tasks, such as making Romesco (see page 321) or Chinese-style fish paste (see page 218). There are several variations on the design, but they all consist of a container about the size of a small saucepan, with a bottom perforated with tiny holes, and a rotating spring-loaded handle attached to one or more angled blades. As you crank the handle, the blades gather food pieces and force them down against the bottom. The soft part goes through the holes, while pieces of skin, seeds, bones, and other tough parts remain inside. Some fancier models have interchangeable plates with different sizes of holes for finer and coarser purées. A new one costs about $30, and fancy versions much more, but chances are you can find one for a few bucks at a garage sale or thrift store.

Notes on Ingredients

Many of the ingredients that give modern Pacific Coast cooking its flavor are Asian in origin, and have become more widely available as Asian specialty stores move into more cities and suburbs, and supermarkets increase their selection of Asian foods. Following are some of the less familiar ingredients used in this book (not all of them Asian by any means).

BEAN THREADS Thin, translucent, brittle noodles made from mung bean starch, used in southern Chinese and Southeast Asian cuisines. Their flavor is neutral, but they soak up other flavors well. They go by lots of names, including Chinese vermicelli, glass noodles, and cellophane noodles. Some rice noodles may have similar names, so check the label to make sure they are made from bean starch and not rice. The packages containing several small bundles are most convenient, as separating a larger bundle is difficult. Bean threads are soaked in hot water, rather than boiled, to prepare them for use. They need no further cooking, though they will keep their shape through cooking in dishes like Salmon with Three Beans (page 63), Steamed Butterfish with Bean Threads (page 189), and Shark Braised with Cabbage (page 160).

BLACK BEANS, CHINESE These soft, slightly shriveled black beans, unrelated to the black turtle beans of the New World, are one of the fundamental ingredients of Cantonese cooking. In a process related to the manufacture of soy sauce, miso, and other soy condiments, soybeans are inoculated with a special mold that partially digests their protein, then they are salted and dried for storage. They give a flavor sometimes described as "winy" to many southern Chinese dishes, especially vegetables and seafood. Fish, crab, lobster, shrimp, clams, oysters—if it lives in the water and it's edible, chances are a Cantonese cook has prepared it with a black bean sauce (see page 203).

Black beans are sold in Chinese groceries in plastic bags of various sizes, but most experts recommend the Pearl River Bridge brand from China, sold in a half-kilogram cardboard canister labeled "Yang Jiang Preserved Beans with Ginger." Transfer the beans to a jar for storage after opening; they will keep indefinitely.

BUTTER Butter in these recipes means unsalted butter. This is sometimes referred to as "sweet" butter, but don't rely on this term, as some packages of salted butter have the words "sweet cream" on the label. Unsalted butter is more perishable than salted, so stores have to turn it over faster and it tends to be fresher when you buy it. Plus, it adds no salt to the overall dish, allowing you more leeway with other salty ingredients.

CHESAPEAKE SEAFOOD SEASONING A style of blended spices, less hot and more complex than a Creole blend, with celery seed and mustard among the dominant ingredients. The best known brand is Old Bay Seasoning, which many cooks in the Chesapeake region consider an absolute necessity in making crab cakes. Old Bay and similar blends from the major spice houses are sold in nearly every supermarket, but if you prefer to grind whole spices as needed for the freshest possible flavor, you might want to make your own. Recipes are trade secrets, but the following blend tastes pretty close to the packaged versions.

MAKES ABOUT ⅓ CUP

2 teaspoons kosher salt

2 tablespoons celery seed

2 teaspoons peppercorns

2 teaspoons mustard seed

4 bay leaves

6 cloves

¼ teaspoon ground ginger

½ teaspoon mace flakes, or ¼ teaspoon ground mace

½ cinnamon stick

1 teaspoon paprika

¼ teaspoon cayenne, more or less, to taste

¼ teaspoon cardamom seed (about 2 pods)

➤ Combine all the ingredients in a spice grinder and grind to a coarse powder. Store in a tightly sealed jar.

CHILES The recipes generally specify which variety of chile, fresh or dried, to use. For fresh green chile to spike a salsa or relish, I usually use serrano if I can get it, otherwise jalapeño, which packs about the same amount of heat per chile. Hero chile eaters might want to substitute the Scotch bonnet pepper of the Caribbean, which is the same as or nearly identical to the *chile habanero* of Yucatán and is the hottest of all chiles, about 50 times hotter than a jalapeño on the Scoville scale of chile intensity. There's much more to the flavor of any chile than just its Scoville rating, and the Scotch bonnet/*habanero* has plenty of sweet, rich chile flavor to balance the heat.

Fresh red chiles are to their green counterparts what red bell peppers are to green—that is, fully ripe, sweeter, and just plain more flavorful. I grab some whenever they are available, but find they don't keep as well as the green ones. However, roasting the chiles—really roasting them, not just blistering the skins for peeling—renders the thick flesh soft enough to strain through a food mill or sieve, leaving the seeds and waxy skins behind. The result is a bright red paste, the color of Sriracha sauce or Vietnamese chile paste, but milder, so you can use more of it. Add some salt and a little vinegar and the paste will keep for several weeks in the refrigerator. See Baked Curried Lingcod, page 125, for the procedure for making fresh red chile paste.

Most of the heat in chiles is in the whitish inner tissues around the seeds (the veins or ribs). Removing the seeds and ribs allows you to use more of the flesh of the chile without making the sauce unbearably hot. Of course, if you like it really hot, you can leave some of the ribs attached.

"Red pepper flakes" refers to flakes of small dried red chiles, usually serrano or a similar variety, chopped or crushed to various degrees of fineness. They are sold in supermarket spice racks, but if you head for the Mexican foods aisle, you can buy the same thing in cellophane envelopes for a fraction of the price, or, cheaper still, buy them in bulk at an Indian store.

COCONUT MILK This staple of Southeast Asian and South Indian cooking is not the liquid inside a coconut, but a thick extract made by grating the coconut meat, blending it with water, and straining it to squeeze out every drop of flavor. Most markets carrying Asian ingredients, including many supermarkets, carry good canned coconut milk from Thailand, Malaysia, or other countries.

Coconut milk always brings up a dilemma for me. It tastes so good, but it's full of saturated fat, so it's become an occasional indulgence these days rather than a staple. After years of using just half a can, and throwing out the rest when it went bad, I now throw out most of the fat right off the bat. Here's how: Keep the can in the same upright position in which it sat on the shelf. Open it, trying not to shake it too much, and pour the contents into a pint glass measuring cup (or a pint canning jar with ounce markings). Let it stand until the cream rises to the top, then spoon cream from the top back into the can until you get down to the quantity of milk you need for the recipe. Take a look at the cream, ask yourself if you really want to save it, and if not, toss it.

CRÈME FRAÎCHE A form of thick ripened

cream, less sour than sour cream, with excellent cooking qualities. To make your own, combine whipping cream (preferably the kind without gums and other additives) with 1 tablespoon of cultured buttermilk per cup of cream. Warm the mixture to body temperature in a double boiler, transfer it to a glass jar or bowl, cover, and let stand at room temperature 24 hours. Refrigerate until ready to use.

CREOLE SEAFOOD SEASONING A blend of red, white, and black pepper with salt and herbs, typical of Louisiana cooking. There are several commercial brands, including Paul Prudhomme's Cajun Magic and Tony Cachere's, but it's easy and cheaper to make your own: Combine 1 teaspoon each paprika, California or New Mexico chile powder, and kosher salt (less if using table salt). Add ½ teaspoon each black and white pepper, ¼ teaspoon crumbled thyme leaves, and a pinch of cayenne. Store in a spice jar.

CURRY PASTE Pounded mixtures of spices, chiles, herbs, and other aromatic ingredients are the foundation of a huge range of dishes called curries from India through Southeast Asia. Thai cooking has developed several archetypes, described by color (among them red, based on dried chiles, the very hot green variety made with fresh chiles, and the milder yellow, with little or no chile). I used to make my own, lovingly grinding my own galangal, lemongrass, and coriander roots in a mortar, but every time I went shopping for these ingredients I saw cans and jars of prepared curry pastes from Thailand at attractive prices. I finally decided that the packaged versions are quite good, and now I only rarely make my own. A plastic tub holding a little under a pint of red curry paste goes a long way, and keeps very nicely.

FISH SAUCE Like soy sauce in Chinese and Japanese cooking, fish sauce provides one of the basic flavors of most Southeast Asian cuisines. This thin, salty, brown liquid is made from salted anchovies, and has a powerful smell when uncooked. But cooking (or even mixing with some boiling water, as in the dipping sauce on page 326) releases the strong smell, leaving a deliciously deep flavor behind. Most brands, even those with Vietnamese-looking labels, come from Thailand. Unless you use a lot of this condiment and need to watch every penny, look for a more expensive (but more delicately flavored) premium variety like the Viet Huong "Flying Lion" brand sold in glass bottles. It costs about three times as much as the cheaper variety in square plastic bottles, but it's still no more expensive than good soy sauce or, for that matter, decent wine, good olive oil, or many other quality ingredients.

OILS For sautéing, unless a specific oil is called for, use one with a pleasant to neutral flavor and a high smoking point, such as peanut or corn oil. Canola oil will work, if you like it. With the lowest level of saturated fat of all vegetable oils, as well as the highest percentage of monounsaturated fatty acids, especially the omega-3 variety (see page 35), it shot to the top of the charts in the '90s. I just don't care for the taste. This may sound like an odd criticism in a seafood cookbook, but canola oil smells and tastes a little fishy to me. Besides, if you are eating fish regularly, you are probably getting plenty of omega-3s from the fish and don't need to worry about squeezing in every milligram you can at the expense of flavor.

Two varieties of olive oil are called for in the recipes. Extra virgin olive oil is cold-pressed and unrefined to preserve its greenish color, aroma, and flavor. It gives a wonderful flavor to dressings and marinades, but much of its special flavor and aroma evaporate when the oil is heated. For sautéing and other cooking, I recommend the more common, less expensive variety sold in 3-liter or gallon cans and labeled "pure olive oil." Starting with a lesser grade of oil that has been refined to strip away the harsh flavors, most packers add back a small amount of virgin oil for flavor. Good brands of both grades of olive oil are available from all over southern Europe as well as California; they vary widely in quality and intensity of flavor. Like wine, price is only a general indicator of quality, and the quality differences among the most expensive bottles may be noticeable only to an expert.

A few dishes call for Asian-style sesame oil. Made from toasted rather than raw sesame seeds, this medium-brown oil has a powerful aroma and, like the best extra virgin olive oil, it's more of a finishing flavor than a cooking medium. Look for sesame oil in Chinese and Japanese markets. Be sure you are getting pure sesame oil, as some brands are blended with peanut or other oils to stretch them (but not proportionally to their price).

PEPPERS, ROASTED AND PEELED Any good-sized sweet pepper or chile bigger than a jalapeño will be more pleasant to eat if you remove the waxy outer skin. The easiest way is by roasting, which also happens to add a delicious flavor. Whatever the heat source—a broiler, a grill, a very hot oven, the open flame of a stovetop burner, or a propane torch—heat the skin until it blisters and begins to separate from the flesh beneath, then enclose the hot pepper (some use a bag, but I prefer a covered bowl) so it steams for a while and the skin slips off with little effort. If you are grilling, you can roast peppers on the same fire you will use later for the fish, but the timing can get tricky, so it's probably better to do it ahead of time. Or use today's fire to roast some peppers for another meal—they will keep for several days in the refrigerator.

PRESERVED LEMONS Curing fresh lemons with salt in the Moroccan style turns them into something else entirely, as different from the fresh fruit as marmalade is from fresh oranges. With salt and time, the bright, snappy acidity of the juice and the slightly bitter skin oils combine into an intensely flavorful whole, which can be used in small amounts as an accent ingredient.

Like many cooks on this side of the Atlantic, I first learned about preserved lemons from the cookbooks of Paula Wolfert, and the procedure here is based on hers. Many cooks in California make them with the fragrant, thin-skinned Meyer lemon, which is a popular home-grown variety here (and available in some markets), but Paula recommends against preserving Meyers, as they don't last very long before turning too soft. If you do use Meyers, bear in mind that they are lower in acid than ordinary lemons, so you should use standard lemons for the juice.

Choose organic or certified pesticide-free lemons if at all possible. Wash and dry them. Set aside about half of the lemons for juicing. Cut the rest into 6 wedges if small, 8 if average size. Sprinkle a little kosher salt into a large clean glass jar. Add a layer of lemon wedges, sprinkle generously with salt, and continue adding lemons and salt, pressing down with a spoon to eliminate air pockets. Some juice will soak out of the lemons right away; top up with additional lemon juice to barely cover the lemon wedges, then cover the jar and let it stand at room temperature for a week, inverting the jar once a day to redistribute the salt and juice. Pour in a half-inch layer of olive oil and store in a cool pantry or in the refrigerator for up to 4 months.

RICE Several kinds of rice are called for in the recipes in this book. Most are defined by the length of the grain, although it is the relative amounts of two different starches, not the shape, that determine the cooking qualities of a given variety. The long-grain rice most familiar to Americans is best for jambalaya and other regional American dishes, and is preferred by most Chinese for everyday white rice. Japanese taste runs to a shorter, softer grain, such as the medium-length Calrose variety grown in California. Italian risotto and Spanish dishes of the paella family use a short-grain type, of which Italian arborio is the best known example; you might also find a Spanish variety packaged as paella rice, which is nearly identical. (Confusingly, Italian books often refer to the best grades of arborio rice as "long-grain," because they have longer grains than other Italian rices, but they are still what we would call a short-grain variety.) In a pinch, Calrose will make an acceptable risotto or paella, though an aficionado could tell the difference.

RICE PAPERS Edible sheets of a sort of dried rice pasta, used as a wrapper for spring rolls and other Asian dishes. The brittle, translucent sheets, bearing the marks of the woven bamboo mats on which they are dried, are especially popular in Vietnamese and Cambodian cuisines, and they are sold in Southeast Asian and some Chinese groceries. They come in rounds and wedge shapes of various sizes, of which 6-inch rounds or quarter rounds are the most convenient size and shape. A brief soaking with water makes them flexible and edible without any further cooking, as in the Fresh Rice-Paper Rolls with Crab on page 233. They may also be used as edible wrappers for fish to be sautéed, trapping herbs and other seasonings inside a translucent layer that gets crisp and brown where it touches the hot oil.

SALT Salt has gotten a bad name in recent decades, to the point that its virtues are in danger of being lost. It has become a victim of a peculiarly American overreaction: If too much is bad, then less is better, and none is best of all. Admittedly, a lot of sodium (even the amount in the average diet) can be dangerous to those with high blood pressure. Even for the otherwise healthy, there is such as thing as too much salt. Short of that, salt is one of the cook's best friends. Used judiciously, it makes most foods taste better. With seafood in particular, it can improve both flavor and texture (see page 15). So unless your doctor dictates otherwise, don't leave out the salt.

IMPORTANT NOTE Where salt is used in measured quantities, as opposed to salting pasta water or seasoning "to taste," bear in mind that the recipes have been developed with KOSHER SALT, which, teaspoon for teaspoon, is only about half as salty as granulated or "table" salt. Like countless other Northern California cooks, I was first alerted to the difference among salts by Barbara Tropp, chef, author, and teacher of Chinese cooking. I agree with her that this coarse, flaky salt (in particular, the Diamond Crystal brand) has a cleaner, more pleasant flavor than the granulated kind. It has become my preferred salt for seasoning foods during cooking.

The reason kosher and granulated salt measure differently has less to do with chemical composition than with the size and shape of the salt crystals. Kosher salt consists of coarse, flattish, flaky crystals that fit together more loosely than the fine granules of table salt; a teaspoon or tablespoon of kosher salt contains a lot more air than the equivalent volume of granulated salt. If you compare weights, granulated salt weighs just about twice as much as kosher salt per unit of volume. So, if you are preparing the recipes in this book with granulated salt, start with half as much salt as called for and adjust to taste.

I frankly don't know where **SEA SALT** fits into this equation. Although some cooks swear by its flavor, I've never found anything special about it, and most brands I have seen are so expensive that I haven't been tempted to experiment. (Besides, virtually all salt is sea salt; even if it comes from mines, it originally precipitated out of seawater, albeit eons ago.) If you use sea salt regularly, you probably have your own formula about how much to use.

SOY SAUCE Unless another kind is specified, use a "thin" or "regular" soy sauce like Kikkoman, or one of the thinner Chinese brands like Koon Chun Thin Soy Sauce or Pearl River Bridge Superior Soy. Chinese labels can be confusing, however; widely different varieties can have nearly identical labels, at least in English. If in doubt, swirl the bottle and look at the neck; thin soy runs quickly down the inside of the bottle, while the more syrupy "dark" or "black" soy sauce leaves a stain that takes 15 seconds or more to disappear.

TOMATILLOS These small green fruits, which look like unripe tomatoes but are not at all related, are increasingly common fresh in supermarkets. Their flavor is basically tart and, like lemon and sorrel, it complements seafood. If you can't find them fresh, the canned version (usually found in the Mexican foods aisle) makes an acceptable sauce, though it needs less cooking.

TOMATOES Many recipes call for peeled, seeded, and chopped tomatoes. When ripe, tasty fresh tomatoes are available, by all means use them; otherwise use good canned tomatoes (I particularly like the organic Muir Glen brand from California).

To peel fresh tomatoes, slash an X in the skin of each with a sharp knife tip, plunge them into a pan of boiling water for 30 seconds to loosen their skins, then transfer them to cold water to stop the cooking. The skins should slip off easily. Halve the tomatoes crosswise, then gently squeeze and shake the seeds out of each half (working over a sieve set over a bowl if the recipe calls for the juice).

VINEGAR A dash of vinegar gives a tart accent to several dishes in this book. All vinegars are made by inoculating an alcoholic beverage (wine, beer, cider, distilled spirits) with bacteria that convert the alcohol into acetic acid. Usually the vinegar retains some of the character of the base liquid. The vinegar I reach for most often for fish dishes is authentic Spanish sherry vinegar, which retains some of the roundness and nuttiness of that wine.

Balsamic vinegar is a special vinegar made from boiled grape must rather than ordinary wine. It's aged in a succession of barrels of different woods for a rich, deep, slightly sweet flavor that is less acid than other vinegars. It is not interchangeable with other vinegars, and is used in a limited role in this book.

Seafood and Safety

Depending on whom you listen to, eating more fish is either a life-saving or a life-threatening habit. On one hand, we are told that reducing the overall amount of fat in our diets and replacing saturated fats with unsaturated fats can reduce the risk of heart disease and certain forms of cancer. Besides being low in fat overall, seafood is especially high in unsaturated fats. A growing body of evidence shows that a particular form of unsaturated fat, the omega-3 fatty acids found in fish, is especially effective in reducing the risk of heart disease.

On the other hand, we are warned about the dangers of carcinogenic chemical contaminants in fish, and of bacteria and viruses that can cause serious or even fatal diseases. Attention-grabbing headlines like "Is Our Fish Safe to Eat?" and "Death on the Half Shell" may give

pause to those who are looking for a healthy diet based on seafood.

Weighing the risks and benefits sometimes comes down to a mathematical exercise, but it is also a matter of common sense. Knowing the risks and how to minimize them is more than half the battle. The health hazards associated with seafood mostly fall into three areas: naturally occurring toxins, pathogens (disease-causing organisms), and chemical contamination.

NATURAL HAZARDS Several forms of plankton contain small amounts of toxins which, when sufficiently concentrated by the food chain, can cause serious or even fatal food poisoning in humans who eat the fish and shellfish near the top of the chain. The best-known example is the plankton commonly but incorrectly known as "red tide." Occasionally, mainly in the summer months, oceanic conditions can cause rapid growth in the population of a particular dinoflagellate (a one-celled form of plankton). Plankton-feeding organisms, especially mollusks like clams and mussels, can concentrate a toxin found in the dinoflagellates to the point that eating the shellfish can produce a dangerous neurological syndrome called paralytic shellfish poisoning (PSP). To minimize the danger, California authorities routinely impose a quarantine on wild mussel harvesting in the warmer months, and monitor the waters where shellfish are grown commercially, suspending harvests whenever signs of red tide appear.

Another neurotoxin carried by another form of plankton is domoic acid, which when sufficiently concentrated by the food chain can cause amnesic shellfish poisoning. Domoic acid was first identified in 1987 in mussels from eastern Canada, in an outbreak that caused several cases of illness and a few deaths. It has since been found periodically in certain West Coast fish and shellfish, including crab, razor clams, and anchovies, leading state health authorities to shut down the sport harvest of razor clams in Washington. At first, state health authorities issued a blanket warning recommendation against eating Dungeness crab fat and viscera; but extensive monitoring by California in the early 1990s turned up only one crab in 1,400 that exceeded the regulatory action level of 30 parts per million. Most of the crabs surveyed showed no detectable levels of domoic acid. Authorities continue to watch the levels of domoic acid-producing plankton as part of the PSP monitoring mentioned above, but for now there are no warnings associated with Dungeness crab.

A third plankton-based toxin that is of concern in some parts of the world is ciguatera, associated mainly with tropical reefs in places like the Caribbean, Hawaii, and Australia. Large predatory fish in these regions can accumulate enough ciguatera toxin to cause food poisoning to humans who eat the fish. Ciguatera is not a problem in West Coast waters, but it could affect certain fish imported from tropical areas; fortunately, ciguatera is a local phenomenon, and where it is prevalent, commercial fishermen are usually aware of the "hot spots" and avoid them.

PATHOGENS that can be found in seafood include bacteria, viruses, and parasites. **BACTERIA** are unavoidable in a watery environment; every fish and shellfish that comes out of the water carries with it various species of bacteria. The presence of bacteria in itself does not constitute a health hazard; many bacteria are benign, and those that can cause illness are killed by normal cooking. In time, growth of bacteria will decrease the quality of raw seafood, but this kind of spoilage is an aesthetic rather than a safety issue. In other words, a piece of spoiled fish may look, smell, and taste bad, but it won't necessarily make you sick if you have cooked it enough to kill the bacteria that are there. (One important exception is discussed on page 38).

However, since some of us eat certain seafoods raw or partially cooked, bacterial contamination can be a serious health concern. By far the greatest proportion of food-borne illnesses traced to seafood can be blamed on one category, raw mollusks. Oysters in particular can carry several dangerous bacteria of the genus *Vibrio*, which if consumed alive in enough quantity can cause diarrhea and other gastrointestinal illness. One of these, *V. parahaemolyticus*, is found in Northwestern waters, and increases to potentially dangerous levels with some regularity in summer months. In the late summer of 1997 and again in 1998, vibrio illnesses connected to raw or undercooked oysters from certain inland waters in Washington led state health authorities to shut down shellfish harvests in some localities for several weeks. At the request of authorities, oyster processors in other nearby areas voluntarily halted shipments of oysters and clams to the half-shell trade during these alerts. By mid-September, the water cooled off, the bacteria levels dropped, and raw harvest resumed, but the pattern can be expected to recur in coming years.

Even more dangerous is *V. vulnificus*, which is

endemic in the Gulf of Mexico but so far unknown in West Coast waters. When eaten raw by healthy persons, this species can cause symptoms similar to those of parahaemolyticus, but in those with certain health conditions (including chronic liver disease, cancer, diabetes, and AIDS and related immune system disorders), vulnificus can also cause blood infections that are frequently fatal. People in these risk groups are generally advised to avoid raw shellfish altogether.

Like other bacteria, all forms of vibrio are killed by normal cooking, so the risk is limited to raw or undercooked shellfish.

VIRUSES responsible for hepatitis and other diseases can be a concern in shellfish from waters contaminated with untreated sewage. Fortunately, this is not a problem in most shellfish-growing waters in the West. And like bacteria, any viruses that do show up are killed by cooking.

Certain fish are host to **PARASITES** that can be a human health concern. The most common one in our area is a tiny larval roundworm, *Anisakis simplex*, which is widespread in the marine food chain and by some estimates is found in up to 90 percent of some popular fish like rockfish and salmon. If eaten raw, anisakis larvae can cause inflammation of the stomach or intestine, and may have to be removed surgically. As scary as this sounds, actual cases of this kind of infection are quite rare (outside of Japan) and never life-threatening. Some fish found in fresh water, particularly certain varieties of salmon, can also host larvae of a tapeworm that can infect humans if eaten. Tapeworm infections, while often long-lasting, are not

especially dangerous, and may in fact go unnoticed. Still, if only for aesthetic reasons, it's nice to avoid having live worms in your fish.

The two most reliable ways of getting rid of these parasites are commercial freezing (home freezing is not reliably cold enough) and thorough cooking. The problem is, at the internal temperature (140°F) that can be relied on to kill the worms, many fish are dangerously close to overcooked, at least from an aesthetic standpoint. Many of us prefer fish cooked slightly less, to about 130° (see page 16), which can present something of a dilemma. Do we sacrifice flavor and texture in the name of safety, or accept a slightly higher risk to enjoy the fish the way we like it? It's a difficult question, and one you need to answer for yourself.

One way to reduce, but not necessarily eliminate, the occurrence of anisakis in fish fillets is by prompt cleaning of fish after landing. In many cases, the larvae are confined to the fish's digestive tract, at least until the fish dies, at which point they migrate into the flesh. In theory, cleaning the fish immediately after it is landed (as is typically done with top-quality salmon, but less often with rockfish) gets rid of most or all of the larvae, but it does not guarantee worm-free flesh.

When anisakis larvae are present, they are often visible to the naked eye. They are an inch or so in length (but usually tightly curled in a spiral) and about the thickness of paper-clip wire. A light cream color, they can be difficult to spot in salmon and other dark-fleshed fish, but somewhat easier to see in rockfish and other white-fleshed fish. In some large processing plants, fillets are "candled" by running

Seafood Safety: The New Regime

For years, a variety of consumer-advocacy groups and publications decried the lack of a mandatory U.S. federal inspection system for seafood, with the implication that lack of inspection meant a risk to public health. While the extent of such risk has always been debatable, and evidence wildly conflicting, Congress finally acted in the 1990s, creating a new mandatory federal seafood safety program under the Food and Drug Administration. Under the new regulations, which went into force in late 1997, all seafood processors and importers are required to have systematic food safety plans based on the principle of HACCP (pronounced hass-ip), which stands for Hazard Analysis-Critical Control Point.

Pioneered by Pillsbury in the 1960s as a way of ensuring safe foods for the space program, HACCP is a system of preventive controls built into food processing. In essence, it consists of identifying potential health hazards in a given product or process and the most effective point in the process to intervene to prevent the hazard from occurring. At the heart of the system is the HACCP plan, a written series of procedures that each processor must have in place for each category of seafood it handles.

Scombroid poisoning, a hazard associated with tuna, mackerel, and certain other dark-fleshed fish, offers an example of the HACCP approach. When any fish is exposed to warm temperatures (by sitting on the deck of a fishing boat in the sun, or in shipping without proper refrigeration), bacteria can grow rapidly. Where in most fish this kind of spoilage affects only taste and aroma, bacterial action on a particular amino acid in the meat of fish of the family Scombridae (tunas and mackerels), as well as mahi-mahi and certain other dark-fleshed fish, can produce high levels of histamine in a matter of hours. If ingested in sufficient quantity, histamine, which is not affected by cooking, can cause serious and sometimes fatal symptoms similar to a severe allergic reaction. Under HACCP, processors of tuna and similar fish must have a system in place to eliminate or at least minimize the histamine hazard.

Once a hazard like histamine is identified, the processor's HACCP plan identifies the critical control point (CCP), the point at which something can be done most effectively to prevent or minimize the hazard, and establishes critical limits for the controls. For scombroid fish, the critical variables are time and temperature. Chilling the fish as quickly as possible after harvest and keeping it cold throughout storage and processing minimize the growth of the offending bacteria. The first CCP in a plan for tuna is checking the internal temperature of the fish on receipt. If the fish is just a few degrees above 40°F, a typical critical limit, the plan may include corrective action, such as quick chilling in an ice slush bath; but much warmer temperatures, visible spoilage, or high histamine levels detected by chemical testing will cause the whole lot to be rejected. After passing the receiving CCP, the fish simply need to be kept on ice until they leave the plant.

Much of what is new under HACCP has to do with monitoring and record keeping. Where before, everyone just looked at the refrigerator thermometer when there was a question about the temperature, and kept mental track of how long a batch of fish had been sitting out on a pallet, HACCP plans typically specify who will check what, how often, and what records will be kept. Verification, the last step of the plan, can be as simple as daily and weekly reviews of the receiving and storage records, or may involve lab testing of samples.

The system is not perfect. In one of the most controversial aspects of the current HACCP regulations, boats are not required to have HACCP plans (nor are retailers at the other end of the chain). In practice, this means the handling practices on the boat and the attendant record keeping become an extension of the first processor's plan. Ideally, the HACCP system provides a paper trail that allows each processor to demonstrate to the next one that the product is safe.

As described by FDA officials, HACCP represents "a fundamental change in the relationship between the industry and FDA." Instead of relying on government inspection to uncover problems and take regulatory action to address those problems, HACCP "places primary responsibility upon the industry to demonstrate that hazards are understood and are being prevented." While HACCP has its critics, I believe it is a scientifically sound approach that will increase the safety and quality of our seafood supply. The government is also looking at the HACCP model as the future of meat and poultry inspection.

As sweeping as the changes may seem, the basic practices in the seafood industry have not changed dramatically under HACCP. Throughout the industry, good firms have always followed good sanitation and seafood handling practices, most of which can be summarized as "keep it clean, keep it cold, and keep it moving"; now they simply have to demonstrate and document these practices more consistently. Processors of raw shellfish, one of the higher-risk seafood categories, did not wait for a federal mandate to learn how to identify and minimize the safety risks associated with their products. When the HACCP requirements came along, they simply adapted the successful voluntary safety guidelines that had been in place for years under the Interstate Shellfish Sanitation Commission into their HACCP plans.

them over light tables, which makes any worms easier to see and remove; but this is also less than 100 percent reliable. If you encounter a lot of worms in a piece of fish, you should return it to where you bought it for a refund.

Although the risk of infection is still small, raw preparations like sashimi and gravlax are probably the riskiest way to use a lot of wild West Coast fish. The high salt level in pickling recipes like the Pickled Herring on page 187 may be sufficient to kill any worms present, but the acid in Sierra en Escabeche (page 177) is not. The safest fish to use for these recipes are frozen or farmed. (Because they are fed a controlled diet, farmed fish are not exposed to parasites through the food chain.)

CHEMICAL CONTAMINATION Decades of pollution of our rivers, estuaries, and oceans have introduced hundreds of chemical compounds into the marine food chain, some of which are extremely toxic or carcinogenic. Many, such as polychlorinated biphenyls (PCBs), DDT and related compounds, and dioxin, are also quite long-lived in the environment. Some of these chemicals enter fish and shellfish by direct absorption, but the vast majority come from eating smaller organisms, which in turn received them from their food sources. Since most food fish are near the top of the marine food chain, contaminants present in only minute quantities in the environment can become concentrated to measurable levels. To further complicate matters, these contaminants are often highest in fattier tissues and in older, fatter fish, the very ones that contain the highest levels of beneficial omega-3s.

Cancer risk is cumulative, and proportional to the concentration of the carcinogen. So eating fish from heavily contaminated water on a regular basis presents a substantially higher risk than an occasional meal or regular consumption of fish from cleaner waters. However, the overall risk of cancer from eating seafood is considerably lower from cleaner waters. (Unfortunately, we have to talk about "cleaner" rather than "clean" water, because pollutants eventually spread far beyond their source. Even fish taken from ocean waters far from any major pollution source show measurable "background" levels of PCBs and other toxins that translate roughly to a cancer risk in the neighborhood of a few cases per hundred thousand.)

While no level of artificially introduced cancer risk is really acceptable, a dispassionate analysis would have to go in favor of more seafood consumption. For every person who gets cancer from eating a diet rich in fish, there are probably thousands who have been spared a heart attack. These odds may be little consolation to the cancer patient, but they remain a good bet.

While much of the research on synthetic chemicals in the diet has focused on cancer, a far more troubling issue has emerged in recent years, as scientists have realized how many of these chemicals, even in tiny concentrations, can interfere with normal hormone functions. Many pesticides work precisely because they are similar enough in chemical structure to hormones in the bodies of target pests that they disrupt their development or reproduction. As these persistent chemicals work their way through the food chain, it doesn't take a leap of imagination to see the risk in tinkering with the finely tuned system of hormones that control growth, development, and reproduction in non-target species—including us.

Research on contaminants in seafood and the related health risks is based on limited data, and much more study needs to be done. The best estimates will always be estimates, however refined and well supported they may be. In the meantime, we must continue to reduce the risks whenever possible. In the short term, this means better monitoring of contaminants in certain localities, and shutdowns of fisheries where necessary. But the long-term solution is to decrease, and as soon as possible eliminate, the introduction of new contaminants into the air and water. Anyone interested in seafood should support stringent and vigorously enforced clean-water and clean-air legislation (the latter because many contaminants enter the ocean from the atmosphere).

The main thing home cooks can do to ensure the safety of the seafood we eat and serve to our families and guests is to follow good basic food handling practices: Keep raw seafood cold (see page 8), and cooked seafood either hot or cold; try to minimize the amount of time either spends between 40° and 140°F, the range in which bacteria grow most rapidly. When in doubt, throw it out. Keep storage and preparation surfaces clean, and avoid cross-contamination by handling raw and ready-to-eat seafoods separately, and by washing hands, tools, and surfaces thoroughly after handling raw products.

salmon & trout

What better way to begin a book about Pacific Coast seafood than with salmon? In addition to it being one of the most delicious foods our part of the Pacific has to offer, no other fish is a better symbol of the natural resources of the region, and of its human history and traditions. And no other fish more clearly ties together the land, the rivers, and the sea, the impact of man's activities on this interrelated environment, and the challenges facing us and the fish in the present and future.

Arctic Char

Chinook

Chum

Coho

King

Pink

Rainbow Trout

Red

Silver

Sockeye

Steelhead

Pacific Salmon

King or chinook salmon, *Oncorhynchus tshawytscha*
Coho or silver salmon, *O. kisutch*
Sockeye or red salmon, *O. nerka*
Chum or "silverbright" salmon, *O. keta*
Pink salmon, *O. gorbuscha*
Steelhead (rainbow trout), *O. mykiss*

On any day of the year, most any supermarket or fish market in the West is likely to be offering some sort of salmon. The selection can include anything from whole fish at under a dollar per pound to fillets and steaks at ten dollars or more. The fish may be any of six or seven different species, caught in the wild or raised on a fish farm, all varying considerably in size, flavor, fat content, range, and season.

Most of this chapter will be devoted to the differences among the various salmons, and how to use each to its best advantage. But first, a look at the basic life cycle of all salmons, which is useful in understanding those differences.

Salmon, along with many trouts, are anadromous fish, which means their life cycle includes phases in both fresh and salt water. Because both salmon and trout are so valued by both commercial and sport fishermen, and because much of their life takes place in full view of man in rivers and creeks rather than in some unknown region of the ocean, the Salmonidae are one of the most studied families of fish, and salmon observers have developed a rich and specialized vocabulary for their developmental stages.

Salmon begin their lives as eggs laid on the gravelly bed of a river or creek. After hatching, which may not take place for several months, the immature fish spend anywhere from a few weeks to two years in fresh water, depending on the species. During this period, they grow and develop through various stages, from the newly hatched fry called "alevins," to the immature "parr" with their camouflage markings, and finally to the "smolt" that are preparing for the conversion to salt water as they migrate to the ocean.

After one to four years in the ocean, feeding and constantly growing, salmon reach sexual maturity and return from the ocean to the river of their birth to spawn and complete the cycle. In one of the miracles of instinctive behavior, fish that have spent years in the open ocean find their way across hundreds of miles, back to the same stretch of gravel in the same branch of the river where they hatched, to lay the eggs that will be the next generation. How they do it is still a mystery, but it may involve a neurological "inner compass" attuned to the earth's magnetic field, changes in day length that define the seasons, and a sense of smell that can detect incredibly subtle differences in the water from one creek fork to another.

Unlike Atlantic salmon and some other salmonids, which can spawn several times and return to the ocean afterward, Pacific salmon make a single spawning return in their lifetime, and undergo irreversible physical changes in the process. They also stop feeding once they enter fresh water, relying on accumulated body fat for the energy needed to swim upstream, sometimes hundreds of miles.

If she has managed to escape predation by whales, sea lions, and brown bears, not to mention fishing humans, a female salmon locates a suitable spot on the stream bed, makes a hollow in the gravel, and lays hundreds of eggs. Nearby male salmon add sperm (milt) to fertilize the eggs. After spawning, all the adults die. Those that are not eaten by gulls or bald eagles decompose in the stream, providing nutrients to the food chain that will ultimately nourish their own offspring.

Because salmon spawning is so site-specific, the stocks in one river rarely if ever cross-breed with those of another river. Even within the same stream, different stocks have evolved that enter the river and spawn at different times of year. Thus each salmon "run," a particular combination of species, river, and season, represents a genetically distinct population,

A Note on Names

In addition to common names, many species of fish and shellfish in this book are identified by their Latin or "scientific" names. To avoid confusion among common names in many languages, as well as multiple common names within a single language, the eighteenth-century Swedish botanist Linnaeus established a Latin-based system of classification of living things that is still in use today. This system assigns a unique, two-part, Latinized name to each species while identifying groups of closely related species.

For example, chinook (king) salmon is known scientifically as *Oncorhynchus tshawytscha.* The first part of the name, always capitalized, identifies the genus, a group of species having certain traits in common. *Oncorhynchus* (Greek for "hooked nose," a reference to the distorted jaws of spawning salmon) covers all varieties of Pacific salmon as well as several trouts native to the Pacific Rim. The second part of the name, the species, is not capitalized, and applies uniquely to chinook salmon. Sockeye salmon is *Oncorhynchus nerka,* coho salmon is *O. kisutch,* and so on (where the genus is clear from context, it is sometimes reduced to an initial). Species names sometimes refer to a discoverer (*pallasi*), or a geographic location (*californicus*), or some anatomical feature (*melanops,* "black-eyed"). In the case of Pacific salmon, they come from native Alaskan and Siberian names for the fish.

Several genera (plural of genus) may be grouped together into families, the names of which end in -idae (such as Salmonidae, salmons and trouts, or Pleuronectidae, right-eyed flounders). Families in turn belong to orders such as Salmoniformes (the Salmonidae plus the Osmeridae, smelts) or Gadiformes (cods and their relatives). These terms occasionally show up in the form of adjectives such as "salmonid" and "gadiform."

adapted to the precise conditions of its spawning grounds and ocean range.

With this specialization comes vulnerability. If a particular spawning run is interfered with, it can become threatened with drastic decline or even extinction. And Pacific salmon have faced plenty of threats. Dams on many rivers block access to upstream waters. Erosion of watersheds from logging, grazing, or other activity can cover spawning gravel with silt, smothering eggs and reducing the attractiveness to future spawners. Water diversions can result in water that is too shallow, too slow-moving, or too warm for salmon that have evolved to match conditions unchanged for millennia. Unscreened irrigation pumps can pull in juvenile salmon by the thousands, a major problem in California's Sacramento Valley.

In the case of chinook salmon, which spawn at three to four years of age, one year of spawning failure can make a serious dent in the population, but there are still younger fish out in the ocean that may do better next year. However, if the spawning grounds are unreachable or unusable four or five years in a row, that's it. One of the first major irrigation projects in California's Central Valley, the Friant Dam completed in 1942, cut off the spring run of chinooks on the San Joaquin River from its only spawning grounds, and within a few years the run was extinct. The story has been repeated on other Western rivers, especially in the Columbia River system, in which more than 200 historic salmon stocks have become extinct and at least 75 more are threatened or endangered. In fact, only a handful of wild salmon runs from California to British Columbia can be called healthy.

The exception to all this gloom is Alaska, which has continued to produce large harvests of all five Pacific salmon species year after year. The Alaska salmon fisheries are characterized by a relatively pristine environment and effective management, augmented by aggressive hatchery production. With abundant freshwater flow in largely undammed rivers, and little of the environmental degradation that has depressed or destroyed so many salmon runs in the Lower 48, Alaska's wild-spawning salmon stocks are in good shape for the present. Fishery managers have also figured out how to allow large catches while ensuring sufficient spawning return to the rivers, so the wild stocks are maintaining their numbers from year to year.

Add to that the many millions of juvenile salmon released each year by the state's salmon hatcheries, some of which survive to return to the river of their birth two to four years later. It's the truest form of "ocean ranching," a little like turning cattle loose on the open range, except that you don't need to herd them in; the salmon return on their own, driven by the same spawning impulses as their wild-born cousins.

Together, Alaska's wild-spawned and hatchery salmon make up fully 90 percent of all the wild-caught salmon taken in U.S. waters. As long as current management and hatchery policies remain the same, this is one fishery that should be sustainable at the high levels that have characterized the last decade.

If anything, Alaska's salmon fishermen sometimes face problems from too many fish. Processors have tried various forms to deal with the excess supply, some of which are succeeding in the marketplace (salmon burgers) while others (salmon ham, breaded portions) have struggled.

SHOPPING FOR SALMON

Salmon is available in steaks, fillets, whole and half fish, and sections or "roasts" of various sizes. Fillets of a given type usually sell for slightly more than steaks, because the latter includes bones and belly flaps that are removed in filleting. If you can use the quantity, buying a whole or half salmon will save you some money (if the price is less than two-thirds the price of fillets, it's a better deal). There's nothing quite so impressive as a whole roasted, poached, or grilled salmon for feeding a crowd. Even if you plan to cook it in pieces, cutting your own salmon allows you to create portions of just the size and shape you want, something you can't always count on finding at the fish market. As a bonus, you have the head and bones for chowder or other uses (see page 75).

Knowing your salmon species can help you get the best bargain, and cook your salmon to the best advantage. Here is a rundown of the various salmons that can be found in our markets, in terms of size, color, texture, and the fat content that is one of the main variables in flavor.

CHINOOK IS KING King, or chinook, is the least numerous of the Pacific salmons, but the most valuable. From California to Alaska, this is the species that produces the largest salmon (fish of 20 pounds or more are common in some areas), and for my money the best flavor. Kings generally spawn in larger rivers, often hundreds of miles inland, which requires large reserves of fat. The fat content of a given king

salmon will depend on the location, time of year, and food supply, but in general kings are among the fattest wild salmon. This makes them ideal for grilling, broiling, and other dry-heat cooking methods, although they are also delicious poached, steamed, or baked.

King salmon are fished commercially from central California to northwest Alaska, and are virtually the only salmon caught commercially south of British Columbia. (Chinook is the official name in field guides and regulations, but just about everyone in the trade calls them kings.) Perhaps it's partly local loyalty, or just the fact that these were the first salmon I learned to cook, but for me a midsummer king salmon caught off Bodega Bay, San Francisco, Half Moon Bay, or Monterey will always be the definition of salmon flavor. Thanks in part to aggressive publicity, the large, rich kings from Alaska's Copper River, available fresh in late May and June, command the highest prices in the market; some aficionados prefer the even fatter kings from the Yukon.

COHO = SILVER Silver, or coho, salmon comes close to king in size and flavor, and can be used interchangeably with king in recipes. Once fairly common all up and down the coast, coho mainly spawn in shorter coastal rivers and have suffered more loss of critical spawning habitat than any other species. Coastal stocks in Oregon and California are officially "threatened" under the Endangered Species Act, and both sport and commercial fishermen must release any silvers they catch. Some relatively healthy runs of coho remain in Alaska, especially in the southeastern region, and there is some commercial fishing for cohos in Canada as well. Peak coho catches are in July and August; look for fresh coho specials in late summer, or frozen fillet portions other times of year.

SOCKEYES SELDOM SEEN Though one of the smaller varieties of Pacific salmon, sockeye is among the most important commercially. In some years it is the most numerous salmon species caught in Alaska, and it brings in by far the most dollar value. Yet this fish can be hard to find in local markets in any form other than canned.

Sockeye, or red, salmon are found as far south as California, but mostly range from the Columbia northward. Where they occur, they can occur in huge numbers. In Bristol Bay in southwest Alaska, home to the world's largest sockeye runs, as many as 60 million of these fish return to their spawning streams each summer, and fishermen harvest tens of millions of fish year after year. (One hopes that two successive bad seasons in Bristol Bay in 1997 and 1998 had to do with weather cycles, and are not signs of a long-term decline.) Another major sockeye fishery occurs at the mouth of the Copper River, where the reds outnumber the famous kings twenty to one.

These large, apparently sustainable catches of sockeye are even more remarkable in that, unlike some other Alaska salmon fisheries, the fish are all from natural spawning populations, not augmented by hatcheries.

For years, the best Alaska sockeye salmon went frozen to Japan, and the rest into cans or smokehouses. (Sockeye is the premium canned salmon variety, commanding twice the price of pink salmon.) In the late 1990s, however, Japanese enthusiasm for Alaska reds waned for a variety of reasons, including a sagging economy in Japan, the growing world supply of cheap farmed salmon, and lingering resentment over a lawsuit brought by a group of Bristol Bay fishermen against the key buyers. If this pattern continues, sockeye processors may look to the domestic market to sell more of their fish both fresh and frozen, which would be fine with me.

Sockeye rarely top 6 pounds, but they pack a lot of flavor. Where bigger salmon often feed on small fish like anchovies and herring, the sockeye diet runs to zooplankton, including larvae of crabs and other shellfish as well as the tiny shrimplike krill. The result is a distinctive, especially "wild" flavor, as well as an especially strong meat color—like other salmon but more so. Although the common name "red salmon" refers to the bright skin color of spawning fish, it also reflects the deep red-orange of the meat. Those unaccustomed to sockeye sometimes think the color looks odd or fake.

CHUM AND PINK: BARGAIN-BASEMENT SALMON For those with the money to spend, it's hard to beat king, coho, or sockeye salmon. But two other species, chum and pink, also offer good eating, at a lower price. Both are plentiful, particularly in Alaska, and both are common in supermarkets as a less expensive alternative to the glamour salmons. In fact, they can be downright cheap, with whole fish sometimes selling for around a dollar a pound. As long as you remember not to expect the same flavor and fat content as in the other types, these cheaper salmon can be among the best buys in the fish market.

Chum salmon makes up 15 to 20 percent of the total Alaska salmon tonnage most years, versus about 10 percent for king and coho combined. Similar in size to coho, but considerably leaner, chum is perhaps the most variable salmon in the quality of the fish that come to market. At its best it can be a delicious, attractive fish; at its worst, it is disappointingly pale and bland.

Although chum salmon is the official name for this species, you would hardly know it from advertisements or package labels. A few products use the name "keta," but almost all of the fresh and frozen chum sold outside Alaska goes under the attractive-sounding label "silverbright," sometimes spelled "silverbrite." Although it sounds more like a brand name for toothpaste or metal polish, and certainly invites confusion with "silver" (coho) salmon, "silverbright" actually has a specific meaning within the fish trade.

When caught out in the ocean, when they are still feeding actively and their fat content and flavor are highest, chum salmon are as silvery in color as real silver salmon, though they lack the identifying black spots of the latter. Fish in this condition, known as "silverbright," offer the best eating and command the highest prices. However, most chums are caught not in the open ocean, but in river mouths and estuaries as they concentrate before spawning. Like other salmons, a chum stops feeding and lives on its stored fat once it heads into fresh water. In a matter of days, the meat becomes noticeably paler and lower in fat, with a corresponding loss of flavor and eye appeal. Hormonal changes cause the skin color to get progressively darker and marked with vertical bars and irregular splotches of red and green. Fishermen and processors rely largely on these color

changes, described in a range of terms like bright, semi-bright, and dark, to decide on the market value of a given batch of fish.

Unfortunately, the distinctions in skin color are not always followed at the retail market, where chums of any shade are likely to be labeled "silverbright." I have yet to see a chum salmon in a supermarket that matches the color of a true silverbright. Still, I have had plenty of very good meals from these fish. Just choose the ones with the brightest skin and the reddest meat.

Smaller, more plentiful, and even cheaper than chum is pink salmon, typically sold as a frozen headed and gutted fish of 2 to 3 pounds. Pinks are by far the most numerous salmon species in Alaska, with annual landings as high as 100 million fish, outnumbering all other species combined. Even with their smaller size, this amounts to 35 to 40 percent of the state's total tonnage of salmon. Pink salmon is the least typical of the Pacific salmons; it's relatively lean, with a finer flake and milder flavor than the other varieties. In fact, the best way to approach this species may be to forget that it is a salmon, and treat it as a salmon-colored alternative to various white-fleshed fish.

A whole thawed pink salmon is one of the easiest of fish to fillet, and yields almost 75 percent of its weight in edible meat. The fillets can fill in nicely in any recipe calling for lean, moderately flavored fish with a fine texture, such as rainbow trout, weakfish, redfish, or corbina. Sautéing, steaming, and baking are among the best cooking methods. The fillets take on seasonings readily; a liberal sprinkling of a packaged Chesapeake or Louisiana-style spice mix is an easy way to jazz up their flavor.

A whole pink salmon or half of a chum is also a good candidate for baking or roasting. Both chum and pink salmon carry most of their fat just under the skin, rather than throughout the meat as the other salmons do; cooking them with the skin on, so the fat bastes the meat as it cooks, maximizes both flavor and moisture. Leftovers are useful in salads, salmon cakes, stuffings for mushrooms, or any other way you might use canned salmon.

To select a frozen pink, look for one that has most of its scales intact; a lot of missing scales, especially in vertical marks that come from a net, are signs that the fish may be bruised. The fish should be rock-hard, with no ice crystals in the bag that would indicate thawing and refreezing. Allow at least 24 hours for the fish to thaw in the refrigerator (set it in a pan to catch the inevitable drippings). Rinse the inside of the fish well before cooking, and remove any traces of blood along the backbone.

STEELHEAD IS SALMON, TOO Rainbow trout, which has recently been reclassified to the same genus as the Pacific salmons (see page 55), is mainly a freshwater fish, but a certain percentage of the fish migrate to the ocean one or more times in their lifetime. There, they adopt the diet and habits of salmon, in the process losing their rainbow colors and taking on a salmonlike color in both the skin and the meat. On their return to the river of their birth, these fish are known as steelhead, a favorite quarry of sport anglers. Although they are strictly game fish in most of their range, and limited to catch-and-release fishing in some areas to preserve threatened stocks, there is a

small commercial take of steelhead as part of the in-river salmon fisheries on the Columbia, and also on some Indian reservations. It's a controversial fishery, and some restaurants and retailers in Washington and Oregon refuse to buy these fish out of sympathy with (or fear of boycott from) sport fishermen. I haven't heard of this happening in California, which may be why some of the Columbia catch winds up here. In any case, it's a fine-tasting fish, a bit paler and milder than salmon.

Wild steelhead is rare in the market. Most of what is sold as "steelhead" is rainbow trout raised on farms, either in salt water (see below) or fresh (see page 53).

FARMED SALMON

Not too many years ago, if you saw fresh salmon in a West Coast fish market, you could assume it was caught somewhere along the Pacific Coast. Today, it's just as likely to have come from a fish farm, possibly one halfway around the world.

The salmon farming that has revolutionized the world salmon market originated in Norway, with the species native to the north Atlantic (*Salmo salar*). Seeing the catch of wild salmon in decline, due to the familiar combination of overfishing and habitat alteration, the Norwegian salmon industry changed its focus in the 1970s from catching salmon to raising them in captivity. From a few Norwegian fjords, the technology of saltwater salmon farming has spread around the world to various coldwater sites in northern Europe as well as Washington, Maine, both coasts of Canada, New Zealand, and Chile.

The typical salmon farm consists of an array

of circular or rectangular floating net pens, accessible by boats or piers, in a sheltered saltwater site such as a fjord or deep bay. The pens are stocked with 6-inch juvenile salmon called smolts, usually spawned in the farm's own freshwater hatchery from its own broodstock. Several times a day, either manually or through automated systems, the farmer scatters pellets of feed based mainly on fish meal over the surface of the pen, and they are gobbled by the salmon as they slowly sink. In 14 to 18 months—the time keeps getting shorter as farmers breed for faster growth and feed producers refine their formulas—the fish grow to market size (4 to 10 pounds).

As salmon farming has grown more efficient, the fish have become less expensive. When farmed salmon first hit the market twenty years ago, they were mainly an off-season replacement for wild salmon, sold to those who would pay the price for a fresh salmon during the winter. Once the wild Pacific salmon season opened in the spring, the farmed fish could not compete in price. By the late 1980s, however, the cost of farmed salmon had dropped to the level of the wild fish, and farmed salmon gradually became a year-round alternative. Over the last decade, as supply has continued to grow and production costs have continued to fall, farmed salmon has actually depressed the price of wild, and fishermen routinely settle for prices lower than those that would have sent them out on strike in past years.

Atlantic salmon remains the most popular species with saltwater farmers, although various Pacific species can be raised by the same methods. Coho salmon was an early favorite with Northwestern farmers, and remains so in Chile, but these days it is mainly a niche item for some freshwater farmers. King salmon performs nearly as well as Atlantic in British Columbia, and a stalwart group of B.C. farmers has stuck with this native variety while others have switched to the slightly more profitable Atlantics. In Washington farms, as in Maine and eastern Canada, Atlantics are the rule. Maybe it's just my regional palate, but given the choice between a farmed Atlantic and a farmed king, I'll take the latter.

The one Pacific species that has succeeded worldwide in salmon farms is rainbow trout, which has come on very strong over the last decade in nearly every growing region. Rainbows have been aquacultured far longer than any other salmonid, though mainly as small fish in fresh water; but it turns out they will also grow to salmon size (up to 8 pounds) in net pens, in either fresh or salt water, and if fed like salmon their meat looks and tastes a lot like salmon. Chile in particular is producing a lot of saltwater rainbows, which are variously sold as salmon trout, sea trout, or steelhead, although their rainbow-striped skin makes them easy to tell apart from wild steelhead (see page 50).

All the farmed salmons share some basic advantages and disadvantages. If nothing else, being available every week of the year in fresh form would give them an advantage, but many chefs and retailers choose them even when wild fish are available because of their consistent quality, size, and shape. And as already noted, the price has gotten more and more attractive. Flavor is a bit more subjective; some tasters find the flavor of farmed fish inferior

How to Grow a Salmon-Colored Salmon

One of the distinguishing traits of all salmons is orange-red meat. But this color is not inherent in the fish; it comes from its diet. Most crustaceans contain a natural pigment called astaxanthin (which is, incidentally, the reason the shells of crab, lobster, and shrimp turn bright red when cooked). In the ocean phase of their life, wild salmon eat large quantities of small shrimp and their smaller relatives called krill, and in the process accumulate the astaxanthin in their flesh.

Captive salmon can survive quite nicely on a diet of fish meal, so long as it has an appropriate mixture of protein and fat. But without a source of dietary astaxanthin (or other carotenoid pigments) the meat will never develop that appealing "salmon" color; it will have the ivory color of farmed trout, or of that small minority of wild salmon that are genetically unable to deposit the pigment in their meat. Conversely, trout fed a diet containing xanthins will develop a salmon color, even in fresh water.

So, to grow a salmon that looks like salmon, farmers need feed with some form of pigment added. One source of pigment for feed manufacturers is shrimp or crayfish meal, but these are relatively expensive. Another option is canthaxanthin, a related pigment found in many plants, including carrots and marigolds, and widely used in food products from ketchup to poultry feed.

Both astaxanthin and canthaxanthin can be synthesized in the laboratory, producing molecules chemically identical to the natural form but at a lower cost. Synthetic astaxanthin, although the more expensive of the two, is also the more effective, and by the early 1990s it had become the standard pigment used by most salmon farmers around the world. The United States Food and Drug Administration did not approve the use of synthetic astaxanthin in fish feed until 1995, but when it did, many farmers and feed producers quickly converted from canthaxanthin to astaxanthin.

Shellfish are not the only natural source of astaxanthin; among the other organisms that produce this pigment is a yeast, *Phaffia rhodozyma,* which can be grown commercially on a large scale. Phaffia may turn out to be a more economical source of pigment than the synthetic form, with a possible marketing advantage in claiming a more "natural" product.

to wild, while others prefer it.

The biggest disadvantage (and this goes for salmon, steelhead, and arctic char alike) is that with the "high-energy" feed formulas that yield rapid growth, these fish deposit a lot of excess calories in the form of fat. Now, some fat is a good thing; just as in beef, fat means flavor in salmon, and a lot of the most prized wild salmon, like Alaska's Copper River and Yukon River kings, are favored precisely because they are fatter than others, in preparation for longer upstream migration. And I know it's "good fat" of the omega-3 variety. But one can have too much of a good thing, and for my money most farmed salmon simply tastes and feels too fatty (especially the belly meat, which can cook up downright greasy). Perhaps if enough of us who feel this way speak up about it, the word will get back to the farmers and feed manufacturers and they can find a way to "finish" the fish with a little less fat.

On the other hand, all that fat means it's a lot harder to overcook farmed salmon. Even when cooked to the fully opaque stage, farmed salmon remains juicy throughout, giving it a much wider margin of error than many leaner fish. Still, in a recipe where the drippings from the fish are retained in the dish, I much prefer wild salmon to farmed.

Trout and Char

Rainbow trout, *Oncorhynchus mykiss*
(formerly *Salmo gairdneri*)
Arctic char, *Salvelinus alpinus*

Through all the booms and busts and next-big-things of the aquaculture industry, one species has remained in steady supply: rainbow trout. A daily staple of the fresh fish market, these fish range in size from single-serving fish of around half a pound to 3-pounders perfect for the poaching pan. Processors now supply this fish in various forms (whole, fillets, boned, preseasoned), and even in different colors.

Native to western North America, rainbow trout is among the world's most widely transplanted fish species. Wild populations have been established (mainly for sport fishing purposes) in most of the temperate parts of the world, across North America and northern Eurasia as well as New Zealand, Tasmania, South America, and South Africa. It's proven just as adaptable as a farmed fish; in fact, most of the world's production comes not from the United States but from northern Europe.

U.S. trout production has remained fairly constant in recent years at around 25,000 metric tons per year—nearly 60 million fish. Approximately 80 percent of that comes from one state, Idaho. Most of Idaho's farms are located near the Snake River, where there is an abundant supply of clean, cool water. An extensive aquifer gathers runoff from snowmelt in the northern Rockies and the Snake River Plateau, transporting it through the porous volcanic rock and releasing it in springs that feed into the river. Some of this water is impounded in ponds and raceways (flow-through channels) where the trout are raised from hatchery fingerlings to market size.

While raceway trout rarely top 2 to 3 pounds, a few farmers on larger freshwater lakes are growing trout to larger sizes, up to 8 pounds, in floating net pens like those used in saltwater salmon farms. One of the largest of these farms is in eastern Washington, in one of the series of long, narrow lakes behind dams that make up the middle reaches of the Columbia River. Their fish, which has rainbow skin but is otherwise more similar in appearance, flavor, and fat content to farmed salmon than to other trout, can be used interchangeably with salmon.

In the wild or on the farm, in fresh water or salt, the color of a trout's flesh depends on its food supply. The vast majority of farmed rainbow trout get a diet based on fish meal, and they have pale-colored meat that cooks up to an ivory color, similar to that of a wild trout in a freshwater stream. However, feeding the same trout a salmon diet containing xanthin pigments (see page 52) will give the meat a reddish-orange color like that of its seagoing cousins, and, to my taste, a somewhat fuller flavor. Many freshwater trout farmers have added red-meated rainbows to their product line.

The most colorful trout of all, and also the least common, are "golden" rainbow trout. Originally developed in West Virginia as a sport fish, these strikingly colored fish represent not a separate species, but a particular color strain of the familiar domesticated O. mykiss. (Despite what some fishmongers might claim, golden rainbows have nothing to do with the wild golden trout of California [O. aguabonita], a separate species native to a few streams in the southern Sierra Nevada.) By crossing and back-crossing descendants of a single golden-colored mutant rainbow spawned in 1954, breeders were able to create a true-breeding stock of trout with a brilliant golden-yellow skin, marked with the characteristic lengthwise rainbow stripes of normally pigmented rainbow trout. Farmed golden rainbows, usually with red flesh, are sometimes found alongside other farmed rainbows in fish markets and supermarkets. Besides being pretty to look at, they are comparable in taste to other red-meated trout, meaning slightly fuller in flavor than ordinary rainbows.

All the small farmed trouts have moderately rich flesh, with a fat content of around 7 percent. Whole fish are ideal for pan-frying or grilling if small, and poaching, roasting, or baking if larger. The restaurant trade demands uniformly sized 6- to 8-ounce fish; in the retail market, fish are more randomly sized. A fish of 1 to 1½ pounds is a convenient size to serve two, a 2- to 3-pounder to serve four. Some small trout are sold as head-on boneless fish, ideal for stuffing or for cooking butterfly style (with both fillets attached by the skin, generally with the head removed). Larger trout are sometimes sold in fillet form, with some processors removing the pin bones for a completely boneless fillet. I always cook trout with the skin on; it helps hold the meat together, as well as providing flavor (most of which is in the thin fat layer just under the skin). I also like to eat the skin, but some prefer to leave it behind on the plate.

If you can't find trout fillets in your market, you can always buy a whole trout and have it cut into fillets at the fish counter, or do it yourself (see page 12). If you want your fillets to be completely boneless, run your fingertips down the middle of the fillet from the head end to locate the strip of tiny pin bones; they continue about halfway to the tail end. With a fillet knife or a thin boning knife, cut as close as possible along one side of the pin bones, cutting down to but not through the skin. Repeat on the other side of the pin bones, then cut under the bones to remove them. This leaves a narrow channel in the meat that mostly disappears in cooking as the skin shrinks.

You might also find live rainbow trout of anywhere from a pound on up in markets with freshwater tanks. For now that means mostly Asian markets, although more full-service Western fish markets are adding live seafood tanks. The classic use for live trout is in Truite au Bleu (page 81), but it's also a good way to ensure the freshest possible fish for any recipe.

The newest member of the salmonid family to enter the aquaculture mainstream is ARCTIC CHAR. Part of a branch of the Salmonidae that includes brook trout, lake trout, and Dolly Varden, arctic char is native to the far northern reaches of North America and Eurasia, and also occurs in smaller form in the Alps and some English lakes. Among those lucky enough to have tasted it, a wild arctic char enjoys a reputation as one of the finest tasting fish in the world. I haven't had that experience, but the farm-raised char I have sampled from farms in

Trout or Salmon?

Originally found in the rivers of North America west of the Continental Divide, rainbow trout is usually identified in older books by the Latin name *Salmo gairdneri,* part of the same genus as Atlantic salmon and various Eastern and European trouts. However, the name has been a subject of debate for more than a century, with many scientists arguing that rainbow trout (especially in its seagoing form, steelhead) has important anatomical and behavioral traits more in common with the Pacific salmons (genus *Oncorhynchus*) than with other *Salmo* species. Others observed that rainbow trout was nearly identical to the Kamchatka trout of northeast Asia, identified in 1792 by Johann Walbaum as *S. mykiss.* Genetic mapping studies in the 1970s and '80s confirmed both these arguments, and in 1988 ichthyologists Gerald R. Smith and Ralph F. Stearley proposed to reclassify rainbow and Kamchatka trout as a single species of *Oncorhynchus;* retaining Walbaum's prior species name yielded *O. mykiss.* The American Fisheries Society adopted this usage in 1989.

the Yukon Territory and western Washington have been among the best farmed fish I have ever tasted. Imagine a very big trout, but richer in flavor and finer in texture, or a small salmon, but paler in color with less fat and a more delicate flavor, and you have a pretty good idea of arctic char. Any cooking methods suitable for either trout or salmon will work with char, although poaching seems especially right for its delicate flavor and texture. If you have occasion to cook a whole arctic char, you'll find that it's one of the prettiest of the salmonids, with skin of a pale coppery or rosy sheen, yellowish highlights, and faint pink spots. As a bonus, a typical fish of 4 to 5 pounds is the perfect size for a 24-inch fish poacher.

Steamed Salmon with Tarragon Mignonette

Here is one of the purest expressions of salmon flavor, and with zero added calories from the tart herbal sauce. For a discussion of the basic steaming technique and apparatus, see page 24.

SERVES 4

1 tablespoon finely minced shallots

2 tablespoons vinegar (white wine, champagne, or sherry)

1 tablespoon water

Freshly ground black pepper, to taste

1 tablespoon minced fresh tarragon

4 salmon steaks or fillets, about ¾ inch thick

Salt and pepper

Fresh tarragon leaves

➤ In a small bowl, combine the shallots, vinegar, water, pepper, and minced tarragon and set aside 30 minutes for flavors to combine.

➤ Season the salmon steaks lightly with salt and pepper and top with whole tarragon leaves. Place them on a plate that will fit inside your steamer and cook until a skewer easily enters the thickest part, 7 to 8 minutes. Serve from the steaming plate(s) at the table, spooning a little of the plate juices over each steak and topping with a little of the tarragon sauce.

Salmon Steamed in Spinach with Sorrel

With a generally milder flavor than salmon caught later in the season, spring chinook salmon lends itself to more delicate cooking treatments like poaching and steaming. Here it is steamed with a topping of sorrel, a leafy herb that looks like spinach but has a distinctive tart flavor that goes wonderfully with fish. One of sorrel's few drawbacks is that it turns an unappetizing olive green when cooked, but adding a layer of spinach helps with the color. Fresh sorrel is sometimes sold in the fresh herb section of produce markets. It can be expensive, but it is easy to grow at home, so you might ask gardening friends if they have any to spare.

SERVES 2

1 bunch (1 ounce) fresh sorrel

Leaves from 1 small bunch fresh spinach (about 6 cups)

2 salmon fillet portions, pin bones removed, 6 to 7 ounces each

¼ teaspoon salt, in all

Freshly ground white pepper, to taste

2 tablespoons fruity olive oil

► Trim off any tough stems from the sorrel. Blanch the leaves in boiling water for 30 seconds (the water in the bottom of the steamer is fine for this purpose); they will turn dull green. Lift them out of the water with a skimmer, rinse with cold water, drain well, and chop finely.

► Choose a deep plate that will fit inside your steamer and line the bottom with a single layer of spinach leaves. Place the salmon skin side down on the spinach and season generously with salt and pepper. Spread the chopped sorrel evenly over the top of the fish. Scatter the rest of the spinach over the top in a mound and sprinkle with a little more salt.

► Bring the water in the steamer to a rolling boil, add the plate, cover, and steam until a skewer easily enters the thickest part of the fish, about 10 minutes per inch of thickness. Drain the excess liquid from the plate, drizzle with olive oil, and serve from the steaming plate at the table.

NOTE Multiplying this recipe to serve more people is simple, as long as you have the steamer capacity. A plate large enough to cook four portions should fit on a steamer rack inside a 14-inch wok; otherwise, use two plates in a two-layer stacking steamer. For that matter, you could steam individual portions in a stacking steamer and serve them in the steaming plates.

VARIATION Omit the sorrel. Thinly slice one-fourth of a small onion crosswise, and slice the peel of 2 wedges of Moroccan-style preserved lemon (see page 32) into fine shreds. Combine and spread over the fish, top

with the spinach, and steam as above. For the final oil drizzle, use a teaspoon of the mixed oil and lemon juice from the top of the lemon jar.

Salmon and Asparagus Chawan-Mushi

This Japanese-style savory custard makes an elegant hot or cold first course for an Asian or Western meal. Individual servings are steamed right in their serving bowls, to be eaten with a spoon and chopsticks. Porcelain bowls and spoons give the most authentic look, but ordinary custard cups or ramekins and teaspoons will do. I use 4-ounce French ramekins, which hold exactly half an egg's worth of chawan-mushi apiece.

SERVES 4 TO 6 AS A FIRST COURSE

1 large salmon steak (10 to 12 ounces),
  OR 8 ounces salmon fillet

Kosher salt

1-inch knob fresh ginger (preferably thin-skinned young ginger)

8 spears medium asparagus, trimmed and cut diagonally into 1-inch pieces

3 large eggs

1½ teaspoons soy sauce

2 teaspoons mirin (sweet cooking sake)

Scant 2 cups thin chicken stock

► Remove any skin and bones from the salmon and divide the meat into 12 pieces. Salt the salmon lightly and set it aside in the refrigerator for 1 hour.

► Choose 4 to 6 individual heatproof bowls or custard cups that will fit inside your steaming pot. Peel the ginger, cut 4 to 6 good-sized slices, and lay one in the bottom of each bowl. Pat the salmon pieces dry with a paper towel and divide them among the bowls. Scatter the asparagus over the salmon.

➤ Bring the water in the steaming pot to a rolling boil. In a large bowl, beat the eggs, soy sauce, and mirin together until well combined but not foamy. Stir in the stock, being careful not to create bubbles. Ladle the mixture into the bowls to within about ¼ inch of the tops. Cover the bowls tightly with plastic wrap and place them in the steamer. Cover and cook 20 minutes, or until the custard is set; there will still be some liquid showing in the bowls, but the egg mixture should be jelled around the fish and asparagus.

➤ Remove the bowls from the steamer with tongs, unwrap (carefully—open them away from you to release the steam), and serve in the bowls, to eat with chopsticks and a spoon. The ginger slice is meant to be left behind in the bowl. To serve cold, unwrap the bowls after steaming and refrigerate at least 1 hour.

Poached Whole Salmon

The principles of poaching fish are the same whether you're dealing with a whole 10-pound fish or a couple of steaks or fillets: Use a well-flavored poaching liquid (court-bouillon), cover the fish completely in the simmering liquid, and don't let it boil. The proportions here are for a whole or headless fish of about 4 pounds in a home-size fish poacher. Any large enough pan will do, but the wider the pan the more liquid will be needed.

SERVES 6 TO 8

1 quart water

1 cup dry white wine, OR ¼ cup white wine vinegar

½ onion or 2 green onions, sliced

2 or 3 sprigs fresh parsley

1 bay leaf

12 peppercorns, cracked

¼ teaspoon anise or fennel seed (optional)

1 small whole salmon or chunk of a larger fish, about 4 pounds

➤ Combine the water, wine, and seasonings in a nonreactive saucepan or fish poacher and bring to a boil. Simmer 15 to 20 minutes. Strain if convenient.

➤ With the fish lying on its side, measure the thickest part. Lower the fish gently into the court-bouillon and cook, with the liquid never exceeding a simmer, 10 minutes per inch of thickness. Or cook until the center of the meat reaches 130°F on an instant-read thermometer. Drain and serve hot or cold. The court-bouillon may be strained and saved in the refrigerator for up to 3 days, or frozen for a month or more; boil it down if desired to save space, and reconstitute next time with more water.

NOTE Good sauces for poached salmon include Sauce Verte (page 324) and its stronger cousin Salsa Verde (page 317); the dill butter sauce on page 83; Beurre Blanc (page 325); and Basil Aioli (page 320).

Poached Salmon with Mussel Sauce

A sweet-briny essence of mussels combines beautifully with the rich but mild taste of early summer salmon. Try it also on halibut or white seabass.

SERVES 4

24 to 32 small mussels (about 1 pound)

¾ cup dry white wine

1 tablespoon chopped shallots or green onions (optional)

A handful of green onion tops

Sprig of fresh tarragon or chervil, OR
   ½ teaspoon dried

1 pound salmon fillet, in 4 diagonal slices
   (see page 14)

Salt and pepper

2 tablespoons butter

➤ Scrub and debeard the mussels, discarding any open ones that do not close when handled. Place them in a small saucepan with ¼ cup of the wine and the shallots. Cover, bring to a boil, and steam just until the shells open. Remove immediately, let cool, and shuck the mussels. Reserve the steaming liquid. (May be done several hours ahead of time.)

➤ Make a simple court-bouillon by combining the remaining wine, green onion tops, herbs, and enough water to fill a 10-inch skillet to a depth of at least 1 inch. Bring almost to a boil, simmer 15 minutes, strain, and return to the skillet.

➤ Season the salmon slices with a little salt and pepper. Slide them into the simmering court-bouillon and poach until a skewer easily enters the thickest part, 3 to 5 minutes depending on thickness. Meanwhile,

bring the reserved mussel broth to a boil and reduce it by half. Transfer the salmon pieces when done to a warmed platter or individual warm serving plates and set in a low oven to keep warm.

➤ When the mussel broth is reduced, add the butter and cook, swirling or stirring the pan, until the butter melts. Return the mussels to the sauce, taste for seasoning, and adjust if necessary. Blot away any accumulated liquid from the salmon plates and spoon the mussel sauce over the fish.

NOTE The court-bouillon can be strained and frozen for future use. If you have some already on hand, use it in place of the version here.

Fennel-Scented Salmon with Mushrooms

Most recipes using fresh fennel, also known as sweet anise, call for the celery-crisp "bulb" (not a true bulb, but the thick base of the stem just above the ground level). The upper stems and feathery green tops are usually thrown away. Here, they make an aromatic bed for salmon braised in wine. If wild fennel grows where you live, you can use the green tops and thinner stalks gathered from a clean source (preferably not alongside a highway or a path heavily used by walkers with dogs). Fresh dill, either the tender salad variety or the more substantial stalks sold in summer for pickling, will work in place of fennel.

SERVES 2

2 tablespoons butter or olive oil

½ pound mushrooms, thickly sliced

1 green onion, minced

Salt and pepper

2 thick crosscut slices salmon fillet (10 to 12 ounces in all)

3 or 4 sprigs fresh fennel tops

1 ounce dry white wine

➤ Heat the butter in a nonstick skillet and sauté the mushrooms over medium heat until they begin to brown. Add the green onion when the mushrooms are nearly done and season to taste with salt and pepper.

➤ Season the salmon lightly on both sides. Push the mushrooms to the edges of the pan, lay the fennel in the middle, place the salmon skin side down on top of the fennel, and add the wine. Cover and cook until the center of the thickest part of the fish is just slightly underdone when probed with a skewer, 5 to 7 minutes. Transfer the fish to warmed plates, discarding the fennel. Scrape the mushrooms and pan juices over and around the fish.

Chard-Wrapped Salmon Packets with Onion Confit and Lentils

How long to cook the onion mixture, called a confit in French, is a matter of how much time you have. Half an hour is enough to make it tender, but another hour or so of simmering gives it the melting texture of marmalade. You can make the confit days ahead of time, and can probably think of lots of other uses for it.

SERVES 4

2 tablespoons olive oil

1 large red or yellow onion, sliced thin

Scant ½ cup red wine

1 teaspoon wine vinegar

½ teaspoon sugar

Salt and pepper, to taste

1 bunch red or green chard

½ cup finely diced carrot

½ cup finely diced celery

4 crosscut salmon fillet portions, 5 to 6 ounces each

½ cup dry lentils, preferably the French green variety

1 tablespoon minced garlic

1 tablespoon chopped parsley

¾ cup Brown Veal or Poultry Stock (page 331), or reduced chicken stock

1 tablespoon lemon juice

➤ Heat 1 tablespoon of the oil in a medium skillet, add the onion, cover, and cook until it begins to wilt. Add ¼ cup of the wine, the vinegar, and sugar, and bring to a boil. Reduce to a simmer, cover, and cook until tender, at least 30 minutes. Season to taste and let cool.

➤ Choose 8 of the largest, most perfect chard leaves and trim off the stems, including an inch or two of the thickest part of the central rib, with a V-shaped cut. Reserve the stems. Blanch the leaves one at a time in boiling water (just until wilted, about 5 seconds) and transfer them to a bowl of cold water to stop the cooking. Drain and pat dry. Finely dice enough of the stems to make 1 cup and set aside with the carrots and celery.

➤ Remove any pin bones from the salmon portions and season lightly with salt and pepper. Lay out 2 chard leaves in oppo-site directions, slightly overlapping. Lay a salmon portion across the middle, skin side up (if the belly flap is especially long or thin, fold it double for a more compact, even shape). Arrange a quarter of the onion mixture alongside the salmon. Fold the near end of the leaves over the fish, tuck in the sides, then fold the whole thing over, forming an envelope. Trim off the remainder of the leaf to form a neat package. Repeat with the remaining salmon portions.

➤ Cook the lentils according to package directions; drain and season to taste. Heat the remaining oil in a large skillet and sauté the diced vegetables and garlic until just tender and well flavored. Stir the mixture and the parsley into the lentils, taste for seasoning, and keep warm.

➤ Add the stock and remaining wine to the same skillet and bring to a simmer. Lay the salmon packages in the pan, seam side down, cover, and cook at a simmer until a skewer easily enters the center of the fish, 8 to 12 minutes depending on thickness.

➤ Spread a quarter of the lentil mixture on each plate and top with a portion of wrapped fish. Turn the heat under the skillet to high, and reduce the stock slightly. Add the lemon juice, adjust the seasoning, and pour over the fish.

VARIATION In place of the lentil mixture, serve the salmon packets on a bed of lemon-scented couscous, or with a fragrant variety of white or brown rice alongside.

Risotto with Salmon and Peas

When your budget requires a little bit of salmon to go a long way, or you arrive late at the fish market and there is only one steak left, or you just don't feel like eating a lot of fish, try this one-dish meal. It can also be made with leftover salmon, simply stirred in at the end to reheat, but I prefer the flavor and texture of salmon cooked right in the risotto.

SERVES 4

1 large salmon steak, 8 to 10 ounces, OR 7 to 8 ounces salmon fillet

Salt and freshly ground white pepper, to taste

1 tablespoon dry vermouth

4 cups (approximately) mild chicken stock

2 tablespoons olive oil

3 green onions, white and pale green parts, thinly sliced

1⅓ cups arborio rice

1 cup petite peas, fresh or thawed

1 teaspoon grated lemon zest

Lemon juice, to taste

➤ Cut the meat away from the central bone if using a steak; remove the skin and pin bones. Put the fillet on a plate, season lightly with salt and pepper, and sprinkle with vermouth. Set aside to marinate briefly while preparing the rest of the ingredients.

➤ Have the stock at a simmer in a saucepan. Heat the oil in a deep skillet over medium heat. Add the green onions and sauté until soft and fragrant. Stir in the rice, coating it well with the oil. Add enough stock to cover the rice by about ⅛ inch, ½ teaspoon salt, and a pinch of pepper. Cook, stirring occasionally, until the liquid drops below the level of the rice. Add stock to cover again and cook down again. Repeat with successive additions of stock until the rice has swollen and the grains are opaque. Meanwhile, cut the salmon crosswise into squares a little less than ¼ inch thick, and if the peas are still frosty, warm them in the stock.

➤ When a grain of rice has only a tiny trace of a raw center, add one more addition of stock and the peas and salmon, and cook until the liquid is reduced to a thick, gravy-like consistency. Stir in the lemon zest and juice, adjust the seasoning, and serve immediately in warm pasta bowls.

Seared Salmon with Cucumber and Brown Butter

Cucumbers and salmon are a classic combination, although they are usually combined in cold dishes. Here, sautéed cucumber makes a delicious, pale green vegetable accompaniment to simply cooked slices of salmon fillet. Serve with mashed potatoes, steamed new potatoes, or a simple risotto.

SERVES 4

1 to 1½ pounds salmon fillet (center cut or head end), in one piece

Salt and pepper

1 medium or ½ large cucumber, split lengthwise, peeled, seeded, and sliced (about 2 cups)

2 tablespoons butter

1½ teaspoons lemon juice

Whole or chopped chives, for garnish

➤ Slice the salmon on a diagonal into 8 equal pieces about ½ inch thick (or have it cut at the fish market). Season the slices lightly on both sides with salt and pepper. Heat a large nonstick skillet over medium-high heat and cook the salmon slices until just slightly underdone, about a minute and a half per side. Transfer to warm plates.

➤ Add the cucumber to the skillet and cook until lightly browned. Add the butter, a pinch of salt, and the lemon juice, and cook until the butter browns slightly. Remove the pan from the heat, arrange the cucumber alongside the salmon, and drizzle the browned butter over the fish. Garnish with chives.

Spicy Sautéed Pink or Chum Salmon

A generous spice rub adds a layer of flavor to these two milder, leaner varieties of salmon. This will also work with most other lean and mild fish. For a Louisiana version, substitute a Creole-style spice mix like Paul Prudhomme's Cajun Magic, or make your own by the recipe on page 31.

SERVES 4

4 skinless pink or chum salmon fillet portions, 4 to 6 ounces each

½ teaspoon Chesapeake-style seasoning mix, bought or homemade (page 29)

¼ cup flour (approximately)

1 generous tablespoon peanut or mild olive oil

2 tablespoons butter

1 tablespoon chopped parsley or chives

Lemon wedges

▶ Season the fish portions evenly on both sides and let them stand 5 to 10 minutes. Coat them lightly with flour and shake off the excess. Heat the oil in a nonstick skillet over medium-high heat. Add the fish, skin side up, and cook until golden brown, 2 to 3 minutes. Turn and cook until a skewer easily enters the thickest part, another 2 to 3 minutes.

▶ Transfer the fish to warm plates and dab the oil out of the skillet with a paper towel. Add the butter and parsley and heat until bubbly. Spoon over the fish and serve immediately, with lemon wedges.

Salmon with Three Beans

It had never occurred to me to stir-fry salmon when, in the spring of 1988, I tasted a dish of salmon and asparagus made by a talented young Chinese-American chef. San Francisco-born Yujean Kang, then just a few years out of restaurant school, was making quite a name for himself combining Chinese and Western traditions in a small restaurant near Berkeley. He has long since moved to Southern California, where he has two successful eponymous restaurants in Pasadena and West Hollywood.

Before he moved south, Yujean kindly showed me how to make the salmon and asparagus dish, including the key technique of slowly cooking the salmon slices in still-warming oil. A variation on his recipe, with scallops added, appears on page 296; here is another. The three beans in the title are preserved black beans, fresh green beans, and bean threads, the transparent noodles made from mung bean starch, also known as cellophane noodles or Chinese vermicelli.

SERVES 2 AS A MAIN DISH, 4 OR MORE WITH OTHER DISHES

1 ounce bean threads

1 thick salmon steak, 9 to 10 ounces

1 egg white

4 teaspoons Shaoxing rice wine or dry sherry

½ teaspoon cornstarch

Pinch of salt

1 tablespoon Chinese fermented black beans

½ cup well-seasoned chicken stock

1 tablespoon soy sauce

½ teaspoon Chinese or Japanese sesame oil

¼ teaspoon sugar

1 teaspoon minced ginger

1 teaspoon minced garlic

1 tablespoon minced green onions (white parts only)

2 cups (approximately) peanut or other vegetable oil

½ pound green beans, trimmed and cut into 2-inch lengths

½ teaspoon cornstarch dissolved in 1 teaspoon water

▶ Put the bean threads in a bowl, cover with boiling water, and soak for 30 minutes. Cut the two fillet pieces away from the central bones of the salmon steak. Remove the skin and any pin bones from each piece. Slice the fillets crosswise (parallel to the backbone) into small ⅛-inch-thick rectangles. Stir the egg white, 1 teaspoon of the wine, cornstarch, and salt together in a small bowl; add the salmon pieces, and toss lightly to coat. Set aside to marinate 20 minutes.

▶ Rinse and coarsely chop the black beans and combine them with the remaining wine. Add the stock, soy sauce, sesame oil, and sugar and stir to dissolve the sugar. Combine the ginger, garlic, and green onions in another bowl. Drain the bean threads, cut them into 2-inch lengths, and arrange them in a bed on the serving dish or individual plates.

➤ Drain any excess marinade from the salmon and stir in a tablespoon of peanut oil. Set a clean, dry saucepan or other heatproof container near the stove with a heatproof strainer across the top. Place the remaining oil in a wok over high heat. Heat the oil to about 250°F (when a clean wooden chopstick plunged into the oil just begins to bubble from the tip) and add the salmon pieces, stirring gently to separate the slices. Cook just until the raw color disappears, then quickly retrieve the pieces with a wire skimmer and transfer them to the strainer. Continue heating the oil until the bits of salmon remaining behind are sizzling like mad, then add the green beans. Cook until just tender and slightly blistered, 2 to 3 minutes.

➤ Carefully pour the contents of the wok through the strainer. Return the wok to the heat, add the ginger, garlic, and onion, and stir-fry 30 seconds. Add the black bean mixture, bring to a boil, and reduce slightly. Return the green beans and salmon to the pan, stir in the cornstarch mixture, and cook until the sauce begins to thicken, about 1 minute. Ladle the contents of the wok over the bean threads.

NOTE The oil from cooking the salmon and beans can be strained through several layers of cheesecloth and reused a couple of times. It's probably best to use it for frying other seafoods.

Planked Salmon or Halibut

Planking is the modern descendant of the Northwest Indian method of cooking salmon in front of a fire, spread out in a frame of aromatic red cedar. Several Northwest-based firms manufacture specialized baking planks in various sizes, or you can fashion your own by routing or chiseling out a shallow basin in a plain 1-by-8 plank of red cedar, incense cedar, or alder.

Although baking and serving fish on a cedar plank will fill your kitchen and dining room with a cedary aroma, the actual transfer of flavor or aroma to the fish itself is subtle, to say the least. However, cooking on a plank can make a dramatic difference in the texture and moisture of the fish. Even when preheated, a thick slab of wood does not transmit the heat of the oven very efficiently; if anything, it acts as a heat sink rather than a radiator, moderating the oven heat and slowing down the cooking time. A piece of fish that might bake in 8 to 10 minutes in a metal, earthenware, or glass pan can take as much as 20 minutes to cook to the same degree on a plank, yet it still comes out tender and moist.

The instructions here are for steaks, but work equally well with fillets anywhere from ½ to 1½ inches thick.

SERVES 4

Olive oil

2 large salmon or halibut steaks, 10 to 12 ounces each

Salt and freshly ground pepper, to taste

1 teaspoon dried dill, OR 1 tablespoon chopped fresh dill, OR 1 teaspoon fresh thyme leaves

Zest of ½ lemon

➤ Rub a baking plank with a little olive oil and place it on the middle or upper oven shelf. Preheat the oven to 350°F. Meanwhile, season the fish on both sides with salt, pepper, and dill. Measure the thickness of the steaks in inches.

➤ When the oven is ready, scatter half the lemon zest on the plank, place the fish on top, drizzle with a little oil, and scatter the remaining zest on top. Bake uncovered, turning after 8 minutes. Start checking for doneness after 15 minutes total cooking time per inch of thickness; cook to 130°F on an instant-read thermometer, or until done by the skewer test. Serve from the plank.

Basic Grilled Salmon

I have probably cooked thousands of meals of grilled salmon—on charcoal and gas-fired grills in restaurant kitchens, over concrete picnic-area grills, on a catering-size rental grill at the edge of a vineyard, on a backyard hibachi or kettle-shaped grill, in the fireplace . . . but I have never before sat down to describe just how to do it. So here goes.

First, see the general discussion of grilling equipment and techniques on pages 18 to 21. I like to grill salmon (and most fish) in an uncovered grill, over a moderately hot fire—hot enough to keep me on my toes, but not so hot that the fish chars on the outside before it cooks through. I usually don't bother with wood chips for the short amount of time that salmon will be on the grill, but I sometimes toss a sprig of thyme or some dried thyme leaves on the coals just before adding the fish.

Given the choice, I'll always cook salmon in fillet form. Steaks have many advantages for the cook; their compact shape allows you to cook more per square foot of grill, and the skin and bones help hold the meat together. Also, both sides of a steak look equally nice, so if you mess up one side you can present the other side up. All in all, steaks are probably the better choice for less experienced grillers. However, steaks mean more work for the diners, dealing with the skin and bones. Fillets are simpler to eat, especially if you remove the pin bones before cooking. And when cut on the diagonal, fillets provide more surface area for browning and grill marks. So although it takes a little more skill on the part of the cook to get fillets off the fire in one attractive piece, I still prefer fillets.

Skin-on or skinless fillets? Some cooks prefer to leave the skin on, reasoning that if something is going to stick to the grill it might as well be the skin and not the meat. The skin, and especially the layer of fat just under the skin, also provide a little more flavor to the fish as it cooks. But I've never found salmon lacking in flavor without it, and after all these years I still can't figure out how to make a skin-on piece look as nice as a skinless one, let alone get the skin off the grill with any consistency.

Although you can add flavor to salmon with a marinade like the Noyo Harbor barbecue version on page 68, a little salt and pepper is really all you need. I've never found that oil in a marinade makes any difference in whether a piece of salmon sticks to the grill or not.

To my eye, a perfectly grilled piece of salmon fillet is one served bone side up, with one nice, clear set of grill marks on a surface lightly crisped by the heat. To get this appearance, you typically need to do more than half of the cooking with the bone side down. It really doesn't matter if you cook the bone side first or last, so long as the timing is right, but I always start with the bone side against the heat, as it seems to brown better that way.

The magic moment when the fish is ready to turn varies with the heat of the fire and the thickness of the fish, but 3 to 5 minutes on the first side is about right. When the fish looks nicely opaque at the thinnest edge, slide the long edge of a spatula under the long edge of the fish and lift gently; if the fish lifts away cleanly, it's time to turn it. If it sticks, wait another 30 seconds and try again; sometimes it needs to cook a bit longer before it is ready to release. If necessary, scrape the edge of the spatula against the grill to force it under the fish, and flip the fillet over onto the other side. Remove when done by the skewer test (see page 17).

As long as you have the grill going, think about other things to cook on the same fire, preferably before the fish goes on. You can roast peppers for peeling, tomatoes for a sauce, and all manner of vegetables for a side dish: corn on the cob, potato wedges, eggplant or zucchini slices—you can even make a whole ratatouille of vegetables grilled in slices, cut up into bite-size pieces, and tossed with olive oil. Just make sure you have enough fire to last through cooking the fish!

Here are three sauces for grilled salmon. Other possibilities include flavored butters (page 326), Beurre Blanc (page 325), Sauce Verte (page 324), or an herb vinaigrette (page 316).

Cucumber-Mint Raita

Serve with grilled salmon, tuna, sea bass, or other full-flavored fish.

MAKES ABOUT 3 CUPS (6 SERVINGS)

3 large cucumbers, peeled, split lengthwise, seeds removed, sliced ⅛ inch thick

1 teaspoon kosher salt

2 cups plain yogurt

1 tablespoon minced or grated fresh ginger

½ teaspoon crushed or ground cardamom seed

¼ cup fresh mint leaves, finely shredded

➤ Sprinkle the sliced cucumbers with salt and place them in a colander for 15 minutes to drain. Combine them with the remaining ingredients, cover, and let stand 1 hour to overnight in the refrigerator. Remove from the refrigerator when you start cooking the salmon.

Summer Vegetable and Tomatillo Sauce for Salmon

As salmon season progresses, I gradually switch from the plainer-is-better approach to pairing salmon with other high-summer flavors. Here, salmon is served with an assortment of seasonal vegetables in a sauce based on Mexican tomatillos. Use a colorful assortment of summer vegetables, at least two or three varieties from the following list: yellow or green summer squash, cucumbers, chayote, Anaheim or poblano chiles, sweet yellow peppers, green beans, and corn kernels. (While I might automatically include red peppers, keeping the vegetables in the yellow to green spectrum makes the orange salmon stand out beautifully on the plate.) Roasted new potatoes or couscous make a good accompaniment.

Try this with king, coho, sockeye, or top-quality chum salmon.

SERVES 4

1 pound fresh tomatillos, papery husks and stems removed

2 tablespoons olive oil

1 clove garlic, peeled and halved

2 green onions, sliced

½ teaspoon salt

1 cup diced onion

1 teaspoon minced garlic

4 cups diced assorted summer vegetables (see above)

Salt and freshly ground pepper, to taste

4 salmon steaks or fillets, about 6 ounces each

¼ cup chopped fresh basil or cilantro

➤ Quarter the tomatillos and place them in a saucepan with 1 tablespoon of the oil, the garlic clove, green onions, and salt. Cover and cook over moderate heat, stirring occasionally, until the tomatillos are quite soft, about 25 minutes. Let cool, then purée in a blender and set aside. (May be prepared ahead of time).

➤ Heat the remaining oil in a large skillet over medium heat. Add the onion and minced garlic and cook until the onion begins to soften. Add the vegetables in reverse order of their cooking time (slowest-cooking first) and cook until just done, seasoning to taste with salt and pepper. Meanwhile, season the salmon lightly and cook by your favorite method. Spoon the tomatillo sauce onto a platter or individual plates, arrange the sautéed vegetables around the outside, topped with basil or cilantro, and lay the salmon in the middle.

TECHNIQUE NOTE If you are grilling the salmon and you have room on the grill, you can cook the vegetables in a skillet right on the grill, as in the roasted tomato sauce in the next recipe. Or you can simply bake the salmon uncovered on a lightly oiled pan in a hot oven, and roast some new potatoes while you're at it. Broiling, like baking, keeps the top of the stove free for the sauce and other dishes. If you don't want to heat up the kitchen that much, consider using a stovetop grill or simply searing the fish in a nonstick skillet. Poaching and steaming somehow seem too delicate for the robust flavor of late-summer salmon, but feel free if you want.

➤ You might be tempted to save a pan by cooking the salmon directly in the sauce, but I don't recommend it. I've tried it with various combinations of fish and sauce, and it sometimes brings out a fishy aroma even in the freshest fish.

Grilled Tomato-Basil Sauce

Here's another late-summer grilling favorite, with the sauce cooked right on the same grill as the fish. Choicest salmon varieties are the same as in the previous recipe; the sauce goes equally well with swordfish, tuna, or any of the "summer fish" described on page 165 and 166.

SERVES 4

1 pound ripe tomatoes

3 tablespoons olive oil

1 unpeeled garlic clove, cracked

1 cup (loosely packed) fresh basil leaves

4 diagonal slices (about 6 ounces each) salmon fillet

Salt and pepper

➤ Build a hot charcoal fire in an open or covered grill. While the fire is still at the flaming stage, grill the tomatoes around the edge of the fire until the skins burst and begin to blacken. Remove the tomatoes to a shallow dish, and when cool enough to handle, remove the skins and chop the tomatoes as finely as possible with a knife and fork or metal spoon. Discard any large clumps of seeds.

➤ Set a wok or deep skillet on the grill and add 2 tablespoons of the oil and the garlic. Cook until fragrant, then add the chopped tomatoes with their juices. Set aside 4 large basil leaves; chop the rest and add them to the sauce. Cook, stirring, until the sauce is well reduced. Meanwhile, season the salmon with a little salt and pepper and sprinkle with the remaining oil.

➤ When the tomato sauce is well reduced, season to taste, discard the garlic, and set the pan aside. Grill the salmon pieces until done, 5 to 7 minutes depending on

thickness. Spoon a little tomato sauce onto each plate and set the grilled salmon on top of the sauce. Cut the reserved basil into chiffonade and scatter it over the salmon.

Noyo Harbor Barbecued Salmon

Every July 4, the fishing harbor on the Noyo River at Fort Bragg, California is the site of what the organizers call "the world's largest salmon barbecue." While I can't swear there isn't a larger one somewhere, they do feed generous portions of grilled salmon (plus corn on the cob and other trimmings) to upwards of 5,000 people each year, in a fundraiser for salmon hatcheries and habitat restoration on the Northern California coast.

The event involves a truckload of skin-on salmon fillets, and many gallons of their "famous basting sauce" (the recipe for which is happily shared with anyone who asks for it). In that kind of quantity, it's necessary to use shortcuts like garlic powder and dried herbs, but here is a scaled-down recipe for a backyard barbecue using fresh herbs. It will work fine with other fish beside salmon.

SERVES 6

Marinade-Basting Sauce

2 cloves garlic

Large pinch of salt

½ cup vegetable oil

¼ cup lemon juice

1 teaspoon soy sauce

1 teaspoon Worcestershire sauce

2 tablespoons minced parsley

1 tablespoon minced basil leaves

½ teaspoon dried oregano

Salt and freshly ground pepper, to taste

2 to 3 pounds skin-on salmon fillet, in individual portions

▶ Chop the garlic, sprinkle it with a little salt, and mash it repeatedly with the side of a knife blade until it is reduced nearly to a paste. Scrape up the paste into a bowl or a jar with a tight lid, add the remaining marinade ingredients, and stir or shake well.

▶ Marinate the salmon fillets for about an hour in two-thirds of the sauce; reserve the rest for basting. Prepare a medium-hot fire in a charcoal or gas grill. Lift the fish out of the marinade, let drain briefly, and start cooking with the skin side up. Grill (see Basic Grilled Salmon, page 65) until nicely marked, turn, and baste with the reserved marinade.

▶ Serve with corn on the cob, green salad, and crusty bread.

Baked Salmon Fillet with Sesame-Ginger Crust

Either thin steaks or fillet cuts will work for this recipe. Square-cut fillet portions that are more than about ¾ inch thick are probably best cut butterfly-style (see page 15).

For a more colorful coating, use black sesame seeds for up to half of the total.

SERVES 4

2 quarter-size slices fresh ginger, peeled

1 teaspoon mild vegetable oil

¼ cup raw sesame seeds

4 salmon fillet portions (6 ounces each), plain or butterflied, OR 4 steaks (8 ounces each)

1 egg white, beaten with a pinch of salt and white pepper

▶ Preheat the oven to its maximum setting (500° to 550°F). Meanwhile, slice the ginger into long shreds and place it on a foil-lined baking sheet. Drizzle with the oil and place in the oven as it heats up. Bake until you hear the ginger sizzle and it is beginning to brown. Remove, chop it fine, and combine it with the sesame seeds.

▶ Brush the tops of the fish (the bone side if using fillets) with a little egg white. Spread the seed mixture evenly on top and place the fish seed side up on the sheet pan. Bake until the seeds are golden brown and a skewer easily enters the thickest part of the fish, 7 to 10 minutes depending on thickness. Serve with a delicate vegetable like braised sliced leeks or leek-potato purée.

Salmon, Wild Rice, and Mushrooms en Papillote

This dish is a cousin several times removed—all right, a bastard cousin—of the classic Russian coulibiac. *The latter is an elaborate presentation of a large piece of salmon or sturgeon fillet enclosed in brioche pastry with kasha (buckwheat groats) and hard-cooked eggs. In* The Chez Panisse Menu Cookbook, *Alice Waters gives a recipe for a salmon* coulibiac *Jeremiah Tower made during his years there, with wild rice and buckwheat crepes replacing the kasha, and a mushroom duxelles added.*

As impressive and delicious as a real coulibiac *is, it is a lot of work. Eliminating the pastry altogether and enclosing individual portions of the fish with wild rice and mushrooms in baking parchment probably removes any claim of legitimate relation to the original, but it still makes a delicious dish.*

For the rice, use all wild rice if you can afford it, or try a blend of wild rice and a fragrant long-grain variety such as basmati or the wonderful brown Wehani variety grown by Lundberg Farms in the Sacramento Valley. Ordinary white button mushrooms are fine, but I prefer the slightly fuller flavor of the brown-capped type.

SERVES 4

1 cup wild rice, OR half wild rice and half fragrant long-grain rice

2 cups water

½ teaspoon salt

2 tablespoons butter

4 green onions, minced

1 clove garlic, minced

½ pound button mushrooms, thickly sliced

½ pound oyster mushrooms, thick stems removed, caps split lengthwise if large

1 teaspoon minced fresh savory, OR ¼ teaspoon crumbled dried savory

Salt and pepper, to taste

4 diagonal slices salmon fillet, 4 to 6 ounces each

➤ At least 2 hours ahead of serving, wash the wild rice in a bowl of cold water, swirling to release any bits of dust and hulls. Pour the water off through a sieve. Repeat until the water remains clear. (Some clean batches of wild rice need only a single rinse.)

➤ Bring the water to a boil in a small saucepan and add the salt and rice. Bring to a boil again, then reduce to a simmer, cover, and cook until the water is all absorbed, 50 to 60 minutes (uncover the pan and tip it to see if any water runs out from under the surface). Let stand covered 15 minutes, then remove the cover and let cool.

➤ Melt the butter in a skillet over medium heat. When the foam subsides, add the green onions and garlic and cook until fragrant. Add the mushrooms and savory and cook, stirring or shaking the pan, until the mushrooms have rendered a lot of liquid. Turn the heat to high and cook until the liquid is nearly evaporated. Season the mushrooms to taste and set aside to cool.

➤ Preheat the oven to 450°F. For each serving, fold a 12-inch square of baking parchment on the diagonal. Crease the corners, but not the entire fold. Open the square and spread ½ cup of the rice on one side of the fold, place a portion of fish over the rice, and top with a quarter of the mushrooms. Fold the other side of the paper over all and seal with a series of creases, starting with one corner and forming a half oval. Finish with a twist at the opposite corner.

➤ Bake the packages on a baking sheet until puffy and browned, about 10 minutes. Transfer to individual plates and serve with a simple vegetable.

NOTE In most cases of cooking fish in parchment, I like to slide the contents of the finished package out of the paper and onto the plate, but here the rice on the bottom makes that impossible. Just serve the packages on the plates, with steak knives for slashing open the paper, and have a platter available to receive the excess paper from each person's plate.

➤ Like other dishes baked in parchment, these packets can be assembled a couple of hours ahead of time, and the rice and mushroom components can be made a day or more ahead. Be sure the rice and mushrooms are completely cooled before assembling the packets or the heat will begin to cook the fish prematurely.

Salmon Baked in Filo with Fennel and Pancetta

I developed this recipe years ago, when farmed salmon (most of which still came from Norway) was generally leaner than it is today. Now the idea of adding bacon to farmed salmon makes little sense. It works very nicely, however, with the leaner pink and chum salmon, or with California king salmon caught early in the season,

which tends to be a little leaner and milder than mid-summer fish.

An even thickness of fish is important, so if you're using tail pieces, fold the thinnest tail section under the rest. This recipe can also be prepared with boned salmon steaks up to ¾ inch thick. To bone steaks, remove the skin, separate the two halves from the central bone, reverse one half, and press the halves together in a yin and yang pattern.

SERVES 4

½ pound fennel bulb (also known as sweet anise)

2 tablespoons mild olive oil

Salt

12 sheets (14 by 18 inches) filo dough, thawed if frozen

3 tablespoons melted butter or vegetable oil

1 to 1½ pounds salmon fillet, ½ to ¾ inch thick, in 4 equal pieces

3 ounces pancetta (Italian-style bacon), thinly sliced and cut into 1-inch squares

1 tablespoon grated or shredded lemon peel

➤ Split the fennel lengthwise and slice it crosswise as thinly as possible. In a skillet with a tight-fitting lid, sauté the fennel briefly in the oil, reduce the heat, cover, and cook until tender. Add salt to taste, allowing for the saltiness of the pancetta, and allow to cool. (May be prepared ahead of time.)

➤ Preheat the oven to 450°F. Lay out a sheet of filo dough on the table (keep the remaining sheets covered with a barely damp towel to prevent drying out) and brush it lightly all over with melted butter. Lay another sheet on top of the first and brush again. Top with a third sheet. Center a piece of salmon 6 inches in from one end. Top with a quarter of the pancetta, fennel, and lemon peel. Fold the long sides over the fish, covering the toppings. Fold the short end of the dough over the fish, then roll the package up in the remaining dough, ending up with the stuffings on top and the seam on the bottom. Repeat with the remaining portions.

➤ Place the packages on an ungreased baking sheet and bake 10 to 12 minutes depending on thickness.

Kurt's Salmon with Oyster Stuffing

This dish has been in my repertoire since my days in the retail wine business twenty-odd years ago. It was created by Kurt Stiehl, a friend and colleague with whom I shared many a good bottle and many a good meal. At a backyard barbecue for a bunch of other wine lovers, he stuffed a whole boned salmon with oyster dressing and roasted it in foil in a covered grill. Nothing very revolutionary there, except for the inspired touch of lacing the dressing with a couple of ounces of good French Sauternes. The sweet, fragrant wine gave an extra dose of moisture and a heady perfume to both the stuffing and the fish. It's a dish we have both served many times since.

This stuffing will enhance any salmonid, including trout, arctic char, and salmon. The recipe here is for a dinner-party presentation of a whole salmon, but it can be cut in half for a single large trout or small char, or a center-cut salmon roast of about 2 pounds to serve four.

SERVES 8

1 pint small shucked oysters

3 tablespoons butter, plus more for buttering the foil

¼ cup minced green onions

1 large clove garlic, minced

⅔ cup fresh bread crumbs

2 tablespoons chopped parsley

Salt and freshly ground pepper, to taste

1 whole salmon or char, 4 to 6 pounds, OR 2 red-meated trout, 2 to 3 pounds each

2 ounces Sauternes or Barsac

➤ Preheat the oven to 400°F. Drain the oysters, reserving the liquor, and chop the oysters coarsely unless they are very small. Melt 3 tablespoons of butter in a skillet, add the green onions and garlic, and sauté until just cooked. Add the oysters and their liquor, bread crumbs, and parsley and cook over low heat until the crumbs absorb the liquid. Season to taste and let cool slightly.

➤ Bone the fish if it has not already been done (see step 2, page 73). Butter the middle of a large sheet of aluminum foil (or coat the foil with oil or nonstick spray if you prefer). Season the inside of the fish lightly and lay it open on the foil. Moisten the stuffing with the wine and pack it loosely into the cavity and head. Fold the fish around the filling, maintaining as natural a shape as possible. Wrap the foil tightly around the fish and seal it well. Place it in a shallow baking dish and bake to an internal temperature of 145°F, about 35 minutes. Transfer the fish to a serving platter and carefully unwrap it, sliding the foil out from underneath. To serve, cut in crosswise slices with stuffing.

NOTE In the past, Sauternes, like Champagne, was used by some California wineries as a generic label, but here we are talking about the real thing. Genuine Sauternes (look for the official words "appellation Sauternes [or Barsac] contrôlée" proudly printed on the label) is a lusciously sweet white wine from the southern stretches of Bordeaux, made from late-harvest sémillon and sauvignon blanc grapes infected with botrytis, the "noble mold." Like other sweet wines, Sauternes is usually thought of strictly as a dessert wine, but a good example has plenty of acidity to balance the sweetness, and you might find, as I do, that it is perfectly delicious alongside the fish. Otherwise, serve the rest of the bottle along with dessert, or by itself as dessert.

Pink or Chum Salmon with Kedgeree Stuffing

Kedgeree is a Scottish dish, a kind of hash of curry-flavored rice with flaked cooked salmon. Turning it inside out, you can use a similar rice stuffing for a small whole salmon or a chunk of a larger fish. Of course, this will taste even better with a more expensive salmon.

SERVES 6

2 tablespoons butter or oil

3 green onions, sliced, green and white parts separated

1 teaspoon good curry powder

2 cups cooked rice

½ cup fish stock or water

Salt, to taste

1 whole pink salmon or center cut from a chum, 2½ to 3 pounds

Lemon wedges

Melted butter (optional)

➤ Melt the butter in a skillet over low heat and cook the white parts of the green onions until soft. Stir in the curry powder, cook until fragrant, and add the rice and stock. Cook until the rice is well colored with curry powder and the liquid is nearly absorbed. Season to taste, remove from the heat, and stir in the green onion tops. Let the stuffing cool while preparing the fish.

➤ Preheat the oven to 400°F. With a boning or fillet knife, cut the meat on one side of the fish away from the backbone and ribs. Carefully fold back the skin and meat. Cut the bones free from the other side and open the fish out flat. Remove any remaining bones clinging to the meat. (You may be able to get the fishmonger or butcher to bone the fish for you.)

➤ Spread the boned fish out skin side down on a large sheet of lightly oiled aluminum foil. Sprinkle with salt. Spread the rice mixture over one side, letting the excess spill out of the ends. Fold half the fish over the stuffing and wrap in the foil, sealing with a drugstore wrap (see page 16). Set the package in a baking pan, measure the thickest part of the fish, and bake 30 minutes, or to an internal temperature of 130°F. Remove from the oven and let rest, wrapped, for 10 minutes. Serve with lemon wedges and, if a sauce is desired, a little more melted butter.

Sautéed Salmon with Morels and Peas

Morels, one of the few wild mushrooms to peak in late spring, go particularly well with salmon. Combining a generous portion of morels—cut with commercial mushrooms if your budget dictates—with peas and cream makes a rich vegetable and sauce accompaniment for simply sautéed salmon. Given both the cost of the mushrooms and the richness of the sauce, smallish portions of salmon are in order; the large fillet cuts typical of many fish counters can be cut in half.

SERVES 4

½ to ¾ pound morels, or half morels and half commercial brown mushrooms

1 pound shelling peas, OR ¾ pound sugar snap peas

1 tablespoon butter

2 tablespoons minced green onion

Sprig of fresh thyme, OR pinch of dried thyme leaves

Salt and freshly ground pepper, to taste

2 tablespoons dry Madeira or sherry

Dash of soy sauce

½ cup cream

4 diagonal slices salmon fillet, 4 to 6 ounces each

1 tablespoon mild olive or peanut oil

➤ Slice the morels in half lengthwise and brush or shake off any debris; wash only if absolutely necessary, and drain thoroughly. Slice the brown mushrooms ¼ inch thick. Remove the peas from the pods; if using sugar snaps, trim and string the pods. Blanch the peas in lightly salted water until crisp-tender and rinse with cold water to stop the cooking.

➤ Melt the butter in a medium skillet over medium-high heat and add the mushrooms. Sauté until the mushrooms begin to color, then add the green onion, thyme, and a pinch of salt and pepper. When the mushrooms begin to release their liquid, add the wine and soy sauce and cook until nearly dry. Add the cream and peas, bring to boil, and reduce to a simmer.

➤ Meanwhile, season the salmon lightly with salt and pepper and heat the oil in another skillet (preferably nonstick). Sauté the salmon over high heat until nicely browned and done by the skewer test (see page 17), 3 to 4 minutes per side. Transfer the salmon to a serving dish or individual plates. Correct the seasoning of the mushroom-pea mixture and spoon it around the salmon. Garnish with more fresh thyme if desired.

Gravlax

Gravlax, a Scandinavian specialty of cold-cured salmon delicately flavored with fresh dill, started out like smoking and other forms of curing fish and meats, as a way to prevent spoilage without refrigeration (see page 26). But like Scottish smoked salmon, Italian salami, or Smithfield ham, gravlax has evolved over the centuries into a distinctive regional specialty, to be enjoyed not just for its convenience. Like the finest smoked salmon, it can be sliced extremely thin, thinner than either raw or cooked fish. And more than any other method, the gravlax cure preserves the clean, rich, fresh-from-the-sea flavor of salmon.

The traditional way to serve gravlax is in very thin slices on a plate, with a sauce like a thick mustard vinaigrette. But it's equally good served like smoked salmon, with slices laid on top of tiny rounds of buttered rye

bread or dense pumpernickel. It's also great on bagels in place of lox.

The recipe here is for 1 pound of fillet, about the minimum worth the effort, but it can be multiplied for anything up to a whole salmon. To double the recipe, consider using both sides of a center cut of salmon, yielding two rectangular pieces that are mirror images of each other; after filleting and removing the pin bones, reverse one fillet (still keeping the skin side outward) and nest them together in a neat yin-yang pattern, the thick dorsal part of one lying against the thin belly part of the other with the dill layer in between. Invert the package every day during the curing stage so the two pieces cure evenly.

SERVES 8 TO 10

1 pound farm-raised salmon fillet, in one piece with skin on, pin bones removed

3 tablespoons kosher salt

3 tablespoons brown sugar

½ teaspoon ground white pepper

½ cup chopped fresh dill

Mustard Sauce, below (optional)

➤ Rinse the fish and pat dry. Place the fillet skin side down in a glass or stainless dish. Combine the salt, sugar, and pepper and spread the mixture evenly all over the fish, a bit heavier where the meat is thickest. Top with a layer of dill.

➤ Cover loosely with plastic wrap and set another pan (such as a loaf pan) on top. Add 2 to 3 pounds of weight inside the second pan (a quart jar of mayonnaise, a bottle of wine, whatever). Place in the refrigerator, with a prop under one end to tilt it slightly. Let cure 2 to 3 days, then brush off any remaining salt crystals, leaving the dill layer intact. Wrap

the gravlax tightly and keep in the refrigerator up to 5 days.

➤ To serve, slice thinly on a diagonal, catching a bit of dill with each slice and leaving the skin behind.

Mustard Sauce

➤ Combine ⅓ cup prepared mustard (the yellow ballpark kind works fine for this purpose), a teaspoon of sugar, a pinch of white pepper, and a tablespoon of chopped dill in a mixing bowl and whisk together. Whisking constantly as if making mayonnaise, slowly add up to ⅓ cup mild olive oil or neutral vegetable oil. Correct the seasoning and serve with sliced gravlax.

Other Serving Suggestions: Salmon

Marinate thin salmon steaks or fillet cuts in Teriyaki Sauce (see Teriyaki Trout, page 86) and broil or grill. Thick fillet pieces are best butterflied, to maximize the surface for the sauce.

Cooked and Canned Salmon Dishes

Like a turkey, a ham, or a beef roast, a whole cooked salmon is a great source of leftovers that can be turned into all kinds of hot and cold dishes. But you don't need to invest in a whole fish to have leftovers; chances are your fish market has just what you need for a very low price, if not free for the asking.

When cutting a salmon into fillets, even the best commercial fish cutters can't get all the meat off the bones with the first cut. Some meat is bound to be left behind on the frame of central bones, and in many markets the frames are routinely thrown away. However, if you poach, steam, or bake the frame from a good-sized salmon, you can recover a cup or more of meat that, to borrow a phrase from butcher-author-TV host Merle Ellis, is "only the thickness of a knife blade away" from the pricey fillets. Add to that the cup or more of meat that can be picked out of the head of a good-sized salmon and you have all you need to make four nice salmon cakes, a pot of chowder, or a tasty salmon salad.

Canned salmon is another option. You'll have to decide for yourself if the cost of sockeye or "red" salmon is worth the price difference over pink. In either case, everything in the can, including skin and bones, is edible.

Salmon Cakes

These can also be served on a soft roll as a sort of salmonburger.

SERVES 4 AS A FIRST COURSE, 2 AS AN ENTREE

2 cups cooked and flaked salmon

¼ cup fresh bread crumbs

1 tablespoon chopped parsley

¼ teaspoon salt, or to taste

Pepper, to taste

1 egg

2 tablespoons butter or oil

1 large onion, diced

➤ Combine the salmon, bread crumbs, and parsley and season to taste. Stir in the egg and form the mixture into 4 hamburger-size patties.

➤ Melt the butter in a large skillet over medium heat and cook the onion until lightly browned. Lay the salmon cakes on top of the onion and cook until the cakes are nicely browned on one side, 4 to 5 minutes. Turn, trapping any loose onion underneath, and cook until browned on the second side. Serve with a green salad and tartar sauce, fresh salsa, or your favorite seafood sauce.

Baked Salmon Filo Roll

This will work with any variety of salmon, not just pink. Canned salmon is another possibility. For an appetizer, make three rolls, each with two sheets of filo and a third of the filling, and slice diagonally.

SERVES 4

1 large onion, finely diced

1 tablespoon butter or oil

3 cups poached or baked pink salmon, flaked, bones removed

1 cup ricotta cheese

1 tablespoon grated or minced lemon zest

3 tablespoons chopped basil leaves

Salt and freshly ground pepper, to taste

2 eggs

⅓ pound filo dough, thawed if frozen

5 to 6 tablespoons melted butter

➤ Sauté the onion in butter until soft but not browned. Transfer to a bowl and add the salmon, ricotta, lemon zest, and basil. Season to taste and stir in the eggs.

➤ Preheat the oven to 375°F. Unroll the stack of filo, pull off one sheet, and lay it crosswise on the table; keep the remainder covered with a slightly damp towel. Brush the sheet lightly with melted butter and top it with another sheet. Brush again with butter and add a third sheet. Brush the top with butter and spread half the salmon mixture along the near edge, stopping an inch and a half in from each edge. Carefully roll the dough and filling just until the filling is covered, then fold in the ends. Roll the rest of the way, forming a neat log. Transfer seam side down to a lightly buttered baking dish.

➤ Repeat with three more sheets of dough and the remaining filling. Brush the tops of the logs with a little more butter and bake until golden brown, 25 to 30 minutes. Allow to cool a few minutes before slicing.

Salmon Scrapple

When I was growing up, one of my family's favorite weekend breakfast dishes was fried grits. We frequently had grits as a side dish for dinner, and my mother would always cook extra and chill the leftovers in tall tumblers. Saturday or Sunday morning, she would slide out the cylinders of firm grits, slice them into thick rounds, and cook them in a skillet to serve with eggs. When as an adult I first encountered Italian baked polenta and Pennsylvania Dutch scrapple—the latter a kind of pork sausage loaf bound with cornmeal—they both seemed familiar.

Leftover baked or poached salmon, or the gleanings from a poached salmon frame, stand in quite nicely for

shredded pork in this seafood scrapple. The seasoning is typical of crab cakes, but also goes well with salmon.

SERVES 4 TO 6

1 tablespoon oil, plus more for reheating

1½ cups finely diced onion

¼ cup minced green onion

1 teaspoon fresh thyme leaves, OR ½ teaspoon dried thyme leaves

2½ teaspoons Chesapeake seafood seasoning, (page 29)

2 cups flaked cooked chum or pink salmon

2 cups cold water

⅔ cup fine yellow or white cornmeal, plus more for dusting

½ teaspoon salt

➤ Heat 1 tablespoon of oil in a skillet and sauté the onion until soft but not browned. Remove from the heat and stir in the green onion, thyme, and seafood seasoning. Stir in the salmon and set aside.

➤ Combine the water, cornmeal, and salt in a saucepan and stir until no lumps of cornmeal remain. Bring to a boil, cover, and cook over medium heat until the mixture is thick and no longer tastes raw, about 5 minutes. Remove from the heat and stir in the salmon and onion mixture. Taste for seasoning and adjust if necessary. Pour into a loaf pan or two straight-sided pint jars or glasses and refrigerate overnight.

➤ Unmold the scrapple and slice about ¾ to 1 inch thick. Dust the slices with a little cornmeal. Cook the slices slowly in a lightly oiled skillet until golden brown and heated through, about 3 to 4 minutes per side.

Salmon and Corn Chowder

Two of my favorite summer foods meet in this simple but delicious soup. Cooking the salmon bones in fish stock will make a richer soup, but a simple court-bouillon works fine.

SERVES 6 TO 8

2 pounds salmon bones and heads

1 quart fish stock or court-bouillon (page 329)

2 ears sweet corn, shucked

1 large onion, finely diced

2 ribs celery, finely diced

½ pound red or white new potatoes, finely diced

2 tablespoons butter

Sprig of fresh thyme

3 cups milk or half-and-half

Salt and white pepper, to taste

➤ Rinse away any bits of blood or organs from the bones and heads and place them in a shallow saucepan. Add stock or court-bouillon to cover. Bring just to a boil, reduce the heat, and simmer 15 minutes. Remove the fish from the broth and allow it to cool. Let the broth settle, then strain it through a fine wire sieve.

➤ When the fish has cooled enough to handle, pull the meat off the bones and break it up into small flakes. Don't miss the meat in the cheeks if using heads.

➤ With a paring knife, cut the outer third of the corn kernels into a bowl. With the back edge of the blade, scrape the cobs to squeeze out the milky centers of the kernels into the bowl.

➤ In a soup kettle, sauté the onion, celery, and potatoes in butter over medium heat until the onion softens. Add the corn, stock, and thyme, bring to a boil, and simmer until the potatoes are tender. Add the salmon and milk, season to taste, and bring almost to a boil. Simmer 5 minutes and serve.

Salmon-Stuffed Mushroom Caps

Serve these stuffed mushrooms as party food, or at the table as a first course or entree. As a first course, try two or three caps with assorted salad greens; for an entree, serve six on a bed of sautéed spinach.

SERVES 8 TO 10 AS A FIRST COURSE,
4 AS AN ENTREE

24 extra-large mushroom caps (about 2 pounds)

2 tablespoons olive oil

Salt and freshly ground pepper

1½ cups cooked and flaked salmon, any bones removed, or canned salmon, drained

3 tablespoons mayonnaise

½ cup minced green onion

1 teaspoon Dijon-style mustard or prepared horseradish

➤ Preheat the oven to 425°F. Place the mushroom caps in a baking dish large enough to hold them in a single layer. Drizzle with the oil, sprinkle with salt and pepper, and toss to moisten evenly. Arrange them open side down and bake until they release their moisture and just begin to shrink, about 12 minutes. Remove from the oven and let cool slightly.

➤ Meanwhile, combine the remaining ingredients and season to taste. Pack the mixture evenly into the mushroom caps and return them to the pan, stuffing side up. Bake until the tops are lightly browned, about 15 minutes.

Tomatoes Stuffed with Salmon Salad

Yes, it's very 1950s—that's just the point. One bite of this and I'm ten years old again, and ready for something more sophisticated than tuna and mayonnaise. I know Mom is sneaking in some vegetables in those bits of diced celery, but I don't mind because they taste okay and are kinda crunchy. And what are those little green things that taste salty and vinegary, like pickles, only softer? "Capers." Like a detective caper? "No, I don't think so. I don't know why they call them capers, that's just what they're called."

These days, a tall can of sockeye salmon seems like quite an indulgence, but this is a perfect way to use the meat gleaned from a salmon head and frame.

SERVES 4

2 cups cooked and flaked leftover salmon, or 1 large can sockeye salmon, drained

3 tablespoons mayonnaise

2 teaspoons prepared mustard

½ cup finely diced celery

2 teaspoons capers, roughly chopped

4 medium tomatoes

Small lettuce leaves or mixed salad greens

➤ Combine the salmon, mayonnaise, mustard, celery, and capers in a bowl and mix well. Keep an eye out for bones if using home-cooked salmon.

➤ Holding a tomato stem side down, cut it almost in half, then crosswise, then each quarter in half, leaving all 8 wedges attached at the bottom. Gently spread out the wedges and place a scoop of salmon salad in the middle. Garnish the plate with a few greens.

Sautéed Trout Grenobloise

This classic treatment for trout takes its name from the city of Grenoble in the French Alps, an area noted for its trout. If you're cooking butterflied trout, two servings is about all you can manage in a skillet at one time; to double the recipe, use four fillet portions from larger fish.

SERVES 2

1 tablespoon oil or clarified butter

2 boneless trout, about 8 ounces each, butterflied, OR 2 trout fillets, about 6 ounces each

Pinch of salt and white pepper

2 tablespoons butter

Juice of ½ lemon

2 teaspoons capers, drained

➤ Heat the oil in a large skillet over medium-high heat. Season the trout lightly with salt and pepper and add it to the pan, skin side up. Cook until lightly browned, about 3 minutes, turn, and continue cooking until the tail meat begins to flake. Remove to a serving platter or individual plates.

➤ Let the pan cool slightly and add the butter, lemon juice, and capers. Brown the butter slightly and pour the sauce over the fish.

Smoked Trout Salad

Here is just one of the ways you can use a relatively small amount of smoked fish to flavor a dish that is mostly vegetables.

Trout of any size and color is delicious smoked; see the procedure on page 174. Fish under a pound can be smoked whole, although for ease in serving you might want to use the boned butterflied form. Larger trout are best smoked in fillet form. If you don't feel like smoking your own fish, this dish can be made with any hot-smoked fish—trout, black cod, salmon, or tuna.

SERVES 4

¼ cup diced red or green onion

Salt and freshly ground pepper, to taste

1 tablespoon red-wine or sherry vinegar

3 tablespoons olive oil

1 pound red-skinned potatoes, steamed, cooled, and cut into bite-size pieces

1 cup diced celery

½ pound smoked trout, skinned and flaked

1 tablespoon chopped parsley, chervil, or dill

➤ If the onion is strong, soak it in cold water for 15 minutes and drain. Dissolve a large pinch of salt in the vinegar in a mixing bowl and stir in the pepper. Add the oil and whisk until combined. Add the onion, potatoes, celery, fish, and herbs and toss to coat everything evenly with dressing. Chill until ready to serve.

Bacon-Fried Trout with Herb Coating

I know lots of vegetarians, semi-vegetarians, and others who avoid eating red meat—but several of them make an exception for bacon. For anyone who grew up with it, there is something very hard to resist about the salty-sweet-smoky flavor of bacon, and nothing is quite like it for adding flavor to mild-tasting fish like farmed trout. Try this with any small boneless trout, red or white, or fillets from a larger trout.

SERVES 4

Oil

1 slice bacon, diced, OR 2 tablespoons diced salt pork or ham rind

¼ cup flour

2 teaspoons dried herbs, crumbled—thyme, marjoram, tarragon, or a blend of these, or use a commercial *fines herbes* mixture

½ teaspoon freshly ground black pepper

4 pan-size boneless trout, about 8 ounces each

Lemon wedges

➤ Generously coat the bottom of a large skillet with oil and add the bacon. Cook over low heat until the bacon has rendered most of its fat; discard the bacon. Meanwhile, combine the flour and seasonings in a wide, shallow bowl or dinner plate.

➤ Remove the heads of the fish if desired, or if necessary to fit the skillet. Open the fish and coat them inside and out with the seasoned flour; shake off the excess. Cook over medium-low heat in the bacon-flavored oil until the skin is golden brown and the meat has lost its raw color, 5 to 6 minutes per side. Serve with lemon wedges.

Golden Trout Stuffed with Couscous

I developed this dish for the beautiful golden-skinned, red-meated trout, but the subtly spiced stuffing can go with any trout, salmon, char, or other mild, fine-textured fish. If the weather is too hot for baking, the foil-wrapped fish can be cooked in a covered grill by the indirect method (off to one side rather than directly over the heat).

SERVES 4

Salt and pepper

3 tablespoons butter or olive oil

1 cup quick-cooking couscous

2 cups diced onion

2 cloves garlic, sliced

½ teaspoon ground cumin

½ teaspoon ground coriander

¼ teaspoon ground ginger

¼ teaspoon cinnamon

Pinch of cayenne

Juice of 1 lemon

⅓ cup sliced or slivered almonds, toasted

3 tablespoons golden raisins (optional)

2 boneless trout or pan-size salmon, about 1 pound each

➤ Combine 1½ cups water, 1 teaspoon salt, and 2 tablespoons of the butter or oil in a covered saucepan. Bring to a rolling boil, stir in the couscous, cover, and remove from the heat. Let stand 5 minutes, covered, then fluff with a fork.

➤ Heat the remaining butter in a skillet over low heat and cook the onion and garlic slowly until soft. Add the spices and cook until fragrant. Remove from the heat, stir in the lemon juice, and add to the couscous.

Add the almonds and raisins, and season to taste with salt and pepper.

➤ Preheat the oven to 400°F. Lightly oil a large sheet of heavy-duty aluminum foil, or coat with nonstick vegetable spray. Place a trout in the center, open it up, and stuff the head and cavity generously with half of the couscous mixture. Fold the fish back over the stuffing and seal the foil with a drugstore wrap (see page 16). Repeat with the other fish and remaining stuffing. Bake in a shallow baking dish 25 to 30 minutes, or to an internal temperature of 145°F. Open the packages and slide the contents out onto a serving platter. To serve, cut the fish in crosswise sections with stuffing.

Truite au Bleu

Many a cookbook or travel book contains an account of a truite au bleu served in a small riverside inn in France or Switzerland. A live trout is taken from a holding tank, disappears into the kitchen, and emerges a few minutes later, poached to perfection, with a bluish haze on the skin. The tail is curled to one side, suggesting one last flip of the tail as the fish gave up the ghost.

There is nothing unique about European trout that makes them turn blue when cooked. What gives blue trout its distinctive color is the protective slime that coats the fish's skin. When a freshly killed trout is cooked in a slightly acidic liquid, the protective slime that coats the skin turns an opaque blue-gray. But within a few hours, it begins to change chemically and will not turn blue. Also, if the fish is handled or washed too much in the cleaning process, much of the slime disappears, and with it the bluing reaction.

The curl in the tail is not a dying spasm, but comes from the shrinkage of the muscles during cooking. Since no fish is perfectly symmetrical, one side generally shrinks more than the other, causing the tail to curl. This effect is lost within a few hours as the muscle tissue relaxes.

Contrary to tradition, truite au bleu *does not require that the fish be cooked within seconds after being killed. If you have a fish market with a live tank within a half hour's distance, you can stop in at the end of the day, buy a live trout, and have it killed and cleaned by the fishmonger. As long as you have it in the poacher within an hour or so after it comes out of the tank, it should turn nicely blue and curl a bit. Even if it doesn't, you will still have a very fresh poached trout. And if you can't find live trout at all, any fresh trout poached in court-bouillon is still a good dish.*

Small trout (½ to 1 pound) can be poached in a skillet; larger fish require an oblong fish poacher or a large oval flameproof roasting pan. The quantities given here are for a 3-pound fish cooked in an 18-inch oval poacher.

SERVES 4 TO 6

Court-Bouillon

1 gallon water

2 cups dry white wine

Juice of 1 lemon

2 tablespoons tarragon-flavored wine vinegar

½ cup sliced onion or green onion

3 or 4 parsley sprigs, OR a handful of celery leaves

1 bay leaf

12 peppercorns, cracked

¼ teaspoon anise or fennel seed (optional)

1 trout, about 3 pounds, OR 2 smaller fish, freshly killed and cleaned

Boiling water, if necessary

Parsley sprigs, for garnish

Buttered new potatoes

Snow peas or sugar snap peas

Hollandaise Sauce (below) or melted butter flavored with lemon juice

➤ Combine the court-bouillon ingredients in a fish poacher. Bring to a boil, reduce the heat, and simmer 15 minutes.

➤ While the court-bouillon is simmering, examine the cavity of the fish for any remaining bits of gills or other organs. If the two long strips of dark tissue alongside the backbone have not been removed, cut them open and rinse well. Handle the fish as little as possible while cleaning, preferably by the head and tail rather than the skin.

➤ Slide the fish into the simmering liquid. If the fish is not completely submerged, ladle some of the liquid over the exposed parts until the skin changes color, then add boiling water to raise the liquid level. Simmer 20 minutes, lift the fish out, and drain well, and serve garnished with parsley and surrounded by the vegetables. Pass the sauce separately.

Hollandaise Sauce

If you're going to the trouble of making truite au bleu, *you might as well go the whole way and make this delicious butter and egg-yolk sauce. No, it's not the sort of thing we eat every day anymore, but it's too good to let the memory slip away.*

MAKES ⅔ CUP (4 TO 6 SERVINGS)

6 tablespoons butter

2 egg yolks

1 tablespoon lemon juice or vinegar

Salt, to taste

➤ Melt the butter gently and let it stand in a warm place until the milky liquid completely separates from the yellow butterfat and settles to the bottom. Skim off any solids floating on the surface.

➤ Place the egg yolks in the bowl of a double boiler or a stainless mixing bowl; bring water to a simmer in the bottom pot, but do not combine the halves yet. Beat the yolks with a whisk until slightly foamy, add the lemon juice and a large pinch of salt, then set the bowl over the hot water. Continue whisking over low heat until the mixture is thick like whipped cream, adjusting the heat so the yolks do not cook to a scrambled-egg texture (at which point they are overcooked, and the sauce will not work).

➤ Remove the bowl from the heat, add a tablespoon of the clarified butter, and beat until all the butter is absorbed. Return the bowl to the heat and continue adding butter gradually, whisking constantly, until all the butter is absorbed. If the sauce is too thick, thin it with a little of the remaining liquid from the butter. Taste for seasoning and keep warm (not hot) until ready to serve.

Charcoal-Roasted Trout

Because the fish is cooked indirectly in a covered charcoal grill rather than directly over the coals, I prefer to call it "charcoal-roasted."

SERVES 4 TO 6

1 whole red trout, 2½ to 3 pounds, skin and
  scales left on

Salt and pepper, to taste
Sprigs of fresh thyme, dill, fennel, or rosemary
Lemon slices

➤ Build a moderate charcoal fire toward one side of a covered grill. Oil the grill and preheat it thoroughly. Season the fish inside and out and stuff the cavity with the herbs and lemon slices. When the fire has burned down to where the coals are beginning to be covered with ash, place the fish on the grill a few inches away from the fire, with the thicker part facing the fire.

➤ Cover the grill and cook 10 to 12 minutes on the first side. Roll the fish over with a spatula or tongs and reverse the grill so that the fish is in the same position relative to the fire. Continue cooking until the meat is opaque orange and a skewer easily penetrates the thickest part, another 8 to 10 minutes. To serve, peel back the skin and pull the meat off the bones with a spoon and fork.

Poached Arctic Char with Dill Butter Sauce

Like its relatives, char has an affinity for herbs with an anise flavor, including dill, fennel, tarragon, and chervil. Feel free to substitute an equal amount of chervil or fennel tops, or a smaller portion of tarragon, for the dill.

SERVES 4

2 cups (approximately) fish stock or
  court-bouillon (page 329)
4 arctic char fillet portions, about 1½ pounds
  in all
¼ teaspoon salt

Freshly ground white pepper, to taste

Additional hot stock or boiling water, if needed

3 tablespoons butter, at room temperature

¼ cup chopped fresh dill

Lemon juice, to taste

➤ Choose a skillet just large enough to hold the fish in one layer and add stock to a depth of about ½ inch. Bring the stock to a simmer. Season the fish lightly with salt and pepper and add to the simmering stock, skin side down. (If the fish sticks up out of the poaching liquid, add more stock, or, as a last resort, boiling water to raise the liquid level.) Cover the pan and simmer until the fish is tender when probed with a skewer, 6 to 8 minutes.

➤ Transfer the fish with a slotted spatula to warm plates or a serving platter; keep warm. Pour off all but ¼ cup of the stock from the skillet and bring the ¼ cup to a boil. Reduce by half, then remove from the heat and add the butter and dill. Swirl the pan or stir constantly as the butter melts. Taste for seasoning and adjust if necessary. (Depending on the acidity of your poaching liquid, no lemon may be needed.) Blot away any liquid that has accumulated on the fish plate and spoon the sauce over the fish. Serve immediately.

Trout with Walnut or Hazelnut Vinaigrette

One of my favorite flavor partners for trout has always been nuts, especially hazelnuts and walnuts. In this recipe, simple broiled trout fillets are sauced with a vinaigrette based on nut oil.

Walnut oil is one the most widely available nut oils, with domestic versions found in most supermarkets, but some of these have only a trace of nut aroma. A better choice is the more expensive cold-pressed walnut oils sold in health food stores. Most flavorful of all, and also the most expensive, are the French hazelnut and walnut oils sold in gourmet specialty shops.

All nut oils are prone to rancidity, especially when exposed to air and heat. Store them in the refrigerator after opening, and plan to use them up fairly quickly in any case.

SERVES 4

1½ teaspoons sherry vinegar

¼ teaspoon salt

White pepper, to taste

Heaping tablespoon chopped celery leaves

2 teaspoons minced shallots or green onions

2 tablespoons walnut or hazelnut oil

2 trout, 1 pound each, boned and butterflied, OR 4 trout fillets, about 6 ounces each

Hot paprika

8 walnut halves or hazelnuts, toasted and chopped

2 cups watercress, arugula, or mixed bitter salad greens

➤ In a small bowl, combine the vinegar, half the salt, and the pepper and stir to dissolve the salt. Stir in the celery, shallots, and oil and mix well. Taste for seasoning and adjust if necessary.

➤ Lay the fish skin side down on an oiled broiler pan (lined with foil if you like). Season with the remaining salt and a little paprika. Broil until the fish is opaque in the center and slightly browned around the edges, about 5 minutes. Transfer to a warm platter or individual plates. Stir the vinaigrette well and spoon it over the fish. Top with chopped nuts and surround with greens.

Cold Steelhead and Asparagus Citronette

This makes an elegant first course for an Easter dinner or Passover seder, and in larger servings it is ideal for a warm-weather lunch. Depending on the time of the season, I have made it with farmed Atlantic salmon, wild Columbia steelhead, and the season's first ocean kings, all of which are available in some portion of asparagus season.

A "citronette" is a salad dressing like vinaigrette, but made with citrus juice rather than vinegar. Try it with the thin-skinned, fragrant Meyer lemons that are common in home gardens in California and increasingly common in the market in late winter and spring. If using regular lemons, use a little less juice, as they are more acid than Meyers.

SERVES 8 AS AN APPETIZER

1 quart court-bouillon (page 329)

1 pound steelhead or salmon fillet

½ teaspoon salt

1 pound slender asparagus

2 or 3 lemons, Meyer if possible

½ teaspoon salt

Large pinch of white pepper

½ cup mild olive oil

Minced chives, for garnish

➤ Prepare the court-bouillon and simmer 15 to 20 minutes, or reheat reserved court-bouillon. Meanwhile, remove the skin and any pin bones from the salmon and cut it diagonally into 8 equal portions. If the end slices are thicker than ⅜ inch, pound them gently with a mallet or the side of a cleaver to thin them slightly.

➤ Lay the slices in a shallow heatproof dish just large enough to hold them in a single layer. Season lightly with salt. Strain the hot liquid over the fish, cover with a sheet of baking parchment or foil, and let stand until the fish is opaque throughout, about 10 minutes. Lift the slices out of the liquid with a spatula, or place a second smaller pan on top to hold them in place and carefully pour out the liquid (reserve and freeze the liquid for another use). Chill the fish. Trim and cook the asparagus according to your favorite method and chill them.

➤ For the citronette, grate the zest from the lemons before squeezing; squeeze the lemons and measure ¼ cup of juice. Dissolve the salt and pepper in the juice, stir in the oil, and adjust the seasoning to taste.

➤ To serve, place a salmon slice on each plate. Toss the asparagus in the citronette and arrange alongside the fish. Drizzle any remaining dressing over the fish and garnish with chives and lemon zest.

VARIATION Thin diagonal cutlets are ideal for this dish, but another option is to buy a couple of large steaks, bone them out, and slice each fillet portion in half horizontally. A pair of chopsticks or the handles of two wooden spoons can help as a guide for this horizontal cut; see page 202.

Teriyaki Trout

The sweet-salty flavor of a teriyaki glaze goes particularly well with the slight richness of trout cooked on the grill or under the broiler. In either method, watch the distance from the heat; the sugar in the sauce should brown deeply, but not burn black.

SERVES 4

Teriyaki Sauce:

2 tablespoons sake

2 tablespoons mirin (sweet cooking sake)

2 tablespoons soy sauce

1 teaspoon sugar

2 teaspoons grated ginger

4 skin-on trout fillets, 4 to 6 ounces each, or butterflied small trout, heads removed

➤ Combine the sauce ingredients in a saucepan and simmer 5 minutes, stirring occasionally to dissolve the sugar. Let cool, then strain to remove the bits of ginger.

➤ Marinate the fish in half of the sauce for at least 30 minutes, turning occasionally. Meanwhile, return the remaining sauce to the pan and reduce it by half (this is the "glaze").

TO BROIL Lay the fish skin side up on a lightly oiled broiling rack about 3 inches from the heat. Broil 2 minutes, turn bone side up, and baste the meat with the glaze. Continue broiling until the tail end is beginning to flake, another 3 to 4 minutes.

TO GRILL Prepare a moderately hot fire in a charcoal or gas grill. Grill the fish skin side up until nicely browned, about 3 minutes. Turn, baste with the glaze, and continue cooking until the tail end is beginning to flake, another 2 to 3 minutes.

Other Serving Suggestions: Trout and Char

Large red-meated trout or arctic char fillets can be cured and served like salmon for Gravlax (page 74).

halibut, sole & other flatfish

This chapter covers a number of species, some so small that it takes several fish to make a serving and others barn-door-size fish that are cut into steaks. However, all of them share a characteristic flopped-over, flattened shape (see page 87), as well as lean, white, delicately flavored meat. Size as much as anything else determines how flatfish are processed and cooked, so I have divided the chapter between the largest varieties in our area, both known as halibut, which are often cut into steaks, and the rest, which are generally sold and cooked as fillets or whole fish.

California Halibut

English Sole

Gray Sole

Greenland Halibut

Pacific Dover Sole

Pacific Halibut

Pacific Sanddab

Petrale Sole

Rex Sole

Starry Flounder

Halibut

Pacific halibut, *Hippoglossus stenolepis*
Atlantic halibut, *H. hippoglossus*
California halibut, *Paralichthys californicus*
Greenland halibut ("Greenland turbot"),
Reinhardtius hippoglossoides

Two large Pacific flounders share the market name of halibut: the Pacific halibut, one of the two largest flatfish species in the world, and the considerably smaller California halibut. While they differ quite a bit in appearance, flavor, and texture, both are among my favorite local fish.

The **PACIFIC HALIBUT** ranges from Northern California to the Bering Sea, but most of the commercial catch comes from British Columbia and Alaska waters. The fishing season runs from late spring to fall, when the fish appear closer to shore and in shallower water than they do in winter. Females can reach giant sizes—6 to 8 feet long and 500 pounds or more in weight—but males are much smaller, seldom topping 80 pounds, and the average size in the commercial fishery is 30 to 40 pounds.

Also known in the market as northern, Canadian, or Alaska halibut (to distinguish it from the smaller and slightly less choice California halibut), Pacific halibut is one of the best eating fish on the West Coast. Its lean, creamy-white meat cooks up sweet, firm, and moist—as

long as it is not overcooked. Crosscut steaks are the most common form, but some markets sell it in skinless fillets, and also in tail sections or "roasts" with the skin on.

For a long time the halibut fishery has been geared to freezing, but an increasing amount of the Pacific halibut catch comes to market fresh these days. Given the remoteness of some of the fishing grounds, however, these fish may be as much as a week out of the water by the time they reach our market. Fortunately, halibut is a durable fish. Its large size and tough skin mean that relatively little of the meat is exposed to the air (which oxidizes the fats, causing a stale flavor) or surface bacteria, which lead to spoilage. The large size also helps it weather slight fluctuations in temperature better than smaller fish. If it was properly handled on the boat and throughout the shipping process, a week-old whole halibut can still be in fine condition. Once cut, the steaks and fillets have a shorter shelf life, and should be used within a day or, at most, two days after purchase.

The other common halibut on the West Coast is **CALIFORNIA HALIBUT,** the second-largest flatfish in our area (up to 3 feet in length and typically weighing 10 to 25 pounds). Although this species is found as far north as British Columbia, the fish is most common from central California to Baja and the Sea of Cortez. In the northern end of its range, halibut numbers fluctuate considerably from year to year, the key variable most likely being water temperatures, as they have been most abundant in El Niño years.

Most cookbook writers dismiss California halibut as inferior to its northern cousin and to

Atlantic halibut, perhaps, but it's still a fine-tasting fish, with a mild, sweet flavor. If you prefer, just think of it as a particularly large flounder. In fact, its closest relative is an East Coast species known as summer flounder or fluke, generally regarded as a fine food fish.

California halibut is available all year, mainly as fresh fillets. If you do find it cut into steaks, they typically constitute an entire crosscut of the fish, with sections of both upper and lower fillets. Where the meat of Pacific halibut is opaque white even when uncooked, raw California halibut is more of a translucent gray.

The biggest difference between California and Pacific halibut is in fat content. While both fall into the lean category, the California variety is certainly the leaner of the two, making it that much more prone to drying out

if overcooked. Both species can be cooked by grilling, broiling, sautéing, roasting, and other dry-heat methods, but gentle, moist methods like steaming, poaching, and braising are perhaps safer with the California variety.

Whatever the cooking method, neither of the halibuts is very forgiving of overcooking. Depending on the thickness of the cut and the heat source, cooking time can be as little as 2 or 3 minutes per side. Be especially careful with frozen halibut steaks, which are easier to overcook and take about 25 percent less time to cook than fresh.

One other halibut occasionally shows up in our markets, but not under that name. A medium-size (to 15 pounds) flatfish of far northern waters (*Reinhardtius hippoglossoides*) is known in field guides as Greenland halibut, and it is

Flopped-Over Flatfish

The distinctive shape that defines the flatfish is a marvelous adaptation to life on the sea floor, but it's not the only approach. Some bottom-dwelling fish, like skates and monkfish, have evolved into a flattened shape, their fins and other body parts becoming large horizontal extensions, while retaining the basic symmetrical, belly-down structure of typical fish. Flatfish, on the other hand, took an asymmetrical evolutionary path—flopping over on one side and twisting parts here and there to make it work.

In the larval stage, flatfish look like other fish, with eyes in the conventional position, one on each side of the head. As they grow and settle into the sideways swimming orientation, their heads become distorted until both eyes are together on the side that faces up. Which way they twist—left or right—is a characteristic of each species, and ichthyologists classify the flatfish into two major families (right-eyed and left-eyed flounders) according to where the eyes end up. The fact that Pacific halibut and most of the Pacific "soles" are all right-eyed, while sanddab, California halibut, and starry flounder are left-eyed, may be of great importance to the scientists, but it really doesn't affect us cooks very much.

fished commercially on a large scale in Greenland and the Canadian Arctic. An anomaly among flatfish, this species has a high fat content, similar to sablefish and Chilean sea bass, and frozen fillets are popular in certain markets. However, U.S. regulations (ostensibly to avoid consumer confusion, but in fact to protect the other halibut fisheries from lower-price competition) require this species to be labeled "Greenland turbot." The only problem with this is that the name "turbot" is also applied to several other species, including one of the most highly prized European flatfish and one of the cheapest of Pacific fish. Across the Atlantic, true turbot (*Psetta maxima*) is second only to Dover sole in reputation and price, and is now being aquacultured in Europe and Chile to meet the nearly insatiable demand. A few fish wholesalers, the kind that fly in Dover sole for upscale restaurants, also feature fresh turbot, and it could become more common in years to come. At the other extreme, "turbot" is the West Coast fishermen's name for arrowtooth flounder, a large and abundant species, but one with a poor reputation for quality. A few other Pacific species known in the field guides as turbot also enter the generic mix of "sole" fillets; see below.

Small Flatfish: Flounder, Sole, and Dab

Petrale sole, *Eopsetta jordani*
Rex sole, *Glyptocephalus zachirus*
Starry flounder, *Platichthys stellatus*
Pacific sanddab, *Citharichthys sordidus*
English sole, *Parophrys vetulus*
Sand sole, *Psettichthys melanostictus*
Pacific Dover sole, *Microstomus pacificus*
Witch flounder or gray sole, *Glyptocephalus cynoglossus*

Quick to cook, delicate in flavor and texture, and widely available, sole is one of the professional chef's favorite fish. It can be a background and platform for other seafood, or it can stand on its own with the simplest of sauces.

About a dozen species of small flatfish caught commercially on the West Coast may be sold as "sole," although strictly speaking there is no sole found in our area. The true soles are found mainly on the European side of the Atlantic; only a few very expensive restaurants actually serve fresh European sole brought in by air. What we have here instead are various members of two families of flounder. However, the best of these Pacific "soles" are delicious in their own right, and can be served without apology in any classical recipe for sole.

The key is to know which sole you are buying, as they vary in quality from fine-textured

90

and delicious to soft and watery. Unfortunately, once cut and skinned, fillets of the various species are difficult to tell apart. Unless you carry a field guide to the market and see the fish before they are cut, you will have to rely on your fishmonger to know which sole you are getting. Better markets label their fish according to species, and others should be encouraged to do so.

One West Coast species, the **PETRALE SOLE** (or just plain petrale), stands above the others in quality. It also commands the highest price, but there's never a shortage of willing buyers for this fine-textured, delicately flavored flounder. Petrale can be one of the larger soles, up to 4 or 5 pounds, although much of the catch is smaller. Fillets may run anywhere from 2 or 3 ounces each to more than half a pound.

ENGLISH SOLE, known in some areas as **LEMON SOLE,** is similar to petrale in appearance and coloring, though generally a bit smaller. A practiced eye can tell them apart by the shape of the head and the mouth: English sole has a longer, more pointed snout, with a small mouth that looks more twisted than in most flatfish, while a petrale's mouth is much larger, extending back to the middle of the eye. Both have a slight point in the center of the tail fin, as opposed to the notched or rounded tails of most other species. English sole fillets sell for a couple of dollars less per pound than petrale, and they offer almost as fine a flavor and texture.

A couple of other West Coast soles, including **SAND SOLE** and several species known as turbot (none of them the true turbot, an Atlantic species), enter the mix of generic "sole" fillets, but are occasionally marketed under their own names. Like English sole, most of these are good fish, though not quite the equal of petrale.

Then there is the Pacific flatfish known as "**DOVER SOLE**." I wish I could find a way to like this fish, as it is one of the most abundant and commercially important species on the Pacific Coast. However, I have always found it soft, watery, and almost devoid of flavor—about as different from the true European sole from the Strait of Dover as sweet two-dollar San Joaquin Valley bubbly is from real French Champagne. Salting (see page 15) does improve its flavor and texture noticeably, but still, if Dover is the only sole available, more often than not I'll reconsider my menu plans.

After petrale, my vote for the best of the Pacific soles is **REX SOLE**. Smaller and slimmer than petrale, it is almost never sold as fillets; the fillets from all but the largest fish would be too small and fragile. The same goes for **SANDDAB**, a small flounder with an olive-brown skin that rarely tops half a pound. Both sanddab and rex sole are time-honored favorites in San Francisco seafood restaurants, where they are nearly always cooked on the bone, which keeps the delicate meat moist and holds it together. However, they can be hard to find away from the immediate coast. One reason is that dabs especially have a very short "shelf life" compared to other fish. While a whole salmon will keep for several days if well iced, and most markets will carry over their supply of rockfish fillets for a day or two after they arrive, figure on cooking sanddabs the day you buy them for the best quality.

Although all the small Pacific flatfish are

actually flounders, the only one commonly marketed as such is the **STARRY FLOUNDER.** This species is the easiest Pacific flatfish to recognize in round form. It is larger than most soles, typically a foot or so in length. The skin on the upper side is a dark olive-brown to nearly black, with wide yellow-orange stripes on the fins and tail. The common name refers to the rough scaly plates scattered like stars over the dark skin. While some writers dismiss starry flounder as of only fair quality, I find it delicious. It has a distinctive, slightly grassy aroma and flavor, which is intensified if the fish is cooked with the skin on. When weather permits, I like to grill whole flounder after briefly marinating it in olive oil with chopped herbs (see page 107). It is more common in fillet form; the fillets are a bit thicker and coarser in texture than those of petrale or other soles, and a little darker in color, though they cook up just as white.

One Atlantic flatfish that has a regular, if limited, market in the West is the **WITCH FLOUNDER,** a.k.a. **GRAY SOLE,** an elongated flounder with light brown skin that looks and tastes like an overgrown version of rex sole, to which it is closely related. For some reason—perhaps the size, which is ideal for cooking and serving whole—Chinese cooks on the West Coast prefer this fish to most local flatfish, and it's a regular item in Chinese markets in California.

In addition to the true flatfish, there are a number of other, unrelated fish, mostly imports, that have a highly compressed shape (i.e., thin bodies that are wide from dorsal fin to belly), but swim in the conventional position. These fish, including tilapia, orange roughy, John Dory, oreo dory, and triggerfish, yield wide, thin fillets similar enough in shape, flavor, and texture to flatfish that they can be used in the same recipes.

Except for a few species like sanddab and rex sole, most small Pacific flatfish are routinely filleted by processors and shipped to stores and wholesalers as skinless fillets. Fillets can run anywhere from 1½ to 8 ounces each, depending on the species and size of the fish, and fillets from the dark-skinned (upper or eyed) side run a little thicker than those from the white-skinned blind side. Another clue to whether you are getting top or bottom fillets is the color; the pigment in the dark upper skin carries over somewhat to the meat, so the upper fillets in a batch tend to be a little darker than the lower.

Why does it matter if you are getting top or bottom fillets? In part because fillets of consistent thickness will cook in a similar amount of time. The other reason is visual: upper and lower fillets from a given species are mirror images of each other in shape. Each fillet is more or less triangular, with the longest edge corresponding to the dorsal fin of the fish and a corner opposite this edge where the belly cavity ends. Since fillets almost always look better on the bone side than the skin side, I like to present them with the bone side up. When two or more fillets make up a portion, it's nice to have them facing in the same direction (with the bellies on the same side). So, although you may not always have a choice, you might want to ask for all top fillets or all bottom fillets when buying a number of pieces.

Rex and dabs, as already noted, are too small to produce durable fillets, so these fish are sold either round or in the form known as pan-dressed, with the head, entrails, tail, and fins removed—essentially, two skin-on fillets attached to the bones. This is the ideal form for pan-frying or sautéing, as well as grilling, broiling, and "oven-frying" with a crust. It's a cut that also works with other flatfish, including petrale, English sole, and flounder; if your fish market does its own cutting, they should be able, with a little advance notice, to hold out a few soles of your chosen size and pan-dress them for you. (Just ask the fishmonger to "trim it like a sanddab," or else do it yourself as described on page 12.) One good-sized petrale or English sole, or a couple of rex, comes to just about a pound, and dresses out to 7 to 9 ounces with the bones, a decent portion at a bargain price.

Depending on your market, pan-dressed dabs and rex sole may or may not have the two long fins still attached, but I recommend removing them before cooking. Find the line where the fillet stops and the small "feather bones" next to the fins begin; you can usually feel a noticeable change in the thickness of the fish at this point, which is a quarter to a half inch in from the fins. Cut along this line with a large knife or kitchen shears and you will remove all those pesky little bones, leaving a neat triangle with two fillets attached to the central bone. (Again, your fishmonger should be able to do this for you if you ask.)

Most recipes that call for fillets of sole can be adapted to pan-dressed sole, and vice versa, by adjusting the cooking time. An exception is grilling, which is ideal for pan-dressed fish but very difficult for fillets.

Eating small flatfish with bones presents no particular challenge; all you need is a knife and fork and a little knowledge of basic fish anatomy. If the fish has been well trimmed along the ventral and dorsal fins, all the bones that remain should be attached to the backbone. Start by making a cut down the middle of the upper fillet, cutting down to the bone. Slide each half fillet off to the side, exposing the whole backbone and its long comblike extensions. Slip the knife under the bone and lift it up and away from the bottom fillet. (Having a plate nearby to receive the bones is a nice touch.) If the trim of the fish was not perfect, you may find strips of the small bones that support the fins along the edges of the fillets; these too are easily removed, but it may take a bit of searching. Return the top fillet halves to their original positions on top, if you like. If you are serving a sauce over the fish, it's nice to keep some of it back to add to the bottom fillets.

Follow the same procedure to divide a larger flatfish into two servings. Note that the two fillet halves are unequal in shape and size; for roughly equal portions, match the larger (dorsal) half of one with the smaller (ventral) half of the other.

European cookbooks and books by European-trained cooks usually give skinning as the first step in pan-dressing a sole. The idea is to begin with an incision near the tail, grasp the flap of skin, and pull it away from the fish. I have tried this with various Pacific soles, and the skin usually tears rather than pulling away cleanly. Besides, the skin is certainly tender enough to eat, and the scales are so tiny as to be negligible, so I don't bother to skin pan-dressed flatfish. Fillets are another matter; if you leave the skin on, it sometimes shrinks quickly as it cooks, causing the fillet to curl up. If you cut your own flatfish fillets, it's best to skin them as well; see page 13.

Sautéed Halibut with Leeks and Anchovy Butter

The opening of Pacific halibut season in the spring usually coincides with an abundance of large leeks, and I often combine the two. Here, the leeks are sautéed first, then the fish is cooked in the same pan to pick up some of the buttery leek flavor. It will also work with California halibut or other flatfish.

If you don't like anchovies, leave them out—the dish is still delicious.

SERVES 2

2 large leeks (to yield 2 cups sliced)

3 tablespoons butter

½ teaspoon salt

White pepper and cayenne, to taste

2 boneless, skinless halibut steak or fillet portions, about ¾ inch thick (about ¾ pound)

2 anchovy fillets, drained, rinsed, and chopped, OR ½ teaspoon anchovy paste

1 tablespoon lemon juice

➤ Slice the white and pale green parts of the leeks crosswise. Place the slices in a bowl of water, break them apart into rings, and agitate them well to wash away any dirt. Lift the slices out of the water, leaving the dirt behind. Drain well.

➤ Melt 1 tablespoon of the butter in a nonstick skillet over medium heat. Add the leeks and a pinch of salt and pepper; cover and cook until tender, about 8 minutes. Meanwhile, combine the salt, pepper, and cayenne and blend thoroughly. Sprinkle lightly on all sides of the fish.

➤ Remove the leeks with a slotted spoon to warm serving plates, leaving as much as possible of the butter behind. Turn the heat to medium-high, add the halibut to the pan, and cook, turning once, until just done in the center when probed with a skewer, about 6 minutes. Transfer the fish to the plates. Reduce the heat to low; add the remaining butter, chopped anchovy, and lemon juice to the skillet and swirl until the butter melts. Spoon over the fish and serve immediately.

Pescado con Rajas y Crema (Fish with Poblano Chiles and Cream)

Many a traditional Mexican dish combines roasted and peeled green chiles, especially the dark green, flavorful poblano variety, with onions and lightly soured cream. In his cookbook Authentic Mexican, *Rick Bayless uses the combination as the sauce for an elegant entree of sautéed fish fillets or steaks. In the following version, adapted from his recipe, the fish cooks directly in the sauce, saving a step and a skillet. It will work with steaks or fillets of any mild-flavored fish, but I especially like it with California halibut.*

There's really no substitute for heavy cream in binding this sauce, but it doesn't use that large an amount of cream. Just watch the fat in the rest of the menu.

SERVES 4

2 teaspoons oil

1 medium onion, julienned

1½ cups roasted and peeled poblano chile strips (about 2 large chiles)

⅔ cup whipping cream or crème fraîche (page 30)

Salt, to taste

1 to 1½ pounds halibut fillet or other white fish fillets or steaks, about ¾ inch thick

➤ Heat the oil in a large nonstick skillet over medium-low heat. Add the onion and chiles and cook until the onion is lightly browned. Stir in the cream, add a pinch of salt, and adjust the heat so the sauce simmers gently.

➤ Push the onion and peppers to the outside of the pan and lay the fish in the middle, skin side down if using fillets. Cover and cook, turning once, until the fish is just done, 7 to 10 minutes depending on thickness.

➤ Transfer the fish to a warmed serving dish. Taste the sauce for seasoning, correct if necessary, and spoon the sauce over and around the fish. Serve with steamed new potatoes and a simple vegetable.

NOTE Poblano chiles, the favorite chiles for roasting in central Mexico, are increasingly available wherever Mexican foods are sold. They are typically 4 to 6 inches long, dark green, and wide at the shoulder, tapering to a point. The flavor varies from fairly mild to fairly hot, depending in part on how much of the capsaicin-containing ribs you include. If you prefer a milder flavor, substitute sweet red bell peppers for part of the chiles, or use a milder chile, such as Anaheim, or hot Italian-style peppers.

Sautéed Halibut with Shredded Vegetables and Cumin

In this dish, an assortment of finely shredded vegetables sautéed in the same pan as the fish becomes the "sauce" for rather thin crosscut slices of halibut fillet, either cut from a whole fillet or boned out from a halibut steak. If the portions are precut, as is usually the case, look for pieces about an inch thick and split them in half, or ask the fishmonger to do it for you.

SERVES 2

½ teaspoon ground cumin

¼ teaspoon freshly ground pepper

¼ teaspoon salt

4 slices halibut fillet, ⅜ to ½ inch thick (10 to 12 ounces total)

2 tablespoons olive oil

1 clove garlic, lightly smashed

2 cups finely shredded assorted vegetables—carrots, zucchini, yellow squash, leeks, or green onions

3 tablespoons fish stock or unsalted chicken stock

½ teaspoon lemon juice or sherry vinegar

1 tablespoon chopped fresh mint

➤ Combine the cumin, pepper, and salt and sprinkle evenly on both sides of the fish. Let stand 15 minutes. Combine the oil and garlic in a 10-inch nonstick skillet over medium heat; cook until fragrant and the garlic begins to brown. Discard the garlic.

➤ Turn the heat to medium-high, add the halibut slices, and cook until lightly browned, about 3 minutes. Turn and cook until they begin to pull apart, another minute or two. Transfer to 2 warmed plates.

Add the carrots to the skillet, cook 1 minute, then add the remaining vegetables. Cook just until the vegetables begin to soften, then add the stock, the lemon juice, and the mint. Bring to a boil, taste for seasoning, and correct if necessary. Spoon the vegetables and sauce over the fish and serve immediately.

Braised Halibut Tail with Leeks and Spring Garlic

This dish can be made with just leeks, but the first month or so of halibut season is also time for "green" or "spring" garlic, partially formed bulbs with green stalks sold in bunches like leeks or green onions. If you can't find them, slice a couple of cloves of ordinary garlic and add them to the pan with the leeks.

For the best flavor, make the hot herb oil at least a day ahead. If you are pressed for time, use more red pepper flakes and it will be ready in a couple of hours.

SERVES 6

½ cup plus 1 tablespoon mild olive oil

1 tablespoon dried *herbes de Provence,* OR ½ tablespoon thyme and ½ tablespoon basil

½ teaspoon red pepper flakes

1 pound leeks

6 to 8 stalks spring garlic

Salt and pepper, to taste

1 halibut tail section or "roast," 2½ pounds

1 ounce dry white wine

One to three days ahead: Combine ½ cup olive oil, the dried herbs, and the red pepper flakes in a small saucepan. Warm slowly over low heat until the mixture begins to bubble, then remove from the heat, cover,

and let stand overnight to 3 days. Strain the mixture into a clean jar, cover tightly, and store in a cool, dark place.

Remove the bruised outer leaves from the leeks, trim the root ends, and cut the white and pale green parts diagonally into ¼-inch slices. Transfer the slices to a bowl of water, separate them into rings, and swirl them around to dislodge any dirt. Let the dirt settle, then lift the slices out with a slotted spoon and drain thoroughly.

Peel off the outer leaves of the garlic and trim the root tends. Cut the bulbs with an inch or so of stalk attached, and split them lengthwise; cut the tender green parts of the stalks diagonally into 1-inch sections.

Season the fish with salt and pepper. In a deep, lidded skillet or Dutch oven just large enough to hold the fish, heat the tablespoon of oil over medium-high heat. Add the fish, white-skinned side down, and cook until lightly browned, about 2 minutes. Turn the fish; if the skin sticks or tears, don't worry about it. Scatter the leeks and garlic around the outside. Sprinkle the leeks with a little salt and pepper, add the wine, cover, and cook until a skewer easily enters the thickest part of the fish (internal temperature of 130°F), another 18 to 20 minutes depending on thickness.

Transfer the fish to a warmed serving platter, spooning the leeks and pan juices over and around the fish. To serve, divide the upper fillet in half along the natural seam down the middle, and slide the halves to the sides. Lift out the central bone and the lower fillet should evenly divide into 2 portions. Spoon a little of the juices over the fish and drizzle each serving with a teaspoon or so of the hot herb oil.

VARIATION You can also use halibut steak or fillet portions, but bear in mind that they cook more quickly and may also call for a wider pan. Start the leeks first, and cook them covered for 3 to 4 minutes or until they begin to wilt before adding the fish and wine.

Grilled Halibut with Roasted Garlic Marinade

Cooking garlic whole tames its harsher nature, adding sweet and nutty flavors. If you already have some roasted garlic on hand, you are ahead of the game, but if not, here is a spur-of-the-moment procedure for roasting garlic on the same fire you will use to cook the fish. The instructions given here are for a covered charcoal grill, which allows you to cook the garlic before the fire gets to the perfect stage for cooking the fish. While you are at it, you might want to roast several heads of garlic, or some peppers for peeling later, or whole eggplant, zucchini, or onions...you name it.

Try this marinade on mahi-mahi, sea bass, or any other mild white fish. It needs no other sauce, just a vegetable that adds color to the plate.

SERVES 4

1 whole, firm head garlic

2 tablespoons extra-virgin olive oil

Salt and pepper

1 anchovy fillet, minced, OR ½ teaspoon anchovy paste (optional)

1½ to 2 pounds halibut steak or fillet portions

➤ Build a good-sized charcoal fire in a covered grill (if in doubt, build a bigger fire than you think you might need). When the charcoal reaches the flaming stage, set the grill in position and roast the whole head of garlic near the edge of the fire. Cook, turning the head occasionally and positioning it so the outside skin browns deeply but does not char, until the outer cloves are soft when pressed gently and liquid bubbles out of the center, 15 to 20 minutes total cooking time. Keep the grill covered with the vents open to extend the life of the fire.

➤ Let the garlic cool slightly, then slice the head crosswise through the thickest part to expose all the cloves. As soon as it is cool enough to handle, peel away any burnt skin, and squeeze the cloves out of each half into a bowl. Mash thoroughly with the back of a spoon. Stir in the oil, a pinch of salt, and anchovy (if used).

➤ Season the fish with salt and pepper and spread the marinade on both sides. Place on the grill and cook 3 to 4 minutes per side depending on thickness. Baste the fish with any oil remaining in the bowl after turning. Continue cooking until done by the skewer test (see page 17). Serve immediately.

Jerk Fish (Jamaican-Style Barbecued Halibut)

I will never forget my first encounter with Jamaican "jerk" barbecue at a Jamaican restaurant in Washington, D.C. To this day, their jerk chicken sticks in my taste memory as the hottest thing I have ever tasted, much hotter than my previous scale-toppers, Thai green curries and Indonesian sambals. It took two tall glasses of sweet ginger punch to soothe my palate, but I was hooked on the subtle interplay of chile and spices.

A really authentic jerk marinade is based on the favorite chile of the Caribbean, the Scotch bonnet or chile habanero (see page 30). But to be perfectly honest, I find a jerk marinade made with pure, whole Scotch bonnets is just plain too hot to enjoy, so I make this somewhat tamer version by removing the ribs and seeds, which are the hottest part of any chile. You can always add some back in if it's not hot enough. Other small hot chiles are also a possibility.

A whole tablespoon of ground allspice in the recipe is not an error. This sweet spice, native to Jamaica, is an equal partner with the chiles, helping to round out the other flavors. In this quantity, it also helps thicken and bind the mixture. If at all possible, use whole allspice berries and grind them freshly for each use; this gives a brighter taste to the marinade.

This recipe makes about twice the marinade you will need for four servings of fish. Tightly sealed in a jar in the refrigerator, the excess will keep for months.

SERVES 4

2 or 3 Scotch bonnet or habanero chiles, OR 4 serrano or jalapeño chiles

4 green onions, trimmed

2 tablespoons vinegar (wine or cider)

1 tablespoon oil

1 tablespoon ground allspice

1 teaspoon salt

½ teaspoon pepper

½ teaspoon cinnamon

⅛ teaspoon nutmeg

4 fillets or steaks of halibut, grouper, or other firm white fish

▶ Split the chiles lengthwise; remove and reserve the white ribs and seeds. Combine the chiles with all the remaining ingredients except the fish in a food processor or blender and blend to a paste. Taste the paste; if you want it hotter, blend in some of the chile ribs and seeds. Spread the paste on the fish and let it marinate in the refrigerator 1 to 4 hours.

▶ Remove the fish from the refrigerator 15 minutes before cooking. Grill or broil until a skewer easily enters the center of the fish, 6 to 10 minutes depending on thickness. Brush once or twice during cooking with the marinade remaining in the bowl.

VARIATION Jerk marinade can go on any firm white fish to be grilled, broiled, or baked in a hot oven. Try it on steaks or fillets of large rockfish or lingcod. It's also suitable for whole fish such as small rockfish; have the fish cleaned and scaled, slash the skin on the sides to allow the marinade to reach more of the meat, and rub it all over the inside and outside of the fish.

Sautéed Halibut with Mushrooms

A lot of halibut steaks are too large for a single serving, yet half a steak can look skimpy on the plate. This dish solves the problem by dividing each half of a steak into two thin pieces of fillet and topping them with a substantial sauce. To double the recipe, you will have to cook the fish in two batches or use a second skillet. Use whatever combination of cultivated and wild mushrooms suits your taste and budget.

SERVES 2

1 large "T-bone" halibut steak (about 12 ounces)

Salt and pepper

1 tablespoon oil

1 cup sliced mushrooms

1 teaspoon minced fresh ginger

2 teaspoons fresh lemon juice

½ teaspoon grated or shredded lemon zest

1 ounce dry white wine

2 tablespoons butter

➤ With a thin-bladed knife, cut both sections of halibut fillet free from the central bone. Holding the skin down against the board, cut the two fillets away from the skin. Discard the skin and bones, or save them for making fish stock. Lay each fillet piece on the board on one flat side. Holding the piece down with the palm of your hand, fingers extended, slice the piece in half across the grain into two thin steaks.

➤ Place 2 dinner plates in a 200°F oven to warm thoroughly. Season the fish lightly with salt and pepper. Heat the oil in a large skillet (nonstick is ideal) over medium-high

heat. Add the fish and cook until the edges are opaque around the upper side and only the center has a bit of raw color, about 3 minutes. Remove with a long-bladed spatula and invert onto the warm plates. Return the plates to the oven to keep warm.

➤ Add the mushrooms and ginger to the pan, turn the heat to high, and cook until the mushrooms begin to release their moisture. Add the lemon juice, lemon zest, and wine and boil until the liquid is nearly gone. Swirl in the butter, taste for seasoning, and spoon over the fish.

Halibut Cubes in Thai Green Curry Sauce

Although halibut is not found within a thousand miles of Thailand, its firm, moist, white meat is perfect for a Thai-style curry. The coconut milk, curry paste, and fish sauce are now widely available in Asian markets and many supermarkets.

SERVES 4 TO 6 ASIAN STYLE, WITH OTHER DISHES

1 can (15 ounces) unsweetened coconut milk

1 to 2 tablespoons green curry paste

¼ cup sliced green onions

½ pound green beans, trimmed and cut into 1-inch lengths

1 tablespoon Thai fish sauce

1 pound halibut steaks or fillets, skinned, boned, and cut into 1-inch cubes

2 firm but ripe tomatoes, peeled, seeded, and coarsely diced

A handful of fresh basil or mint leaves, or a combination

➤ Do not shake the coconut milk before opening the can. Skim ¼ cup of the thick "cream" from the surface of the milk and heat it in a wok or saucepan over medium heat until bubbly. Add the curry paste, green onions, and green beans and cook until the mixture is quite fragrant and the oil begins to separate from the cream.

➤ Discard the remaining cream from the coconut milk if desired, then add the remaining milk and the fish sauce to the pan. Bring to a boil, lower the heat to medium, and reduce the mixture by half. Add the fish cubes and tomatoes and simmer until the fish is done, about 6 minutes. Stir in the basil leaves and serve with rice.

NOTE Coconut milk is very high in saturated fat, so if you're watching calories, discard the oil-rich coconut "cream" and use 1 tablespoon peanut or corn oil in the first step. You will lose just a bit of the coconut flavor.

Pan-Seared Halibut with Dried Mushroom Crust

In a curious but delicious twist on the "surf & turf" idea, the 1990s saw a lot of chefs using meat stocks (especially veal stock) to enhance seafood dishes. In many cases, these sauces also include red wine, mushrooms, or other robust, earthy flavors more typically associated with meats and game. A good brown meat stock also provides enough gelatin to give both richness and body to a sauce without the use of thickeners or added fats.

This recipe is a much simplified version of a dish I first tasted at Aqua in San Francisco: a thick petrale fillet sautéed with a dried porcini mushroom crust and served

on truffled mashed potatoes, surrounded by assorted mushrooms in a sauce based on brown veal stock. Michael Mina's version reflects the resources and staff available to a restaurant chef; for example, they use a different cooking method for each mushroom, to bring out its best flavor and texture.

The most distinctive ingredient in this version is ground dried porcini mushrooms. An electric spice mill or coffee grinder (the type with a spinning blade, not the burr type) quickly reduces a handful of mushroom slices to bits the size of cornmeal, suitable for using as a spice. Better still, use a mini-food processor or a blender equipped with a 1-cup jar (see page 28). Dried button mushrooms will also work, but not shiitakes, which taste like mothballs if they are cooked too quickly.

SERVES 4

½ ounce dried porcini or other dried boletus mushrooms

1 cup Brown Veal Stock (page 331) or strong unsalted poultry stock

3 tablespoons dry sherry or dry Madeira

4 boneless halibut steak portions, ¾ inch thick (5 to 6 ounces each)

¼ teaspoon freshly ground white pepper

1 tablespoon soy sauce

1 tablespoon olive oil, approximately

3 tablespoons butter

Garlic-flavored mashed potatoes and steamed pea pods or green beans

➤ Place the dried mushrooms in a mini-food processor, coffee grinder, or blender fitted with a small jar and chop to a coarse powder. Sift the mixture through a coarse sieve into a bowl, grind the large pieces again, and sift again. When less than a tablespoon of large chunks remains, put the chunks in a small saucepan with the stock and 2 tablespoons of the wine. Bring to a boil, reduce to a simmer, and cook until the liquid is reduced by two-thirds. Strain the mixture and return it to the saucepan; set aside. (May be prepared to this point several hours ahead; cover the ground mushrooms to keep them dry).

➤ Season the halibut steaks lightly with pepper, place them on a plate, and drizzle them with the soy sauce and remaining wine. Turn them to coat them evenly with the marinade. Marinate 15 minutes to a few hours.

➤ Preheat the oven to 400°F. Bring the reduced stock back to a simmer, season it to taste, and keep it warm. Heat a heavy skillet with an ovenproof handle over medium heat and add oil to coat the bottom. Turn the halibut steaks in the marinade one more time, then blot them dry. Press a quarter of the ground mushrooms into the top side of each steak and set them in the hot skillet, coated side down. Cook 3 minutes, turn, and place the pan in the hot oven. Cook until the fish is just opaque in the center and done by the skewer test, 4 to 6 minutes more.

➤ Transfer the halibut portions to warm plates, alongside or on top of the mashed potatoes. Swirl the butter into the stock and spoon this sauce over and around the fish. Garnish with your choice of green vegetable.

VARIATION This can work with a variety of fish, from thick petrale fillets to grouper and even arctic char. Thinner cuts of fish can be cooked entirely on top of the stove, without using the oven.

Grilled Halibut with Fresh Thyme

Simple, but delicious with either northern or California halibut. Broil the fish if grilling is not convenient.

SERVES 4

1½ pounds halibut fillet
Salt and pepper
Heaping teaspoon fresh thyme leaves
Zest of 1 lemon
2 to 3 tablespoons olive oil

➤ Slice the fillet diagonally into 4 equal pieces, ¾ to 1 inch thick. Season them lightly with salt and pepper and place them in a shallow dish. Scatter the thyme and lemon zest over the fish and sprinkle it with oil. Marinate in the refrigerator 30 minutes to several hours.

➤ Build a hot charcoal fire and preheat the grill thoroughly. Remove the fish from the refrigerator 15 minutes before grilling. Turn the fish in the marinade one more time just before cooking, and let the excess oil drip off before putting the fish on the grill. Grill 3 to 5 minutes with the bone side down, turn, and cook until done by the skewer test.

Other Serving Suggestions: Halibut
Both varieties of halibut are excellent baked or braised in Red Onion Confit (page 125).

Substitute Pacific halibut fillet or boned-out steaks in Poached Salmon with Mussel Sauce, page 59.

See Planked Salmon or Halibut, page 61.

Flounder or Sole in Red Wine Sauce

This is a fundamental dish that should be in every seafood cook's repertoire: delicate flatfish fillets poached in a wine-flavored stock, which is then reduced and enriched with a little butter for a sauce. Master this dish and a few variations (see also the next recipe) and you can always put out a delicious fish dinner in less than an hour.

I give the red wine version first because it is the more classic rendition in French cuisine, but the dish is equally good with white wine. If price were no issue, I would use a good California or Oregon pinot noir, but when the budget is more constrained I have had excellent results with inexpensive southern French reds like Côtes du Rhône and Costières de Nîmes, as well as jug zinfandel. Just look for a red that is pleasant to drink and not too tannic and you won't go wrong.

SERVES 2

2 large skinless petrale or starry flounder fillets, 6 to 7 ounces each

Scant ½ teaspoon salt

1 cup not very tannic red wine

1 cup water, unsalted fish stock, or unsalted vegetable broth

1 onion, sliced

4 to 5 sprigs parsley

6 peppercorns

1 teaspoon fennel seed

Heads, bones, and trimmings of lean fish (optional; see note, page 104)

Large pinch of salt and white pepper

A few grains of cayenne (optional)

Lemon juice, if needed

2 tablespoons cold butter, in small pieces

➤ Remove any pin bones from the fish; reserve the trimmings for the stock. Sprinkle the fillets generously with salt and set aside.

➤ In a nonreactive skillet, combine the wine, water, onion, parsley, peppercorns, fennel seed, and fish bones, if used. Bring just to a boil, skim off any foam, reduce the heat, and simmer 20 to 30 minutes. Meanwhile, warm a serving platter or individual plates in a very low oven.

➤ Strain the stock, return it to the skillet, and bring it back to a simmer. Rinse the fillets and pat them dry. Slide the fillets skin side down into the stock and poach until slightly underdone by the skewer test (see page 17). Transfer the fish to the platter and keep it warm in the oven.

➤ Remove all but 1 cup of the stock from the pan. (The rest can be refrigerated or frozen for future use.) Over high heat, bring the stock to a boil with the salt, pepper, and cayenne and reduce it to about 2 tablespoons of syrupy liquid. Taste for seasoning; it should be quite tart. Add lemon juice if necessary. Remove the pan from the heat and swirl in the butter. Drain or dab away any accumulated liquid from the fish plates and pour the sauce over the fish.

NOTE Doubling this recipe gets tricky unless you have an especially large skillet. A better way to make more servings is to use smaller, thinner fillets and roll them up, as in the following recipe. Increase the cooking time for rolled fillets to allow the heat to reach the center of the rolls.

VARIATION To prepare with white wine, choose a not very oaky wine with good fruit and acidity, such as a California or Northwest sauvignon blanc or sémillon. Add some chopped chives to the sauce for a touch of color.

Poached Sole with Summer Vegetables

Here is another way to poach sole fillets, by arranging them (rolled up into the compact cylinders the French call paupiettes) in an empty skillet and then pouring the hot stock over them. With really small fillets (less than 2 ounces each), you may want to use two fillets laid together to make each roll.

This recipe can be varied almost endlessly. Shrimp, oysters, mussels, or other cooked shellfish can be added to the sauce or tucked inside the fish rolls. Mushrooms can be used in place of the vegetables. Pan-dressed rex sole or sanddabs can be used in place of the rolled fillets (adjust the poaching time accordingly).

Timing can be a bit tricky here, as you have to sauté the vegetable garnish separately at the same time as you are poaching the fish and reducing the sauce. If in doubt, it's better for the vegetables to wait a few minutes for the fish than vice versa.

SERVES 4

1½ pounds small sole fillets

¾ teaspoon kosher salt

1 cup dry white wine

2 cups water, unsalted fish stock, or unsalted vegetable broth

½ cup green onion tops

6 peppercorns

½ pound bones and trimmings of lean fish, well rinsed (optional; see note)

½ cup cream

Salt and white pepper, to taste

2 cups finely shredded vegetables, lightly sautéed (use a colorful assortment—zucchini, yellow summer squash, red peppers, and green onions, for example)

➤ Remove any pin bones from the fillets and trim off any ragged ends. Save the trimmings for the stock. Season the fillets generously with salt and set aside.

➤ Combine the wine, water, green onion tops, peppercorns, and fish bones, if used, in a nonreactive saucepan. Bring just to a boil, reduce the heat, and simmer 30 minutes. Meanwhile, lightly butter a deep skillet or baking dish just large enough to hold the fish rolls in a single layer. Warm a serving platter or individual plates in a very low oven.

➤ Rinse the fillets and pat dry. Divide them into 8 portions, doubling the smallest fillets or splitting the largest as necessary. Roll up the fillets skin side inward and place them in the skillet, seams down. Bring the stock just to a boil and strain it over the fish rolls, pouring some directly over each roll. Set the skillet over low heat, cover, and cook at a simmer (do not boil) until just a trace of raw center remains when the fish is probed with a skewer, 2 to 5 minutes depending on variety and thickness. Spoon some hot stock over any exposed parts if necessary for even cooking.

➤ Transfer the barely cooked fish rolls to the platter and keep warm in the oven. Pour the poaching liquid into a measuring pitcher and return 1½ cups to the skillet (reserve the rest for another use). Bring to a boil and reduce by two-thirds. Add the cream, reduce slightly, and season to taste. Pour or dab away any liquid from the fish platter and pour the sauce over the fish. Surround the fish with sautéed vegetables and serve immediately.

VARIATION If you prefer, you can cook the fish rolls right in a bake-and-serve dish or even in a deep enough platter with a cover of aluminum foil. This technique takes some daring, as you have to remove the stock after cooking without destroying the delicate fish rolls. One way is simply to lay your hand against the foil (protected from the heat with a towel) and carefully pour out the liquid. A safer, but much slower, way is to remove the stock with a bulb baster. Whichever method you choose, practice it first for family, not for company!

NOTE Bones and trimmings of sole are ideal for making a richer stock. If your fish market cuts its own sole fillets, they should be able to set aside some bones for you with advance notice.

Sole with Spinach and Hazelnuts

In the classic French sole Florentine, poached sole is served on a bed of sautéed spinach and topped with a creamy sauce. This slimmed-down version uses a lemony vinaigrette made with hazelnut-infused oil.

This recipe may appear complicated at first, but it's mostly a matter of assembling the components so you can put together the finished dish in a few minutes. The timing depends mainly on the fish; if using rex sole or other fish

on the bone, wait a minute or two after you begin cooking the fish to start the spinach. With very thin fillets, you may want to start the spinach cooking, then begin poaching the fish.

SERVES 4

6 tablespoons peanut oil

¼ cup whole hazelnuts

Leaves from 1 pound fresh spinach, washed, spun dry, and shredded

¼ teaspoon salt (approximately)

Pepper, to taste

1½ tablespoons lemon juice

3 to 4 cups fish stock or court-bouillon (page 329)

1 pound fillets of sole, OR 8 pan-dressed rex sole

➤ Combine the oil and hazelnuts in a wok and place over medium-low heat. Cook, stirring, until the nuts are quite fragrant and the meat shows golden brown through cracks in the skin. Pour the contents of the wok through a fine sieve into a heatproof container and set the wok aside. As soon as the nuts are cool enough to handle, wrap them in a clean towel and rub them to remove as much of the skins as possible. Chop the nuts coarsely (cracking them first with the side of a broad-bladed knife helps). Set aside.

➤ A handful at a time, bundle the spinach leaves together and slice crosswise into coarse shreds. (It will look like an enormous amount, about 8 cups, but it will reduce considerably in cooking.)

➤ Dissolve a hefty pinch of the salt and a generous grinding of pepper in the lemon juice, then stir the mixture into the reserved nut-cooking oil. Set aside in a warm place.

➤ Bring the court-bouillon to a simmer in a large skillet. Add the fish in a single layer if possible; if necessary, overlap the thinnest tail sections or the smallest fillets. While the fish cooks, sauté the spinach over high heat in the bit of oil that has clung to the wok, adding a pinch of salt, until thoroughly wilted. Moisten with a tablespoonful or two of the fish poaching liquid.

➤ Spread a layer of spinach on warm plates or a serving platter. Remove the fish fillets with a slotted spoon as they become opaque, beginning with the smallest ones, and arrange on top of the spinach. Give the lemon dressing a stir and drizzle half over the fillets. Garnish with chopped nuts and serve immediately; pass the rest of the dressing separately at the table.

Oven-Fried Sanddabs or Rex Sole

Tender little flatfish are delicious with a crisp crust, and the "Spencer method" of "oven-frying" (see page 123) is the easiest way to achieve it. Use fresh bread crumbs if at all possible. Just put some fresh French bread in a food processor or blender and chop into small pieces. If your bread is a little stale, grating it on the coarse side of a box grater is another easy way to make crumbs.

SERVES 4

1 cup bread crumbs, preferably fresh

1 tablespoon minced fresh herbs, such as basil, parsley, or chives

8 good-sized rex sole or sanddabs, well trimmed (about 2 pounds after trimming)

Salt and pepper

2 tablespoons olive or other vegetable oil
Lemon wedges

➤ Preheat the oven to 500°F. Lightly oil a baking sheet or coat it with nonstick spray. Combine the bread crumbs and herbs. Season the fish lightly with salt and pepper and dip them in the bread crumb mixture. Arrange the fish on the baking sheet with the thicker (dark-skinned) side up.

➤ Drizzle the oil over the top of the fish and put them immediately in the oven. Bake until the meat begins to separate from the bones at the thick ends, 5 to 6 minutes. Serve with a simple squeeze of lemon, or with your choice of mayonnaise-based sauces (see page 323).

Broiled Sole "Stuffed" with Crab

The "stuffing" in this recipe is not an actual stuffing, but rather a thick layer of dressing (much like a crab cake) spread on top of fillets. You will need a large skillet with a heatproof handle so it can go under the broiler. Nonstick is a definite plus, as delicate flatfish fillets might fall apart if they stick. A 10-inch skillet is just barely large enough to hold the fish in a single layer; a 12-inch pan is better. If the largest you have is 10 inches, use tilapia or another compact-shaped fish.

SERVES 4

2 teaspoons oil

¼ cup minced green onion

1 small clove garlic, minced

¼ cup chopped mushrooms

⅓ pound cooked crabmeat, flaked

4 teaspoons mayonnaise

2 tablespoons fine bread crumbs, cracker crumbs, or matzo meal

1 teaspoon Chesapeake seafood seasoning (page 29) or Creole seafood seasoning (page 31), or to taste

4 fillets of sole, flounder, or similarly shaped fish, 4 to 5 ounces each

Paprika (optional)

Lemon wedges

➤ Heat the oil in a small skillet and cook the onion, garlic, and mushrooms until the mushrooms release their liquid; continue cooking until nearly dry. Let cool slightly, then combine with the crabmeat, mayonnaise, and crumbs. Season the mixture to taste with seafood seasoning.

➤ Season the fish fillets lightly with the seafood seasoning and spread a thick, even layer of the crab mixture on top of each. Dust the tops with paprika if desired.

➤ Heat the broiler and heat a large skillet (nonstick or lightly oiled) over medium heat. Place the fish in the skillet, then immediately run the pan under the broiler. Cook until the tops are lightly browned and the fish is opaque around the edges, about 5 minutes. Check the center of the fish for doneness with a thin skewer or toothpick (insert the tip for a few seconds, then immediately touch it to your lips; if it is quite warm, the fish is done). If necessary, return the pan to the top of the stove to cook a bit more from below. Serve with lemon wedges.

Sautéed Sole with Red Pepper–Garlic Butter

This sauce will also work well with rex sole or sanddab, or fillets of flounder or larger soles, or California halibut.

SERVES 2

2½ tablespoons peanut or other vegetable oil

½ large red bell pepper, thinly sliced

1 small clove garlic, peeled and left whole

2 tablespoons softened butter

Salt, pepper, and lemon juice, to taste

2 whole petrale or English sole, ¾ to 1 pound each, pan-dressed

Flour for dusting fish

➤ Heat 1 tablespoon of the oil in a skillet over low heat. (It can be the same pan you will use later to cook the fish.) Add the pepper strips and garlic and cook until the pepper is quite soft, adjusting the heat so it does not burn. Remove the pepper and garlic with a slotted spoon and put through a sieve or food mill, straining out the pieces of skin. Let cool, then whisk into the softened butter. Season to taste with salt, pepper, and lemon juice. Set aside. (Can be prepared to this point an hour or two ahead of time.)

➤ Heat the remaining oil in a large skillet over medium-high heat. Meanwhile, dredge the fish in flour and shake off the excess. Add the fish to the skillet dark side down; cook until well browned, about 5 minutes. Turn and cook until the meat has shrunk back noticeably from the bones on both sides, about another 3 minutes. Transfer to warm plates. Spoon half the red pepper butter over the fish and serve the rest in individual ramekins.

Falafel Flatfish

Looking around the pantry one day for something other than flour or cornmeal for coating fish fillets, my eye landed on a jar of falafel mix. This blend of ground chickpeas and seasonings is normally reconstituted and fried in balls or patties for that Middle Eastern snack. In its plain dry form, it turned out to make a delicious coating for mild-flavored fish. Falafel mixes are sold in supermarkets and health-food stores, both in boxes and in bulk; brands vary in flavor, so try several to find one you like.

This recipe will work with any small to medium-size flatfish fillets, as well as similarly shaped fish like orange roughy and tilapia. If using the smallest sizes, those thin fillets that run an ounce or two apiece, you might want to press two fillets together back to back to create a thicker piece. Serve with a simple squeeze of lemon or a fresh tomato salsa.

SERVES 4

½ teaspoon salt

¼ teaspoon paprika

1 to 1½ pounds skinless flounder or sole fillets

1 cup (approximately) dry falafel mix

2 to 3 tablespoons mild olive or peanut oil

➤ Combine the salt and paprika and sprinkle evenly over the fish. Spread the falafel mix in a plate or shallow bowl. Heat the oil in a large skillet, using high heat for thinner fillets, medium-high for thicker ones.

➤ Dredge the fillets in the falafel mix, shake off the excess, and lay them in the pan skin side up. Cook until golden brown, turn with a large spatula, and cook on the second side until a skewer easily enters the thickest part. Total cooking time will range from 4 to 8 minutes depending on thickness; figure about half as long on the second side as on the first.

Whole Flounder with Herb Marinade

Grilling or broiling a whole flatfish with the skin on is a great way to maximize its flavor, whether it's a half-pound sanddab or a 2-pound starry flounder. I like to cook the former as plainly as possible, but the latter enjoys a flavor boost from an herbal marinade.

How you orient the fish has to do with whether you are broiling or grilling. On the grill, start with the dark side down, toward the heat, where it cooks first; under the broiler, start with the white side toward the heat first. Either way, you should turn the fish once and finish with the dark side up, and that's the way it goes on the plate.

SERVES 2

3 tablespoons olive oil

2 tablespoons chopped fresh herbs (parsley, chives, chervil, tarragon, or a blend)

1 teaspoon minced garlic (optional)

¼ teaspoon salt

Freshly ground pepper, to taste

1 large or 2 small whole flounder (2 pounds in all)

➤ Combine the oil, herbs, garlic, salt, and pepper and set aside for up to 2 hours for the flavors to blend.

➤ Dress or pan-dress the fish (see page 10), rinse well, and pat dry. Slash the thicker part of both fillets with one or two shallow diagonal cuts through the skin and into the meat. Set aside 1 tablespoon of the marinade and rub the rest all over the surface of the fish and into the cuts. Set aside in a shallow bowl or plate for 15 minutes.

TO GRILL Build a medium-hot fire in a charcoal grill or preheat a gas grill. Oil the grill rack and place the fish dark skin side down. Grill 4 minutes, or until the skin releases easily from the grill, and turn. Baste with any marinade remaining in the fish dish (not the separately reserved part, which will become the sauce). Continue grilling until a thin skewer easily penetrates the thickest part of the fish (poke through past the bones to the underside), another 2 to 4 minutes.

TO BROIL Oil a broiling pan and rack and preheat the broiler. Start the fish cooking with the white-skinned side toward the heat and broil until the meat begins to show opaque white at the cuts, 2 to 4 minutes. Turn, baste with any marinade in the fish dish, and broil on the dark side until done by the skewer test.

Transfer the fish to a warm serving dish or individual plates, dark side up. Drizzle with the reserved marinade.

VARIATION Charmoula (page 318) makes a particularly nice marinade and sauce for starry flounder.

Other Serving Suggestions: Small Flatfish

Pan-dressed sanddabs or rex sole are delicious cooked à la meunière; see Tilapia Meunière with Julienne Leeks and Carrots, page 209.

Any good-sized sole and flounder fillets can also be cooked meunière style. If you dip the floured fish in beaten egg before cooking, it becomes Sole Doré, another old San Francisco favorite.

Substitute thicker sole or flounder fillets in Sautéed Halibut with Shredded Vegetables and Cumin, page 95.

lean, mild & white fish

In the wholesale seafood business, "whitefish" does not refer to the freshwater fish of the same name, a member of the salmon and trout family. Instead, it is shorthand for "lean, white-fleshed, mild-flavored fish." Worldwide, the most important of these "whitefish" belong to the order Gadiformes, which includes the cod family and several closely related families. But the larger share of the Pacific white fish market has historically belonged to the rockfishes, which is where this chapter begins.

Alaska Pollock

Bocaccio

Cabrilla

Cabezon

Chilipepper

Goldeneye

Greenling

Grenadier

Grouper

Lingcod

Pacific Cod

Pacific Whiting

Rockfish

Skate

White Seabass

Wolffish

Rockfish

Rockfish, *Sebastes* spp.

Walk into a Chinese fish market from Orange County to Vancouver and you may see a dozen or more varieties of whole fish in a rainbow of colors. Unless you are familiar with the fish, however, you might never guess that half or more of them are considered a single item in most Western fish markets.

If you look a little closer, you might recognize a basic similarity in shape among many of the fish, as well as other details—a heavy head with spiky points on the gill covers, sharp spines on the dorsal fins, large eyes. These anatomical details identify the 60-odd members of the genus *Sebastes*, the rockfishes, and the closely related thornyheads (*Sebastolobus* spp.). Although rockfish is the proper name for these fish, they are better known in the market under pseudonyms such as rock cod and "Pacific red snapper," even though they are neither cods nor snappers. A couple of species of *Sebastes* from the north Pacific and north Atlantic are also known as ocean perch.

While Western markets tend to group many species of rockfish together, Chinese fishmongers and their customers are more discerning. To take just two varieties as an example, a Chinese market might charge upwards of $4.00 per

pound for the blackish-green variety with a wide yellow stripe known as China rockfish, while the similarly sized black rockfish lying next to it might command only $1.50 per pound. To someone looking for a whole fish to steam Cantonese style, the finer texture and flavor of the former makes all the difference. This is not to say the black rockfish is a bad fish; it's just not as nicely textured and flavorful. It's fine for many uses, including frying, grilling, or making soup.

This "varietal" labeling of rockfish is spreading in Western fish markets as well, especially in the Northwest. A few fishermen willing to go to the trouble of separating their catch into species and handling the best varieties with extra care have found that they can get a premium price, at least from a few retailers who know the difference. The retailers in turn can offer the fish to their customers as something more than generic "snapper." It's like selling chardonnay rather than "chablis"; the producer gets a higher price, and the consumer gets a better product.

One of the first rockfish species to make a name for itself in Western markets was yelloweye or goldeneye (*Sebastes ruberrimus*), a large, red-skinned species with a prominent, bright yellow eye. A bit smaller but also choice is the canary rockfish (*S. pinniger*), with mottled orange and gray skin. Quillback rockfish (*S. maliger*) is strikingly colored, bright orange around the face and dark brown to black near the tail. And the most distinctively colored of all, the China rockfish (*S. nebulosus*) is black with a bright yellow streak from above the head to the tail. Any of these species, as well as the smaller and plainer-looking copper (*S. caurinus*) and brown (*S. auriculatus*) rockfish, deserves to be sold under its own name, rather than lumped together as "snapper."

These "fancy" rockfishes tend to be loners, and often inhabit rocky reefs, so they must be caught by hook and line rather than in nets. This adds somewhat to the price, as it is not possible to catch them efficiently; but it pays off in the condition of the fish, which do not get handled as roughly as they would in nets. Some fishermen go a step further, bleeding the fish shortly after they land on deck, a step that improves the flavor.

Other, and generally less expensive, rockfish are schooling fish, often caught in trawl nets. This category includes Pacific ocean perch, which is the only variety typically sold as skin-on fillets. It also covers a handful of species, all staples of the West Coast commercial fishing industry, that are usually sold under the generic label of "snapper" or "rock cod," including yellowtail rockfish, chilipepper, bocaccio, widow rockfish, and black rockfish. Unfortunately, increases in both the intensity and efficiency of fishing for these species have put some species of rockfish into serious decline. Fearing another Atlantic cod situation, West Coast authorities issued catch quotas on several individual species of rockfish in the 1990s, and more will likely be added in the near future.

Short of carrying a field guide to the market, how do you know whether you are getting one of the fancy or one of the everyday varieties? In a Chinese market, you can generally go by price; the higher price of the choice varieties is a matter of mutually agreed value between buyer and seller, representing years of experience on both sides of the sales counter. The overall shape of a rockfish is another general indicator; the choicest varieties tend to have deeper bodies, i.e., the distance from the chin to the top of the head is larger relative to the length of the fish. The less expensive varieties are slightly more elongated.

Lingcod

Lingcod, *Ophiodon elongatus*

When the first English-speaking fishermen came to the West Coast, one of the fish they found was a rather large bottom-dwelling fish with an elongated shape and firm, white meat. It looked a lot like the familiar cod of the north Atlantic, as well as its slimmer cousin the ling, and it became known as lingcod. Biologists long ago realized that it's not at all related to the cod family, but the name has stuck. And it remains one of the best white-meat fish found in these parts.

A mostly solitary, predatory fish distantly related to rockfish, lingcod is found all along the Pacific Coast from Baja to Alaska. Together with their close relatives the greenlings (*Hexagrammos* spp.), smaller lingcod are caught all year in rockfish trawls. The larger adult fish are most common in the market from late summer into the fall, when they move into rocky areas of shallow water in preparation for early winter spawning. However, in recent years the season has been cut short before the end of the year when the annual catch quotas have filled by mid-November.

Lingcod's white, lean meat is similar in appearance to that of the larger rockfish, but denser, with a finer flake. The meat of some individuals can show a pale to strikingly deep blue-green tint, but this coloration is harmless and disappears in cooking and the two color phases are indistinguishable in flavor.

Many people consider lingcod superior in flavor to any rockfish. It's my first choice among West Coast fish for frying in a batter, and its firm texture makes it ideal for baking in a sauce. Grilling and broiling are also good choices, if your piece is not too thick.

Whatever the cooking method, lingcod can take a surprisingly long time to cook. In my experience, a piece of lingcod usually takes half again as long to cook over the same heat as a similarly shaped piece of rockfish, salmon, or most other fish. It's a good example of how simplistic rules like "10 minutes per inch" should be treated as guidelines only, to be adjusted to the particular fish you are cooking.

Most of the lingcod found in fish markets is in the form of fillets, but you may find whole fish in Asian markets. If you can find them, the heads and bones are especially good for making fish stocks and soups. Chinese markets are your best bet for finding lingcod heads, but don't be surprised if the head of a good-sized ling costs you five dollars or more; it will produce plenty of meat from the cheeks and the back of the head. It's harder to find the heads in most Western fish markets, but if you ask ahead of time they may be able to supply one for you.

Although it is unrelated to lingcod, cabezon (*Scorpaenichthys marmoratus*), a large sculpin, is similar in texture and flavor, and even shares the occasional blue-green tint to the meat. Cabezon fillets (often spelled cabazone) can be used exactly like lingcod.

Cod and Its Relatives

Pacific cod, *Gadus macrocephalus*
Walleye (Alaska) pollock, *Theragra chalcogramma*
Pacific whiting, *Merluccius productus*
Pacific grenadier, *Coryphaenoides acrolepis*

In the world of seafood, "cod" without a qualifying name means North Atlantic cod, the target of one of the world's most important commercial fisheries since the Middle Ages. However, Atlantic cod (and its equally valuable cousin haddock) have fallen on hard times in the late twentieth century. Too many years of too many boats catching too many fish have sent stocks into a deep decline, from which it is hoped the species will eventually recover. In the meantime, many East Coast processors who traditionally relied on Atlantic cod have switched over to its Pacific cousin, which is still relatively abundant in Alaskan and Russian waters. An expert can tell the two apart, but for most purposes Pacific cod can stand in for Atlantic without apology.

Pacific cod alone cannot satisfy the world demand, and the world fish market continues to clamor for something as close as possible to cod: an abundant species yielding similarly lean, firm white-fleshed fillets with a mild flavor and a fine flake. The most successful of these cod surrogates have been other gadiform (cod-related) fish from northern waters, especially Alaska pollock, and a couple of close relatives from the colder oceans of the Southern Hemisphere.

Alaska pollock is now the largest single fish species taken in Alaska waters, and while much of the catch goes into value-added products and surimi shellfish analogues, some is sold as fresh and frozen fillets.

A newer entrant in the a-lot-like-cod contest is grenadier, part of another family of gadiform fish with a distinctive shape. Instead of the typical fish profile, with a flaring tail fin at the end of a tapered tail, grenadier tapers constantly from the head to the tail, with the dorsal and anal fins coming together in a pointed tip. The long, rather slender fillets reflect this shape, though processors routinely trim off the thinnest part of the tail meat for a more compact and conventional shape.

Grenadiers are found mainly in the deeper waters off the continental shelves. One place where these deep waters occur quite close to the North American coast is the submarine Monterey Canyon off central California. Boats fishing the canyon slopes for other species have always caught some grenadier, but only in the mid-1990s did they find a ready market for this fish. The fillets, though on the small side, can stand in nicely for other codlike fish.

Increasingly, the northern world has looked across the equator to cod's relatives among the hake family to fill the gaps in the fillet market.

The genus *Merluccius* includes several of the most important commercial fish species of the temperate and polar oceans. A couple of these species are unique to the Southern Hemisphere, where they are the ecological counterparts of cods and pollocks in the north. Many are available here, sold either as whiting or under confusing names like "Antarctic queen" (the South American *M. australis*) or "Cape capensis" (*M. capensis* from South Africa). Hoki, a grenadier-shaped relative from New Zealand, is usually found under its own name.

The local cousin of these hakes is Pacific whiting, a smallish variety found along the north Pacific rim from Baja California to Japan. For as long as I can remember, whiting has been one of the great bargains among West Coast fish. It has the lean, flaky white meat typical of the cod family, though it's perhaps a little stronger in flavor than its cousins. Because of a unique enzyme reaction that can cause the fish to soften quickly, most of the catch is frozen at sea, some of it by large factory trawlers that process the fish all the way to the finished form (including surimi, page 226).

The most common market form for Pacific whiting is pan-dressed or "H&G" (headed and gutted) whole fish, typically a half pound to a pound apiece, packed in 5-pound boxes and frozen. Frozen H&G whiting still sell for around a dollar a pound, and only slightly more thawed. Despite its bargain price, whiting can be hard to find outside of ethnic markets, where it is often sold under the Spanish name *merluza*. Frying and baking in a sauce are the best cooking methods.

Skate

Skate, *Raja* spp.

The French love it. Julia Child has been promoting it. It's abundant, underutilized, versatile, and cheap. So why isn't skate an everyday item at your local fish market? Maybe it's the odd appearance, maybe it's a fear of "stingrays," or maybe it's just because few people have ever tried it.

Skates and rays are a worldwide family of distinctively shaped fish related to sharks. Their characteristic shape comes from the enlarged pectoral fins, which are attached by skin all along the length of the body to form the characteristic "wings." The family includes the giant manta rays so popular with underwater photographers, and the stingrays, with venomous defensive spines on their tails.

Smaller, less dramatic, and more abundant are the skates, several species of which are native to the Pacific Coast. A few species, the California, longnose, and big skates, are common in nearshore waters at shallow to moderate depths, the same habitat that produces most of the sole, flounder, and halibut catch. Every haul of the flatfish nets brings up a few skate, making these species a small but regular bycatch of flatfish trawl fisheries. However, skate can be tough to sell, and many skate still go back over the side for lack of a market. This

is too bad, because skate is a delicious fish; its lean white meat is as mild in flavor as that of shark, and much more tender.

Anytime there is more of a fish than the market demands, the result is a bargain price. With a wholesale price around a dollar per pound, and an edible yield of better than 50 percent after boning and skinning, skate wings compete with squid as one of the best buys in the seafood market. Maybe that's part of its problem—it's too cheap. Compared to salmon, halibut, sole, and all the other varieties of fish that are readily available, easy to cut, and easy to sell at a higher price, the occasional skate may seem like small potatoes to some fishmongers. If you have a choice between these familiar species and something more obscure, it's easy to go with the favorites.

Skate fillets can be sautéed, broiled, fried, or poached and served with your favorite sauce. Getting at the meat of a skate is not difficult, once you understand its unique structure. Most of the meat is in the wings, which is typically the only part landed, the rest being discarded at sea. Filleting a skate wing, like filleting any other fish, is a matter of separating the meat from both the skin and the skeleton. Like their cousins the sharks, skates and rays have a skeleton of cartilage rather than bone. Each wing consists of two layers of muscle, one above and one below a row of parallel cartilaginous supports (the "bones"). Again like sharks, the muscles are covered by a thick, inedible skin.

To fillet a whole wing, use a fillet knife or a long, thin-bladed boning knife, sliding the blade along the top of the bones from the thick side out toward the point. Flip the fillet over on its skin side, hold the skin, and scrape the knife along the skin at a shallow angle to cut away the meat. Turn the wing over and repeat on the other side.

Poaching is an even easier way to deal with whole skate wings. Once the fish is cooked, peel away the skin, leaving the meat attached to both sides of the bone, then pull the meat away from the bone. The meat is ready to be served hot with a sauce, or used warm or cold in a fish salad. It also makes a fine and inexpensive addition to cioppino, bouillabaisse, and other fish stews; poach the whole wings first, then skin and bone them, and add the meat to the stew at the end, just to reheat.

Like shark, skate can sometimes develop an ammonia smell due to nitrogen compounds in the meat, which can be dealt with by soaking in acidulated water (see page 149). While most fish should be cooked as fresh as possible, skate keeps very well under refrigeration. In fact, some authorities claim that letting skate age for two to three days before cooking makes the meat more firm.

Other White-Fleshed Fish

Wolf-eel or Wolffish, *Anarrichthys ocellatus*
White Seabass, *Cynoscion nobilis*
Grouper and Cabrilla, *Epinephelus* and *Mycteroperca* spp.

A scary-looking fish that turns out to be surprisingly mild and gentle in flavor, **WOLF-EEL** is found around the north Pacific rim from California to Japan, usually lurking in rocky reefs at moderate depths. That's the same habitat favored by lingcod, and the wolf-eels that occasionally show up in the fresh fish market are probably caught incidentally to other fisheries.

Wolf-eel is the local representative of the wolffish family, the rest of which live in the north Atlantic. True to its name, the wolf-eel combines the long tapering tail of an eel with the head of a predator. It can grow to 6 feet in length and 40 pounds, but the fish in our market are usually smaller, in the 3-foot and 5-pound range. The large head, powerful jaws, and many heavy teeth are adapted for crushing shellfish, a diet that gives the meat a sweet, mild flavor.

Unlike true eels, which are among the fattiest fish in the sea, wolf-eel is on the lean side. Its meat is white to pale pink when raw, and

A Note on Names, Part 2:
Of Bass, Trout, and Toothfish

When is a bass not a bass? When the U.S. Food and Drug Administration decides it is a trout. If you're confused, welcome to the club.

While scientists and regulators may prefer to use Latin names to identify fish and shellfish (see page 45), the rest of us use common English names most of the time. The problem sometimes is in agreeing on what those names mean. Here on the West Coast, a lot of what is sold as "snapper" or even "red snapper" is rockfish, no relation to the true red snapper of the Southeast. Now there's not much real red snapper sold around here, and "snapper" is widely understood to mean rockfish, so nobody is really being deceived. Ship the same fish to the Midwest, however, and there is a real potential for consumer confusion.

In an attempt to bring some nationwide uniformity to fish names, the FDA publishes a book listing hundreds of species by their official "acceptable market names," as well as by scientific (Latin) names, common names, and for reference only, various vernacular names, many of them regional in use. For the most part, the FDA list is well organized and performs a much-needed service. The list corrects some naming practices which, while they may have years of local tradition behind them, are ultimately misleading to the consumer. However, there are a few mysterious choices of market names. One example is the delicious California fish known around here as white seabass (*Cynoscion nobilis*). Several species of the genus *Cynoscion* occur in the Atlantic and Gulf of Mexico, where they go under various names including sea trout, speckled trout, weakfish, and squeteague. In fact, they are not trout any more than white seabass is a true bass; they belong to the drum or croaker family. True, the Eastern species are somewhat troutlike in shape and superficial appearance, and the name seatrout has a long history there. But it has virtually no meaning on the West Coast, and I doubt very much that you will ever see white seabass sold under that name. Still, the FDA has decided on one market name, seatrout, for all North American species of the genus, although it does allow white seabass as a common name for *C. nobilis*.

Sometimes the facts of the marketplace dictate policy, as in the case of the popular Southern Hemisphere fish nearly everyone knows as Chilean sea bass (*Dissostichus eleginoides*). The FDA's official market name of this species in the 1993 edition is Patagonian toothfish, and the book does not even mention sea bass as a vernacular name. However, the agency has since said it will accept the use of Chilean sea bass as a common name, even though a lot of this fish now comes from other nations like Argentina and New Zealand. Frankly, I don't see any chance of "Patagonian toothfish" ever catching the public's imagination, but we'll see.

cooks up snow-white, with a fine flake. It's quite firm, perhaps even bordering on tough if cooked too quickly; poaching, moist baking, and other gentle moist-heat methods are best. Or cut the fillets into thin fingers for frying in a batter. Like monkfish, which it resembles in firmness if not in flake, it makes a fine addition to a fish soup or stew. At a price comparable to lingcod and rockfish, it's certainly worth a try.

Although it can be hard to find, one of my all-time favorite West Coast fish is **WHITE SEABASS.** A cousin of the famous Louisiana redfish, as well as several smaller Eastern species known as seatrout, white seabass is about the size and shape of a good-sized salmon, with silvery skin and large, heavy scales. While it is sometimes found as far north as Vancouver Island, especially in warmer years, most of the catch comes from Southern California and Mexico. In Mexico, this fish is known, along with a couple of smaller relatives, as either corbina or corvina.

In color, flavor, and fat content, white seabass falls somewhere between the other lean and mild fish in this chapter and the darker, more full-flavored fish in the next—a perfect compromise, to my taste. The firm, fine-textured meat is a distinctive gray color with strong red markings when raw, but cooks up pure white; its moderate fat content makes it juicy without seeming at all oily. And the flavor strikes the perfect balance between mild and assertive—you know you are eating fish, but there's nothing "fishy" about the flavor or aroma. Perhaps the closest equivalent is a wild East Coast striped bass of similar size.

Fillets, especially when cut into diagonal slices no more than ¾ inch thick, are ideal for grilling, broiling, sautéing, or any other dry-heat cooking method. One recipe specifically for this fish appears on page 134; see also the "summer fish" recipe on page 178. Seabass bones make a particularly good fish stock, so a call ahead of time to your fish market could yield a seabass frame that would be the basis for a fine pot of chowder.

Several related species of the true sea bass family, mostly tropical or subtropical in origin, are favored by chefs for their lean, firm, sweet meat and sometimes quite large fillets. **GROUPERS** are especially associated with Florida and the Caribbean, but the growing popularity of that area's regional cuisine means more of those fish are being consumed close to home. A small amount of grouper from the west coast of Mexico shows up in West Coast markets, often under the Spanish name **CABRILLA;** it is a fine choice for any recipe calling for firm, white fish.

Braised Fillets with Red Pepper and Sherry Sauce

When I come across really big rockfish fillets, from species like goldeneye or cowcod, I treat them like grouper, to which they are similar in size and texture. The head end of a large rockfish fillet will yield the ideal cut of fish for this recipe, a chunk at least a pound in weight and 1 to 2 inches thick. Browned in garlic-flavored olive oil, then smothered with pimientos and moistened with dry sherry, it comes out juicy, flavorful, and tender. A splash of sherry vinegar and a sprinkling of the browned garlic bits give just the right lift to the sauce. If fresh pimientos are not available, use the canned (preferably Spanish) variety or roasted and peeled red bell peppers. Be sure to use a good, bone-dry Spanish sherry.

SERVES 4

3 tablespoons olive oil

3 cloves garlic, sliced

1 to 1½ pounds rockfish fillet, in one thick piece

Salt and freshly ground black pepper

¼ cup fino or manzanilla sherry

2 roasted and peeled pimientos, diced (about ¾ cup)

1 teaspoon sherry vinegar

➤ Heat the oil in a deep, heavy skillet over medium-low heat. Add the garlic and cook slowly, stirring constantly, until golden brown. Strain the oil through a fine sieve and return it to the pan; set aside the garlic.

➤ Season the fish with salt and pepper. Turn the heat to medium-high and brown the fish lightly on both sides. Add the wine to the pan and scatter the pimientos over the top. Cover, reduce the heat, and simmer until the fish is just tender when probed with a skewer. Total cooking time will be about 12 to 20 minutes, depending on the thickness of the fish.

➤ Transfer the cooked fish to a platter with a large spatula. Bring the pan juices to a boil and reduce by a third. Stir in the vinegar, taste the sauce for seasoning, and spoon it over the fish.

ALTERNATIVE SPECIES Braising is suitable for other dense fish, including lingcod, monkfish, tilefish, halibut, or grouper. Even with moist heat, however, any fish will dry out eventually, so be sure to test the fish periodically with a skewer or toothpick. Cooking time could vary as much as 10 minutes according to the texture of the fish.

Baked Whole Fish with Okra and Tomatoes

Some of my best seafood inspirations come from the produce market. In this case, it was a shopping trip to Chinatown on a day in late summer, when tomatoes, okra, and chiles were all at their seasonal peak. I was thinking about the classic red snapper Veracruz style, with its tomato, green chile, and green olive sauce, but some beautiful okra caught my eye, and it took the place of the olives in this one-dish fish and vegetable combination.

SERVES 3 TO 4

½ pound small okra

2 tablespoons olive oil

1 large onion, chopped

2 cloves garlic, sliced

1 poblano chile, seeded and diced

1 teaspoon salt

Freshly ground pepper, to taste

1 whole rockfish, about 2 pounds, cleaned

2 large tomatoes, peeled, seeded, and coarsely chopped

➤ Trim off the caps of the okra, and any brown tips. Spread the oil in an oval baking dish just large enough to hold the fish and scatter in the onion, garlic, chile, and okra. Season with about ½ teaspoon salt and a little pepper. Turn the oven on to 375°F and set the baking dish inside to begin cooking as the oven heats up. Meanwhile, give the fish a final cleaning and inspection, rinse well, pat dry, and season inside and out with salt.

➤ When the vegetable mixture is aromatic and beginning to soften, stir in the tomatoes. Push the vegetable mixture to the sides of the dish and lay in the fish. Top loosely with a sheet of oiled aluminum foil and bake 15 minutes. Remove the foil, baste the fish with some of the pan juices, and continue baking uncovered until the thickest part of the fish is opaque, another 5 to 8 minutes. Serve from the baking dish, with rice or couscous.

VARIATION For a hotter flavor, use a couple of diced serrano or jalapeño chiles in place of the poblano.

ALTERNATIVE SPECIES Any lean, mild-tasting whole fish of a convenient size—snapper, tilapia, porgy, hybrid bass, snook, or whiting, to name a few possibilities. Also crosscuts of larger fish like lingcod or tilefish.

Whole Fish Steamed Cantonese Style

A whole fish steamed with the typical seafood seasonings of ginger and green onion is one of the classic dishes of Cantonese cooking, and in our area the fish is usually a rockfish. However, any similarly sized fish, including farmed freshwater varieties like catfish, striped bass, and tilapia, can be presented the same way.

It's a good idea to make sure your fish will fit on the steaming plate, and that the plate will fit inside your steaming pot, before the water is boiling and the guests are waiting. Of course, you could remove the head and tail, but that spoils the appearance to the Chinese eye. If the fish is just an inch or two too long, you can position

it upright, the way it swims, and bend the tail around to fit onto the plate. Scoring the sides of the fish with deep gashes almost to the bone every couple of inches makes it more flexible; it also helps the heat and the seasonings penetrate the flesh more quickly.

SERVES 3 TO 4, WITH OTHER DISHES

1 whole rockfish, 2 to 3 pounds

¼ cup shredded fresh ginger

3 or 4 green onions, cut into 2-inch lengths and shredded

¼ cup dry sherry or Chinese rice wine

2 tablespoons soy sauce

Scant tablespoon Asian sesame oil

Cilantro sprigs, for garnish

➤ Have the fish cleaned and scaled, with the head left on. Rinse and dry the fish and score the sides with diagonal slashes 2 inches apart and almost to the bone. Place the fish belly side down on a heatproof plate that will fit into the steamer.

➤ Bring the water in the steamer to a rolling boil. Scatter the ginger and green onions over the fish and pour on the wine and soy sauce. Set the plate on the steaming rack, cover, and steam until the fish is just done at the thickest part, about 15 minutes.

➤ Serve the fish from its steaming plate or transfer it to a warm serving platter, scattering the onions and ginger over the fish. Just before serving, sprinkle sesame oil over the fish and garnish with cilantro.

VARIATION Steamed Fish with Black Bean Sauce

Equally classic, and equally good.

➤ Prepare a double recipe of the black bean sauce in the oyster recipe on page 286 and spoon it over the fish before steaming. In place of the sesame oil, heat a little plain oil in a skillet and pour it over the fish just before serving.

VARIATION Steamed Fish with Basil and Tomato

This is one of my favorite Western adaptations of this Eastern technique.

➤ Omit the ginger, green onions, soy sauce, and sherry; season the fish with salt and pepper, set it on the plate, and scatter 1 cup peeled, seeded, and chopped tomato, 2 thinly sliced cloves of garlic, the grated zest of ½ lemon, and a handful of fresh basil leaves over the fish, tucking a basil leaf into each cut in the sides. Steam as above; just before serving, drizzle a tablespoon or two of extra virgin olive oil over the fish.

Provençal Fish Soup

Buying rockfish whole doesn't save you any money over buying fillets at a Western fish market; it may in fact be more expensive. It makes sense only when you can make use of the whole fish, either by cooking it whole or by using the head and bones in a stock.

You could call this soup bouillabaisse, but that is just asking for trouble from the experts who insist that there is only one right way to make the specialty fish soup of Marseilles. Like all fish soups and stews, this one is endlessly variable. Use other varieties of fish and shellfish according to taste and availability. The only rule is to avoid really strong-tasting fish, as they will overpower the others.

SERVES 6

3 to 4 pounds whole rockfish, dressed

6 green onions

¼ cup olive oil

4 to 6 cloves garlic, chopped

¼ cup chopped fennel leaves, OR 8 fennel seeds

2 pounds ripe tomatoes, OR 1 large can peeled tomatoes

1 cup dry white wine

2 quarts water

2-inch strip of dried orange peel

Pinch of saffron

Bouquet garni (see note)

½ pound firm, white fish fillet such as monkfish, shark, swordfish, or halibut

Rouille (below)

12 mussels, scrubbed and debearded

➤ Fillet the rockfish and discard the skin. Set the fillet aside with the other fish. Clean the carcass thoroughly, removing any traces of blood along the backbone. Split the head open, and if the carcass is large, chop it into several pieces.

➤ Trim the green onions, set aside the white parts, and chop the green tops and trimmings roughly. Heat the oil in a large pot and sauté the green onion tops, garlic, and fennel without browning. Chop half the tomatoes and add them to the pot. Add the fish heads and bones, wine, and water and bring to a boil. Reduce to a simmer and skim off any foam that rises to the surface. Add the orange peel, saffron, and bouquet garni to the pot and simmer 45 minutes.

➤ While the stock is simmering, peel, seed, and chop the remaining tomatoes and set them aside. Add the peels, seeds, and juice to the stockpot. Cut the green onions into ½-inch slices. Cut the fish fillets into bite-size pieces. Prepare the rouille.

➤ When the stock is ready, put the mussels in a 4-quart covered saucepan with the tomatoes and green onions. Strain a cup or so of the stock into the pan, cover, bring to a boil, and steam the mussels open. As soon as they are open, strain in the remaining stock, add the fish pieces, and simmer until the fish is firm, about another 5 minutes. Serve in shallow bowls with French bread, adding rouille to each serving to taste.

NOTE For the bouquet garni, bundle a few celery leaves, several parsley sprigs, a bay leaf, and a sprig each of fresh thyme and oregano or marjoram together and tie with cotton twine.

VARIATION In place of a whole rockfish, you can use 3 to 4 pounds of fish heads or bones (monkfish bones are especially nice for this purpose), and buy a little extra of the mixed fillets to put in the soup.

Rouille

This sauce, a spicy relative of aioli (page 320), is traditionally stirred into soups, but there is no reason why you cannot use it as a sauce for any white-fleshed fish.

MAKES ABOUT 1 CUP

4 cloves garlic, peeled

Salt, to taste

2 egg yolks

¼ teaspoon hot paprika (or sweet paprika with a pinch of cayenne)

1 cup olive oil

➤ Combine the garlic and a pinch of salt in a mortar and pound to a smooth paste. (If you don't have a mortar and pestle, mince the garlic on a cutting board, sprinkle with salt, then mash to a paste with the side of a broad-bladed knife, leaning on the blade with the heel of your hand and rubbing in a circular motion. Scrape up the paste with the knife and transfer it to a mixing bowl.)

➤ Add the egg yolks and paprika and blend thoroughly. Add the oil a tablespoon at a time, stirring in each addition thoroughly before adding more, until the sauce is thick (not all the oil may be needed). Let the sauce sit 10 minutes or more for the flavors to blend, then taste and correct the seasoning, if necessary.

Steaks or Fillets Braised with Artichoke Hearts

I am going to let you in on a secret: I have been known to use the liquid from a jar of marinated artichoke hearts as an emergency salad dressing, or in this case, for cooking and seasoning a mild-tasting fish. There's usually a bit of oil floating on top, which gets used for the preliminary browning step.

SERVES 4

1½ pounds fillet of lingcod or large rockfish, in one piece, or 1 or 2 large steaks

Salt and pepper

1 (6-ounce) jar marinated artichoke hearts, drained (reserve marinade)

¼ cup dry white wine

1 tablespoon chopped parsley

➤ Season the fish lightly with salt and pepper. Spoon 1 to 2 tablespoons of the oil from the artichoke jar into a skillet over medium-high heat. Lay in the fish bone side down and cook until lightly browned. Turn, reduce the heat, add the wine, cover, and simmer 5 minutes. Add the artichokes, replace the cover, and continue cooking until the fish reaches an internal temperature of 140°F.

➤ Remove the fish to a warm platter, return the pan to high heat, and reduce the liquid by half. Taste for seasoning, and if a little more flavor is needed, add a bit of the artichoke marinade. Stir in the parsley and pour the sauce over the fish. Serve with a colorful vegetable.

L'Aioli Garni

If you can't manage a summer trip to southern France, here is a way to enjoy the flavors of the Mediterranean in a feast of summer produce, seasonal fish and shellfish, and the heady garlic sauce called aioli.

Sometimes called "the butter of Provence," aioli (see page 320) is more than a sauce, it is a food that in itself connotes a celebration. In southern France it is served at holidays throughout the year, including Christmas Eve and Ash Wednesday, but especially in the summer. In the communal form known as grand aioli or aioli monstre, whole villages come together at large tables in the central square or on the village green to enjoy a feast of assorted fish and shellfish, boiled meats and chicken, ripe tomatoes, peppers, eggplant, squash, and other summer vegetables, all dunked in the garlicky sauce.

In a more modest form, the meal is known as aioli garni, "garnished" with a somewhat smaller selection of seafood and vegetables, and perhaps hard-boiled eggs. Use whatever assortment strikes your fancy and your budget. Here on the West Coast, rockfish, lingcod, Pacific cod, California halibut, whiting, or shark might take the place of the traditional Mediterranean fishes (or the even more traditional salt cod). Among shellfish, fresh squid from Monterey, Manila clams or Mediterranean mussels from Puget Sound, or tiny Oregon pink shrimp would all be appropriate.

In Provence, a robust red wine is traditional with aioli, although it is likely to be cut to taste with iced water. With this all-seafood version, you may prefer a well-chilled dry white or rosé, or a white zinfandel on the drier side than most.

Use the following procedure as a general guide. If you insist on serving everything piping hot, you will need many pans and many hands at the last minute. However, this sort of meal tastes fine at room temperature, so it's much easier to cook the vegetables a little bit ahead of time, and concentrate on cooking the fish and squid to perfection.

SERVES 6

2 cups Aioli I or II (page 320)

An assortment of blanched or steamed vegetables, such as:

> small new potatoes ("creamers")
> broccoli or cauliflower florets
> green beans
> carrots, peeled and sliced diagonally
> zucchini or other summer squash, cooked whole and sliced
> artichoke hearts
> small beets, stems trimmed short, cooked and peeled

An assortment of raw vegetables, such as:

> celery stalks, cut in 2-inch lengths
> cherry or yellow pear tomatoes
> sweet red or yellow peppers, cored and sliced

1 whole rockfish, about 3 pounds, OR 1½ pounds rockfish or lingcod fillet

Court-bouillon (page 329)

1½ pounds squid, cleaned and cut into rings or strips

Crusty French bread

➤ Prepare the aioli as directed. Prepare all the vegetables shortly before serving and arrange them on large platters or in individual bowls.

➤ Poach the fish in court-bouillon until a skewer easily enters the thickest part; remove and drain. Remove half the court-bouillon and bring the remainder to a boil; add the squid and cook just until opaque, about 30 seconds after the liquid returns to the boil. Transfer the fish and squid to a warm serving platter. Serve family style, dipping everything into aioli.

Fish & Chips from the Oven

If you like the crispness and flavor of traditional fish & chips but don't want to be bothered with deep-frying, here is an alternative cooking technique known as "oven-frying." This method, often called the "Spencer method" after its originator, Mary Evelene Spencer, uses a very hot oven and a bread-crumb coating to give an effect like frying the fish but without the excess calories. In the original Spencer method published in 1934, the fish fillets are first dipped in salted milk, then rolled in bread crumbs, then drizzled with a little oil, melted butter, or bacon drippings before baking. A revised version of oven-frying (I don't know who invented this variation) uses mayonnaise instead of milk for the first dip and omits the external oil; the oil from the mayonnaise soaks out into the bread crumbs to the same effect. The amount of fat is still modest compared to deep-fried fish and potatoes, and it's certainly less messy.

SERVES 4

1 pound thin-skinned russet potatoes (Kennebecs are even better, if you can find them)

2 tablespoons olive oil

Salt and freshly ground pepper, to taste

1 to 1½ pounds lingcod, rockfish, or halibut fillets

3 tablespoons mayonnaise

Water

1 tablespoon minced fresh basil or chives

1 cup bread crumbs, preferably fresh

Lemon wedges

➤ Preheat the oven to 400°F. Scrub the potatoes, but do not peel them. Cut them lengthwise into wedges; the number doesn't matter so much as making them of an even size. Place them in a shallow baking ban, drizzle with 1 tablespoon of the oil, and sprinkle generously with salt. Turn the potatoes to coat them evenly with the oil and leave them with one cut side down. Bake 20 minutes, or until the bottoms are nicely browned and release easily from the pan. Turn the other cut side down and continue baking. Meanwhile, rinse the fish fillets and pat them dry. Cut them into 4 or 8 portions as equal in thickness as possible. Season with a little salt and pepper. Lightly oil a baking sheet or coat with nonstick spray.

➤ When the potatoes are nicely browned on two sides, turn them skin side down and turn the oven up to 500°F. Place the mayonnaise in a shallow bowl and thin it with a little water to the consistency of yogurt. Stir in the minced herbs. Place the bread crumbs in a second shallow bowl. With one hand, dip a piece of fish in the mayonnaise mixture and turn it to coat evenly, draining off the excess. Transfer the fillet to the crumb bowl, and with the other (dry) hand scoop and pat crumbs onto the top to cover the fish evenly. Shake off the excess and place the fillet skin side down on the baking sheet. Repeat with the remaining pieces, keeping one hand dry to keep from wetting the crumbs or knocking off the crumb coating.

➤ Remove the potatoes from the oven and put the fish pan on the uppermost shelf. Bake until the crumbs are golden brown and the fish is done by the skewer test (page 17), 7 to 10 minutes depending on size. Serve with lemon wedges.

Fish Baked in Peanut Sauce

This sauce is derived from the spicy, peanut-thickened stews of West Africa and eastern Brazil. Chiles, tomatoes, and peanuts, all native to South America, were introduced into Africa by the Portuguese in the early years of European exploration. African cooks combined these ingredients with ginger and okra to develop a characteristic style of stew, usually with chicken or seafood. Slaves from West Africa then brought these dishes back across the Atlantic to Brazil, the Caribbean, and the American South.

Reversing the proportions of the typical stew, this dish consists of a large piece of fish fillet topped with a peanut sauce and baked. It will work with any thick piece of mild white fish.

SERVES 4

1 tablespoon peanut or other vegetable oil

⅓ cup diced onion

1 teaspoon minced garlic

1 tablespoon minced fresh ginger

½ teaspoon ground ginger

¼ teaspoon red pepper flakes

¾ cup peeled and chopped tomatoes, with juice (canned are fine)

1½ teaspoons dried shrimp, ground in a mortar or spice grinder

¼ cup smooth peanut butter

½ cup boiling water

Pinch of salt (if using unsalted peanut butter)

1 to 1½ pounds lingcod, cabezon, or wolffish fillet, pin bones removed, in one piece

➤ Heat the oil in a large skillet over medium-low heat. Add the onion, garlic, both kinds of ginger, and red pepper flakes and cook, stirring, until the onion begins to color. Add the tomatoes and dried shrimp. In a bowl, dissolve the peanut butter in the boiling water and add it to the pan. Simmer until slightly thickened. Taste for seasoning and adjust if necessary. (The sauce may be prepared to this point several days ahead of time and refrigerated.)

➤ Preheat the oven to 400°F. Lay the fish fillet in a lightly oiled baking dish and spoon the sauce over and around the fish. Cover tightly and bake until a skewer easily enters the thickest part of the fish, about 15 minutes. Serve with rice.

Fillets Baked in Red Onion Confit

This dish is rooted in the kitchen of Berkeley's famous Chez Panisse, where red onion confit—a kind of marmalade of onions slowly braised with red wine, vinegar, and sugar or honey—has been a signature ingredient from the earliest days. It was at a dinner sometime in the early 1980s in the home of Sibella Kraus, then a cook at Chez Panisse and later a driving force behind the revival of farmers' markets in the Bay Area, that I first tasted fish fillets baked in an abundant amount of onion confit. I have been cooking all sorts of firm, white fish, including rockfish, grouper, and halibut, that way ever since.

SERVES 4

3 tablespoons olive oil

1½ pounds red or yellow onions, sliced as thinly as possible

1 cup zinfandel or other dry red wine

4 tablespoons red-wine or raspberry vinegar

2 teaspoons sugar

1 pound fillet of lingcod, wolffish, or other mild white fish

➤ Heat the oil in a heavy covered casserole or skillet over medium heat. Add the onions, cover, and cook until they begin to soften, about 5 minutes. Add the wine, vinegar, and sugar and bring to a boil. Reduce the heat as low as possible, cover, and cook until the onions are quite soft, 1 to 2 hours. Remove the cover, turn up the heat, and cook, stirring, until the liquid is nearly evaporated. Remove from the heat. (May be prepared to this point ahead of time.)

➤ Preheat the oven to 450°F. Slice the fillet diagonally into ½-inch slices. Spread a quarter of the onion mixture on the bottom of a deep baking dish just large enough to hold the fish. Arrange the fish slices on top, overlapping if necessary. Cover with the remaining onion mixture. Bake until the center of the fish is tender, 10 to 20 minutes depending on thickness.

TECHNIQUE NOTE The onion mixture should cook as slowly as possible, so you might want to make it a day or two ahead of time. If the dish is assembled while the onion mixture is still hot, it will bake in about a third less time.

Baked Curried Lingcod

Call it coincidence, or the luck of the draw, or maybe some grand cosmic design, but year after year, I find certain combinations of seafood and produce winding up in my shopping basket. Dungeness crab and avocados just happen to be at their best and cheapest in late winter, and they just happen to go together beautifully. The same is true in summer for California halibut and green chiles. Local king salmon is a little more fickle; it comes to the

125

dance in May with the last of the local asparagus, but spends all summer changing partners—peas, cucumbers, basil, sweet corn, and finally September's tomatoes. By late September, when lingcod is hitting its peak, so are fully ripe red peppers, running the gamut from sweet to searingly hot. Little wonder that a lot of lingcod recipes in my files involve red peppers in some form or another. Here, the fish is baked in a curry-style sauce based on puréed roasted red chiles.

SERVES 4

½ pound red-ripe poblano or Anaheim chiles
¼ teaspoon salt, or to taste
1 cup canned coconut milk
1 large onion, grated (about 1 cup)
1 tablespoon grated ginger
1 clove garlic, minced
½ teaspoon turmeric
1 to 1½ pounds lingcod fillet
Salt and freshly ground pepper, to taste

➤ For the chile paste, bake the chiles in a shallow pan at 400° to 450°F, turning once, until the flesh is soft and the skins are separating, about 30 minutes. Let cool slightly, then pull off the stems. Force the chiles through a food mill or sieve, straining out the seeds and skins. Season the purée with salt. Makes about ⅓ cup, more than needed for this recipe; store in the refrigerator and use within a few weeks.

➤ Turn the oven to 400°F. Spoon about 2 tablespoons of cream from the top of the coconut milk into a small skillet. Add the onion, 1 tablespoon of the chile paste, and the ginger, garlic, and turmeric. Simmer over medium-low heat, stirring often, until the liquid evaporates, leaving a thick paste. Add the remaining coconut milk and a pinch of salt and simmer until slightly thickened, about 5 minutes.

➤ Slice the fish diagonally into 4 portions. Season with salt and pepper and lay in a baking dish. Taste the sauce for seasoning and correct if necessary. Spoon the sauce over the fish, cover, and bake until a skewer easily enters the thickest part of the fish, 12 to 15 minutes depending on thickness. Serve from the baking dish, with a side dish of sautéed spinach or chard.

NOTE The longer, smoother Anaheim chiles are a good second choice if poblanos are not available; they are generally milder but also more variable in heat, so taste the paste and adjust the amount accordingly. Red jalapeños also work, but the result is much hotter. If you're really timid about heat, you could use a red bell pepper or pimiento for color and flavor, with just a dash of liquid pepper sauce.

➤ To save some calories, you might want to discard some of the cream remaining in the coconut milk after adding the first part to the skillet.

"Unblackened" Seabass

The following recipe is adapted from Paul Prudhomme's famous Blackened Redfish, which is made with a close cousin of California white seabass (or was until it became too popular and the redfish was nearly fished out). Like redfish, white seabass has a way of drawing the flavor of a dry spice rub into the fish more thoroughly than some other fish do. I call this version "unblackened" because the fish is sautéed over moderate heat, browning the surface slightly rather than charring it.

SERVES 4

1½ pounds white seabass fillet, cut into 4 serving pieces

1 tablespoon Creole seafood seasoning (page 31)

2 tablespoons oil, or half oil and half butter

1 clove garlic

Juice of 1 lemon or lime

2 tablespoons butter (optional)

Lemon or lime wedges

➤ Dust the fish all over with the seasoning mixture and shake off the excess. Heat the oil in a skillet over medium-high heat. Flatten the garlic clove with the side of a large knife or cleaver and add it to the pan. When the garlic begins to sizzle, add the fish. Sauté until the fish is lightly browned on both sides and a skewer easily enters the thickest part.

➤ Transfer the fish to a serving dish or plates. Remove the pan from the heat, deglaze with lemon juice, and swirl in the butter for a sauce if desired. Serve with additional lemon or lime wedges.

Soy-Braised Fish Steak

Braising, in French and other European cuisines, means cooking with moist heat in a covered pan, sometimes with a preliminary browning with dry heat. But "braised" on a Chinese menu does not exactly match the Western definition; it is used to translate various cooking methods labeled on the Chinese part of the menu as stir-fried, red-cooked (simmered in soy sauce), or even dry-fried (cooked in oil and then in liquid seasonings, which are boiled dry). This is one Chinese dish that is braised in the Western sense: the fish is cooked first with oil, then with moist heat.

The recipe is written for the thick crosscut steaks, which sometimes run a pound or more, of large rockfish, lingcod, East Coast tilefish, and similar fish often found in Chinese markets. It will also work with halibut or salmon steaks (especially the leaner salmons), not to mention thicker fillets of seabass or any of the varieties already mentioned.

SERVES 4 CHINESE STYLE, WITH OTHER DISHES

1 pound center-cut fish steaks, 1 to 1½ inches thick

½ teaspoon salt

Cornstarch

1 tablespoon peanut or other mild vegetable oil

2 tablespoons soy sauce

1 tablespoon dry sherry or Chinese rice wine

2 tablespoons chicken stock

2 green onions, cut into 2-inch lengths and shredded

2 tablespoons shredded fresh ginger

Cilantro sprigs or shredded green onions for garnish

➤ Sprinkle the fish on both sides with salt and let stand 5 minutes. Rinse and pat dry. Dust with cornstarch, shaking off the excess.

► Heat the oil to near smoking in a non-stick skillet or flat-bottomed wok. Add the fish and cook until lightly browned on both sides, about 2 minutes per side. Add the liquids and scatter the green onion and ginger shreds around the fish. Cover and simmer over medium-low heat until a skewer easily enters the thickest part of the fish, 3 to 5 minutes depending on thickness. Transfer the fish to a warmed serving plate. Bring the liquid in the pan to a boil and reduce by a third. Pour over the fish and garnish.

VARIATION Other vegetables, such as julienne bamboo shoots or sliced reconstituted black (shiitake) mushroom caps, can be added along with the onions and ginger.

Fish Cakes

Cooking a whole fish, or a large piece like the braised halibut tail on page 96, will often generate leftovers. Here is one way to use them, in one of many possible variations on fish cakes, in this case bound with potato. If the fish leftovers contain onions or leeks, by all means include them.

SERVES 4

¾ pound russet potatoes (2 medium)
½ cup cooked chopped onion or leek
1⅓ cups flaked cooked fish
2 tablespoons dry bread crumbs or matzo meal
½ teaspoon Dijon-style mustard, or to taste
Salt and freshly ground pepper, to taste
1 egg
1 to 2 tablespoons olive oil

► Scrub or peel the potatoes and boil them in lightly salted water until tender. Meanwhile, if you do not already have cooked onion on hand, sauté a heaping ½ cup of finely diced onion in a little oil until tender. Drain the potatoes, peel if you have not already done so, and mash. Pick over the fish carefully and discard any remaining bones. Combine all the ingredients but the egg and oil, adjust the seasoning, and stir in the egg. Form the fish mixture into 8 cakes, ½ to ¾ inch thick. Refrigerate if not cooking within 20 minutes.

► Heat a 12-inch skillet (preferably non-stick) over medium heat with a generous coating of oil. Cook the cakes until heated through and golden brown, 3 to 5 minutes per side. Serve over mixed salad greens, with a dollop of Aioli (page 320), one of the flavored mayonnaise sauces on page 323, or plain mayonnaise on the side.

VARIATION The seasonings can be varied just about infinitely: with Chesapeake or Creole-style seasoning blend (pages 29 and 31), or curry powder, or chopped fresh herbs, or horseradish, or a Thai curry paste . . . use your imagination. Just remember that some of these mixes supply salt while others do not. Curry powders and pastes will benefit from a preliminary cooking in oil with the onions; raw, they can give a harsh taste to the finished cakes.

► If you prefer a crunchier exterior, press the cakes in additional bread crumbs just before cooking.

Broiled Cod, New England Style

The first time I went to a seafood restaurant in Boston, I wanted to try some local fish as plainly cooked as possible. So I ordered broiled cod, with the sauce on the side. The sauce came on the side all right, but on top of the fish was a substantial layer of buttered, seasoned bread crumbs! That, by local standards, is plainly cooked fish; if you want it truly au naturel, *you have to ask them to leave off the topping as well. Once I got accustomed to the idea, however, I found it a perfectly good way to prepare cod and other lean fish.*

SERVES 4

1½ pounds cod fillet, in 4 equal portions

Salt and freshly ground pepper, to taste

2 tablespoons butter, softened

¾ cup sifted fresh bread crumbs

1½ teaspoons chopped fresh herbs (marjoram, thyme, Italian parsley, or a combination), OR ¼ teaspoon crumbled dried herbs

1 tablespoon grated Parmesan or asiago cheese

Lemon wedges

➤ Season the fish lightly and place it on a foil-lined broiling pan, skin side down. Combine the salt, pepper, butter, bread crumbs, herbs, and cheese, and spread the mixture evenly over the top of the fish. Broil 4 inches from the heat until the fish is tender in the center when probed with a skewer, 6 to 8 minutes depending on thickness. Serve with lemon wedges.

Fish Fillets with Pasta and Summer Vegetables

It's hard to think of a fish, from rockfish or halibut to tuna or salmon, that won't show well in this dish, surrounded by a warm salsa-like mixture of vegetables and small pasta.

SERVES 4

½ pound gemelli, small shells, or other small dried pasta

3 tablespoons olive oil

1 red bell pepper, diced

2 small zucchini, cut into ½-inch dice

1 bunch green onions, sliced

Kernels cut from 2 ears of corn

1 jalapeño chile, quartered and seeded

½ cup chicken stock

Salt and freshly ground pepper, to taste

1 to 1½ pounds fish fillets, in 4 portions

1 to 2 tablespoons Basil Oil (page 324)

➤ Start the pasta cooking in a pot of salted water. Meanwhile, heat 2 tablespoons of the oil in a wok or large skillet over medium heat, and preheat a second skillet for the fish on another burner. Add the red pepper to the wok and cook until it begins to soften, then add the zucchini, onions, corn, and chile. Add the stock and season with salt and pepper.

➤ Season the fish with salt and pepper, add oil to lightly coat the fish skillet, and add the fish skin side up. Continue cooking the vegetable mixture, stirring or tossing, until it is heated through and well flavored. Turn the fish once during cooking. When the pasta is done, drain it and add it to the vegetable pan.

129

Serve the fish surrounded with the vegetable mixture, with basil oil drizzled over all.

TECHNIQUE NOTE Although this is a one-dish meal, it involves three different cooking processes in three different pans. If juggling that many pans worries you, the pasta can be cooked ahead of time, rinsed with cold water to stop the cooking, lightly oiled, and reheated along with the vegetables.

Baked Fish with Celery and Apple

Celery is both a vegetable and the dominant herb in this dish, its assertive taste mingling with the sweetness of apple and onion. If your apple is not especially tart, toss the slices with a little lemon juice before cooking.

SERVES 4

2 to 3 tablespoons butter

2 ribs celery, thinly sliced

1 small tart apple, cored and sliced

1 teaspoon lemon juice, if needed

1 small onion, thinly sliced

Salt and freshly ground pepper, to taste

1 pound cod, whiting, or similar fish fillets

➤ Turn on the oven to 400°F. Choose a bake-and-serve dish just large enough to fit the fish fillets in one layer, but don't put the fish in yet. Rub the dish with 1 tablespoon of the butter. Scatter the celery, apple, and onion in the dish with a pinch of salt and place it uncovered in the oven (no need to wait for it to fully preheat). Bake until the vegetables are sizzling and almost tender, 10 to 15 minutes. Meanwhile, remove the fish from

the refrigerator and season it with a little salt and pepper.

➤ Remove the baking dish from the oven, push the vegetables to the sides, and lay in the fish. Spoon the vegetables over and around the fish and dot with the remaining butter. Cover with foil and bake 10 minutes per inch of thickness, or until the fish is tender when probed with a skewer. Serve from the dish, spooning some vegetables and buttery juices over each serving.

Whiting Baked in Cider

In Asturias, the Celtic region of the northern coast of Spain, the local "wine" is a lightly sparkling fermented apple cider, and it's used as a cooking liquid for hake (whiting) and other fish. (The same combination of hake and cider is found on the west coast of Ireland, another area where hake is plentiful.) To make a truly authentic merluza a la sidra, you would need a dry fermented cider like that made in northern Spain, northwest France, or the British Isles. These ciders are not easy to come by around here, but they can be found in some well-stocked wine shops. Or try a hard cider from one of the newer North American microbreweries, if you can find one that is not too sweet.

If you have a shallow flameproof casserole that can go from the stovetop to the oven to the table, it's ideal for this dish. Otherwise, start in a skillet and finish in a baking dish.

SERVES 4

3 tablespoons mild olive oil

2 large white new potatoes, scrubbed and diced

1 large onion, thinly sliced

2 cloves garlic, sliced

½ teaspoon salt

Freshly ground pepper, to taste

1½ to 2 pounds pan-dressed whiting (2 large
or 4 small fish)

Juice of 1 lemon

1 cup dry hard cider

2 tablespoons chopped parsley

➤ Heat the oil in a large skillet over medium heat. Cook the potatoes until they begin to brown. Add the onions and garlic, season lightly with salt and pepper, and cook until the onion softens. Meanwhile, preheat the oven to 350°F and season the fish with the remaining salt, pepper, and lemon juice.

➤ Transfer the potatoes, onion, and garlic to a shallow baking dish large enough to hold the fish. Nestle the fish in among the potatoes and onions. Pour in the cider, sprinkle with parsley, and cover with a lid or foil. Bake until the fish and the potatoes are tender, about 30 minutes. Serve from the baking dish.

Caribbean Fish Chowder

Fish soups don't get much easier than this chile-spiked chowder. It doesn't require fish stock or even fish bones; half an hour of simmering cubes of cod, whiting, or other gadiform fish provides plenty of richness and flavor to the broth, enhanced by the slight thickening power of the potatoes.

SERVES 6

5 cups water

1½ cups diced onion

1 medium red or green bell pepper, diced

2 cloves garlic, minced

1 small green or red chile, seeded and minced

1 pound tomatoes, peeled and chopped,
with juice

1 pound (2 medium) white potatoes,
scrubbed and diced

½ teaspoon oregano

1 bay leaf

1 teaspoon salt, or to taste

1 pound fillets of cod, pollock, or other lean
white fish, cut into 1-inch cubes

Hot pepper sauce (optional)

➤ Combine all the ingredients except the fish in a large pot. Bring to a boil, reduce the heat, and simmer 15 minutes. Add the fish cubes and simmer until the potatoes are tender and the fish is falling apart, about 30 minutes. Check the seasoning and adjust if necessary. Serve with hot pepper sauce if desired.

Fish Paillards with Tomato-Mint Sauce

Jeremiah Tower introduced the technique of fish paillards cooked on a plate to San Francisco with the opening of Stars in 1984. A paillard is a thin slice of fish fillet pounded so thin that it will cook just from the heat of a preheated plate and a hot sauce poured over the top. It's an easy way to make a small amount of fish go a long way; sliced thin and spread out on a plate, 2 to 4 ounces of fish looks like much more, and together with a well-seasoned sauce, the portion is just as satisfying as a larger portion cooked by another method.

As Tower notes in his cookbook New American Classics, *from which this recipe is adapted, fish paillards lend themselves to all sorts of improvised sauces. This version is Southeast Asian in inspiration.*

SERVES 4 AS A FIRST COURSE

8 ounces fillet of fancy rockfish or other firm white fish, preferably in one thick piece

3 tablespoons oil (approximately)

1 clove garlic, minced

2 teaspoons minced ginger

½ small green or red chile, seeds and ribs removed, minced

½ cup peeled, seeded, and chopped tomatoes

Pinch of sugar

1 tablespoon Thai or Vietnamese fish sauce

Juice of ½ lime

⅔ cup fish or chicken stock

Salt, to taste

¼ cup fresh mint or basil leaves

Lime wedges

➤ Rub 4 heatproof plates with a little oil and place them in a 250°F oven to preheat thoroughly; they should be too hot to hold barehanded.

➤ Slice the fish diagonally into 1- to 2-ounce pieces no more than ¼ inch thick. Place between sheets of plastic wrap and pound gently with a mallet or the side of a cleaver to a thickness of ⅛ inch.

➤ Combine the oil, garlic, ginger, and chile in a small skillet and heat until fragrant. Add the tomatoes, sugar, fish sauce, lime juice, and stock. Bring to a boil and reduce by a third. While the sauce is reducing, lay out the fish slices on the hot plates, skin side up. Season the sauce to taste and stir in the mint or basil. Turn over the fish slices and spoon the hot sauce over the fish. Serve with lime wedges.

Fish and Sweet Pepper Hash

One of the best ways to get another meal out of the last of a roast, or a piece of corned beef or a ham or a roast turkey, is to combine it with diced potatoes and onions in a hash. It may come as a surprise that leftover fish also makes a delicious hash.

Mediterranean, and especially Iberian, cuisines have many dishes in which fish is cooked together with potatoes. They often include liberal amounts of olive oil, garlic, and hot or sweet peppers. It doesn't take a great leap of imagination to take these ingredients apart and reassemble them in slightly different form as hash.

Unlike a meat hash, where the meat and potatoes are cut fairly fine and cooked together for a relatively long time, this hash uses rather large chunks of both potatoes

and fish. The secret of a fish hash is to cook the potatoes and other vegetables until they are nearly done, then stir in the fish and cook just long enough for it to reheat.

SERVES 2

½ pound cooked fish

1 pound thin-skinned potatoes (red, yellow Finn or Yukon gold, purple, or a combination)

2 tablespoons olive oil

2 large cloves garlic, sliced

Large pinch red pepper flakes

⅓ cup sliced green onions

2 tablespoons water, stock, or reserved fish juices

½ teaspoon salt, or to taste

2 large red or yellow peppers, roasted and peeled, with juices

1 tablespoon chopped parsley

➤ Remove the fish from the refrigerator at least 30 minutes before cooking to allow it to warm slightly. Scrub, but do not peel, the potatoes; cut them into ¾-inch pieces. Heat the oil in a 10-inch nonstick skillet over medium-low heat and add the potatoes, garlic, and pepper flakes. Cook, stirring occasionally and turning the potatoes well in the oil, until they just begin to brown, about 5 minutes. Add the green onions, water, and salt, cover the pan, and cook until the potatoes are almost done, 8 to 10 minutes. Meanwhile, pull the fish apart into flakes and remove any bones. Cut or tear the peppers into bite-size pieces.

➤ When the potatoes are almost done, remove the cover, stir in the fish, peppers, and parsley, and cook over medium-high heat until the liquid is gone and the potatoes get nicely browned in the oil. Turn the hash gently with a wide spatula (or toss the mixture in the skillet) to brown evenly, but try not to break up the fish and potatoes any more than necessary. Correct the seasoning and serve on warm plates.

NOTE As with any other hash, the flavor will be only as good as the fish you start with. Almost any leftover fish cooked by any method will do, but it works best with the more flavorful varieties and cooking methods. A lean, mild fish such as rockfish may need some help in the flavor department, in the form of a strong marinade or grilling with some smoke chips or herbs added to the fire. Fish with a little more richness and flavor, such as mahi-mahi, yellowtail, spearfish, seabass, or grouper, are a better choice. Even some of the tunas, especially albacore and bonito, would work, though I wouldn't especially recommend the darker, beefier tunas for this treatment. Salmon doesn't seem right for this dish either, though leftovers from a large trout ought to work well.

Seabass with Oyster Cream Sauce

This rich, Creole-inspired recipe is ideal for white seabass or corvina, West Coast cousins of the Gulf redfish. Try it also with trout, pink or chum salmon, hybrid striped bass, or top-quality rockfish like goldeneye or quillback.

SERVES 4

1 jar (10 ounces) small oysters

1 pound fish fillet, cut diagonally into 4 pieces no more than ¾ inch thick

2 teaspoons Creole seafood seasoning (page 31)

1 tablespoon oil or clarified butter

¼ cup chopped green onions, including tops

1 cup whipping cream, at room temperature

▶ Drain the oysters, reserving the liquor. If they are on the large side, chop the oysters roughly; otherwise leave them whole.

▶ Dust the fish slices with the seasoning mixture and shake off the excess. Heat the oil or butter in a nonstick or well-seasoned cast iron skillet over medium-high heat. Sauté the fish just until done, about 2 minutes per side. Remove to a warm serving platter or individual plates.

▶ Add the onions to the pan and cook, stirring, until they begin to wilt. Add the oyster liquor and cream, bring to a boil, and reduce by half. Add the oysters to the pan and continue cooking until they begin to curl at the edges and the sauce is well reduced. Taste the sauce for seasoning and adjust if necessary. Spoon the sauce and oysters over the fish and serve immediately.

Fish-Stuffed Peppers with Orzo

This variation on the chiles rellenos *model is another example of fish, vegetables, pasta, and sauce cooked separately but combined on the plate. Just about any firm white fish is suitable for this treatment. It's a good way to add flavor to naturally mild fish like rockfish and lingcod, but it's also delicious with more flavorful "summer fish" like white seabass, yellowtail, or ono.*

Use whatever sort of pepper you like, as long as it is large enough to be stuffed after roasting and peeling: Anaheim or poblano chiles for a hotter flavor, or various long, sweet roasting peppers or bell peppers in your favorite color for a milder taste. Cutting bell peppers in half after roasting will provide wrapping pieces to approximate the size of chiles. The size and shape of the fish piece will be dictated by the peppers, so it's best to buy one or two large pieces of fillet and cut them up accordingly.

SERVES 4

8 large chiles or long, slender sweet peppers, OR 4 large bell peppers

¾ to 1 pound rockfish or lingcod fillet

1 tablespoon minced garlic

½ teaspoon salt

1 tablespoon lemon juice

½ teaspoon ground coriander seed

Freshly ground pepper, to taste

3 tablespoons everyday olive oil

½ cup loosely packed basil leaves

2 ounces orzo, rosmarino, or other rice-size dry pasta

3 cloves garlic, sliced

1½ cups seeded and coarsely chopped tomato

2 tablespoons extra virgin olive oil

▶ Roast, peel, and seed the peppers. Rinse the fish, pat it dry, and cut into pieces to fit comfortably inside each pepper (but don't put them there yet).

➤ Combine the minced garlic and salt in a medium bowl and mash to a paste with the back of a spoon. Add the lemon juice, coriander, pepper, and 1 tablespoon olive oil and stir to combine. Bruise 3 or 4 of the basil leaves and add them to the marinade. Add the fish pieces, toss gently to coat evenly, and marinate 1 to 2 hours. Cook the pasta until just done, drain, and rinse with cold water.

➤ Warm the peppers (loosely covered to prevent drying) and serving plates in a low oven. Heat two skillets over medium-high heat, one for the fish (nonstick if possible) and one for the sauce. Remove the fish from its marinade and add it to the dry skillet. Put the remaining 2 tablespoons of olive oil in the other skillet, add the sliced garlic, and cook until it begins to color. Immediately add the tomatoes and pasta and toss to coat evenly. Add the basil leaves, remove from the heat, and season to taste. Spread the pasta mixture evenly on the plates and lay the peppers on top. As the fish pieces are done, tuck them inside the peppers. Drizzle or brush the tops of the peppers with the extra virgin oil and serve.

NOTE Because the fish and the sauce need to be cooked at the same time, the logistics can get a little complicated. Broiling the fish while you cook the sauce in a skillet is the easiest method, but if you have room on top of the stove, searing the fish in a skillet gives it a little more flavor. You can also grill the fish, as long as you have someone helping in the kitchen with the sauce.

Poached Skate Salad

This tastes equally good with skate still warm from the poacher or chilled. Salsa Verde (page 317), a garlicky vinaigrette with an abundance of chopped herbs, is another good choice for the dressing.

SERVES 4

2 pounds whole skate wings

Water

1 teaspoon salt (approximately)

1 tablespoon Dijon-style mustard

2 teaspoons wine vinegar

Freshly ground pepper, to taste

4 tablespoons olive oil

4 cups mixed salad greens

2 cups cooked seasonal vegetables—steamed and sliced new potatoes, poached asparagus, roasted and peeled peppers, or blanched green beans

➤ Soak the skate wings in acidulated water if needed (see page 149); drain and rinse. Fill a deep skillet, just large enough to hold the skate, with water. Add 1 teaspoon salt. Bring just to a boil, add the skate, and poach until a knife or skewer easily enters the thickest part. Remove from the pan, peel off and discard the skin, and cut the meat away from the bone. Let cool slightly, or chill if desired.

➤ Combine the mustard, vinegar, a pinch of salt, and pepper in a salad bowl and stir to dissolve the salt. Add the oil gradually, whisking to combine. Thin with a little water if desired, and adjust the flavors to taste. Remove half the dressing and set aside. Toss the greens in the dressing remaining in the bowl and arrange it on plates. Toss the vegetables in a little more dressing and add them to the individual salads.

➤ Pull the skate meat apart into bite-size pieces and toss it in the remaining dressing. Arrange a portion in the center of each plate and drizzle any remaining dressing over all.

Skate Tacos

You can cook the skate by whatever means is most handy—broiling, pan-frying, even grilling in the skin. The poaching method given here yields the most delicate flavor and texture.

SERVES 4

1 whole skate wing, about 1 pound

Salt and freshly ground pepper, to taste

¼ teaspoon oregano, or to taste

Lime juice, to taste

8 corn tortillas

1 cup hot cooked black beans

1 cup shredded lettuce

½ cup Fresh Tomato Salsa (page 327), or good bottled salsa

➤ Soak the skate wings in acidulated water if needed (see page 149); drain and rinse. Poach, peel, and shred the meat as in the previous recipe.

➤ Season the meat to taste with salt, pepper, oregano, and lime juice. Warm the tortillas on a dry griddle or skillet until pliable. To serve, spoon some fish, beans, lettuce, and salsa into a tortilla and fold in half.

Pan-Fried Skate with Herb Butter

In the classic French preparation for skates and rays, raie au beurre noir, skate wings are poached in court-bouillon and served with a brown butter sauce enlivened with lemon juice and capers. In this dish, described to me years ago by Seattle restaurateur Robert Rosellini, skinned fillets are pan-fried instead, to add a crisp texture to the otherwise rather soft meat.

SERVES 4

2½ pounds whole skate wings, filleted and skinned (see page 114) (or 1¾ pounds trimmed and skinned)

2 tablespoons oil

Salt and freshly ground pepper

Flour

¼ cup water

Juice of 1 lemon

2 cloves garlic, minced

2 tablespoons chopped herbs—Italian parsley, thyme, marjoram, chives, or a combination

3 tablespoons butter

➤ Soak the fillets in acidulated water if needed (see page 149). Rinse, drain thoroughly, and pat dry.

➤ Heat the oil in a large skillet over medium heat. Season the fillets lightly with salt and pepper. Dredge them in flour and shake off the excess. Starting with the thicker (top) fillet pieces, add the fillets to the skillet and cook until lightly browned on the first side, about 4 minutes. Turn, increase the heat to medium-high, and cook until the center of the thickest part is opaque. Transfer to a warm platter or plates and keep warm. Cook the thinner bottom pieces last.

➤ Remove any excess oil from the skillet with a paper towel. Deglaze the skillet with the water, scraping up any browned bits. Taste the drippings; if they taste at all burnt, discard them and wipe the skillet clean. Return the skillet to the heat and add the lemon juice, garlic, and herbs. Cook until nearly dry, remove the pan from the heat, and swirl in the butter and a hefty pinch of pepper. Stir constantly until the butter is melted, add salt to taste, and pour the sauce over the fish.

tuna, shark, swordfish & other steak fish

Many varieties of fish are described as "meaty," but none quite so deservingly as swordfish and tuna. Together with shark and a few other large fish, these fish make up a category I call "steak fish"—firm, meaty fish, typically cut crosswise into steaks that are suitable for grilling, broiling, and other dry-heat cooking methods. Most of the marinades, sauces, and other treatments in this chapter are assigned to one fish or another, but will work equally well with the others.

Ahi

Albacore

Angel Shark

Bigeye Tuna

Bluefin Tuna

Bonito

Leopard Shark

Mako Shark

Marlin

Opah

Skipjack Tuna

Spearfish

Swordfish

Thresher Shark

Tombo

Yellowfin Tuna

Tuna

Albacore, *Thunnus alalunga*
Yellowfin tuna, *T. albacares*
Bigeye tuna, *T. obesus*
Bluefin tuna, *T. thynnus*
Skipjack tuna, *Euthynnus pelamis*
Pacific bonito, *Sarda chiliensis*

I can't think of another fish that is as symbolic of the way Pacific Coast cookery has been affected by Asian cuisines (specifically Japanese) as tuna. Thanks largely to the spread of Japanese sushi bars and the Japanese influence on world cuisine, top-quality fresh tuna has become an everyday commodity in the fish market. While some tuna is caught near our shores, most of it comes in refrigerated containers in the belly of commercial airliners from Honolulu, Taiwan, Fiji, or Guam, not to mention Miami or New Orleans.

One might expect Japanese tuna terminology to come into common use along with the tuna trade, but that's not the way it has worked out. Instead, Hawaiian names like *ahi* and *tombo* have become increasingly common on restaurant menus and in retail stores, reflecting the role of Hawaii as a major shipping point in the tuna business.

Ahi is the Hawaiian name for two large, highly valued red-meated tuna varieties. The most common and numerous is yellowfin tuna, a species found all around the warmer oceans of the world. The nearly identical bigeye tuna, which is more common in Hawaiian waters in winter than yellowtail, is also known as ahi. The two species are fairly easy to tell apart as whole fish, but once they are cut up, it's hard to tell which is which. Fortunately for the cook, they are similar enough in cooking qualities to be treated as one variety.

A favorite fish for sushi and sashimi, yellowfin tuna has a beefy red color when raw, and its rich texture and not-at-all-fishy flavor make it a popular choice for first-timers and sushi-bar veterans alike. Ahi steaks, grilled medium rare like good beef, have been a staple of West Coast seafood restaurants for years, and have been more recently joined by "seared ahi," tuna cooked crisp and brown on the outside but still sashimi-raw in the center (see Seared Tuna Salad with Wasabi Mayonnaise, page 150).

Most top-quality ahi, whether from the mid-Pacific or the Gulf of Mexico, is caught on longlines (floating lines with many branches, each with a baited hook). There is also a good-sized net fishery for yellowfin off Southern California and Mexico, but most of the net fish go into cans.

Larger, scarcer, and even more valuable in the Japanese trade is bluefin tuna, which shows up only occasionally in our markets. Bluefin has a deeper color than yellowfin, especially when cooked, as well as a fuller flavor.

As much as I like the dark-meated tunas, I often prefer the smaller, paler, and leaner albacore. This species, the one known as "white" tuna when canned, is highly migratory like other tunas, but favors the colder waters north and south of the tropics. The annual migrations of the north Pacific population typically bring juvenile albacore within a hundred miles of California and Oregon in late summer, where they are caught by hook and line by both commercial and sport fishermen. (The timing works well for some salmon trollers, who as the salmon season is winding down simply head out farther to sea to find albacore before re-rigging their boats for the winter crab fishery.)

Traditionally, most West Coast albacore went into cans, but as mainland canneries have closed, fishermen have had to look for other markets. Much of the catch is frozen at sea, and converted by a few big shoreside processors into frozen individual portions. The fresh fish

A One and a Two . . .

A lot of restaurants and stores boast of "sashimi-grade" or "number 1" tuna. What do these terms mean, and who assigns them?

As one tuna importer explains it, most tuna destined for the Japanese restaurant trade and other high-end markets are individually graded, like beef carcasses. By inserting and removing a small hollow tube, the tuna buyer extracts a thin core of meat, which he examines visually. If the sample meets his standards—for ahi varieties, brilliant red in color and slightly translucent, making it especially attractive in sashimi or other raw presentations—the fish is graded number 1, and may command a premium of up to 50 percent over a number 2 fish that is only slightly duller and more opaque. Although a lot of money is at stake, the distinctions are subtle and certainly subjective; ultimately, a tuna is a number 1 if the buyer and the seller agree that it is.

The visual edge of a number 1 tuna disappears as soon as the fish is heated, so it makes little sense to pay the extra price for sashimi-grade fish if it is destined for the grill or the sauté pan. A number 2 tuna is certainly fine for these purposes. Still, some chefs will specify a "1½" or "high 2" grade for their nearly raw presentations, and pay a little extra for carefully chosen fish that fall just short of the number 1 mark.

If the quality difference between number 1 and number 2 tuna is subtle, the difference between those that make the number 2 grade and those that don't can be striking. A fish that struggles when caught and expires on the deck of the boat can get quite heated up in the process. Without the benefit of water to cool it down, it can release large amounts of enzymes, which begin breaking down the meat, reducing its fat content and giving it an almost cooked appearance. Depending on how far the condition progresses, the "burned" meat near the backbone changes from red to a mauve or even a manila color, and cooks up unpleasantly dry. With proper handling, burned meat is rare in the longline tuna that dominates the fresh tuna market.

market has generally been a low priority for the albacore fleet, apart from some fishermen selling their fish directly at dockside and in farmers' markets. But that seems to be changing, with more fresh albacore showing up in restaurants and retailers in recent years.

West Coast albacore has a tough competitor in tombo, as albacore are known in Hawaii. A relatively new fishery in the south Pacific, especially around Fiji, has been sending good quantities of large albacore into the Hawaiian market since the early 1990s, and a lot of the fish gets sent on to the mainland. Paler in color and a little leaner than ahi, tombo is still quite pink and rich compared to the smaller "peanut" albacore found off the West Coast. Its size is comparable to ahi, with half-fillets or "loins" running at least 6 pounds each, suitable for cutting into steaks. The price started out quite a bit less than ahi, but the gap has narrowed as tombo has become better known.

Local albacore loins rarely run larger than 4 pounds, and 1½ to 3 pounds is more typical. This small size might be a disadvantage to a restaurant chef, but it's perfect for a home cook looking to create a dramatic dish. A whole loin fits nicely on a charcoal grill or in a roasting pan, and the result looks great on a platter, ready to be "carved" at the table. Leftovers make a fine *salade niçoise*, and cubes of albacore can also be used for anything from grilling en brochette to sautéing for a pasta sauce to simmering in a Thai-style curry. Of course, you can always cut an albacore loin into inch-thick steaks, although they will need to be cut diagonally to be of decent size.

The Southern California tuna fleet also catches a couple of smaller, more strongly flavored tunas, most of which go into cans or into the freezer for export, but some occasionally show up in our market. Pacific bonito gets its common name (Spanish for "beautiful") from its attractive appearance. It has the familiar bullet shape of the family, and silvery skin with diagonal blue-black lines on the upper side. Frozen whole bonito of 5 pounds and up can be found most of the year in Asian markets, and is often quite cheap. Fresh bonito show up sporadically, as bycatch from other fisheries.

In shopping for any tuna, look first at the color, which should be in the pink to red range rather than tan or brown. In perfectly fresh fish the blood line, the band of darker, blood-rich meat running through the middle of each side (thus on one edge of a triangular loin), will be a darker shade of the same basic color. If it has turned noticeably brown, it can have an unpleasantly strong or even bitter flavor, and it should be removed before cooking.

All the tunas are perfect for grilling, broiling, and other dry-heat cooking methods. As long as it is not cooked past the medium stage (130°F internal temperature), when the meat is just turning opaque throughout, tuna is practically guaranteed to be juicy. Cooked past this point, however, even the richest tuna can taste dry. Of course, as the Japanese have shown us, tuna is delicious raw, and most experts agree that the large tunas are free of the kind of parasites that can make some raw or undercooked fish dangerous. So feel free to enjoy your tuna as rare as you like.

Swordfish

Swordfish, *Xiphias gladius*

Broadbill swordfish, a single species that constitutes its own fish family, is found throughout the tropical and warm temperate oceans of the world. A large predatory species, swordfish migrate widely in the ocean in search of other fish to eat. They most often find their prey in "frontal zones" where ocean currents bring colder and warmer waters together, providing ideal conditions for the plankton that are the basis of the marine food chain.

In the north Pacific, the seasonal locations of these frontal zones, and therefore of the swordfish, are roughly predictable. While not as reliable as the swallows returning to Capistrano, swordfish can usually be counted on to show up in good numbers in the open ocean north of Hawaii in spring and summer, and close to the California and Oregon coast in early fall.

Some swordfish may be found off our coast any time of year, but the season typically starts early in September when the broadbills begin to congregate within 200 miles of the Southern California coast. Over the next two to three months a fleet of fishing boats based in various West Coast ports follows the fish, landing their catch in the nearest suitable port. Depending

on the year and time of the season, that port may be as far south as San Diego, as far north as Astoria or Ilwaco, or just about any major fishing port in between. Each year's exact pattern is unique, but landings are typically heaviest in the south early in the season and farther north as the season progresses.

For most of the twentieth century, California's commercial fishermen went after swordfish in the traditional Sicilian way, harpooning the big billfish as they basked near the surface. Harpooning remained the dominant method of catching swordfish until around 1980, when gillnet fishermen targeting large pelagic sharks began to catch swordfish as well. Within a few years, most of the West Coast swordfish fleet switched over to gillnets, which are now responsible for about 90 percent of the catch (the rest comes from the few remaining harpoon boats).

Unlike the notoriously massive drift nets used by some Asian countries in international waters, swordfish nets are modest in size, with a maximum length of one nautical mile. Their large mesh size (14 inches minimum, and typically 18 to 22 inches) allows undersize fish and most smaller species to escape. The nets are typically set late in the day to "soak" overnight, then retrieved at dawn. In addition to swordfish, these nets capture other large pelagic species such as sharks (especially thresher), some large tunas, opah, and louvar (see page 167). To avoid catching dolphins and other marine mammals, swordfish drift nets are now required to carry acoustic devices called "pingers," which have proven very effective in scaring away the mammals. Other restrictions

The Mercury Question

Talking about swordfish inevitably brings up the question of mercury contamination. Mercury is a metallic element that occurs widely in nature. Around the world, trace amounts of mercury are constantly leaching out of the soil or evaporating into the atmosphere, and trace amounts of mercury are found everywhere in the oceans. In the water, bacteria convert some of this mercury to a toxic organic compound, methyl mercury.

Fish absorb some methyl mercury directly from the water, and more from the other marine organisms they eat, and the amount accumulates over time. This accumulation is mainly of concern in fish at the top of the marine food chain, including swordfish, various sharks, and the largest tunas. In sufficient concentration in the human diet, mercury can cause neurological damage in adults as well as developing fetuses.

Since the 1960s, when the dangers of mercury in seafood were first documented, the mercury spotlight has been trained especially on swordfish, as this is the species most likely to exceed the FDA "action level" of 1 part per million (ppm) of methyl mercury in the edible portion. (Most other commonly eaten fish contain smaller amounts, in the range of 10 to 500 parts per billion.) According to the FDA, the action level was set at 1 ppm "to limit consumers' methyl mercury exposure to levels 10 times lower than the lowest levels associated with adverse effects."

While there has never been an overall ban on swordfish, U.S. authorities have periodically tested swordfish for mercury content, and fish exceeding the action level were rejected. Under the new HACCP system (see page 38), the onus is on importers and processors to prevent fish with excessive mercury levels from reaching the market. In practice, the easiest way to avoid the action level is to specify smaller swordfish. The older and larger the individual fish, the more fish it has eaten in its lifetime, and the more mercury it is likely to have absorbed. Swordfish of more than 100 pounds are much more likely to approach or exceed 1 ppm than smaller fish, so some buyers simply don't want to take a chance with the larger fish.

So should you worry about mercury in swordfish? As usual, the answer is maybe. It's probably not a good idea to eat it all the time—the usual guideline for any species of concern is no more than one meal per week. For women who are pregnant (or planning to be anytime soon), FDA seafood specialists advise no more than one meal per month of swordfish or shark, to avoid possible exposure of a fetus to excessive levels of mercury, especially during the critical first trimester.

on fishing areas and seasons are designed to protect shark stocks and to avoid interaction with migrating gray whales.

The Hawaiian connection is an even newer one. Beginning in the late 1980s, Hawaiian longliners fishing for tuna and other pelagic species began to find swordfish in good numbers in the ocean north of Oahu, especially in late spring. By the mid-1990s, Hawaiian swordfish landings had increased from a few hundred tons to 6,000 tons—three times the catch in all other U.S. waters, and most of it air-freighted fresh to the mainland. Peak season for Hawaiian sword is April to July; other times of year, fresh swordfish may come from various locations, including Chile and various Pacific island nations. Frozen swordfish is available all year.

Most swordfish is sold in ½-inch- to 1-inch-thick steaks, usually with the gray skin attached. Rather than a whole fish, retailers generally begin with "blocks," thick crosscut sections of several pounds. Each nearly circular block divides neatly into four roughly triangular muscle segments or "loins," which are then sliced crosswise into steaks. However, because of the variations in size of the fish and the location on the fish, those loins can range in size from 3 or 4 inches on a side to 6 inches or more. Simply cutting them into slices of the same thickness will yield steaks of anywhere from 6 ounces to nearly a pound. If you insist on serving perfectly shaped, quarter-round restaurant-style steaks, it may take some hunting to find the size you want. An easier approach is to decide on the number of ounces you want to serve per portion (4 to 6 ounces is a good range), and if they don't have steaks

that size, look for larger pieces in multiples of that size, then divide them into portions before or after cooking.

The color of swordfish meat varies from a pale ivory to a definite pinkish-orange shade, depending on diet, but I haven't found any corresponding differences in flavor. It's more important to look at the "blood line," the dark meat running near one edge of each loin. The color, while never really red, should be more red than brown, and perhaps more important, the line should be as thin as possible. The browner the dark meat and the more the color has diffused into the surrounding meat, the older the fish.

Opah

Opah, *Lampris guttatus*

Every once in a while, my local fish market displays a whole opah in the front window, and it never fails to attract attention. Around 3 feet long and nearly as wide from back to belly, with silvery skin covered with rose-pink spots and bright red fins, this very large (60 pounds and up) deep-sea fish is one of the most colorful fish in the sea. It's also one of the tastier fish around, with a flavor and texture somewhere between swordfish and tuna.

Opah, also known as moonfish for its nearly round profile, is found throughout the tropical and temperate oceans of the world, as far north as the Gulf of Alaska, but it is more commonly caught in warmer latitudes. Loners rather than schooling fish, opah are never especially abundant, but they are caught in regular numbers by the mid-Pacific longline tuna fleet, and in smaller quantities in the California swordfish and shark gillnet fishery. Most of the fish in our market comes in fresh by air from the Honolulu fish auction, at a price comparable to fresh tuna.

Because of its large size and its unique shape, an opah provides several distinct cuts, each with different cooking qualities. Most mainland buyers get just the most popular and expensive cut, known in the trade as the "loin," the large muscles on the dorsal (upper) side of the fish, above and on either side of the backbone. (The fatter, paler belly meat, which is less valuable even though some consider it the better-tasting part of the fish, usually stays behind in Honolulu.) In color, texture of the meat, and approximate shape, the loin looks like a pale piece of tuna, and it cuts neatly into pieces about the shape of a New York steak.

Opah can be cooked in any recipe and by any method suitable for tuna. Simple sauces are probably best; try a flavored butter such as ginger-lime (page 326), or for a fat-free version, a tomato or fruit salsa.

Hawaiian Billfish

Shortbill spearfish, *Tetrapturus angustirostris*
Striped marlin, *T. audax*
Pacific blue marlin, *Makaira nigricans*

Although these three fish, with their upper jaws elongated into swordlike bills, bear a superficial resemblance to swordfish, they belong to an entirely different family. Most fish cookbooks that mention them at all discuss them in terms of swordfish, but in the appearance, texture, and flavor of the meat they are closer to jacks, tunas, and mackerels.

In mainland waters, the large billfish are reserved for the sport fishery, and never enter commercial channels. However, a fair number of them are taken in the Hawaiian commercial longline tuna fishery, and they sometimes find their way into our markets. Spearfish, the smallest member of the family, is also the one that most commonly comes here, especially in summer. Its dense, firm, rich meat falls somewhere between albacore and the darker tunas in color and flavor. The shape of the fish is slimmer than tuna or swordfish, yielding fillets that are typically about half as thick as they are wide, usually cut into long and narrow steaks.

Just about any recipe for tuna will work with spearfish and marlin; see also the recipes for "summer fish" on pages 178 to 183. Grilling is perhaps the best cooking method, but searing, broiling, and sautéing are fine. Spearfish is a highly regarded sashimi fish in Japan and Hawaii, and some local chefs use it for this purpose. Marlin is often smoked.

About the only drawback of spearfish, apart from its unfamiliarity, is the color of the raw meat. Like Atlantic bluefish and king mackerel (also delicious dark-meated fish), it's a dull grayish brown when raw, although it cooks to a pleasant light color like that of veal or pork.

Shark

Leopard shark, *Triakis semifasciata*
Thresher shark, *Alopias vulpinus*
Shortfin mako (bonito shark), *Isurus oxyrinchus*
Pacific angel shark, *Squatina californica*
Spiny dogfish, *Squalus acanthias*
Smoothhounds, *Mustelus* spp.

Once valued only for their fins or their liver oil, and otherwise considered unfit for the table, sharks have become extremely popular food fish in recent decades. Perhaps too popular, as many species are now in declining numbers around the world (see page 148).

Several sharks in our area are fished commercially, at rates that appear to be sustainable. Most are not specifically targeted by fishermen, but show up as incidental catch in other fisheries. The closest thing to a targeted shark fishery is for thresher shark, a large species that gets its common name from its extremely long upper caudal (tail) fin, which resembles a flail used for threshing grain (although it's often mispronounced and even misspelled "thrasher"). Threshers are caught in the same large gillnets used in the California swordfish fishery, and serve as an advance guard for the swordfish, typically appearing a few weeks ahead of the swords in the same waters. Until the swords show up, thresher shark offers fine eating as well as important income for the swordfish fleet. When you are waiting for swordfish steaks to show up in the market, you could do a whole lot worse than to grill or broil thresher steaks instead.

Another excellent-tasting shark is mako, most of which comes in as bycatch in the long-line tuna fishery out of Hawaii. Pinker in color and more tender than thresher, mako is also a fine choice for grilling or broiling. A little smaller than thresher and mako, and a notch below in quality, is blacktip shark from Florida, fairly common in supermarkets.

Leopard shark, a small species with distinctively marked skin, is common in nearshore waters and bays in California, and it is one of my favorites. It has fine-textured, tender meat with a mild, almost chicken-like flavor. Because of its size, typically in the 3-foot range, leopard shark is often sold as fillets rather than steaks. A couple of other small species known as smoothhounds are also likely to show up as fillets rather than steaks.

One shark from Southern California that was once quite popular and may be again is angel shark, a peculiarly shaped variety somewhere between typical sharks and skates in shape. In the 1980s, at the peak of the gillnet fishery for halibut and white seabass, angel shark went from an annoying bycatch usually discarded at sea to one of the most popular sharks of all, surpassing thresher in overall landings in at least one year. There were signs that the population was already under stress when the gillnets were outlawed in 1990, but with nearly a decade to recover, I wouldn't be surprised to see angel shark landings from other gear creep back up in the years to come. Angel shark meat is particularly tender.

If there is one type of shark in North America that is underutilized, it would be spiny dogfish. This small shark is apparently abundant on both coasts, and may even be increasing in some areas as larger sharks become more scarce. New England processors have for some time been promoting dogfish taken incidentally in other trawl fisheries as "cape shark," and

The Shark Dilemma

I must admit to having mixed feelings about including shark recipes in this book. Sharks are some of the best eating fish in the sea, but in some ways they are among the worst candidates for targeted fishing.

The main reason sharks are so vulnerable to overfishing is their slow reproductive rate, which is more like that of mammals than other fish. Sharks are slow to mature, with some species not reaching reproductive age for 20 years or more. Add the fact that they produce many fewer eggs than other fish (especially the live-bearing varieties, which incubate their young internally rather than laying eggs) and you have a population that can take decades to recover from a few years of overfishing.

By contrast, most other fish are extremely prolific, releasing huge numbers of eggs into the ocean when they spawn. As John McCosker, senior scientist with the California Academy of Sciences and one of the world's foremost shark experts, explains it, "If you got down to the last two cod in the world, they could in theory produce a million offspring. The last two angel sharks might produce four or five."

Does this mean we should stop eating shark? I don't plan to, and neither did McCosker the last time we spoke. Several species of shark are excellent food fish, and they provide important income to the fishing and fish handling industries. A lot of shark is caught not as the target species but as a bycatch in other fisheries. Now that U.S. regulations have outlawed the practice of "finning," removing just the fins of a shark and discarding the rest of the carcass at sea, more of the shark bycatch can be expected to come to market, and if it does it should not go to waste. However, we can try to become aware of which sharks are more and less appropriate to catch than others, and especially try to shift to those species that are under the least pressure.

although dogfish is common on the West Coast as well, I've never seen it for sale here. Apparently the main market value is in export to Europe.

Most shark is cut into skinless steaks, suitable for grilling, broiling, braising, and adding to fish stews. Some shark steaks have a darker patch of meat near the bone; this meat contains more blood, and will be stronger in flavor. As long as the fish is fresh (when the dark meat is beefy red), the dark meat tastes fine; but a dark brown color is a sign that the fish is not very fresh and that the flavor may be unpleasantly strong. Some markets routinely cut away the dark part.

Sharks are primitive fish, with a different circulatory system from most fish. As a result, their flesh contains nitrogen compounds that gradually convert to ammonia after the fish is cut, and the ammonia smell gets stronger with age. However, it is easy to eliminate by soaking the fish for an hour or so in a mild acid solution (1 part vinegar or lemon juice to 10 parts water). Really fresh shark may not need any acid bath at all; if there is no trace of ammonia odor, you can skip the soaking step.

Grilled Tuna with Onion and Red Jalapeño Confit

Fresh, red-ripe jalapeño or Fresno chiles have a sweeter, fuller flavor than their green counterparts, and they give a piquant touch to an onion confit to top tuna or other rich, meaty fish. Look for red chiles from local sources in fall, or for imported ones in Asian markets most of the year.

SERVES 4

4 red jalapeño or Fresno chiles

2 tablespoons mild olive or peanut oil

1 medium onion, quartered and sliced crosswise

1 tablespoon red wine vinegar

1 teaspoon honey

Salt and pepper, to taste

4 ahi or tombo steaks, ¾ to 1 inch thick

➤ Cut off the stem ends of the chiles and split the chiles lengthwise. Carefully remove all traces of the seeds and pale ribs. Slice the chiles lengthwise into thin julienne. Combine the oil, onion, and chiles in a skillet over medium heat. Cook until they just begin to sizzle, then turn the heat to low and add the vinegar, honey, and salt. Cover and cook, stirring occasionally, until the onion is very soft and beginning to disappear into the liquid, about 1½ hours. If the mixture appears to be drying out before the onion is fully cooked, add a tablespoon of water to prevent scorching. Adjust the seasoning and keep warm.

➤ Season the fish steaks with a little salt and pepper and grill or broil 2 to 3 minutes per side. Spoon the warm onion mixture over and around the fish.

Seared Tuna Salad with Wasabi Mayonnaise

This treatment of tuna, which combines the silky texture of sashimi with a thin crust of browned meat, has become a standard of Pacific Rim cuisine. The ideal cut of tuna for this dish is a crosscut from the smaller end of a tuna loin (essentially a double-thick steak) weighing 12 ounces to a pound. This roughly triangular block divides neatly into three-sided logs that can be seared on the long sides, then cut across the grain to expose the raw-to-rare centers.

SERVES 4

2 teaspoons wasabi powder (see note)

¼ cup mayonnaise

¾ to 1 pound ahi or tombo, in one piece

2 tablespoons soy sauce

2 teaspoons grated fresh ginger

Pinch of sugar

2 teaspoons rice vinegar

Pinch of salt and pepper

2 tablespoons mild vegetable oil, plus more for the skillet

1 teaspoon Asian sesame oil

3 cups mixed salad greens

8 small red new potatoes, cooked, cooled, diced, and sprinkled with 2 teaspoons rice vinegar (optional)

1 tablespoon toasted sesame seeds

➤ Combine the wasabi powder with an equal amount of water and stir to make a thin paste. Stir half the wasabi paste into the mayonnaise and let stand 1 hour. Taste for seasoning and add more wasabi if desired.

➤ Skin the tuna and trim off the dark meat. Divide the block lengthwise into 4 equal portions, triangular in cross section. Combine the soy sauce, ginger, and sugar in a shallow bowl. Marinate the tuna pieces in the mixture 15 to 20 minutes. Combine the vinegar, salt, and pepper in another bowl and stir to dissolve the salt. Add the oils, whisk to blend, and taste for seasoning.

➤ Preheat a heavy skillet thoroughly. Meanwhile, toss the greens in the sesame oil dressing and divide them among the plates, off center. Top each portion with potatoes, if used. Remove the tuna from the marinade. Add oil to generously coat the skillet. For seared-sashimi style, cook the fish over highest heat just until browned on all sides, about 1 minute per side; for medium-rare fish, cook on a slightly cooler fire for 2 to 3 minutes per side. Let cool slightly, then cut crosswise into ⅛-inch-thick slices. Fan the slices out next to the salad and place a spoonful of wasabi mayonnaise on one side. Garnish with sesame seeds.

NOTE Look for powdered wasabi, the green horseradish used with sushi and sashimi, in little cans in Japanese markets. Unless you use it frequently, buy it in the smallest can possible. When the green color has faded, so has the flavor, so it's time to discard it and get a fresh can.

VARIATION Omit the wasabi mayonnaise and add a spoonful of Orange-Serrano Salsa (page 179).

Grilled Whole Albacore Loin with Corn-Potato "Risotto"

Albacore loins are roughly triangular in cross section, thus the instruction to cook on "all three sides." Steaks may be substituted for the whole loin; cook them over a hotter fire, about 3 minutes per side. This dish will also work with individual cuts of larger tuna, salmon, or any of the "summer fish" on pages 165 and 166.

SERVES 4 TO 6

¼ cup plus 1 tablespoon fruity olive oil

2 tablespoons fresh oregano or marjoram leaves, roughly chopped

2 cloves garlic, one cracked, one minced

Lemon juice, to taste

½ teaspoon salt

Freshly ground pepper, to taste

1 whole albacore loin, 1½ to 2 pounds

3 medium red potatoes, scrubbed and finely diced

1½ cups chicken or vegetable stock

3 ears sweet corn

½ cup sliced green onion

1 red bell pepper, roasted, peeled, seeded, and diced

1 poblano or Anaheim chile, roasted, peeled, seeded, and diced

➤ Combine ¼ cup of oil in a small bowl with the herbs, cracked garlic, lemon juice, salt, and pepper. Remove the skin from the albacore loin and trim off any loose ends; if there is a substantial belly flap, tie it to the rest with butcher's twine. Place the fish in a roasting pan and pour half of the marinade over it; reserve the rest of the marinade as a sauce. Marinate 30 minutes to several hours in the refrigerator, turning occasionally.

➤ Heat 1 tablespoon of oil in a large skillet over medium heat. Add the potatoes and cook until they begin to color and stick; add the minced garlic part way through cooking. Add the stock (and a pinch of salt if using unsalted stock) and adjust the heat to maintain a simmer. Cut the kernels off the corn cobs into a bowl and scrape the cobs with the back of a knife to extract the remaining milky hearts of the kernels. When the potatoes are still just a bit crunchy, add the corn, onion, and both peppers to the pan and continue simmering until the potatoes are tender. Adjust the seasoning and keep warm.

➤ Grill the albacore over a medium-hot fire on all three sides, 2 to 3 minutes per side for a rare center, 3 to 4 minutes per side for medium-rare. Brush with the reserved marinade during cooking if using a covered grill. Divide into portions at the table and serve over the corn-potato mixture, drizzled with the reserved marinade.

NOTE Even more than other tunas, albacore is prone to drying out if overcooked. An internal temperature of 120°F on an instant-read thermometer corresponds to the medium-rare stage, as far as I would recommend cooking it. The natural tapering shape of the loin means the thinner tail portion will be more cooked than that, so you should be able to accommodate the tastes of those who like their fish more cooked.

VARIATION For a simpler dish, omit the corn-potato risotto and serve the fish over boiled *conchiglie* or other small pasta. Prepare extra marinade to act as a sauce for the pasta as well. If you like, you can pound the oregano, garlic, and oil together in a mortar to make a kind of thin pesto.

VARIATION Instead of grilling, roast the fish in a hot oven (450° to 500°F). After marinating, be sure to allow time for the fish and the roasting pan to come back to room temperature before putting them in the oven, or transfer the fish to a second roasting pan to cook. In any case, cooking time will vary according to the size, shape, and weight of the roasting pan, so start checking the internal temperature after 10 minutes.

Spaghetti al Tonno

Adding tuna to the southern Italian pasta sauce alla puttanesca *makes for a more substantial dish which can serve as a main course. It can also be served in smaller portions as a first course. Marinated Poached Tuna Belly (page 153) is ideal for this dish, but any leftover poached or grilled tuna, or canned, will work fine. You can also use raw tuna; just cut it into small cubes and sauté it along with the peppers and garlic until it turns opaque.*

SERVES 2 AS A MAIN DISH, 3 TO 4 AS A FIRST COURSE

6 to 8 ounces spaghetti or other long dried pasta

3 tablespoons olive oil

¼ cup finely diced sweet pepper

1 large clove garlic, minced

1 anchovy fillet, chopped (optional)

Pinch of red pepper flakes

1 cup peeled and chopped tomatoes, with juice

6 ounces cooked tuna, flaked, OR 1 can (6½ ounces) tuna, drained and broken into small chunks

1 heaping tablespoon pitted and chopped green olives

1 teaspoon capers

➤ Cook the spaghetti in boiling salted water.

➤ While the spaghetti cooks, heat the oil in a large skillet over medium heat. Add the sweet pepper, garlic, anchovy (if used), and red pepper flakes and cook until the peppers begin to soften. Add the tomatoes, tuna, olives, and capers, turn the heat to high, and cook until the tomatoes have given off plenty of liquid. Taste for seasoning and correct if necessary. Simmer until the pasta is done. Drain the cooked pasta (not too thoroughly—it should still be a little wet), add it to the skillet, and toss with the sauce. Serve immediately.

Marinated Poached Tuna Belly

*Most of the value in a tuna is in the loins, those meaty half-fillet cuts that divide so neatly into steaks. But the same fish can also produce two substantial cuts of belly meat, which are different enough in flavor and texture that they really constitute another type of fish. Japanese sashimi and sushi chefs understand the special qualities of tuna belly meat, and treat it as an entirely different item (*toro, *as opposed to* maguro, *the redder loin meat). Otherwise, there is a limited market for tuna bellies and, unfortunately for both cooks and dealers, some of this delicious meat goes to waste.*

If you can find it, the paler belly meat from a yellowfin or similar tuna is one of the tastiest kinds of fish anywhere. Its higher fat content ensures a juicy result, whether grilled, broiled, or poached. Belly meat is also a relative bargain, selling for a little more than half the price of grilling-grade steaks.

One reason many uninitiated cooks may be hesitant to try cooking tuna belly is its appearance. The layers of pink muscle in a tuna belly are separated by heavy white bands of connective tissue that look like they are going to be tough, but this appearance is deceptive. Even where it is relatively thick, the connective tissue in fish (myocommata) is much more delicate than that of terrestrial meats. Unlike the membranes surrounding the muscles in red meats and poultry, which toughen initially when cooked, this tissue converts to gelatin at relatively low cooking temperatures. By the time the meat turns from pink to tan, most of the myocommata has "melted" away, leaving the meat in the familiar flakes.

Poached tuna belly can be served warm, but it's even better in this chilled treatment, known as à la grecque, *in which the poaching liquid is reduced after the fish is done to provide a slightly acid marinade. Try it in a salade niçoise (page 154) or anywhere else you would use top-quality canned tuna.*

SERVES 3 TO 4

3 cups water

1 cup dry white wine, OR 2 tablespoons white vinegar plus water to equal 1 cup

2 or 3 sprigs parsley

1 bay leaf

½ teaspoon peppercorns, cracked

1 green onion, sliced, OR ¼ cup sliced onion

¼ teaspoon salt

2 tablespoons olive oil

1 pound skinless tuna belly

➤ Combine all the ingredients except the tuna in a stainless or enameled saucepan. Bring to a boil, reduce the heat, and simmer 15 minutes. Add the fish to the poaching liquid and simmer until the center is slightly pink (bend a piece open slightly to peek at the center). Remove the fish to a bowl.

➤ Bring the liquid to a boil and reduce by two-thirds. Strain it over the fish and refrigerate until ready to use.

VARIATION Regular tuna steaks, as well as fillets of bonito, mackerel, and other rich fish, are also suitable for cooking *à la grecque*. If the fish is in large pieces, cut it into ¾- to 1-inch-thick slices before cooking.

Salade Niçoise

I always thought tuna was de rigueur *in a niçoise salad, but looking back into the classic recipe books, I found many versions have only a bit of anchovy in the dressing of what is otherwise a vegetable salad. Still, the name to me will always mean a substantial, entree-size composed salad featuring poached tuna atop an assortment of summer vegetables, the way I learned to make it twenty years ago at the Hayes Street Grill. Here is a general outline of the style; use as many or as few items as fit the season, your mood, and the selection in your produce basket.*

Mustard Vinaigrette

2 tablespoons tarragon-flavored wine vinegar

Salt and freshly ground pepper, to taste

1 heaping tablespoon Dijon-style mustard

¼ cup olive oil

Mixed salad greens, washed and spun dry, plus some large outside lettuce leaves

Green beans, strings removed, split lengthwise if large, boiled in salted water and cooled

Poached, grilled, or canned tuna or bonito, 2 to 3 ounces per serving

Hard-boiled eggs, quartered

Canned anchovy fillets

Capers

Small red potatoes, boiled and cooled

Sliced cooked or pickled beets

Red bell pepper strips, sautéed slowly in olive oil with chopped garlic and oregano until tender, seasoned with salt and pepper

Niçoise, Kalamata, or other brine-cured black olives

Cherry tomatoes, or larger tomatoes cut in wedges

➤ For the vinaigrette, combine the vinegar, salt, and pepper in a large mixing bowl and stir to dissolve the salt. Whisk in the mustard and a few drops of water, then whisk in the oil. Taste on a lettuce leaf and adjust. Pour the dressing into another container for now.

➤ Choose one or two large lettuce leaves per serving, swab them around in the empty bowl to pick up a little dressing, and use them to line each serving plate. Toss the remaining greens in a little of the dressing and arrange them on top. Add the green beans to the bowl, toss with a little dressing, and add to each plate. Break apart the tuna into the bowl, moisten with a little dressing, and place in the center of each salad. Add a couple of wedges of egg to each plate, drape half an anchovy fillet over each one, and scatter some capers alongside. Slice a potato and fan out the slices on each portion. Add some beets, pepper strips, a few olives, and tomatoes to each plate. Drizzle a little more dressing over the potatoes and tomatoes.

NOTE Nothing works better than a clean hand for tossing the elements of this salad in the dressing and arranging them on the plates. Keeping one hand dry for handling the plates and bowl, use the other one to grab a handful of greens, dress them, and transfer them to the plates; then the same with the beans, then the tuna. Now you can wash the dressing off your hand if you like before assembling the rest of the salad.

Other Serving Suggestions: Tuna

Serve grilled tuna with Herbed Tomato Salsa (page 328), a flavored butter such as Red Pepper–Garlic Butter (page 106), or any of the suggested toppings for swordfish (following pages).

Basic Grilled or Broiled Swordfish

No other fish is quite as meaty and succulent as a swordfish steak cooked to perfection on a grill, under a broiler, or in a skillet. And none is more disappointing than a swordfish steak that comes off the fire dry because it was cut too thin. The ideal thickness of a swordfish steak for these dry-heat cooking methods is between ½ and ¾ inch. If cut much thicker, the dense meat is hard to cook all the way through without drying on the outside; thinner steaks cook much more quickly, but they lose the thick, succulent core of just-cooked meat that makes swordfish worth its high price.

All the cooking methods and sauces in this section are interchangeable; see Swordfish Medallions with Papaya–Black Bean Relish, page 156, for how to cook the fish in a skillet. Top swordfish steaks with your choice of salsa, or a flavored butter, or one of the vinaigrette variations on pages 317 and 318. Or try the Tomato Explosion Sauce below.

SERVES 4

1 to 1½ pounds swordfish steaks
Salt and freshly ground pepper, to taste
Olive oil
Sprig of rosemary or thyme
Lemon or lime juice (optional)

➤ Divide the steaks into serving portions, or leave them whole for carving at the table.

Sprinkle with salt and pepper, drizzle with a little oil (flavored with a bruised garlic clove if you like) and add the herbs and a squeeze of lemon. Marinate 15 minutes at room temperature, or up to several hours in the refrigerator. Remove the steaks from the refrigerator at least 15 minutes before cooking.

➤ Grill the steaks over a medium-hot fire or on a ridged stovetop grill until just done by the skewer test, about 4 minutes per side for ¾-inch steaks. For a single set of grill marks, turn the fish only once; if you prefer the cross-hatch style, be sure the grill bars are thoroughly preheated, turn the fish after about 2 minutes, cook 3 to 4 minutes, then turn it again to the first side, rotating it so the new marks are at a 60° angle to the first. Turn the double-marked side up when serving.

➤ To broil, set the broiler rack so the fish is about 3 inches from the heat and cook about 3 minutes on the first side; turn and finish with a little longer cooking on the second side, which should be served face up.

Tomato Explosion Sauce

Peak California swordfish season is also peak tomato season, and a good fresh tomato salsa (or the grilled tomato sauce on page 68) is always a good bet with simply grilled or broiled swordfish. But if you want something more intense in tomato flavor, try this sauce based on tomatoes partially dried in the oven. I think you'll agree that it just explodes with tomato flavor. (A note of thanks to Barbara Tropp, from whose China Moon Cookbook *I first learned the oven-drying technique, which miraculously combines the fresh flavor of raw tomatoes with the concentration of dried.)*

SERVES 4

1 pound Roma or other plum tomatoes

¼ teaspoon salt

½ cup finely diced onion

4 tablespoons olive oil

2 teaspoons minced garlic

Heaping ¼ teaspoon cumin seed

2 teaspoons fresh oregano or marjoram leaves, coarsely chopped

Pinch of freshly ground pepper or red pepper flakes

1 teaspoon sherry or other wine vinegar

➤ Quarter the tomatoes lengthwise and remove the stem bases. Lay the wedges skin side down on a baking sheet and bake in a 250°F oven for 2 hours. If time permits, leave them in the turned-off oven another hour or two to continue drying. Refrigerate if not using the same day.

➤ Dice the tomatoes, place them in a heatproof mixing bowl, and add the salt. Soak the diced onion in cold water for a few minutes, then drain thoroughly and add to the tomato bowl. Combine the oil, garlic,

cumin, oregano, and pepper in a small skillet or saucepan and heat over low heat until quite fragrant. Pour over the tomatoes, sprinkle with vinegar, and toss to combine. Taste for seasoning and adjust if necessary. Serve warm or at room temperature, spooned over grilled, broiled, or sautéed fish.

NOTE Oven-drying tomatoes takes about 4 hours, but the timing given here is not the only possibility. Feel free to adjust the method to fit your schedule; for example, you could put the tomatoes in the oven for an hour first thing in the morning, turn it off when you leave for work, and leave them there all day without drying them too much. Or you can dry them the night before or a day or two ahead of time; they will keep for several days in the refrigerator.

Swordfish Medallions with Papaya–Black Bean Relish

Since Hawaii supplies us with so much swordfish, we might as well look to a Hawaiian recipe. This one, from the state agency that promotes seafood, was originally developed for aku (skipjack tuna), but it also compliments swordfish and other meaty fish. It represents the kind of East-West blend of ingredients typical of island cookery these days: olive oil and basil meet rice wine and ginger in a relish based on papaya and black beans. Note that it uses ordinary black beans (turtle beans), not the salted and fermented Chinese black beans.

By the way, "medallions" is just a fancy restaurant term for small steaks. The sauce is equally appropriate for bigger steaks or brochettes.

SERVES 4

4 skinless medallions of swordfish, tuna, or similar fish, 6 ounces each

Salt and freshly ground pepper, to taste

6 tablespoons olive oil

2 teaspoons chopped basil leaves

1 medium papaya, peeled, seeded, and diced

¾ cup cooked black beans, drained

4 teaspoons minced ginger

4 teaspoons shredded basil leaves

2 teaspoons mirin (sweet cooking sake)

2 teaspoons rice vinegar

Juice of 1 lime

➤ Season the fish with salt and pepper and place it in a bowl with 2 tablespoons of the oil and the chopped basil. Marinate 15 to 30 minutes.

➤ Combine the papaya, beans, and remaining ingredients in a mixing bowl and set aside at least 15 minutes for the flavors to combine.

➤ Heat a nonstick skillet thoroughly over medium-high heat. Turn the fish one more time in the marinade to coat it with oil, let the excess run off, and add to the skillet. Cook until just done by the skewer test, about 3 minutes per side, and transfer to warm plates. Serve with the papaya-bean relish (a radicchio leaf makes an attractive cup for the relish).

➤ (Recipe courtesy of Ocean Resources Branch, Hawaii Department of Business, Economic Development, and Tourism.)

Hoisin-Glazed Swordfish Brochettes

While it's hard to deny the appeal of a big, thick swordfish steak, its price makes it a bit of a splurge. However, the oddly shaped chunks that come from the edges of those perfectly shaped steaks, as well as from farther down toward the tail, often are not. Some fish markets sell these chunks for as little as half the price of steaks. With a little careful cutting, they can make fine brochettes or stewing pieces.

Whatever the shape of the chunks you begin with, the first step is to cut them across the grain to a single thickness; once they are of a uniform thickness, it doesn't really matter if the pieces are large or small, rectangular or triangular. You may have to remove some of the gristly fibers that run down the middle of the muscles, but even so, it should be cheaper than a prime steak from farther forward on the fish. The flavor will certainly be the same.

SERVES 4

2 tablespoons hoisin sauce

2 teaspoons Chinese or Japanese sesame oil

1½ pounds swordfish chunks

Salt and white pepper, to taste

➤ Combine the hoisin and sesame oil and blend thoroughly. Remove any skin from the fish and cut into pieces of uniform thickness (¾ to 1 inch). Thread the pieces together on 4 skewers.

➤ Season the fish lightly with salt and pepper. Grill or broil, brushing with the hoisin mixture after the first turn, until a skewer easily enters the center of the meat. Total cooking time is 6 to 10 minutes, depending on thickness and heat of the fire.

Swordfish "Pie"

Here's another way to make your swordfish dollar go farther, by combining the fish with a substantial amount of vegetables. A 3- to 4-ounce portion makes a satisfying serving in this rustic fish "pie" inspired by the fish and shellfish teglie *(casseroles) of southern Italy.*

Like its French and English equivalent, casserole, the word teglia *(tail-ya)—*tiella *or* tiedda *in some dialects—refers to both the baking dish and the food cooked in it. Most seafood* teglie *combine at least one kind of fish or shellfish with seasonal vegetables plus potatoes, rice, or both. Other firm, meaty fish, including the thresher shark caught in the same fishery, can stand in for swordfish, and are usually cheaper. East Coast monkfish is another good choice. Smaller, flakier fish are less suited to this kind of long baking, unless in large cuts held together with skin and bone.*

Italians would serve teglia *as a first course rather than an entree, but it makes a fine supper dish by itself.* Teglie *are traditionally served warm or at room temperature rather than hot from the oven. This, together with the leisurely cooking time, makes this dish better suited to a weekend than a busy weeknight.*

SERVES 4

1 medium onion

3 tablespoons olive oil

1 clove garlic, minced

¾ cup Italian short-grain rice

1 teaspoon salt, or to taste

1 thin-skinned white or yellow potato (about ½ pound), scrubbed and sliced very thin

2 small or 1 medium zucchini, sliced ⅛ inch thick

1 pound peeled, seeded, and chopped tomatoes, with juice

¾ pound swordfish steak or chunks, skin removed, in ¾-inch cubes

Freshly ground pepper, to taste

2 tablespoons chopped Italian parsley

➤ Slice the onion about ⅛ inch thick; mince the end and any odd pieces to make ¼ cup. Set the slices aside. Heat 1 tablespoon of the oil in a skillet, add the minced onion and garlic, and cook until fragrant. Add the rice and cook 2 minutes, stirring to coat it with the oil. Add 2½ cups of hot water and ½ teaspoon of the salt to the skillet and cook, stirring occasionally, until the rice has nearly absorbed the water and is about 80 percent done. Remove from the heat.

➤ Preheat the oven to 375°F. Spread the rice evenly in the bottom and partly up the sides of an 8-cup casserole dish. Make a layer of half the onion slices, then half the potato, then half the zucchini, then half the tomatoes. Add the fish cubes in a layer, seasoning them with a little salt and pepper and half of the parsley. Add the remaining onion, then potato, then zucchini in layers, and season again with salt and pepper. Top with the remaining tomatoes, letting their juice run down over all. Carefully add boiling water until it just covers the top layer of potatoes. Drizzle with the remaining oil and bake until the potatoes are tender, 1 to 1¼ hours. Let the pie rest at least 30 minutes out of the oven before serving, garnished with chopped parsley.

TECHNIQUE NOTE A mandoline-type slicer is handy for cutting even slices of the vegetables; if you have one, use the thinnest setting (about ¹⁄₁₆ inch) for the potatoes, and a slightly thicker one for the zucchini. Otherwise, slice by hand as evenly as possible.

Other Serving Suggestions: Swordfish

Broiled Sturgeon "Pasta e Fagioli," page 204.

Any of the shark dishes on the following pages, particularly Shark Scaloppine with Capers and Lemons, page 161.

Charcoal-Grilled Shark

A simple olive oil and citrus marinade does wonders for any kind of shark, large or small. No sauce is really needed, but top the cooked fish with a little lemon butter if desired.

SERVES 4

1½ pounds skinless shark steaks or fillets, cut ½ to ¾ inch thick

2 tablespoons distilled or cider vinegar

Salt and pepper

2 tablespoons extra virgin olive oil

Juice of 1 lemon or lime

1 tablespoon fresh thyme, oregano, or marjoram leaves, OR ½ teaspoon dried

Dried thyme or oregano leaves for the fire (optional)

➤ Place the shark steaks in a glass or earthenware dish, cover with water, and add the vinegar. Soak 15 minutes, turning occasionally. Drain, pat dry, and season lightly with salt and generously with pepper. Combine the oil, lemon juice, and herbs in a small bowl, stir to combine thoroughly, and pour over the shark. Marinate 30 minutes to several hours, turning several times so both sides marinate evenly.

➤ Grill the shark on a preheated grill over a hot charcoal fire, 4 to 5 minutes on the first side and another 2 to 4 minutes on the second side (break a piece partway open to check for doneness). Baste once or twice during cooking with the remaining marinade. For an extra touch of flavor, throw some dried herbs through the grill onto the coals while the fish cooks.

Shark with Peas, Roman Style

This is my loose interpretation of the Roman dish palombo coi piselli. Palombo is the Italian name for a small shark related to leopard shark, typically cooked and served with peas. This recipe makes just enough sauce to moisten the fish; if you want to serve it over couscous, add another cup or so of tomato juice.

SERVES 4

3 tablespoons olive oil

½ cup minced onion

1 pound ripe tomatoes, peeled, seeded, and chopped, with juice

2 cups fresh or thawed peas

½ teaspoon salt, or to taste

Freshly ground pepper, to taste

4 portions skinless leopard shark fillets, or small shark steaks (1½ pounds in all)

3 tablespoons chopped fresh mint leaves

➤ Combine the oil and onion in a large skillet and cook over medium heat just until the onion begins to color. Add the tomatoes, fresh peas, salt, and pepper and cook until the tomatoes release their juice, about 5 minutes. Add thawed peas at the end, just to reheat.

➤ Season the shark pieces with a little more salt and pepper and lay them in among the vegetables. Cover and cook until the shark is tender, 6 to 8 minutes depending on thickness. Transfer the fish to warm plates, stir the mint into the skillet, correct the seasoning, and spoon the sauce and peas over and around the fish.

Shark with Braised Eggplant Topping

Eggplant, tomatoes, sweet peppers, and other late summer vegetables make a good match for shark. The topping in this recipe, derived from caponata, the Sicilian sweet and sour eggplant relish, will work on thresher and other sharks as well as swordfish and other fish steaks.

SERVES 4

½ medium eggplant (about ½ pound), unpeeled, in ½-inch dice

1 teaspoon salt

2 medium tomatoes

1 tablespoon olive oil

1 cup finely diced onion

1 clove garlic, minced

Pinch of red pepper flakes

1 tablespoon raisins, chopped

1 tablespoon pitted and chopped green olives

½ cup chicken stock

1 teaspoon balsamic or aged red wine vinegar

Salt and pepper, to taste

4 shark steaks, about 6 ounces each

➤ Toss the eggplant cubes with the salt, place in a colander, and let stand 30 minutes to drain. Slice the stem ends off the tomatoes and grate the flesh against the coarse side of a box grater into a bowl; discard the skin.

➤ Combine the oil and onion in a non-stick skillet and place over medium-high heat. Cook until the onion begins to color, then add the garlic and pepper flakes. Cook a few seconds, and add the eggplant. Stir or shake the skillet until the eggplant cubes begin to brown (they will absorb nearly all the oil quickly). Add the raisins, olives, tomatoes, and stock and simmer, loosely covered, until the liquid is nearly gone and the eggplant is tender, about 10 minutes.

➤ Remove the lid, sprinkle in the vinegar, and cook until the mixture is thick. Taste for seasoning and correct if necessary (no additional salt may be needed if you use salted canned stock). Remove from the heat and replace the cover.

➤ Season the shark steaks lightly with salt and pepper; grill, broil, or sauté until a skewer easily enters the center, 3 to 4 minutes per side. Serve with the eggplant mixture on top.

Shark Braised with Cabbage

This recipe draws on widely different sources: a baked casserole of monkfish with shredded Savoy cabbage at New York's Le Bernardin, and a Taiwanese stew of fish steaks, tofu, and aged vinegar in Barbara Tropp's first cookbook.

If you have one, a Chinese clay pot or "sandy pot" is ideal for this dish, but any flameproof covered casserole will do.

SERVES 4 CHINESE STYLE, WITH OTHER DISHES

½ pound shark fillet or steak

1 ounce bean threads (also known as cellophane noodles or Chinese vermicelli)

½ pound nappa or Savoy cabbage

1 ounce tasty ham such as Westphalian, Smithfield, or prosciutto, sliced

1 green onion, cut into 1-inch sections

5 slices ginger

½ package firm (Chinese-style) tofu, drained

1 cup water or unsalted chicken stock

¼ cup soy sauce

1 tablespoon Chinese black vinegar or balsamic vinegar

➤ If using shark fillet, cut crosswise into ¾-inch slices. If the shark has any ammonia aroma, soak in acidulated water (see page 149) for 30 minutes, drain, and rinse.

➤ Soak the bean threads in hot water until soft; drain. Line the bottom of a 2-quart flameproof casserole with outside cabbage leaves. Thinly slice the rest of the cabbage and scatter it over the leaves. Spread the bean threads in an even layer, top with the ham, green onion, and ginger, then lay in the shark slices. Cut the tofu into 8 triangles and arrange around the outside. Combine the water, soy sauce, and vinegar and pour over all.

➤ Cover the casserole and bring just to a boil over medium heat (start with low heat and increase gradually if using a Chinese clay pot). Reduce the heat to maintain a lively simmer and cook 15 to 20 minutes, or until the shark is opaque and tender. Serve from the casserole, spooning the mixture over individual bowls of rice.

Shark Scaloppine with Capers and Lemons

This recipe also works with swordfish, sturgeon, halibut, or albacore. Swordfish takes a few seconds longer per side; albacore is better on the rare side, so turn it a few seconds sooner.

SERVES 4

2 cups unsalted chicken or veal stock

1 pound shark, cut into ¼-inch scaloppine (see note, page 202)

Salt and pepper

Flour

1 to 2 tablespoons oil or clarified butter

1 tablespoon minced shallots

2 tablespoons lemon juice

1 tablespoon capers

1 tablespoon softened butter (optional)

➤ In a small saucepan, bring the stock to a boil, reduce the heat to medium, and cook until reduced to less than ½ cup. Set aside.

➤ Season the scaloppine lightly with salt and pepper (allowing for the saltiness of the capers) and dredge them in flour, shaking off the excess. Heat a large skillet over high heat and add 1 tablespoon of oil, swirling the pan to coat the bottom. Add as many scaloppine as will fit in the pan and cook until they begin to shrink and brown, about 30 seconds. Turn and cook 20 to 30 seconds on the other side. As they are done, transfer the scaloppine to a warm serving platter or individual plates and continue cooking the rest.

➤ When all the scaloppine are done, add the shallots to the pan and sauté briefly. Add the lemon juice, capers, and reduced stock and cook, scraping the pan to loosen any browned bits, until the sauce is reduced by a third. Taste for seasoning and correct if necessary. If a richer sauce is desired, remove the pan from the heat and swirl in the softened butter. Pour the sauce over the fish and serve.

Grilled Shark, Yucatán Style

One of the most delicious shark dishes I have ever tasted was on a boat trip out of Isla Mujeres, off Mexico's Yucatán Peninsula. On our way out to view an island bird sanctuary, we trolled for our lunch. A barracuda became ceviche, and we also had an assortment of small fried fish. But the real highlight was made from a small shark called cazón. *Our skipper spread the shark fillets with a thick red seasoning paste and grilled it in a folding wire grill over a charcoal fire, then folded bites of the fish in warm tortillas to make memorable fish tacos.*

The following version of shark a la yucateca *can be made with steaks, fillets, or skewered cubes of leopard shark or any other variety. The traditional seasoning paste is made from ground achiote (annatto seed), chile powder, oregano, cumin, garlic, and citrus juices. The rock-hard achiote seeds are a pain in the neck to grind unless you have a sturdy electric spice grinder; fortunately, pre-seasoned ground achiote is available in Latin American markets in bricks labeled* achiote condimentado. *Black beans cooked with a little chile powder and cumin are a nice accompaniment.*

SERVES 4

½ cake (2 ounces) prepared achiote paste
3 cloves garlic, pressed or mashed
⅛ teaspoon cayenne, or to taste
Juice of ½ orange and ½ lime
1 tablespoon vegetable oil
1½ pounds shark fillet or steaks
8 warm corn tortillas
Fresh Tomato Salsa, page 327 (optional)

➤ Crumble the achiote paste into a blender or mortar, add the garlic, cayenne, citrus juices, and oil, and blend to a smooth paste. Rub the mixture all over the shark and marinate in the refrigerator several hours; remove from refrigerator 30 minutes before cooking.

➤ Grill or broil the fish until just done, cut it into chunks, and fold it into warm tortillas to eat with your fingers. Season the tacos to taste with additional lime juice or salsa, if desired.

Other Serving Suggestions: Shark

Marinate shark steaks in orange juice for 30 minutes; grill or broil and serve the meat as in Skate Tacos (page 136).

Swordfish "Pie," page 158.

full-flavored fish

While some of the fish in previous chapters might be called "fish for people who don't like fish," the ones in the following pages—ranging from tiny anchovies to 4-foot mahi-mahi—are definitely for those who want to know they are eating fish. While they differ in a lot of particulars, the fish in this chapter are generally higher in fat and darker of meat, with a more fully developed flavor that invites a heavier hand with spices and salt, smoke and herbs, chiles and garlic . . . makes me hungry just thinking about it!

Mackerel

Pacific or chub mackerel, *Scomber japonicus*
Atlantic mackerel, *Scomber scombrus*
Sierras, *Scomberomorus* spp.
Wahoo or ono, *Acanthocybium solanderi*
King mackerel ("kingfish"), *Scomberomorus cavalla*
Spanish mackerel, *Scomberomorus maculatus*

The cosmopolitan family Scombridae, the tunas and mackerels, encompasses dozens of species of fish ranging in size from half-pound chub mackerels to half-ton bluefin tuna. It also spans the economic spectrum, with some of the world's most expensive fish as well as some of the cheapest. The exact qualities vary from one species to another, but all the scombrids are fast-swimming, predatory pelagic (found near the surface in the open ocean) fish with relatively dark, flavorful meat. Tunas are dealt with on page 140, the small and medium-size members of the family, here.

Small mackerels of the genus *Scomber* are found in both the Atlantic and Pacific, and range farther north than most of their cousins. These fish usually weigh less than a pound apiece, and can often be cooked whole. While they are often amazingly cheap, they tend to be the strongest in taste of all the scombrids, so they might not be the best choice if you're shy about serving fish that are full of flavor.

"Fancy mackerels" is not a recognized name in the market, but my own description for several larger members of the family, a few of which are second only to the tunas in culinary esteem. Most of these fish belong to the genus *Scomberomorus,* including the East Coast king mackerel (kingfish) and Spanish mackerels, and various subtropical and tropical species known in Spanish as *sierra*. Wahoo, a fish better known on the West Coast under its Hawaiian name *ono,* also belongs in this league. Most of these fish run large enough that a single fillet will yield several portions; king mackerel are sometimes large enough to steak like tuna. All these fish have meat that is paler and more delicate in flavor than that of the smaller mackerels.

In Mediterranean cooking, mackerel is often combined with olive oil, tomatoes, garlic, strong herbs, and other ingredients to match (or perhaps to mask) its robust flavors. Of course, no marinade or sauce will restore the flavor of fish that is no longer fresh, and of all fish, the mackerels are among the quickest to show their age. Only a market that turns over its stock quickly and is ruthless about discarding less-than-fresh fish is likely to be a good source of fresh mackerel. Look for bright red gills, an unbroken skin, and firm flesh that springs back when touched gently with a fingertip.

Miscellaneous Full-Flavored Fish

Yellowtail or yellowtail jack, *Seriola lalandi*
California, or Pacific, barracuda, *Sphyraena argentea*
Dolphin, mahi-mahi, or dorado, *Coryphaena hippurus*
Sablefish, *Anoplopoma fimbria*

The following section brings together a number of fish that are not related to one another, but more or less similar in their culinary qualities. All these fish are moderately rich, with more fat than cod or rockfish but less than tuna or salmon. Their meat is neither snow-white nor as beefy red as tuna, and mostly cooks up to an ivory shade. They mostly have firm meat, more toward fibrous than flaky in texture, and the flavor also falls into the middle—not as strong as some, but you certainly know you're eating fish.

What all these traits add up to is fish that taste great cooked by dry-heat methods like grilling, broiling, sautéing, and searing, and take well to sauces with some punch from chiles, ginger, citrus, and tomato. As a sort of mental shorthand, I think of all of these as "summer fish"—not necessarily because they are available in summer, though most are, but because they take so well to cooking and eating outdoors.

Most of the fish in this section are fast-swimming predatory fish, and they tend to have a good-sized strip of dark red, blood-rich meat running down the center of each fillet. This meat is the first to go if the fish is not perfectly fresh. If it is more brown than red, the fish is showing its age. Some cooks prefer to remove the dark meat before cooking; to do so, skin the fillet, place it skin side up on the board, and shave away the dark meat with several long strokes, leaving a shallow V-shaped channel.

If you want a milder flavor overall, or if you have to keep the fish in the refrigerator for a day before cooking it, you can reduce any strong flavor by soaking the fish in a light brine for a half hour before cooking.

Yellowtail and mahi-mahi share the same basic shape as salmon, and white seabass, which lends itself to diagonal slices no more than 1 inch thick, preferably closer to ¾ inch. If all you can find is thick, square-cut slices, then I recommend the butterfly cut (see page 15).

A member of the jack family, which also includes pompano and several other valuable food fishes, **YELLOWTAIL** is a popular sport and commercial fish in Southern California, and one that deserves to be better known. A long, slender fish about the size of a salmon, it has firm, meaty, moderately rich flesh of a distinctive color, light brown with an orange tint, though it cooks to a creamy color like albacore. In the kitchen, yellowtail can function as a leaner and milder version of tuna, ideal for dry-heat cooking methods such as grilling and broiling. Yellowtail also makes an excellent, though strong-flavored, ceviche. It is also popular in Japan, where it is known as *hamachi*, and large amounts of aquacultured yellowtail are served raw as sashimi or sushi.

CALIFORNIA BARRACUDA is a relatively small member of this worldwide family of predatory warm-water fishes. The typical size is 2 to 3 feet long, and the weight is usually less than 10 pounds. Its normal range is from about Santa Barbara to the tip of Baja, although it ranges farther north in El Niño years. Spring and early summer is the main season, and most of the catch goes into Asian and Hispanic markets.

Like many other predatory fish, California barracuda has moderately rich meat that is on the dark side when raw but cooks up nearly white. The flavor is also in the middle range, stronger than most mild white fish but less so than mackerels and tunas. Whole headed and gutted fish is the most common form, to be cooked whole or cut into steaks or, less commonly, fillets. The flesh is a little soft, so if cooking fillets, leave the skin on to help hold the meat together.

Whole fish or large chunks can be baked in a sauce, and steaks or fillets are suitable for grilling, broiling, baking, or frying. I have also tasted it as a delicious ceviche. Tomato-based sauces and chiles are both good matches for the flavor of this fish; try baking the fish surrounded with a chunky tomato and chile sauce, or serve grilled or broiled barracuda with a simple raw tomato salsa or the fruit-based salsa given on page 179.

Although the field guides list this fish as **DOLPHIN,** nearly everybody uses the Hawaiian name **MAHI-MAHI** to distinguish it from the marine mammal. (The Spanish name, *dorado*, which means "golden," has never caught on

here.) Even the FDA has adopted mahi-mahi as the official market name. Still, I run into people who avoid mahi-mahi because they think someone is trying to get them to eat Flipper!

A medium-size fish of warm oceans, mahi-mahi is more likely to come to our markets from South America than from Hawaii these days, especially during our winter. Both fresh and frozen mahi have become common in supermarkets, although the quality varies widely; I have seen "fresh" mahi so old that it has turned a most unappetizing shade of brown, enough to make me mistrust everything else in the case. Fresh mahi does have a grayish tint, but the darker markings on the meat should be more pink than brown.

The meat of mahi-mahi is firm and fine-textured, both leaner and a bit milder in flavor than either white seabass or yellowtail. Sautéing seems a better bet with this species than grilling or broiling, but, in any case, don't overcook it.

One of the treasures of Northwestern seafood is a long, slender, salmon-size fish found in cold waters from California and Japan to the Bering Sea. However, this fish suffers from an identity problem. California supermarket shoppers know it as **BUTTERFISH**—smallish, slender fillets usually well under a pound apiece. In old-style Seattle or Portland seafood restaurants, it's known as **BLACK COD** and is more likely to appear as a good-sized square of smoked fish, reheated by poaching or steaming. Only east of the Rockies is it commonly known as **SABLEFISH.** Yet to my mind, sablefish is the perfect name: like the lustrous black fur of the same name, it suggests something luxurious, an impression borne out by the rich, moist texture and sweet-nutty flavor of this fish.

Part of the difference between "black cod" and "butterfish" is size. In general, the fish caught father north are larger than those typical of California. Most California "butterfish" are smaller, younger fish (2 to 3 pounds is typical) caught by flatfish trawlers in relatively shallow waters from Fort Bragg to Crescent City. Farther north, the same species is caught in deeper water, mostly with traps and long-lines. In Alaska, which produces three-quarters of the U.S. sablefish catch, the majority of the fish are taken by longline, and include a high proportion of fish of 5 pounds or more.

With a greater range of sablefish sizes to choose among, shoppers in the Northwest show a strong preference for larger fish, which

Rich and White

While most rich fish have a darker meat color, a few combine snow-white meat with a high fat content that makes them quite forgiving of a little overcooking. Sablefish, or black cod, is the prime example in our area, although Chilean sea bass is probably better known these days. A couple of other rich white fish, especially suitable for grilling and other dry-heat methods, are caught incidentally on longlines or in nets set for target species like swordfish and tuna, and are worth trying if they show up in the market.

Among the incidental catch species in the swordfish fishery is the occasional louvar (*Luvarus imperialis*), a large fish vaguely tunalike in shape, but with a small mouth adapted to feeding on jellyfish and other small gelatinous invertebrates. The snow-white meat of louvar is mild in flavor, and while I don't know about its fat content, it tastes especially juicy.

Perhaps the most controversial fish of this type is escolar (*Lepidocybium flavobrunneum*), another oceanic fish of an overall size and shape similar to tuna. Caught by the same long-lines that take tuna in the Pacific and Gulf of Mexico, escolar (its name is Spanish for scholar, perhaps because its golden eyes against the dark purple-brown skin make it look like it is wearing glasses) was routinely thrown back until a decade ago, but when a few chefs and diners tried it they loved it. The tuna-size steaks cook up pure white, tender, and moderately flavorful, and the high fat content keeps it juicy. However, the fat in escolar is made up of some very large molecules that are difficult to digest, and there have been some reports of this fish having a pronounced laxative effect. Other reports say the problem is with a close relative, the oilfish (*Ruvettus pretiosus*), and that true escolar can be eaten with no ill effects. (It hasn't given me any trouble on the few occasions I have eaten it.) The FDA has made some attempts to discourage the sale of escolar, but has never outlawed it, and it remains popular on many restaurant menus.

tend to have firmer flesh and a higher fat content. This preference is shared by chefs and diners in upscale Chinese restaurants in California, where a roasted or smoked fillet of "black cod" is a centerpiece entree. The Chinese trade in San Francisco and Los Angeles largely ignores the California fish, preferring to pay a premium price for larger fish flown in from Vancouver.

With its rich flavor and high fat content, sablefish is perfect for dry-heat cooking methods. Its biggest drawback is its soft and fragile texture, which can make it one of the most challenging of local fish to cook just right. When pressed with a fingertip, a perfectly cooked piece of sablefish will offer some resistance and spring back, but the flakes will not separate. Cook it half a minute longer, however, and the whole thing begins to fall apart, leaving a jumble of small pieces sitting in an amazing amount of liquid. The trick, then, is to cook it just until it firms up and the very last flakes on the tail end are starting to separate, then whisk it off the fire. Once it sits on a warm serving plate for a couple of minutes, the flakes will slide apart with the gentlest nudge of a fork or chopsticks.

Sablefish fillets can be made a little more manageable by a preliminary dry cure like those used for smoked fish. Two methods are given on page 182, a quick cure and an overnight version. Both rely on salt and sugar to draw excess moisture out of the fish, making the meat firmer. I'd still recommend a cooking method where the fish doesn't have to be turned during cooking, such as broiling, baking, or hot-smoking. Only the most confi-dent grillers will want to try sablefish on the grill, at least without a safety net of foil under the fish, which more or less defeats the purpose of grilling. If you can find the fish in crosscut steaks, they are a better choice for grilling, as the bones and skin help hold the meat together.

The demand for sablefish, especially larger fish, usually exceeds the supply, which is one reason the market has been so quick to embrace Chilean sea bass. The latter fish, which is not really a bass, is in many ways the Southern Hemisphere equivalent of sablefish: both are large, slow-growing fish found in relatively deep, cold waters at high latitudes, and have rich white flesh. The texture of the meat is different—Chilean sea bass is more steaklike and less flaky—but they take well to the same flavorings. Feel free to substitute Chilean sea bass in these recipes.

Little Pelagic Fish

Pacific sardine, *Sardinops sagax*
Northern anchovy, *Engraulis mordax*
Pacific herring, *Clupea pallasii*
Jack mackerel, *Trachurus symmetricus*
Jacksmelt, *Atherinopsis californiensis*

One way to save some money on seafood is to eat lower on the oceanic food chain (see page 170). Many of the smaller types of fish that are food for larger, more expensive fish also offer the adventurous cook good eating at a bargain price.

To commercial fishermen, a lot of the value in small pelagic fish like anchovies and sardines is not as human food, but as forage and bait for other fish, or as the raw material for fish meal that finds its way into everything from poultry feed to fish-oil capsules. Still, shoppers may from time to time come across displays of small, slender, silvery fish, usually at an attractive price. Depending on the season and the particular batch of fish, you may be looking at a single species or up to half a dozen, ranging in size from 5 inches to a foot long.

Although they are superficially similar, these little fish (sometimes lumped together under the generic name whitebait) represent many different families. It can be confusing to tell the different species apart, so I've given a summary of the important "field marks" that distinguish each fish.

Several of these fish belong to the herring family, which is characterized by loose, silvery, rather large (for fish of this size) scales. The largest variety is also the easiest to identify: the **PACIFIC SARDINE,** up to 8 inches long with a conspicuous row of dark spots running back from the head about halfway to the tail.

The return of the sardine to Central and Southern California is one of the few good news stories about fish in the 1980s and '90s. To those who associate sardines only with little flat tin cans, fresh sardines cooked on a grill or in the oven can be a delicious revelation.

In one of the classic boom-and-bust fishery stories of this century, the Pacific sardine once supported huge catches, most of which went into cans in Monterey and San Pedro. At the peak of the fishery in the 1930s, annual landings sometimes exceeded a billion pounds. Predictably, the population crashed under this intense fishing pressure (coupled perhaps with increasing water pollution); by the end of the '40s the species was "commercially extinct"—too scarce to bother fishing for. Some sardines survived, however, and without fishing pressure, their numbers gradually recovered. In the 1980s, biologists from the California Department of Fish and Game began to notice a growing incidental catch of sardines in the squid, mackerel, and anchovy fisheries, and the agency allowed a resumption of commercial sardine fishing.

Catches have grown steadily since then, and with Cannery Row having long since been converted to other uses, a lot of these tasty little fish have gone into the fresh market (although one Monterey area processor actually got back into the business of canning sardines in 1998!). For much of the '80s the going price for fresh sardines was around a dollar a pound, but since they have been discovered by a growing number of chefs and home cooks, they have more than doubled in price. They are still a bargain in my book.

Some of the increase in sardine stocks has to do with cyclical changes in the temperature of the North Pacific. Warmer ocean conditions, such as those that have prevailed since the late 1970s, favor sardines over anchovies, which do better in cold-water periods. A sustained cold-water cycle is believed to have contributed to the California sardine crash. If and when the wheel turns and we have several years of colder water, the sardine population can be expected to decline. In the meantime, let's enjoy them.

The sardine's more northerly cousin, the **PACIFIC HERRING,** is one of the most commercially valuable fish on the West Coast, yet it seldom shows up in the market. Despite the tremendous popularity of fresh herring in other parts of the world, herring fisheries from San Francisco Bay to Alaska are geared almost entirely to the Japanese passion for herring roe, and the good price these fish will bring when shipped to Japan or Korea for processing. What doesn't go to Japan is mostly used for bait in sport fishing. Only a tiny amount of the catch is available to the fresh fish market, but it's worth buying when it shows up. Pacific herring look quite similar to sardines, but run a bit smaller and lack the spots. Fresh herring can be used in any recipe for sardines, and are also popular pickled (see page 187).

Closely related to the herrings but considerably smaller and slimmer is the **NORTHERN ANCHOVY.** The anchovy's range overlaps that of the sardine in California, but anchovies mostly occur farther north and seem to prefer slightly colder water. As mentioned above, in warm-water years sardines tend to be more common, while in colder conditions the anchovies are more numerous.

Anchovies are big business on the West Coast, but unlike anchovies caught in other

Grazers and Predators in the Marine Food Chain

Many of the small pelagic fish covered in this section are related, while others are not, but they all occupy a similar ecological niche in various Pacific Coast waters. Along with squid and certain shrimp, many species of small fish—among them herring, sardines, anchovies, and smelt—constitute an essential link in the oceanic food chain off the Pacific Coast. If salmon and swordfish are among the lions and leopards of this watery Serengeti, then the small pelagic fish are the enormous herds of antelope and wildebeest, and plankton are the grass on which the latter feed.

The analogy is far from perfect, as there are many more levels to the marine food chain, but the principle remains the same: predators at every level consume many times their weight in smaller animals, and the whole thing depends on plants, in this case, phytoplankton, free-floating microscopic plants that occur near the ocean surface.

Eating fish from lower on the food chain makes sense, in terms of extracting the maximum amount of protein that the ocean can produce sustainably. Most of the middle-level fish grow quickly, and replace their numbers in a shorter time than fish that take years to mature. However, we have to be careful; take too much of any resource and you will starve the other species that also rely on it. If we catch all the anchovies, there will be nothing there for the salmon to eat.

parts of the world, relatively little of the West Coast catch winds up as salted fillets in cans; instead, these little fish are used mainly as fishing bait or aquarium feed, or are reduced into fish meal. But a small amount of the catch comes into the fresh fish market. Fresh anchovies are easy to tell apart from sardines and herring; look for the smaller overall size (4 to 6 inches long), smaller scales, and especially for the long mouth that opens to well behind the eye. They can be used interchangeably with sardines, bearing in mind their smaller size.

Two other small pelagics sometimes found in the market are jacksmelt and jack mackerel. Despite the name, the jacksmelt is not related to the true smelts (see page 172); it's also larger than most, up to a foot long, with a definite contrast between the greenish upper parts and the paler belly. The meat is on the mild side, and suitable for pan-dressing and frying like smelt, or baking in a sauce like sardines or mackerel.

Just as jacksmelt is not a true smelt, jack mackerel is not a true mackerel. Instead, it belongs to the jack family, which includes the famous pompano of the Southeast and the large yellowtail of Southern California. Like many members of the family, the jack mackerel has a distinctive row of scutes, thick scale-like plates, running down the middle of each side. Its meat is strongly flavored, and can be used like mackerel.

SHOPPING AND PREPARATION

When buying small pelagic fish, avoid any that look beat up or have swollen or ruptured bellies. The fish should be well iced, just like the more expensive fish on the counter. Lift the gill covers and look at the gills; they should be bright red or pink, never gray or brown. Above all, go by the smell. If they smell fishy, they are

Salting Your Own

Because sardines and anchovies appear sporadically in stores, when you do find them it may be too late to change your menu plans for that night. The solution? The age-old method of preserving with salt. By generously salting the fish, you can keep them in the refrigerator for several days longer than you could in fresh form. After soaking in fresh water, they come out somewhere between fresh sardines and canned anchovies in flavor and texture—not right for every use, but certainly suitable for dishes like the pasta sauce on page 186 or the potato gratin on page 185.

Once you have done it a time or two, boning or filleting a small batch of these fish takes just a few minutes. After boning and rinsing, pat the fillets dry and lay a single layer in a glass, ceramic, or stainless steel bowl and sprinkle generously with kosher salt, enough to cover all the fish about one salt crystal deep. Continue adding fillets in layers, topping each with salt. Cover the bowl, refrigerate overnight, and pour off the liquid that accumulates in the bowl. Keep tightly covered and use within a week.

not fresh. If at all possible, plan to cook them the day you buy them; otherwise, clean them (or have them cleaned at the shop, if this service is available) and cook them by the next day, or else salt them (see page 171).

Cleaning these little fish is relatively easy. Start by rubbing off the scales, which is easiest to do in a bowl of water. Working on several layers of newspaper, lay a fish on its side with the belly away from you, cut through the bone just behind the head, slide the knife in along one side of the belly cavity to the vent, and cut outward to slit open the belly. The entrails should pull away easily with the heads. Transfer the cleaned fish to a bowl, and when you are done, use the newspaper to wrap up and discard the heads and trimmings. Slit open the reddish strips of tissue along the backbone of each fish (the kidneys), and rinse the cavities thoroughly until no traces of blood remain. The fish are now ready for grilling or baking whole.

To bone sardines, as in the recipe for Baked Sardines with Gremolata (page 185), head and gut the fish as described above, but don't bother with the kidney strip. Lay a fish belly side down on the cutting board and press gently with the heel of your hand to force the two sides apart. Flip the fish over and the whole backbone should peel away easily. Cut the bone free from the tail or remove the tail with the bone as you prefer. You will be left with the two fillets attached at the back by the skin. The same cleaning and boning instructions will work with herring, anchovies, jack mackerel, and other small fish. You can also fillet these fish with a knife, just as you would a salmon or trout; the bone structure is identical.

Other Little Fish

Smelts, *Spirinchus, Hypomesus, Allosmerus* spp.
Pacific butterfish or "California pompano,"
Peprilus simillimus

If your small, slender fish are not sardines, herring, or anchovies, they are likely to be one species or another of **SMELT.** Like the small pelagic fish, smelts are important prey for larger fish as well as popular food fish. Several species occur in our area, and are caught when they come to spawn on sandy beaches at various times of year. There is also a somewhat larger variety from eastern Canada and the Great Lakes which is widely sold frozen. The smelts are rather nondescript, with no dramatic stripes or other color marks, but as a group they can be identified by the presence of an adipose fin, a small, soft, boneless fin between the dorsal fin and the tail also found in salmons and trouts, to which they are related. Smelt are leaner and milder than the other little fish, and are best simply fried (see page 188).

Chinese fish markets in California frequently display piles of small, silvery, almost disc-shaped fish invariably labeled **"POMPANO."** While these little fish are not related to the true Florida pompano, the similarity in appearance is obvious—the compressed shape ("tall" from dorsal fin to belly, and quite thin from side to side), the blunt snout, deeply forked tail, and raked fins—and given the fine reputation of real pompano, it's no surprise that they are sold under that name rather than their proper name, **BUTTERFISH.**

Another reason for the pompano tag is that the name butterfish causes some confusion around here. Ask for butterfish in most California markets and you will get fillets of the much larger sablefish (see page 166). The two couldn't be more dissimilar; sablefish is a large, rather codlike fish, producing long, thick, narrow fillets a foot or more in length. Butterfish is a small fish, needing several to make up a single pound, and the compressed shape yields thin fillets almost as wide as they are long. About the only thing the two share is a soft texture and high fat content, thus the name butterfish.

Butterfish are caught commercially on the West Coast, but the supply is sporadic, and the fish in the market are more likely to be a very similar species of butterfish from Florida, brought in frozen and thawed for sale in the "fresh" market. Although it's not the equal of true pompano, butterfish does have rich, fine-textured meat that starts out dark but cooks up white and sweet. At 2 to 3 ounces each, butterfish are usually treated as pan fish, simply dusted with flour or cornstarch and fried in deep or shallow oil. But they are also good broiled, grilled, steamed in the Chinese style, or baked in a sauce as in Baked Mackerel with Tomatoes and Salsa (page 178). In any case, the thin skin is likely to come apart in cooking.

The scales are so tiny they can be eaten along with the skin.

At Asian fish markets, the price may or may not include cleaning, which usually means with the heads left on. If you have to do it yourself, it's a lot easier to pan-dress the fish like small flatfish (see page 12). Either way, be sure to rinse away any traces of blood from the back of the cavity, or it will spoil the flavor.

Salt-Grilled Mackerel with Ginger Sauce

The Japanese approach to mackerel is a little different from the Western: instead of adding a lot of competing flavors, a Japanese cook will focus on the flavor of the fish alone, "cleansed" with a bit of salt (see page 15) and enhanced by the heat of the grill and a very simple dipping sauce.

SERVES 4

2 whole Pacific mackerel, 1 to
   1¼ pounds each

½ teaspoon kosher or sea salt

1 teaspoon grated ginger, with juice

1 teaspoon sugar

4 teaspoons unseasoned rice vinegar

1 tablespoon water

2 teaspoons soy sauce

1 tablespoon peanut oil

▶ Have the fish filleted, with the skin left on. Rinse well. Cut 3 diagonal slashes in the skin side of each fillet. Sprinkle a little of the salt in the bottom of a shallow baking dish, lay in the fillets skin side down, and sprinkle

Smoking Allowed

One of the most delicious ways to cook any fish, but especially the richer varieties, is with aromatic smoke. Smoking fish was once a matter of survival, a way to preserve a seasonal catch to feed the family or tribe during leaner times. But it has remained popular even in the days of refrigeration for a very simple reason—smoked fish tastes good.

The kind of smoking I am talking about here (and in the recipe below) is hot-smoking, where the temperature inside the smoking chamber is high enough to fully cook the fish. Cold-smoking, the kind that produces the moist, velvety texture of delicatessen lox, requires maintaining a temperature of 60° to 110°F for many hours, something that is practical only on the large scale of commercial smokehouses (although cold-smoking fish in old refrigerators and other improvised smokers is a time-honored tradition in salmon country). Hot-smoking occurs in a much more manageable temperature range, and while the result won't slice as neatly as cold-smoked fish, it's a tasty dish eaten on its own, or broken up into flakes for salads, pasta dishes, and spreads.

The most reliable way to smoke fish is in a specialized outdoor smoker, of which there are several designs, both electric and charcoal-fired. (For a stovetop alternative, see Wok-Smoked Sablefish, page 183.) If you have one, follow the manufacturer's instructions for hot-smoking fish fillets. I've never owned a smoker, but with a little practice I have found it possible to hot-smoke fish in a covered barbecue kettle. The only trick is getting the fire to smolder without going out or getting too hot. The ideal temperature is as low as your grill can maintain, but no hotter than 200°F. Partially closing the top and bottom vents allows you to damp down the fire to this level, as long as it's not too big or too small to begin with. An instant-reading thermometer dangled through one of the top vents is a good way to monitor the temperature.

If you use your grill frequently, you don't need to build a separate fire for smoking. Try it some evening after dinner is done and the fire is nearly burned out; it may be the perfect temperature to add a handful of smoking chips and smoke a couple of fish fillets. With a little planning ahead, it's a way of getting two meals out of one fire. ➤

the remaining salt on top. Cover and set aside in the refrigerator 30 to 45 minutes.

➤ Combine the ginger, sugar, vinegar, water, and soy sauce in a small bowl and stir to dissolve the sugar. Strain into small individual dipping sauce bowls.

➤ Remove the fish from the refrigerator 15 minutes before cooking. Prepare a char-

coal, gas, or stovetop grill (or broiler) for cooking over medium-high heat. Pat the fish dry and rub lightly with oil. Grill, starting with the skin side up and turning once, until the center just loses its raw color, 3 to 5 minutes per side. Or broil on a lightly oiled broiling rack, starting with the skin toward the heat and turning once when the skin is nicely

Like other methods of preserving fish, smoking usually involves a preliminary curing step with salt (see page 26). As the preserving role of smoking has gradually diminished, so has the amount of salting and drying involved. Most smoked fish today is still a perishable product, although it does have a longer shelf life than fresh fish.

If time permits, after curing and rinsing, dry the fish briefly in the breeze or before a fan until a shiny skin forms. This smooth surface, or pellicle, takes the smoke flavor especially well, helps seal in the remaining moisture during the smoking process, and prevents the fats in the fish from rising to the surface and spoiling.

Alder is the traditional wood for smoking fish in the Pacific Northwest, but other hardwoods including maple, oak, hickory, and various fruitwoods (especially apple) will give fine results. Each wood gives a subtly different flavor, and matching fish and woods can be an interesting exercise, but don't worry too much about getting the perfect match. Just make sure that your wood is suitable for cooking with—fruitwood should come from unsprayed trees if possible, or else have all the bark removed.

browned. Serve immediately with plain rice and the dipping sauce.

NOTE If you have a jar of Japanese pickled ginger on hand, it makes a nice garnish, and the juice from the jar plus a little soy sauce makes an even easier dipping sauce.

Hot-Smoked Fish

Please see Smoking Allowed, above. The instructions here will work with any rich to moderately rich fish. Classic varieties include salmon, trout, char, sturgeon, mackerel, tuna, and sablefish, as well as Eastern "imports" like mullet and bluefish. You can also smoke split herring and sardines, or boned fillets of their bigger cousin shad. Skin-on fillets are the easiest to handle; if your fillets are already skinned, especially softer varieties like sablefish, lay them on a sheet of aluminum foil punctured in many places to allow the smoke to penetrate.

SERVES 4

1 to 1½ pounds fish fillet, with skin on

1½ teaspoons kosher salt

1½ teaspoons brown sugar

½ to 1 cup hardwood smoking chips (alder, apple, maple, hickory)

➤ Cut the fillets into serving-size pieces if desired. Place in a bowl and sprinkle salt and brown sugar generously on both sides. Cover and refrigerate 8 to 24 hours. Drain off the accumulated liquid and add cold water to cover. Let soak 15 minutes, changing the water twice. Drain and pat dry. For best results, set the fish aside on a wire rack in a breezy place to air-dry for 15 minutes or so before cooking.

➤ Build a small fire (10 to 12 briquets) at one edge of a covered grill and let it burn down until the charcoal is covered with gray ash. Meanwhile, soak ½ cup of the smoking chips in water. Cover the grill and adjust the vents on the top and bottom to maintain a temperature of about 200°F. Drain the chips and add them to the coals; replace the grill with one handle nearest the fire, to facilitate adding smoking chips. Lay the fillets on the opposite side from the fire, with the thickest parts nearest the heat. Cover and cook until the fish is opaque, 10 to 40 minutes depending on heat and thickness. Add some dry smoking chips to the fire after 15 minutes or so to maintain smoke and heat. Serve hot, warm, or cold.

VARIATION If you prefer, you can cure the fish with brine rather than dry salt. Place the fish in a shallow pan just large enough to hold it. Add cold water in 1-cup increments to cover, then sprinkle in salt in the proportion of 2 tablespoons per cup of water. Swirl the water to dissolve the salt and let stand 20 minutes. Drain, rinse with a couple of changes of fresh water, and dry and smoke as above.

➤ To add additional flavor to the fish, use a two-step brine as follows. After the first brining, cover the fish again with water, this time adding 1 tablespoon each salt and sugar per cup of water and adding a tablespoon of mixed pickling spices. Let soak 20 minutes, drain, rinse, and proceed with the drying and smoking steps.

Smoked Mackerel Pâté

I have had delicious spreads made from hot-smoked mackerel in England, and from smoked bluefish in Boston. Mackerel is a whole lot cheaper and easier to find around here than bluefish, so it's the natural choice.

SERVES 8 TO 10 AS AN APPETIZER

1 tablespoon butter
½ cup finely diced onion
1 ounce dry sherry
4 ounces smoked mackerel or other hot-smoked fish
1 ounce cream cheese (reduced fat is fine)
Unsalted crackers or thin toast triangles
Pickled Onion Rings, below, or capers, for garnish (optional)

➤ Melt the butter in a small skillet and cook the onion over low heat until golden. Add the sherry and cook until nearly dry. Let cool, then transfer to a food processor.

➤ Discard the skin and any pin bones from the fish and add it and the cream cheese to the processor. Process in pulses, stopping to scrape down the sides of the bowl, until the mixture is well blended but not reduced to a paste. Pack into a ramekin or small bowl and refrigerate. Serve as a spread with crackers or toast and your choice of garnish.

Pickled Onion Rings

➤ Slice a red onion very thinly crosswise. Place the rings in a bowl, cover with boiling water, and soak 5 minutes. Drain and rinse with cold water, then cover again with half water and half cider vinegar plus a large pinch of salt and a few peppercorns. Marinate overnight in the refrigerator. If you don't have red onions, a little juice from canned or pickled beets will add a nice pink color.

1. Early summer is prime time for Risotto with Peas and Salmon.

2. Later in summer, serve Basic Grilled Salmon with Summer Vegetable and Tomatillo Sauce.

3. A simple cure of salt, sugar, and dill turns raw salmon into velvety Gravlax.

4. Slow cooking with herbs in a covered grill yields fragrant Charcoal-Roasted Trout.

5. Ground porcini is the "spice" in Pan-Seared Halibut with Dried Mushroom Crust.

6. Soy-Braised Fish Steak, a Chinese treatment for various fish and cuts.

7. Once trendy, now a classic: Seared Tuna Salad with Wasabi Mayonnaise.

8. Dungeness crab two ways, in Fresh Rice-Paper Rolls with Crab and as Crab-Topped Cornmeal Blini with Guacamole.

9. Serve simmered crab in Provençal Crab Soup with Vermicelli, or as a separate course.

10. Lemon peel truly gives zest to Tagliarini with Shrimp in Lemon Cream Sauce.

11. Tender asparagus and peas highlight Spring Shrimp Soup with Saffron Aioli.

12. Warm Spinach Salad with crisp Pan-Fried Oysters.

13. Spaghetti with Oysters and Bacon is especially good made with Italian-style pancetta.

14. Barbecued Oysters my way—
no cocktail sauce, thank you!

15. Mussel Skillet Paella, a simplified version of the Spanish classic.

16. Tasty, tender squid and seasonal vegetables in Calamari and Fennel Salad.

Sierra en Escabeche

Most sources describe escabeche *as a dish of Spanish origin, although none of my Spanish cookbooks mentions it. Perhaps "Spanish" in this case refers to Spanish-speaking parts of the Americas; the dish is certainly popular in Latin America. It's probably best known around the Caribbean, where the name has evolved into such variations as* escovitch, caveach, *and* escabechi. *All of these sound better to me than the English translation,* soused fish.

As with any traditional dish that has traveled around the world, escabeche *has many local variations. The basic recipe here is a generic version with Mediterranean herbs. In Mexico, the seasonings are likely to include cumin and oregano. Caribbean island cooks usually use allspice, the sweet-spicy dried berry native to the region, and may include ginger or the very hot Scotch bonnet chiles. Where citrus fruits are grown, lime or lemon juice is often used in place of vinegar.*

Serve larger pieces as is, as a cold entree, or combine them with cold cooked vegetables and greens in a composed salad. For bite-size appetizers, cut the fish into small pieces after the initial frying and serve with toothpicks.

SERVES 3 TO 4 AS AN ENTREE, 6 AS AN APPETIZER

3 tablespoons olive oil

1 pound mackerel fillets or steaks

Salt and pepper, to taste

Flour

1 bay leaf

1 sprig fresh thyme

1 small dried red pepper (optional)

1 medium onion, thinly sliced

2 cloves garlic, sliced

⅔ cup good wine vinegar

⅓ cup water

➤ Heat the oil in a skillet over medium heat. Meanwhile, season the fish generously with salt and pepper and dredge in the flour, shaking off the excess. Add the fish to the skillet and cook until just done, about 10 minutes per inch of thickness. Transfer to a heatproof serving dish and add the bay leaf, thyme, and red pepper, if used.

➤ Add the onion and garlic to the skillet and cook over medium-low heat until the onion is soft and beginning to brown. Add the vinegar and water and bring to a boil. Pour the contents of the skillet over the fish and let stand at room temperature until cool. Taste for seasoning and adjust if necessary. Refrigerate if not serving the same day.

NOTE I take some liberty in calling this dish *sierra,* which properly speaking refers to a couple of mackerel species that are rare north of Mexico. Of course, if you can get king or Spanish mackerel, or one of the other fancy mackerel varieties, by all means use them; otherwise, this works with our local chub mackerel, or other rich, dark-meated fish.

VARIATION For a Caribbean flavor, omit the thyme and add 6 whole allspice berries, 6 peppercorns, and 2 slices fresh ginger to the vinegar mixture. Simmer until the seasonings begin to release their fragrance.

Baked Mackerel with Tomatoes and Salsa

A little fresh tomato and some bottled salsa make a quick and easy sauce for baked fish. This will also work with just about any mild-flavored fish fillets.

SERVES 4

1 clove garlic, peeled

1 tablespoon olive or neutral vegetable oil

1 large onion, sliced crosswise as thinly as possible

1½ pounds mackerel fillets, skin left on

Salt

1 large ripe tomato

3 to 4 tablespoons bottled tomato and chile salsa (mild, medium, or hot)

➤ Preheat the oven to 400°F. Rub a shallow glass baking dish with the garlic clove; add oil to coat the bottom. Scatter the onion in an even layer in the bottom of the dish. Season the fish lightly with salt and lay it in a single layer over the onion. Place the fish in alternate directions if necessary to fit the dish.

➤ Slice about ½ inch off the stem end of the tomato. Holding the cut side against the coarsest side of a box grater, grate the tomato over the fish, letting the pulp, juice, and seeds fall through the grater. Discard the skin. Top each fillet with a dollop of salsa, seal the pan with foil, and bake for 12 minutes.

Other Serving Suggestions: Mackerel

Try any of the small or medium-size mackerels in Sable-fish Kasuzuke, page 180; Catfish in Banana Leaf with Chipotle-Orange Marinade, page 206; or Fillets Baked in Red Onion Confit, page 125.

Sautéed Summer Fish with Sweet Corn and Red Pepper Sauce

This recipe will work with any of the "summer fish" described on pages 165 and 166, as well as California or Pacific halibut, lingcod, Hawaiian billfish, and the best grades of rockfish.

SERVES 4

1 large or 2 small red peppers, roasted, peeled, and seeded (reserve any juices)

1 to 1½ pounds firm fish fillet

Pinch of salt and pepper

3 tablespoons olive oil

1 clove garlic, lightly smashed

2 tablespoons flour

2 green onions, sliced

Kernels cut from 2 ears sweet corn (yellow or white)

⅓ cup unsalted chicken or fish stock

1 teaspoon sherry vinegar or red wine vinegar

½ teaspoon salt, or to taste

➤ Puree the red pepper and its juices in a blender or food processor, or chop it as finely as possible by hand. Have the fish cut into 4 equal portions, diagonally if possible. Season lightly with salt and pepper.

➤ Heat 1 tablespoon of the oil and the garlic in a heavy skillet over medium-high heat until the garlic begins to sizzle. Discard the garlic. Dust the fish with flour and shake off the excess. Sauté the fish pieces until almost done in the center and transfer to a warm platter or individual plates.

➤ Add the remaining oil to the pan and add the green onions and corn. Cook until the onions begin to soften, stir in the red pepper purée, and cook 1 minute. Add the stock and vinegar, bring to a boil, and reduce slightly. Add salt to taste and pour the sauce over the fish, pushing the corn to the edges of the fish.

Barracuda Steaks with Orange-Serrano Salsa

Barracuda season peaks in spring, before the local tomatoes come in, so navel oranges make a better choice for salsa. But this piquant relish can go on any firm, meaty, full-flavored fish, any time of year.

SERVES 4

1 large navel orange

1 small fresh chile (serrano or jalapeño), seeds and ribs removed, minced

1 green onion, minced

1 teaspoon minced fresh ginger

1½ teaspoons Chinese or Japanese sesame oil

½ teaspoon salt

1½ pounds barracuda steaks, about 1 inch thick

Freshly ground pepper, to taste

1 tablespoon (approximately) peanut or other vegetable oil

➤ Remove the orange peel and white pith with a knife. Slice the orange crosswise and cut it into fine dice. Combine with the chile, onion, ginger, sesame oil, and ¼ teaspoon salt. Let stand at least 30 minutes for the flavors to develop.

➤ Season the fish lightly with salt and pepper. Heat the oil in a skillet over medium-high heat. Add the fish and cook until nicely browned on the first side, 4 to 5 minutes. Turn and cook until done by the skewer test, another 4 to 5 minutes. Transfer to warmed plates and top each serving with the orange mixture.

VARIATION For boneless portions and an attractively crunchy presentation, buy a center cut of barracuda (be sure to have it scaled, or do it yourself), fillet it, cut it into sections, and cook it skin down in a hot skillet as in Herb-Crusted Striped Bass Fillets, page 214.

Grilled Yellowtail with Avocado-Lime Sauce

This sauce, a sort of thin guacamole without tomatoes or onion, goes well on any rich fish. A food processor, which is all wrong for making guacamole, is ideal for producing the smooth, almost liquid texture of this sauce.

SERVES 4

1 ripe avocado

1 small green chile, seeded and minced

Juice of 1 lime

Salt, to taste

4 pieces yellowtail fillet (about 1½ pounds)

Salt and pepper

Oil

Lime wedges (optional)

➤ Split the avocado, remove the pit, and scoop out the flesh. Combine with the chile, lime juice, and salt and mash with a fork to a smooth paste, or blend in a food processor. Taste for seasoning and adjust if necessary.

➤ Season the fillets lightly with salt and pepper; if they will be grilled, rub lightly with oil. Broil or grill until just the center of the thickest part feels raw when probed with a skewer. Serve with the avocado sauce on the side, with lime wedges if desired.

Mahi-Mahi with Avocado-Grapefruit Relish

This simple topping is suited to any plainly cooked fish. The nut oil, though not essential, goes nicely with the nutty flavor of the avocado. If you don't have any on hand, a plain vegetable oil or a mild olive oil will do.

SERVES 4

1 small ripe but firm avocado, peeled and diced

6 grapefruit sections, peeled and diced

2 tablespoons finely diced red or green onion

3 tablespoons finely diced red or yellow bell pepper

Pinch of salt

1½ teaspoons hazelnut or walnut oil

8 diagonal slices skinned mahi-mahi fillet, ½ inch thick (about 1½ pounds)

Salt and pepper, to taste

Juice of ½ lemon

Oil or vegetable cooking spray

➤ Combine the avocado, grapefruit, onion, bell pepper, salt, and oil; let stand at room temperature for at least 15 minutes. (For a milder onion flavor, soak the diced onion in a cup of cold water for 15 minutes before preparing the relish.)

➤ Season the fish lightly with salt, pepper, and lemon juice. Coat a nonstick skillet with a little oil or cooking spray and

sauté the fish over medium-high heat, 3 to 4 minutes per side. Serve topped with the relish.

Sablefish Kasuzuke

See Kasuzuke, below. How much of the marinade to leave on the fish is a matter of taste. Some cooks scrape most of it off, while others prefer a thick coating. In either case, the sugar in the marinade will cause it to cook to a deep caramel color and flavor.

SERVES 4

1 to 1½ pounds sablefish or salmon fillets, skin on if possible

1 tablespoon kosher salt (approximately)

½ cup (about ¼ pound) kasu

¼ cup granulated sugar

¼ cup sake

➤ Cut the fillets into serving-size pieces. Place them in a bowl and sprinkle salt generously on both sides. Let stand 15 minutes (no longer), then rinse the fish well. Pat dry. Combine the kasu, sugar, and sake and stir to a smooth consistency. Spread the marinade generously over the fish, seal tightly, and refrigerate 24 to 48 hours, or freeze for longer storage.

➤ Prepare a medium-hot charcoal fire in a covered grill or hibachi. Remove the fish pieces from the marinade, leaving a thin or thick layer of marinade on the fish as desired. Grill, starting bone side down and turning once, until the kasu caramelizes and the fish begins to flake at the thin end.

Kasuzuke

In the West, we use byproducts from alcoholic beverages in various ways, from feeding beer grains to cattle and poultry to refining cream of tartar from the crystals deposited in wine barrels. In Japan, a byproduct of brewing sake (rice wine) has been used for centuries to flavor and preserve fish.

Sake kasu, or sake lees, are the particles of rice and yeast that settle to the bottom of the wine after fermentation, which when drained and pressed form a dense, semisolid, and nutritious cake. By first salting pieces of fish and then storing them in a marinade of kasu and sugar, cooks found they could keep fish without refrigeration for weeks. Today, kasu marinades are not as important for preserving fish, but they remain popular for their flavor. *Kasuzuke* (kasu-marinated) fish has a unique and unforgettable taste—sweet and a little salty, slightly beery, and unmistakably Japanese.

Although Japanese-Americans have been using kasu marinades on West Coast fish for decades, it took a few adventurous Western chefs working in Seattle in the late 1980s (especially Tom Douglas) to bring the technique into the mainstream of Northwestern seafood cookery. By happy coincidence, the same period saw the opening of two of the largest sake breweries outside Japan in Northern California, and a third has opened since, making kasu more easily available in this country than ever.

Sablefish is the most popular kasu fish in the Pacific Northwest, but other rich fish can be prepared this way. Salmon is an obvious and popular choice, although some would argue that no marinade can improve on the salmon's own flavor. Mackerel is another suitably rich fish which has the advantage of being much cheaper.

The first step in making kasuzuke fish is to salt the fish, either whole fillets or smaller portions. The amount and duration of salting determines how long the fish may be stored, as in smoking and other curing methods; heavily salted fish will resist spoilage longer, but the high salt content makes it impossible to eat large portions of the fish. Most kasu cooks use a lighter hand with the salt, relying on refrigeration to retard spoilage. The kasu marinade on page 180 will preserve fresh fish for a few days, but for longer storage it's best to freeze it. Freezer-weight resealable plastic bags are ideal containers for one or more portions of fish through the salting and marinating stages, and whatever you will not cook right away can go into the freezer.

Kasu fish is admittedly not for everyone. If you want to try the taste of kasu fish before investing a couple of days in making your own, some Japanese markets also sell kasu-marinated fish in ready-to-cook portions.

Basic Broiled Sablefish

With its natural richness, sablefish does not need any additional fat in the sauce. Try a dipping sauce like Nuoc Cham (page 326), or one based on soy sauce (see page 173), or just a simple squeeze of lemon.

SERVES 4

1 to 1½ pounds sablefish fillet, preferably thick pieces

1 tablespoon kosher salt (approximately)

➤ Cut the fillets into serving-size pieces. Place in a bowl and sprinkle salt generously on both sides. Let stand 15 minutes (no longer), then rinse the fish well. Pat dry. For best results, set the fish aside on a wire rack in a breezy place to air-dry for 15 minutes or so before cooking.

➤ Set the broiler shelf so the fish will broil about 4 inches from the heat and line a broiling pan with foil. Place the fish on the foil skin side down and broil without turning until the flakes begin to spread and a skewer easily enters the thickest part of the fish, 6 to 10 minutes depending on thickness.

VARIATION For fish to be cooked the next day, replace half the salt with sugar, cover, and refrigerate overnight. On serving day, drain off the accumulated liquid and add cold water to cover. Let soak 15 minutes, changing the water twice. Drain and pat dry. Air-dry 15 to 30 minutes before cooking.

Soy-Glazed Sablefish

This is a home version of the roasted black cod fillet served in many Cantonese restaurants, using the broiler to simulate the heat of a commercial roasting oven. The sugar in this glaze will burn as it runs off the fish, so line the broiling pan with foil and do not try to save any of the juices from the pan.

SERVES 4

3 tablespoons dark (preferably Chinese) soy sauce

3 tablespoons Shaoxing (Chinese rice wine) or dry sherry

1 teaspoon brown sugar

6 thin slices fresh ginger

1 to 1½ pounds sablefish fillet, preferably in one piece

➤ In a small saucepan, combine the soy sauce, wine, and sugar. Crush the ginger slices lightly with the side of a knife blade and add to the pan. Bring to a boil, stirring to dissolve the sugar, and reduce by half. Discard the ginger.

➤ Set the broiler shelf so the fish will broil about 4 inches from the heat and line a broiling pan with foil. Place the fish on the foil skin side down and spoon the soy glaze over the top. Broil (without turning) until the flakes begin to spread and a skewer easily enters the thickest part of the fish, 6 to 10 minutes depending on thickness.

VARIATION If your market cuts sablefish into steaks, they will also work in this dish, although the presentation is not as classic. Turn the steaks once and reserve half the soy mixture for glazing the second side.

Wok-Smoked Sablefish

Chinese wok-smoking is a handy technique for home cooks, in which fish or other foods cook on a wire rack in a foil-lined wok. A mixture of dried tea leaves, uncooked rice, and sugar sprinkled in the bottom of the wok provides the aromatic smoke. Other ingredients may include chips of aromatic wood (especially camphor wood) and various spices.

SERVES 4

1 pound large sablefish fillets or steaks

1 teaspoon kosher salt

1 teaspoon sugar

2 tablespoons soy sauce

1 green onion, sliced and lightly crushed

3 slices fresh ginger, lightly crushed

¼ cup tea leaves

¼ cup raw rice

¼ cup brown sugar

1 tablespoon Sichuan peppercorns

2 star anise pods, broken into points

Oil

➤ Rinse the fish and pat dry. Place it in a shallow glass container. Combine the salt and sugar and sprinkle evenly all over the fish. Let stand 15 minutes (no longer), then rinse well and pat dry again. Return the fish to the dish and add the soy sauce, green onion, and ginger. Cover and marinate in the refrigerator 2 to 6 hours, turning once or twice. Remove from the refrigerator 15 minutes before cooking.

➤ Line a wok with heavy-duty aluminum foil, draping the excess over the edges. Line the lid with another piece of foil. Combine the tea, rice, sugar, and spices and scatter the mixture in the bottom of the wok. Lightly oil a round cake rack or other open support that will hold the fish and place it in the wok. Drain the fish and place it on the rack. Turn the heat to high under the wok. When the tea mixture begins to smoke, put on the lid and crimp the edges of the foil together to keep in all the smoke. Turn the heat down to medium, cook 8 minutes, turn off the heat, and let rest another 10 minutes.

➤ With the exhaust fan on, carefully separate the foil layers and open the wok to test for doneness. The fish is done when the tail end is beginning to flake. If it needs more cooking, close the wok and crimp the foil together again before returning it to the heat.

VARIATION This technique will also work with other rich fish, including salmon, large trout, and fish of the mackerel family.

Sardines Grilled in Grape Leaves

Fresh sardines are delicious grilled as plainly as possible and simply sprinkled with salt, but I also like them cooked with a grape leaf wrapping. The leaf both adds flavor and helps protect the skin from sticking to the grill or burning. It's a technique that will work with any similarly sized fish, from trout to small flatfish.

SERVES 4

8 fresh sardines (2½ to 3 pounds)
Salt and pepper
8 large bottled grape leaves
1 tablespoon olive oil
Lemon wedges

➤ Clean and scale the fish, leaving the heads on unless you prefer otherwise. Season the fish inside and out with salt and pepper. Lay out a grape leaf on the table, dull side up. Place a fish across the leaf near the stem end, tuck the stem inside the cavity of the fish, and roll the leaf tightly around the fish. Repeat with the remaining fish.

➤ Brush the wrapped fish with olive oil. Grill over a hot fire or broil 3 to 4 inches from the broiler until a skewer easily enters the thickest part, about 8 minutes. Serve with lemon wedges.

Pesce in Saor

This Venetian specialty, which probably dates at least to Roman times, is a close cousin to dishes known as escabeche *in other Romance languages (see page 177). Although the method originated as a way to preserve fish without refrigeration, it's probably safer to keep it in the refrigerator if marinating for longer than a few hours. The flavor is best if made a day, or at most two days, ahead of serving.*

Pesce in saor can be prepared with various kinds of fish; in Venice a holiday version is made with the delicious Adriatic sole, but the rest of the year it is more common with smaller, richer fish such as sardines or anchovies. A couple of anchovies or a single sardine, served with the traditional slice of polenta, makes a nice appetizer; a larger portion could be a lunch dish, perhaps preceded by a cup of vegetable soup.

SERVES 4 TO 8

2 tablespoons raisins
3 tablespoons olive oil
1 pound fresh anchovies or sardines, cleaned
Flour
Salt and pepper, to taste
1 large onion, thinly sliced
⅔ cup red wine vinegar
2 tablespoons pine nuts

➤ In a small bowl or measuring cup, soak the raisins in water to cover.

➤ Heat the oil in a large skillet over medium heat. Dredge the fish in flour, shaking off the excess, and add as many to the skillet as will fit in a single layer. Fry until the meat begins to peel back from the bones on the belly side, about 2 minutes per side. Remove to a shallow dish and season lightly with salt and pepper.

Add the onion to the skillet and cook over medium-low heat until translucent but not browned. Add the vinegar, bring to a boil, and reduce by about a third. Drain the raisins well and add them and the pine nuts to the fish dish. Pour the contents of the skillet over all. Let stand at least 2 hours at room temperature, or refrigerate for longer storage; remove the fish from the refrigerator at least 2 hours before serving to let it return to room temperature. Serve over slices of cooked and cooled polenta.

Baked Sardines with Gremolata

In Italy, especially along the Adriatic coast, fresh anchovies and other small rich fish such as sardines and mackerel are known as pesce azzurro. *The literal translation of the term is "blue fish," but it has no connection to the bluefish of our Atlantic coast; perhaps it refers to the slight bluish tint in the skin of the fish, or more loosely to the dark color of the meat. Anyway, here is a simple way to enjoy them, as well as fillets of larger mackerel.*

SERVES 4

8 fresh sardines (about 2½ to 3 pounds), headed and gutted

Olive oil

Salt and pepper

3 cloves garlic, peeled

A large handful Italian (flat-leaf) parsley leaves

Zest of ½ lemon, removed with a peeler and cut into thin strips

½ cup bread crumbs from stale bread (not dried crumbs)

Lemon wedges

Preheat the oven to 350°F. Bone the fish as directed on page 00, or fillet with a knife. Oil a shallow baking dish that will hold the fish in one layer. Lay the fish skin side down in the dish. Season with salt and pepper.

Make a gremolata by combining the garlic, parsley, and lemon zest on a cutting board or in a food processor and chopping finely. Sprinkle half the mixture over the fish, top with a thin layer of bread crumbs, and drizzle or spray with more olive oil. Bake for 15 minutes. Sprinkle with the remaining gremolata and serve with lemon wedges.

Potato Gratin with Little Fish

There are certain recipes in this book that I imagine only serious fish lovers will make; this is one of them. Like the soba recipe on page 186, it is a good way to use sardines or similar fish that you have found in the market one day and salted down for use later in the week.

SERVES 2 TO 4

1 pound fresh sardines, herring, or anchovies

Kosher salt

3 medium russet or white potatoes

3 tablespoons olive oil or melted butter

1 small onion, sliced as thin as possible

Freshly ground pepper

1 tablespoon chopped parsley

One to three days ahead of serving: Clean, bone, and salt the fish as directed on page 171. On the day you're going to cook them, rinse off the salt, then soak them in cold water for at least 1 hour, changing the water once or twice.

➤ Peel the potatoes and slice them about ⅛ inch thick. Store in a bowl of cold water if not assembling the dish right away.

➤ Preheat the oven to 350°F. Rub a shallow 6-cup baking dish with a little of the oil. Drain the potatoes and pat dry with a towel. Cover the bottom of the dish with a little less than half the potato slices, then all the sliced onion. Pat the fillets dry and arrange them on top in a single layer. Season the fish and potatoes with a little pepper (the fish should provide enough salt). Top with the remaining potatoes, overlapped in an attractive pattern. Drizzle the remaining oil over the potatoes, sprinkle with more pepper and parsley, and bake until the potatoes are just tender and lightly browned, about 50 minutes. Serve hot or warm.

TECHNIQUE NOTE A mandoline or a food processor with a 4mm disc makes short work of slicing the potatoes; the latter makes slices that are a little thicker than ideal, but they will still work. More important than thickness is uniformity, so they all cook in the same amount of time.

Soba with Sardine or Anchovy Sauce

Mixing Japanese buckwheat noodles (soba) with a northern Italian sauce may sound like a silly East-West experiment, but the result really works. One of the most famous regional pasta dishes of Venice is the spaghetti-shaped whole-wheat noodles called bigoli scuri, *sauced with slowly cooked onions and salt-preserved anchovies. According to Giuliano Bugialli in* Bugialli on Pasta, bigoli *used to be made with buckwheat flour, and still are in some homes, but no longer commercially. The whole-wheat spaghetti sold here in health food stores would seem the logical choice for this dish, but its flavor and texture strike me as boring. Soba, on the other hand, contribute a depth of flavor and a firm texture that make the dish work perfectly.*

In Venice, salt-preserved anchovies are the rule for this sauce; the Milanese version of the same dish oddly, given the inland location, adds fresh sardines. Having tried it both ways, I find what I like best is a compromise: fresh sardines briefly preserved with salt.

SERVES 3 TO 4 AS A MAIN DISH, 6 TO 8 AS A FIRST COURSE

1 pound fresh anchovies or sardines

Kosher salt

½ cup olive oil

1 large onion, sliced very thinly (about 2 cups sliced)

Freshly ground black pepper, to taste

12 ounces Japanese buckwheat noodles (soba)

2 tablespoons chopped parsley

➤ One to three days ahead of serving: Clean, bone, and salt the fish as directed on page 171. On the day you're going to cook them, rinse off the salt, then soak them in cold water for at least 1 hour.

➤ Heat ⅓ cup of oil in a deep skillet over medium-low heat and add the onion and pepper. Cover and cook slowly, stirring occasionally, until the onion nearly melts into a golden mass, 30 to 45 minutes. Toward the end of the cooking time, bring a pot of water to a boil to cook the pasta. Drain the fish and pat dry.

➤ When the onion is quite soft, remove the lid and turn the heat to medium to cook off the liquid and brown the onion a little more. Cook the pasta according to package directions. While the pasta cooks, add the fish to the pan with the onion and cook until opaque, breaking up the fillets with a fork. Stir in the chopped parsley, taste for seasoning, and correct if necessary. Moisten the onion mixture with ¼ cup or so of water from the pasta pot, then drain the cooked pasta and add it to the skillet. Toss to combine the pasta and sauce and transfer to a warm serving bowl; add a little more oil at the table if desired.

VARIATION If using fish bought the same day, simply clean and bone the fillets while the onion cooks; salt generously and let stand 5 minutes, then rinse and pat dry. Add 2 or 3 canned anchovy fillets, rinsed and mashed, to the skillet with the sardines for the traditional flavor.

Pickled Herring

When and if you find fresh herring, you might as well get a good-sized batch and pickle it. Here is a basic pickling technique, courtesy of the University of California Cooperative Extension. For "cut herring," cut each cleaned fish into 1-inch sections; cut off the dorsal fin from the center pieces. The bones will soften somewhat in the pickling process, and they are a good source of calcium. For "rollmops," fillet the fish and discard the bones.

MAKES 4 TO 5 PINTS

Preliminary Cure

5 pounds herring, cleaned and cut up or filleted

2 cups cold water

2 cups distilled or cider vinegar (5 grain strength)

1 cup kosher salt

➤ Place the fish in a glass or stainless steel bowl or a large glass jar. Combine the water, vinegar, and salt, stirring to dissolve the salt. Cover the fish with this mixture. If more is needed, prepare more in small batches, using 2 tablespoons salt to ¼ cup each water and vinegar. Keep track of the volume of liquid needed. Refrigerate 3 to 5 days (at least 4 days for large chunks).

➤ Drain the fish and soak 2 to 3 hours in plain water to remove the excess salt, changing the water 3 or 4 times. The fish are now ready for final pickling by either of the recipes below.

Spiced Herring Pack the herring back into the curing container or into pint glass jars, alternating layers of fish with sliced onions and carrots and ¼ cup mixed pickling spices. Prepare the same volume of liquid as used in the first stage, using 2 parts vinegar to 1 part water, and 2 teaspoons sugar per cup of combined liquid (no salt); cover the herring with this mixture. Refrigerate until ready to serve, at least 24 hours and up to 6 weeks.

Cream Herring Omit the sugar in the spiced herring recipe above, and replace up to half of the liquid with sour cream.

NOTE Because the fish is never cooked in the pickling process, the quantities of salt and vinegar in the first step are crucial to prevent spoilage and kill any parasites that might be in the flesh of the fish. Use a commercial vinegar of at least 5 grain strength (5 percent acetic acid) and pure kosher or pickling salt (see page 33).

Fried Smelt

I can't improve on the standard way of cooking smelt, which is to deep-fry them until crisp. You can use a three-step batter of flour, milk or egg, and bread crumbs if you like, but I prefer a simpler coating that lets me taste more of the fish. See page 25 for general notes about frying.

The traditional way to cook and eat smelt is whole, without any cleaning. If the thought of eating them head, innards, and all offends you, you can head and gut them (the frozen Eastern and Midwestern variety come that way). In either case, after frying, the bones and fins are pleasantly crunchy and quite edible. Of course, you can nibble around the bones, but then you are missing half the fun (not to mention a good source of calcium). Add some steamed asparagus and you have a meal you can eat entirely with your fingers.

SERVES 2

1 pound fresh or thawed smelt
1 cup milk
1 cup flour
1 teaspoon salt
Black or white pepper
Oil for deep-frying
Lemon wedges

➤ Head and gut fresh smelt if desired; otherwise just rinse and drain. Place the fish in a bowl with the milk. In another shallow bowl, combine the flour, salt, and pepper.

➤ Heat the frying oil to 375°F and preheat the oven to 200°F. Have absorbent paper ready for draining the fish (paper towels on top of newspaper works well). Pull a few fish out of the bottom of the bowl, let the excess milk drain off, and transfer to the flour. Keeping one hand dry, turn and toss the fish in the flour to coat; shake off the excess. Fry the fish 4 or 5 at a time until the coating begins to brown, 2 to 3 minutes. Drain well on paper, then transfer to the oven to keep warm. Serve on a plate or in a basket lined with a paper napkin, with a squeeze of lemon if desired.

Steamed Butterfish with Bean Threads

This recipe will also work with various whole fish or steaks from a larger fish. The bean threads, transparent noodles made from mung bean starch, soak up the juices from the fish and mushrooms, yet come out without tasting the least bit fishy. Look for them in Asian markets; they're sometimes labeled Chinese vermicelli. The packages containing several individual bundles of 2 ounces or less are most convenient.

SERVES 2 TO 3 AS A MAIN DISH, 4 WITH
OTHER DISHES

8 to 10 dried shiitake mushrooms

1 bundle (1½ to 2 ounces) bean threads

1½ tablespoons soy sauce

6 small butterfish (about 1½ pounds),
   cleaned or pan-dressed

⅓ cup chicken stock

2 green onions, shredded

1½ tablespoons shredded ginger

1 teaspoon Asian sesame oil

➤ In separate bowls, soak the mushrooms in warm water and the bean threads in hot water until soft, 20 to 30 minutes. Drain the mushrooms, discard the stems, and toss the caps with a teaspoon of soy sauce. Drain the bean threads and place them in a deep heat-proof plate or glass pie pan that will fit inside a wok or other steaming pot. Arrange the fish on top, tucking the mushroom caps in around them. Pour in the chicken stock, scatter the green onions and ginger on top of the fish, and sprinkle with the remaining soy sauce.

➤ Bring the water in the steamer to a rolling boil and place the plate on a rack an inch above the water. Cover and steam 20 minutes. Sprinkle with the sesame oil and serve from the steaming dish.

sturgeon, catfish, shad & other freshwater fish

With a few exceptions, commercial fishing in the West is a saltwater affair. We don't have many large bodies of fresh water like the Great Lakes or the lower Mississippi that can support commercial fishing. Instead, we get most of our freshwater fish from farms rather than from wild fisheries. This chapter focuses on aquaculture perennials such as catfish and carp as well as relative newcomers like tilapia, sturgeon, and striped bass.

Carp

Channel Catfish

Shad

Striped Bass

Tilapia

White Sturgeon

Sturgeon

White sturgeon, *Acipenser transmontanus*

With their thick skins studded with heavy bony plates and long, sharklike asymmetrical tails, the sturgeons look like what they are—a primitive family of fishes that has been around North America and Eurasia since the time of the dinosaurs. Unfortunately, many species of sturgeon worldwide are threatened with going the way of the dinosaurs, due to the usual combination of overfishing and habitat alteration. But at least one species is being saved from extinction by human intervention, giving hope for restoration of other sturgeon stocks around the world, and giving birth to a lucrative aquaculture industry in the process.

White sturgeon is the major West Coast member of the sturgeon family, and the largest freshwater fish in North America, reaching a maximum size of 20 feet and half a ton in weight. Along with the smaller green sturgeon (*A. medirostris*), it is native to larger rivers like the Sacramento, Columbia, and Fraser as well as estuaries up and down the coast. All of these rivers supported intensive commercial fisheries a century ago, but overfishing brought a collapse of most sturgeon populations by early in the twentieth century. Fortunately, with careful management, hatchery breeding, and minimum

and maximum fish size limits (the latter designed to protect fish of breeding age), several remaining sturgeon populations have stabilized and are on the increase.

Sacramento white sturgeon were nearly extinct when California banned commercial sturgeon fishing in 1917, but they have since rebounded. While there is still no commercial fishery, the Sacramento stocks now support a popular sport fishery (with a strong hook-and-release ethic) in the river's delta and San Francisco Bay. British Columbia allowed some commercial sturgeon fishing into the early 1990s, but in 1995 shut the fishery down and required live release of all fish caught in the sport fishery as well.

Columbia River stocks remained relatively strong through the twentieth century, although the dams built in the 1930s and '40s disrupted the migration routes of the sturgeon, isolating the populations in each stretch of river from each other. Today the Columbia still supports good-sized sport and tribal fisheries, as well as a limited non-Indian commercial fishery below Bonneville Dam.

Meanwhile, over the last two decades sturgeon aquaculture has gone from theoretical potential to an economically viable industry. Beginning in 1980, a group at the University of California at Davis, led by Russian émigré Serge Doroshov, developed a sturgeon hatchery system using wild fish from the Sacramento and Columbia Rivers for broodstock. Each spring, as breeding sturgeon headed for their spawning grounds, state authorities allowed a few fish to be captured and brought into hatcheries, where the eggs and milt could be combined (and the adult fish subsequently returned alive to the wild).

As the technology improved, at some point the hatcheries produced more juvenile fish than were needed to replenish the wild stocks, and the fingerlings were made available to nearby commercial fish farmers to grow out to market size in ponds and tanks. A breakthrough came in 1989, when the first captive-born female sturgeon reached sexual maturity and spawned successfully. In the wild, these slow-growing fish do not reach sexual maturity until 15 to 20 years of age; but on the farm, the ideal conditions and food supply result in much faster growth rates, and maturity comes much earlier, as young as 8 years. By the mid-'90s, as the first generation of hatchery-born sturgeon reached breeding age, farmers were finally able to close the production loop, producing eggs entirely from their own stock. Today, a handful of fish farms in the Sacramento area collectively produce more than a million pounds per year of white sturgeon, virtually all of it from captive-bred eggs. A few farmers have even begun large-scale production of the most valuable sturgeon product of all—caviar (see page 194).

So far, farm-raised sturgeon is not exactly a common retail item. But then, there are a number of other foods (baby lettuces and radicchio come to mind) that have made the crossover from specialty crops raised for a few demanding restaurant chefs to almost-mainstream foods sold in many supermarkets. Farmed sturgeon will never be as cheap as catfish, but it could come down to a price closer to that of farmed salmon.

Not all commercially available sturgeon is farmed. The commercial share of the Columbia River fishery produces 12,000 to 15,000 white sturgeon per year, mostly in fall and late winter. Some people prefer the fuller flavor of these wild fish, although they can sometimes have a muddy flavor (which can be minimized by skinning the fillets prior to cooking). To prevent sport-caught fish from sneaking into the market, all sturgeon must be labeled by the processor with their point of origin.

Like sharks, sturgeons have a fairly simple skeleton, much of which is semi-rigid cartilage rather than true bone, with no troublesome pin bones. Wholesale fish dealers typically ship large sturgeon in "blocks" (large chunks, with skin and bone) and smaller farmed fish as "bullets" (whole headed and gutted fish). A few markets simply cut the blocks or bullets crosswise into steaks, but this is not a good idea for two reasons: the skin is likely to shrink during cooking, distorting the steak badly, and as already mentioned, the skin can harbor a slightly muddy flavor. For best results, look for sturgeon that is sold already filleted and skinned.

With white, rather mild-tasting meat and a firm, fine-grained texture, sturgeon reminds me of veal. It takes well to grilling and sautéing, but cooks who blindly follow the "cook 10 minutes per inch" rule will find it quite underdone. In fact, a thick slice of sturgeon will take almost twice as long to cook as a similarly sized piece of salmon. For this reason, I often slice the fillet on the diagonal into slices or "scallops" no more than ¼ inch thick, and serve two or three of them per serving.

Caviar Farming

If you associate the world's finest caviar only with Russia and Iran, think again. Thanks to the work of a small handful of fish farmers, academics, and processors, a new world center of top-quality caviar production is emerging not around the Caspian Sea, but on the outskirts of Sacramento, California.

True caviar, unless identified with another species, means the salted roe (eggs) of sturgeon. Russian and Iranian caviar from Caspian sturgeon have always set the world standard of caviar quality, but political and environmental problems ranging from pollution of the Volga to poorly regulated fishing and the U.S. embargo on trade with Iran have made the supply of Caspian caviar unpredictable at best. Enter California caviar, two commercial brands of which made their debut in the mid-1990s. Like their counterparts in wine, olive oil, and many other food products, California caviar producers are staking their claim to a place among the best in the world.

In the biggest revolution in caviar production, California caviar is coming not from wild fish, but from aquaculture. With the development of reliable, captive-born breeding stock, farmers were able by the mid-1990s to devote some of the eggs to producing caviar rather than baby sturgeon. The first major release in 1996 consisted of less than 1,000 pounds of caviar between the state's two major brands, but both are building up their facilities and production to a combined target of 25,000 pounds per year by 2002.

Although the farming technology is new, the process of curing caviar is the same as with a wild fish. In the spring, the natural spawning season for white sturgeon on the farm as well as in the wild, farmers watch their eight-year-old, 50- to 80-pound females for signs of imminent spawning. The most promising fish undergo biopsy of the ovaries, and when they show eggs not quite ready for release—the perfect stage for caviar—they are scheduled for caviar production.

At a spotlessly clean processing facility, one fish at a time is removed alive from a holding tank, then stunned with a blow to the head and bled from the gills and tail. (While breeding fish can have their eggs removed by a kind of Caesarean section and survive to breed again, caviar requires killing the fish.) Slitting open the belly skin reveals a belly cavity at least three-quarters filled by the two large egg sacs, which average 11 percent of the body weight. The sacs are carefully removed and rinsed, and the body of the fish goes to another part of the plant for use as fresh fish; unlike some spawning fish, spawning sturgeon provide fine meat.

In the traditional hand method, the sacs are slit open and rubbed over a coarse screen, gently breaking the eggs loose from the surrounding membranes and letting them fall into a bowl below. After painstakingly removing any bits of membrane that get through the screen, the processor drains the eggs through a fine sieve, weighs them, and measures out salt to a precise percentage of the egg weight. Sprinkling on the salt by hand, she mixes steadily and fairly quickly by hand for a good 3 minutes. In addition to mixing in the salt evenly, she is feeling for the right texture, as the salt begins drawing moisture out of the eggs. Without this constant mixing, the eggs will become too sticky and clump unevenly. At this point they are caviar.

After a brief draining, the caviar moves on to another table, where it is packed into curing tins of about 1 pound. Packing is an art in itself; the packer heaps the caviar in a dome about an inch above the rim of the tin, and carefully aligning the seams of the tin and the lid, slides the lid onto the tin, then leans on the top to press it until liquid oozes out along the seam. This process expels all the air and any excess salty liquid, which makes all the difference in the quality and shelf life of the finished product.

Once in the tins, the caviar goes into a refrigerator for the initial curing period of several weeks. The processors inspect the tins regularly, inverting them periodically to distribute the salt evenly, and tapping on the tops to make sure no air remains inside. Over the next couple of weeks, the flavor and texture of the caviar will improve as the salt reaches equilibrium inside the eggs and out. The best-quality caviar contains as little salt as necessary to preserve the eggs without overwhelming their flavor; around 3.2 percent, the premium grade known in Russian as *malossol* ("little salt"), is enough to allow storage at 28° to 30°F without freezing. Together, the salt and cold temperature arrest the growth of spoilage bacteria, which cannot be otherwise controlled since the caviar is never cooked.

By about two weeks after harvest, the caviar is ready to eat. With proper storage, kept well chilled and unopened, the caviar can stay fresh for up to two years, but age will not improve it, and experienced tasters will find it at its freshest in the first six months or so.

While I can't claim to be a caviar expert, the California caviar I have sampled seemed very similar to Caspian osetra, to which it also compares in price. Color and size of white sturgeon eggs apparently vary somewhat, but generally match the medium to dark gray color range typical of osetra, with medium-size "berries" that are pleasantly tender but not too soft. The similarity is not surprising, as white sturgeon is a close cousin of the Eurasian species known in Russian as *osetr* (*Acipenser sturio*), source of osetra. Beluga, the Caspian caviar with the highest value, comes from a sturgeon of another genus not represented in North America.

Catfish

Channel catfish, *Ictalurus punctatus*

A lot of people have a prejudice against "bottom fish." Anything that swims and feeds near the bottom of the sea, river, stream, or lake is perceived as less "clean" than other fish that swim higher in the water. Of course this is nonsense; otherwise how could sole, flounder, and halibut—all magnificently adapted for life on the sea floor—have such sweet, mild-tasting flesh? Still, the bottom-fish stigma persists, and catfish is one its chief victims. It's true catfish (in the wild, at least) feed on the bottom; what is more, they can survive in marginal water conditions, and those from muddy waters tend to have a muddy flavor.

However, when raised in clean water with a controlled food supply, catfish can be downright delicate in flavor. Thanks in part to the development of floating feed pellets, which draw the fish to the surface to feed rather than having them forage on the bottom, modern farmed catfish (almost all of it one species, the channel catfish) has uniformly tender, white, moderately rich, mild-tasting meat that will surprise those who think of this fish as tasting muddy. Catfish have also turned out to be very efficient converters of feed into meat, even better than poultry. Together, these qualities have made pond-raised catfish one of the major aquaculture success stories of the late twentieth century. Today, American catfish farmers produce hundreds of millions of pounds per year of fresh and frozen catfish, primarily in the Mississippi Delta and other parts of the South and to a lesser extent in California.

Catfish is available live and as fillets, pan-dressed skinless whole fish, and dressed fish. Most of the California crop is shipped alive, primarily to Asian markets; even in our area, fillets and pan-dressed fish are more likely to come from one of the big southern processors. Even in its minimally treated form, farmed catfish is never likely to be cheap. Despite its rapid growth and feed conversion rates, processing remains labor-intensive and keeps the price from going below a certain point.

Live catfish weigh anywhere from a pound on up, with most falling in the range of 1 to 3 pounds. A whole fish will yield about 50 percent meat, so allow ½ to 1 pound per person, according to taste and the rest of the menu. Killing and cleaning is usually included in the price. Skinning the fish is another matter; catfish skin is thin but tough and firmly attached, and removing it requires very strong fingers or a pair of pliers. If they will do it at all, most markets charge extra for skinning, around a dollar per fish.

Fortunately, it is not necessary to skin catfish for many preparations. The meat separates from the skin fairly easily after cooking, especially if you score the sides of the fish before cooking (see Steamed Catfish with Young Ginger, page 205). In the crosscut steaks used in many Asian soups and stews, both the skin and the bones help the piece of fish keep its shape. Fillets, on the other hand, should be skinned or they will curl up in cooking as the skin shrinks. If skinless fillets are what you want, you might as well buy them that way.

Tilapia

Tilapia, *Oreochromis* spp., *Tilapia* spp., and hybrids

Inspired by the success of trout, catfish, shrimp, and salmon, aquaculturists all over the world continue to search for the Next Big Thing. The fish most ready to move from the fringes to being a high-volume staple of the fresh fish market appears to be tilapia.

A small perchlike fish native to Africa, tilapia has become one of the most widely cultured fish in the world. Because it requires warm water, outdoor tilapia culture is limited to tropical and subtropical areas, but some farmers in colder areas (including many parts of the United States) are growing fish in solar greenhouses or with geothermally heated water.

Tilapia are algae feeders by nature and can survive in marginal conditions, but as with any other fish, water and feed affect the quality of the meat. When raised in the cleanest possible water on controlled feed, tilapia tastes mild, sweet, and a little nutty. Modern tilapia farms, using hybrid fish and a grain-based diet, have turned tilapia into a consistent, high-quality, versatile product. Farmed tilapia has firm, white,

lean meat with a texture somewhere between that of sole and rockfish. The compactly shaped fillets can be cooked by any cooking methods and recipes suitable for sole, flounder, snapper, or orange roughy, and most cooking methods, including steaming Asian style, braising, and baking, work with whole fish.

Tilapia are available live, round, dressed, and as fillets. Whole fish range from under a pound to 2 pounds each. Fillets are generally taken from more uniformly sized fish and run anywhere from 2 ounces on up, with 4 to 6 ounces the most popular size range.

Depending on the species or hybrid, tilapia skin may be gray (actually a fine pattern of black and white), white with orange markings, or mostly red-orange. More important than color, however, is knowing where and how the fish was grown. Fillets sold in supermarkets are most likely to come from high-quality suppliers, either here or in Latin America. One producer in Costa Rica grows two different color forms, one in fresh water and the other in saltwater shrimp ponds, but once filleted they look and taste nearly identical. When it comes to whole tilapia, the source becomes critical. The Chinese markets in my area typically sell live California-grown tilapia (usually the black and white *nilotica* strain) for about three times the price of similar-looking whole tilapia sold on ice, but the difference in flavor is more than worth the difference in price. The cheaper fish, which come frozen from Taiwan, have to my taste a mossy-muddy flavor that no amount of sauce will mask.

When it first appeared, tilapia was a name unknown to most people, and retailers and restaurateurs have tried several aliases including "sunshine bass," "cherry snapper," "sunfish," and "St. Peter's fish." (The last name refers to the Biblical miracle of the loaves and fishes; tilapia are found in the Sea of Galilee, and may have been the fish caught by St. Peter.) However, all these names are frowned upon (rightly) by the Food and Drug Administration as trading on the reputations of other fish, and FDA rules require that tilapia be sold under its own name.

"Striped" (Hybrid) Bass

Hybrid bass, *Morone chrysops* x *saxatilis*

Many aquacultured fish, like Atlantic salmon and channel catfish, are essentially the same species as their wild counterparts. Broodstock may be selected for particular traits, and the gene pool in the captive stock is usually smaller, but the fish are more or less indistinguishable from those in the wild. In some cases, however, the wild fish don't domesticate easily, and farmers have better luck with a hybrid of two species—a sort of swimming mule. One of these is hybrid bass, also known as hybrid striped bass, "sunshine bass," and a few other names.

Striped bass (*Morone saxatilis*) is an anadromous fish native to the Atlantic coast and its rivers that became well established on the West Coast after its introduction a century ago. It

has also been introduced into many inland waters around the country, where it frequently hybridizes with its freshwater cousin the white bass (*M. chrysops*). These hybrid bass, while sterile, are popular as game fish, and hatcheries in several southeastern states have been raising them for years to stock lakes and reservoirs.

In the 1980s, when wild striped bass stocks on the East Coast were at an all-time low (commercial fishing for stripers has never been allowed on the West Coast), a few farmers also began raising hybrid bass for the fresh seafood market. Some of the early efforts produced fish with a slight mossy or muddy flavor, but the Southern California farm that now dominates the market seems to have solved whatever was the problem, and their fish come out with a clean, pleasant flavor. Hybrid bass bear the same flavor relationship to wild stripers as farmed trout do to wild trout—the farmed fish is definitely not as flavorful, but is a fine fish in its own right.

Hybrid bass are sold alive in Southern California, but live fish are not allowed north of the Tehachapis, to prevent their escape into the San Joaquin–Sacramento River system. (Even sterile fish might compete with other fish for food and habitat, and there's always the chance that some individuals may turn out to be fertile.) Elsewhere they are sold round or dressed. Typical size is 12 to 16 inches and 1½ to 2 pounds. They look similar to small stripers, with the distinctive dark stripes running the length of the silvery sides. Experts can tell them apart from pure striped bass of a similar size by the broken, rather than continuous, stripes, as well as by the shape, which is thicker and stockier than a young striper of the same weight.

A typical 1½-pound hybrid bass will serve two if steamed whole, Chinese style, or baked with a stuffing. If you fillet it, expect to get two fillets of 5 to 7 ounces each, a nice single-serving size.

Shad

Shad, *Alosa sapidissima*

During the couple of months in late spring and early summer when salmon and halibut seasons are in full swing, it's easy to overlook other seasonal pleasures of the fish market. Especially fish with a reputation of being difficult to handle, like shad.

A large Atlantic member of the herring family introduced to the Pacific Coast in the 1870s, shad is an anadromous fish, caught mainly when it migrates into rivers to spawn. Although it's strictly a sport fish in most of the West, there is a commercial fishery on the Columbia River, peaking in June, and some East Coast shad typically come in before that, mainly appearing in Chinese markets in my area. Shad typically run 2 to 3 pounds, and up to a foot and a half in length, with a smallish head, large silvery scales, and a reddish-gold tint around the head and gills. Most of the fish in our market are either females that have already been stripped of their more valuable roe, or else "buck" (male) shad. As famous and

valuable as shad roe is, the meat of this fish remains relatively unknown, and therefore relatively cheap. That's good news for lovers of full-flavored fish, and anyone with a fondness for its smaller cousins herring and sardines should find shad an equally delicious choice. Once they get past the bones, that is.

The biggest barrier to the popularity of shad has to be its unique bone structure. Where most fish have a single row of pin bones running partway down the middle of the fillet, shad has three rows, and they curve and branch in a way that puts a potential mouthful of bones in almost every bite.

On the East Coast, where shad is more plentiful and better known than it is here, fish markets that sell a lot of shad fillets generally have experienced fish cutters who bone hundreds of fillets every season, and have the process down to a few minutes' work. Around here, you'll probably have to do it yourself. If you are comfortable with the basic procedure of filleting fish, and are ready for a stretch, I invite you to try your hand at boning shad (see sidebar).

Shad is also quite reasonably priced. At less than two dollars per pound, a typical 3-pound fish will serve five to six diners for about a dollar a serving. Try matching that with most other fish! If you are still reluctant to deal with boning or grinding, there is another way to enjoy shad: very long and slow cooking renders the smaller bones soft enough to eat (see page 214), providing plenty of calcium as a nutritional bonus.

Boning Shad

The trick to boning a shad fillet is to make a series of long cuts that separate each section of the fillet from the nearby row of bones, then lift out the bones, leaving most of the meat attached to the skin. It's not brain surgery, but it takes at least as much care and attention as, say, boning quail.

For four generous servings, select two shad of about 2 pounds each. Have the fishmonger scale and clean the fish, and fillet them if they offer to do so. At home, you will need a sharp boning knife and a cutting board big enough to hold one fillet at a time, but small enough to rotate the board as necessary (rather than trying to move the partially boned fillet). Give yourself the better part of an hour if this is the first time; be prepared to ignore the phone for now, turn on the radio or a favorite CD, and pour yourself a cup of coffee or a glass of wine if that will help.

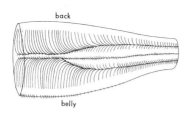

Fillet the fish if it hasn't already been done, leaving the skin on. Lay one fillet skin side down on the board, and keep the remaining fillets in the refrigerator. Using the bone diagram as your guide, locate the various rows of bones by running a fingertip along the fillet toward the tail end. Once you locate a row, make a shallow cut just to one side of the bones, feeling for bones with the tip of the knife as you go. When the bones spread out diagonally, let the knife slide over the bones, cutting at an angle and gently peeling the meat back as you go. When you get to the tips of the bones, stop cutting, leaving the edge of the fillet attached to the skin. Move to the other side of the row and do the same thing. This will expose a triangular strip of darker flesh and forked bones attached to the skin; slide the knife under one end of this strip to loosen it, then grasp and pull the bones away. Continue hunting for strips of bones and repeat the process. You may think you are cutting away a lot of meat, but that's all right.

You will probably mangle the first fillet, and get a little better on the following fillets. As you finish each fillet, fold the strips of meat back into their original positions, and you should have something that looks like a fillet again. Congratulations! Boned shad fillets are delicious simply broiled, with an initial dusting of Chesapeake or Creole seafood seasoning or plain salt and pepper, or hot-smoked in a covered grill or smoker (preferably on a sheet of aluminum foil to keep them intact), or sautéed in bacon fat.

If you make a hopeless mess of the fish, or run out of patience with the boning process, shad makes excellent fish-ball material (see page 218).

Carp

Common carp, *Cyprinus carpio*
Silver carp, *Hypophthalmichthys molitrix*

Carp has been an important food fish in China since Neolithic times, and has been cultivated for around 2,500 years. Several species of these adaptable herbivorous fish can survive in small ponds, rice paddies, and other enclosures, growing to edible size on the algae in the water. The carps remain the most important family of aquacultured fish in Asia, and both they and the technology of fish farming have spread around the world.

Carp is greatly esteemed in central and eastern European cooking, and it is essential in many traditional Jewish dishes, the best known of which is gefilte fish. Introduced into North America in the nineteenth century, carp quickly escaped into the wild and are especially common in the Mississippi River system. They are also farmed, mainly for the Asian market.

Common carp of anywhere from 2 to 8 pounds can be found in Chinese fish markets, especially those with live-fish tanks, and also as steaks and other cut-up pieces. They are easily identified by their very large scales, small downturned mouths, and golden tint. Increasingly common in live tanks these days are the smaller, duller-colored silver carp, which

command a higher price more like that of live tilapia and catfish.

Carp has fine-textured white meat with a mild flavor. It can be cooked by most methods, including baking, poaching, and deep-frying. A whole carp is the traditional choice for frying and coating with a sweet and sour sauce, but because carp contains a lot of small Y-shaped pin bones, Chinese restaurants tend to steer Western customers toward rockfish or other less bony varieties. While the bones are not quite as troublesome as those of shad, I find carp best in dishes where the meat is ground or chopped, to be formed into balls or cakes.

Miscellaneous Freshwater Fish

Sheepshead, *Aplodinotus grunniens*
Bigmouth buffalo, *Ictiobus cyprinellus*
White perch, *Morone americana*
Lake Victoria perch, *Lates niloticus*

A couple of wild freshwater fish from the Mississippi River system and Great Lakes show up regularly in Chinese markets and in those catering to people from the American South. The best of these to my taste is a freshwater drum also known as **SHEEPSHEAD,** but most commonly sold under the Louisiana name gaspergou. It's a rather nondescript fish of 2 to 3 pounds with a silvery color, large scales, and a humped back sloping down to a small head with a blunt nose. A relative of both white seabass and Gulf redfish, it produces fillets with a pleasant flavor, moderate fat content, and a texture that is ideal for grilling or simmering in a fish stew. **BIGMOUTH BUFFALO,** a large fish that is usually sold split lengthwise, has fairly rich white meat with an agreeable taste, as long as you skin it before cooking. **WHITE PERCH,** a small relative of striped bass, is a good fish for pan-frying.

One of the more interesting freshwater fish options comes all the way from Africa. **LAKE VICTORIA PERCH** is a good-sized predatory fish accidentally introduced into Africa's largest lake, where it has upset the ecological balance and threatens many smaller species. Several nations bordering the lake have large-scale fisheries that export high-quality perch fillets about the size of rockfish fillets. This fish has a fine, firm texture, a moderate fat content, and a mild flavor, and has become quite popular in some parts of the United States. So far it has been slow to catch on in the West, but we may see more of it in the future.

Sautéed Sturgeon Grenobloise

This recipe is based on a classic French treatment of trout, a butter sauce with lemon and capers.

SERVES 4

1 pound sturgeon fillet, skinned
Oil or clarified butter
3 tablespoons butter
Juice of 1 lemon
4 teaspoons capers
Pinch of white pepper

➤ Slice the fillet diagonally into thin ($\frac{1}{4}$-inch) slices (see note). Coat a large skillet lightly with oil or butter and preheat it over medium-high heat. Add the sturgeon slices and sauté 3 minutes per side, or until lightly browned. Remove to a serving platter or individual plates.

➤ Let the pan cool slightly, then add the butter, lemon juice, capers, and pepper. Brown the butter slightly and pour the sauce over the fish.

NOTE To cut fillets or thick steaks of meaty fish like sturgeon and shark into scaloppine, try a Japanese trick, using chopsticks as a cutting guide. You will need a pair of Chinese-style bamboo chopsticks, the kind with square handles and little or no taper, sold in bundles in Chinese stores. Lay the chopsticks on the cutting board just far enough apart to set the boneless, skinless meat in between. Press down lightly on the steak with the palm of one hand to hold it in place, and with your slimmest, sharpest knife riding on top of the chopsticks, slice horizontally. Cut as smoothly as possible, ideally with one or two long, drawing cuts, to get a smooth surface. Lift out the slice and repeat. The last slice seldom comes out exactly the same thickness as the others, so remember to give it a few seconds more or less in the pan.

Stir-Fried Sturgeon with Black Bean Sauce

With its dense meat, sturgeon is one of the few fish that will stand up to Chinese-style stir-frying without falling apart. Like some other stir-fried dishes in this book, this recipe actually calls for deep-frying the sturgeon cubes, then building up the sauce in the same pan after the oil is removed. After it has had a chance to cool, the frying oil can be filtered and reused for frying.

SERVES 4 WITH OTHER DISHES

¼ cup cornstarch

½ teaspoon baking powder

3 tablespoons water

12 ounces sturgeon fillet, in ½-inch cubes

¼ teaspoon sugar

Pinch of salt

¼ cup chicken stock

Peanut or corn oil

1½ tablespoons minced ginger

1 teaspoon minced garlic

⅓ cup sliced green onions

½ cup diced mild green or red chiles

1½ tablespoons Chinese fermented black beans, roughly chopped

➤ Combine all but ½ teaspoon of the cornstarch with the baking powder and water and stir just until dissolved. Toss the sturgeon cubes in this batter. Dissolve the remaining ½ teaspoon of cornstarch, the sugar, and a pinch of salt in the chicken stock.

➤ Fill a wok or deep skillet with oil to a depth of 1 inch and heat over high heat until a drop of batter sizzles immediately on contact. Reduce the heat to medium and fry the fish cubes a few at a time until lightly browned. Drain on paper towels.

➤ Carefully ladle or pour the oil into another pot to cool. (The oil that clings to the wok will be enough to make the sauce.) Return the wok to the heat and add the ginger, garlic, green onions, chiles, and black beans. Stir-fry until fragrant but not browned. Add the stock mixture, bring to a boil, and cook until glossy and slightly thickened. Add the fish cubes and toss to coat with the sauce. Transfer to a serving platter.

TECHNIQUE NOTE Although the sturgeon cubes can be stir-fried without any coating, I prefer the method given here. The batter adds a slight crunchiness, but more important, it provides a better surface for the sauce to cling to. If you want to make this dish with the absolutely fewest added calories, skip the battering step, start with a tablespoon or two of oil in the pan, and stir-fry the fish cubes along with the ginger and garlic. When the fish begins to turn opaque, add the sauce ingredients.

VARIATION In place of or in addition to the chiles, add bite-size squares of red, yellow, or green bell pepper to the wok along with the aromatic ingredients.

Tomatoes make a nice flavor addition to a black bean sauce (see the lobster dish on page 249). Sprinkle 1½ cups peeled, seeded, and chopped tomatoes with ¼ teaspoon sugar and a pinch of salt and set aside in a bowl while you prepare the other ingredients; add them to the wok after the black bean mixture.

Broiled Sturgeon "Pasta e Fagioli"

Pasta e fagioli *is Italian for pasta and beans. This one-dish entree demonstrates how those traditional nutrition and flavor partners can help make a modest portion of fish go farther. This recipe is also good with steaks or fillets of other meaty fish such as halibut, swordfish, albacore, lingcod, fancy rockfish—for that matter, just about any lean to moderately rich fish.*

Although this is a one-dish presentation, it does involve several components cooked in different pots and pans and combined at the last minute. However, the sauce, pasta, and beans can all be prepared ahead of time, leaving only the spinach to be sautéed while the fish is broiling.

SERVES 4

2 small cloves garlic

⅓ pound small shell pasta

½ cup chicken stock

1 medium red bell pepper, roasted and peeled

1 tablespoon sherry vinegar

2 tablespoons olive oil

Salt and freshly ground pepper, to taste

1 cup cooked small white beans, with their broth

1 pound sturgeon fillet, cut into 4 equal portions

Leaves from a large (1-pound) bunch spinach or chard, washed and chopped or shredded

➤ Bring a pot of salted water to a boil for the pasta. Blanch the garlic in the pasta water for 1 minute; retrieve and peel. Cook the pasta according to package directions, drain, and rinse with cool water to stop the cooking. Warm the chicken stock (the pasta pot is fine for this purpose).

➤ Seed the pepper, reserving any juices. Combine in a blender with the garlic, vinegar, 1 tablespoon of the oil, and half the warm stock. Blend to a smooth purée, season to taste (canned stock will likely supply enough salt), and keep warm. Add the beans and pasta to the pot with the remaining stock and keep barely warm.

➤ Preheat the broiler with the broiling rack set 3 to 4 inches from the heat. Set a wok or your largest skillet over low heat to preheat. Season the fish lightly with salt and pepper and broil, starting skin side up and turning once, until done by the skewer test (see page 17).

➤ While the fish cooks, turn the heat under the wok to high and sauté the spinach in the remaining oil until wilted. Add the beans, pasta, and stock and cook until heated through. Taste for seasoning and correct if necessary. Divide the mixture among 4 warm plates, place the cooked fish on top, and drizzle the red pepper sauce over all.

Basic Buttermilk Fried Catfish

Although farmed catfish are milder in taste than wild cat-fish, some cooks still prefer to soak the fillets in buttermilk before cooking to remove any hint of a muddy flavor.

SERVES 4

1 to 1½ pounds catfish fillet, or 4 small
    pan-dressed catfish
Salt and pepper
1 cup buttermilk
1 cup fine bread crumbs or cornmeal
Oil for deep-frying or pan-frying
Lemon wedges

➤ Season the fish lightly with salt and pepper. Place it in a shallow glass or stainless steel dish, add the buttermilk, and let stand 15 minutes. Lift out the pieces one at a time, drain slightly, and roll in the crumbs.

TO PAN-FRY Coat a skillet generously with peanut or other vegetable oil and heat until a bit of the crumb coating sizzles instantly on contact. Add the fish and cook until golden brown, 2 to 4 minutes per side for fillets and 3 to 5 minutes for dressed fish.

TO DEEP-FRY Fill a deep pan with oil to a depth of at least 1 inch and heat to 375°F on a frying thermometer (for fillets). Fish on the bone should cook more slowly, at 350° to 360°F. Cook until golden brown, about 4 minutes for fillets, 6 to 7 minutes for whole fish. Serve with lemon wedges.

Steamed Catfish with Young Ginger

Fish and ginger is a classic Chinese combination; the beautiful thin-skinned "young" ginger that appears in the market in early summer is especially nice for this purpose.

SERVES 4 TO 6 WITH OTHER DISHES

1 catfish, 1½ to 3 pounds
2 tablespoons soy sauce
2 tablespoons Chinese rice wine or dry sherry
⅛ cup thinly sliced young ginger
3 green onions, cut into 2-inch lengths
    and shredded
1 teaspoon Chinese or Japanese sesame oil

➤ Have the fish cleaned, with the head left on. Open up the cavity and with the tip of a knife cut open the reddish strips lying along the backbone. Rinse the cavity well. Score the sides of the fish with diagonal slashes almost to the bone every inch or so.

➤ Set up a steaming pan with a way of holding the fish on a plate (see page 24) and bring the water to a rolling boil. Place the fish belly side down on a large heatproof plate that will fit inside the steamer, bending the tail if necessary to fit. Sprinkle the fish with the soy sauce and wine and scatter the ginger and green onions over the top.

➤ Lift the steamer lid carefully away from you to avoid steam burns and place the plate on the rack. Cover and steam 15 minutes, or until a skewer easily enters the thickest part of the meat. Sprinkle the fish with the sesame oil and serve.

Catfish in Banana Leaf with Chipotle-Orange Marinade

Many traditional dishes from Yucatán to Malaysia use rectangles of banana leaf the way we use aluminum foil, as a wrapper for cooking. Like foil, the banana leaf wrapping traps the cooking juices, preserving the moisture and aroma of the foods inside; but unlike foil, banana leaves add a subtle flavor of their own. Here, squares of banana leaf enclose individual portions of catfish in a marinade spiked with chipotle (smoked jalapeño) chiles. The packets can be cooked in the oven or, in true tropical style, over an outdoor fire.

A single fish will make four modest portions, to be served Asian style with an assortment of other dishes. If you prefer a larger serving, use one small catfish per person and cook them whole.

SERVES 4 ASIAN STYLE, WITH OTHER DISHES

1 large orange

1 small onion

3 cloves garlic, minced

2 canned chipotle chiles, seeded and finely chopped

1 tablespoon peanut or other vegetable oil

1 tablespoon rice or cider vinegar

¾ teaspoon salt

½ teaspoon sugar

1 pan-dressed catfish, 1¼ to 1½ pounds

4 (10-inch) squares banana leaf, without any tears (see note)

➤ Grate the zest of the orange into a medium bowl. Cut off the top and bottom of the orange, then cut away the peel and all the white pith. Slice the orange, remove any seeds, and set the slices aside. Squeeze any juice you can from the peel sections into the bowl. Peel the onion and cut half of it into thin rings; set aside. Mince the rest of the onion and add it to the bowl with the garlic, chipotles, oil, vinegar, salt, and sugar.

➤ With a Chinese cleaver or other heavy knife, chop the fish crosswise into steaks about an inch thick; leave the last 2-inch section near the tail whole. Rinse the fish pieces, pat dry, and toss in the marinade; let stand 15 minutes.

➤ Preheat the oven to 450°F, or prepare a medium-hot fire in a covered grill. Lay a few onion slices in the middle of each banana-leaf square, lay 2 fish steaks on top of the onions, and top with orange slices. Fold the edges together over the fish (along, not across, the ribs of the leaf). Fold the ends of the leaf toward the middle and pin shut with a toothpick or short bamboo skewer. Bake seam side up on a foil-lined sheet pan until a thin skewer poked through the leaf easily enters the thickest part of the fish, about 12 minutes. Serve in the leaf packets, with rice on the side.

NOTE Look for frozen banana leaves in Vietnamese, Filipino, or other Southeast Asian groceries. Fresh banana leaves from a florist (or from a backyard tree, if you live in a warm climate) are another option, but be sure they have not been sprayed. If using fresh leaves, cut each side away from the large central rib, and blanch or lightly grill the leaves until pliable. If you can't get any form of banana leaves, the dish will taste almost as good baked or grilled in foil, or baked *en papillote* (see page 22).

Marinated Catfish with Wilted Spinach

In addition to plain pan-dressed fish and fillets, catfish processors offer various "value-added" products, including already-marinated fillets, which come in such "flavors" as lemon pepper, garlic butter, Cajun, "blackened," and barbecued. They are convenient, but you pay a lot for some salt and spices, so I have included a recipe for a simple do-it-yourself marinade.

This proportion of fish to spinach makes a fish-with-vegetable dish. If you prefer a lighter dish, use just one fish fillet, cut the cooked fish into narrow crosswise strips, arrange them artfully on top of the spinach, and call it a warm salad.

SERVES 2

2 tablespoons vegetable oil

2 lemon-pepper or other marinated catfish fillets (about 6 ounces each)

Salt

1 tablespoon lemon juice

Leaves and tender stems from ½ pound fresh spinach, washed and dried

½ cup sliced red onion

➤ Heat 1 tablespoon of the oil in a nonstick skillet over medium-high heat. Add the fish fillets and cook until a skewer or toothpick easily enters the thickest part and the tail end begins to flake, about 3 minutes per side. Meanwhile, dissolve a pinch of salt in the lemon juice in a large bowl, add the spinach, and toss to coat evenly.

➤ When the fish is done, transfer it to a plate. Add the remaining oil and the onion to the skillet and cook until the onion softens. Immediately pour the contents of the skillet over the spinach, toss to distribute the oil and wilt the leaves evenly, and serve onto warm plates. Serve the whole fillets on top of the spinach, or slice into strips and arrange as described above.

Lemon-Pepper Marinade

➤ Combine 1 teaspoon oil, ½ teaspoon lemon juice, 1 teaspoon finely grated lemon peel, and ¼ teaspoon each salt and freshly ground black pepper in a bowl and stir to dissolve the salt. Add the fish fillets and marinate 15 to 30 minutes before cooking. (Do not marinate longer or the lemon juice will begin to "cook" the fish.) Makes enough marinade for 2 servings.

Catfish with Caramel Sauce

If you think sweet when you hear caramel, think again. Sugar cooked to a very dark brown loses most of its sweetening power, but takes on a deep, rich, slightly bitter taste that Vietnamese cooks use to great advantage in combination with salty, pungent fish sauce. At Mama Lan's in Berkeley, my favorite neighborhood restaurant, this syrup is the base of a deeply flavored dish of catfish fillets served in a clay casserole.

The recipe makes a good deal more caramel syrup than you will need for this many servings, because it's easier than making it fresh every time and it keeps well.

SERVES 2 TO 4

⅔ cup (approximately) sugar

⅓ cup plus 2 tablespoons fish sauce

⅔ cup water

½ pound catfish fillet

1 tablespoon finely chopped garlic

½ teaspoon ground black pepper

¼ cup chicken stock

1 tablespoon sliced green onion

1 green or red jalapeño chile, sliced

1 cup blanched cabbage leaves, in bite-size pieces, or blanched bean sprouts, or cucumber slices

➤ At least 2 hours before serving time, make the caramel syrup: Put ½ cup sugar in a dry, heavy-bottomed saucepan (2 quarts or larger). Combine ⅓ cup of the fish sauce and the water in a measuring pitcher and set aside. Place the pan of sugar over medium heat and turn the exhaust fan to its maximum setting. When the sugar begins to melt around the edges, swirl the pan (do not stir)

so it melts evenly. Cook until the syrup darkens to a deep mahogany shade, then remove from the heat. Carefully pour in the fish sauce mixture (see note). The caramel will very likely seize into a solid mass; don't worry. Return the pan to the heat and bring back to a boil, swirling the pan, until the caramel is totally dissolved and the syrup is the color of strong coffee. Let cool, then transfer to a small jar and cover tightly.

➤ Cut the fish into 8 pieces and place them in a bowl. Add ¼ cup of the caramel syrup, the garlic and pepper, and 1 teaspoon sugar. Marinate 30 minutes to overnight.

➤ Combine 1 tablespoon sugar and a tablespoon of stock or water in a medium skillet. Cook over high heat, swirling the pan, until the sugar caramelizes. Add the fish and its marinade, the remaining stock, and the remaining fish sauce and cook over medium-high heat, turning the fish to coat it with the sauce as the sauce reduces. When the fish is fully cooked and beginning to break apart, sprinkle in 1 tablespoon sugar and cook until the sauce becomes thick and glossy. Stir in the green onion and divide the fish and sauce among individual bowls, or serve in one bowl, family style. Garnish with slices of chile. Serve with rice and cabbage leaves to dip in the sauce.

NOTE Caramel gets extremely hot, so be careful to avoid splattering yourself when adding the liquids. The syrup may also boil up violently when the liquid hits the caramel, so try to select a saucepan that is nearly as tall as it is wide. Even so, you might want to put a heat-proof colander over the top of the pan and pour the water through it, to deflect any splatters.

VARIATION This is also good with salmon, but the sauce does not seem to permeate salmon as well as it does catfish. Cut salmon fillet into diagonal slices about ½ inch thick for the best results, and cook only 5 to 7 minutes.

Tilapia Meunière with Julienne Leeks and Carrots

In this attractive presentation, golden-brown fillets are surrounded by a mixture of finely shredded leeks and carrots. To keep calories down, the vegetables are "sautéed" in stock, with just a bit of oil added for flavor. Other vegetables, including summer squashes and peppers of various colors, can be used in season.

SERVES 4

1 large or 2 small leeks

1 medium carrot, cut into fine julienne

¼ cup chicken or vegetable stock

2 tablespoons plus 1 teaspoon olive oil

¼ cup flour

½ teaspoon salt

Pinch of white pepper or cayenne

4 large or 8 small tilapia fillets (about 1½ pounds in all)

Salt and pepper, to taste

1½ ounces dry white wine

4 tablespoons butter

2 tablespoons chopped mild herbs—chervil, parsley, tarragon, or chives

Lemon juice

➤ Wash and trim the leeks and cut the white and pale green parts into 2-inch lengths (discard the tops or reserve for stock). Split the sections lengthwise and cut into thin ribbons. Soak in a bowl of cold water, separating all the pieces and swirling to wash away any dirt. Lift out and drain. Combine with the carrot, stock, and 1 teaspoon of oil in a medium skillet.

➤ Combine the flour, salt, and pepper in a shallow dish. Dredge the fillets in the seasoned flour and shake off the excess. Heat the remaining oil in a large skillet over medium-high heat. Add the fish and cook until lightly browned, about 3 minutes. Turn and cook 2 to 3 minutes more, or until a skewer easily enters the thickest part. Meanwhile, turn the heat to medium-high under the vegetable skillet and "sauté" the leeks and carrot until they are just tender and the liquid is nearly gone. Season to taste with salt and pepper.

➤ When the fillets are done, transfer them to warm individual plates or a serving platter. Deglaze the pan with wine and reduce by half. Remove the pan from the heat and swirl in the butter and herbs. Taste the sauce for seasoning and adjust if necessary with lemon juice, salt, or pepper. Spoon the sauce over the fish and arrange the vegetables around the outside.

TECHNIQUE NOTE Depending on the size and number of your fillets, you may need to cook them in a couple of shifts. Keep the first ones warm in a low oven. If the flour and oil in the pan is in danger of burning, wipe it out and add fresh oil before cooking the second batch of fish.

Baked Fish with Whole Spices

A bed of aromatic vegetables and what may seem like a lot of whole spices gives a subtle flavor and aroma to a light sauce based on drippings. This will work with other whole lean fish, including small rockfish, hybrid bass, and trout, as well as cuts or "roasts" of halibut or pink salmon. Adjust the cooking time according to the thickness and density of the fish.

SERVES 4

2 teaspoons peanut or other vegetable oil

1 medium carrot, peeled and cut into ¼-inch sticks

4 green onions, cut into 3-inch sections

8 quarter-size slices ginger (no need to peel)

1 teaspoon whole allspice

3 star anise pods, broken up

½ teaspoon whole peppercorns

2 small dried chiles, any loose seeds removed

2 tilapia, 1¼ to 1½ pounds each, dressed and scaled

Salt

3 tablespoons white wine

½ cup fish or poultry stock

1 tablespoon butter (optional)

➤ Preheat the oven to 400°F. Rub a baking dish well with the oil, add the vegetables and whole spices, and toss to coat lightly with oil.

➤ Arrange in an even layer. Rinse the fish well inside and out and pat dry. Season lightly inside and out with salt, and place on top of the vegetables. Add the wine and 3 tablespoons of the stock. Make a loose tent of foil over the tails of the fish and place the pan in the oven. Bake, rotating the pan once halfway through the cooking time, until a skewer easily enters the thickest part of the fish and the center reads 145°F, 20 to 30 minutes.

➤ Transfer the fish to a warm serving platter. Strain the contents of the baking dish into a small saucepan; discard the spices and vegetables. Add the remaining stock, bring to a boil, and reduce by a third. Taste for seasoning and adjust if necessary. Swirl in the butter if desired and pour over and around the fish on the platter.

Pecan-Crusted Tilapia Fillets with Beurre Blanc

A crisp coating of ground nuts highlights the slight nutty flavor of tilapia. This works equally well with other fine-textured freshwater fish such as hybrid striped bass, trout, or catfish, as well as sole or flounder.

SERVES 4

½ recipe Beurre Blanc (page 325)

4 ounces (1 cup) pecan halves

4 tilapia fillets, 4 to 5 ounces each

Salt and freshly ground white pepper, to taste

¼ cup (approximately) peanut or mild olive oil

➤ Prepare the beurre blanc and keep it warm. Grate the nuts in a rotary grater, or chop them fine with a knife. Season the fillets lightly on both sides with salt and pepper.

➤ Spread half the grated nuts on a plate. Lay 2 fillets bone side down on the nuts, pressing gently so the nuts adhere. Turn and inspect; fill in any bare spots with the excess nuts remaining on the plate. Repeat with the remaining fish and nuts.

➤ Heat a large skillet (see Technique Note, page 209) over medium-high heat and add oil to generously coat the bottom. Add the fillets, nut-coated side down, and cook until the thick end looks halfway done, about 3 minutes. Turn and cook until done by the skewer test. Transfer to warm plates and drizzle with the beurre blanc, or serve the sauce on the side in small ramekins.

Tilapia en Papillote with Asparagus and Shrimp

The Idaho potato giant J.R. Simplot Company made news in the late '80s with the opening of a huge tilapia farm that used natural hot spring water to raise this tropical fish. But apparently the geothermal heat source beneath the earth was finite, because the water started coming out of the well cold rather than hot. The energy costs of heating the water to 80-plus degrees became prohibitive, and Simplot shut down the operation after a couple of years. Before it went under, the farm produced not only some great fish but also some fine recipes, one of which I have adapted here to the parchment method.

SERVES 4

½ pound thin or medium asparagus

2 tablespoons butter, softened

Grated zest of 1 lemon

Salt and freshly ground pepper, to taste

4 large or 8 small tilapia fillets (1¼ to 1½ pounds total)

2 tablespoons fresh lemon juice

2 ounces tiny cooked shrimp, rinsed and drained

➤ Snap off the thick ends of the asparagus, cut the spears diagonally into bite-size pieces, and blanch in lightly salted water. Drain and cool. Meanwhile, beat the butter until light and blend in the lemon zest; season to taste with salt and pepper.

➤ Preheat the oven to 450°F. For each portion, fold a 12-inch square of baking parchment in half diagonally and crease the corners. Open the parchment and arrange one portion of tilapia fillet on one side of the fold. Season with a little lemon juice and top with a quarter of the shrimp and asparagus. Dot with a quarter of the lemon butter. Fold the other side of the paper over the fish and seal the package into a half oval with a series of creases, starting with one corner and finishing with a twist at the opposite end (see page 22). Repeat for the remaining portions. Bake the packages on a sheet pan until the paper is browned and puffy, 7 to 8 minutes. To serve, slit open each package and slide the contents out onto a plate; or serve in the paper, letting each diner cut open his own.

Baked Whole Tilapia with Curry Paste

In this or any other recipe for whole tilapia, you can make the fish easier to serve and eat by removing all the fins and their supporting bones as described on page 11. In any case, the meat right at the base of the pectoral fins sometimes has a strong flavor, so it's best left behind.

SERVES 4

2 tilapia, cleaned and scaled (2½ to 3 pounds in all)
Salt and freshly ground pepper, to taste
1 lemon or lime, cut into wedges
¼ cup thick coconut milk
1 tablespoon red curry paste

➤ Preheat the oven to 400°F. Cut 3 diagonal slashes on each side of the fish, cutting to the bone. Season the fish and the cut surfaces with salt, pepper, and a bit of lemon juice. Combine half the coconut milk with the curry paste and rub the mixture all over the fish, including into the slashes.

➤ Lay the fish in a shallow baking pan. Thin the remaining coconut milk with a little water and pour it around the fish. Bake uncovered until the meat has shrunk noticeably from the slashes and reads 145°F on an instant-reading thermometer, about 20 minutes. Serve with lemon or lime wedges.

Steamed Striped Bass with Fennel

Bass and fennel are traditional partners in southern French cooking, especially in the classic dish of a whole bass flamed over fennel stalks. This recipe uses the same combination of ingredients, but the cooking technique is Chinese, right down to drizzling the finished fish with sizzling-hot oil.

For the cooking vessel, you will need a large wok or a flameproof oval covered roaster, the largest round or oval plate that will fit inside, and a rack or other means of holding the plate an inch above an ample supply of boiling water (see page 24). If possible, use an attractive plate so you can serve the fish without having to transfer it to another plate, which is always tricky. Although this dish is designed for two, you could always use two fish and double the rest of the recipe to serve four, as long as everything fits into your steamer.

To serve the fish, you can lift off the top fillet and serve it as one portion, then lift away the bones and fins and serve the other half. Or share the top fillet, then share the bottom fillet as second helpings. Baked or steamed potatoes and a colorful vegetable are all you need to complete the plate. If you don't mind repeating the flavor of fennel, crosswise slices of the bulb stir-fried with sliced red bell pepper and a pinch of herbes de Provence makes a nice combination.

SERVES 2

1 hybrid striped bass, about 1½ pounds, cleaned and scaled, head and tail left on
Salt and pepper
5 or 6 thin slices lemon
Leaves and stems from 1 large bulb fresh fennel (sweet anise)
1 small leek, OR 3 large green onions
3 tablespoons olive oil

➤ Rinse the fish well inside and out, removing any remaining bits of blood or gills. Pat dry. Slash both sides of the fish with 2 or 3 diagonal cuts, cutting through the skin and meat almost to the bone. Season the fish inside and out with salt and pepper. Stuff the cavity with the lemon slices and a few sprigs of fennel. Make a bed of the remaining fennel on a large plate that will fit inside your steaming pan and lay the fish on top.

➤ Bring the water in the steamer to a rolling boil and place the fish plate on a steaming rack an inch above the water. Cover and steam until the exposed meat is opaque to the bone, 13 to 15 minutes. Meanwhile, cut the white part of the leek or green onions into 2-inch lengths, split lengthwise, and cut into narrow ribbons. Rinse the leek well in water to dislodge any dirt and drain thoroughly.

➤ When the fish is nearly done, combine the oil and leek in a small saucepan and heat until sizzling. Pour over the fish and serve immediately.

Baked Striped Bass with Country Ham

A little pork, especially a flavorful cured form like ham or bacon, does wonders for the flavor of freshwater fish, as anyone who has had trout cooked in bacon drippings will confirm. Here, a few shreds of intensely flavored ham like Smithfield or prosciutto are the "spice" for a simply baked hybrid bass. Many Chinese meat markets sell crosscut slabs of Smithfield or similar dry-cured Virginia ham as a substitute for the Yunnan ham of China, and at a fraction of the price per pound you would pay for sliced prosciutto in a deli. However, this ham is nearly rock-hard and you will have to slice it yourself. Since you need only an ounce or so per fish, I won't tell on you if you opt for the deli version. Whatever ham you choose, use as much of the fat as you dare—it gives flavor and richness to the dish.

SERVES 4

1 tablespoon olive oil

1 large onion, thinly sliced

2 hybrid striped bass, 1½ pounds each, cleaned and scaled

Freshly ground pepper, to taste

2 tablespoons dry sherry

2 ounces thinly sliced Smithfield ham or prosciutto, cut with fat into thin shreds

➤ Preheat the oven to 400°F. Lightly oil a bake-and-serve dish large enough to hold both of the fish and scatter the sliced onion over the bottom. Rinse the fish inside and out and pat dry. Slash both sides of the fish with 2 or 3 diagonal cuts, cutting through the skin and meat almost to the bone. Season lightly with pepper; the ham should supply enough salt.

➤ Sprinkle the fish on both sides with the sherry and place them in the baking pan, dorsal sides outward. Scatter the ham shreds over the fish, cover with foil, and bake to an internal temperature of 145°F, about 20 minutes. Let the fish rest, loosely covered, for a few minutes before serving from the baking dish.

Herb-Crusted Striped Bass Fillets

This works best with skin-on fillets; the skin gets nicely crisp, and if a little bit of it sticks to the pan, that's the side that is going down against the plate anyway. Having the fish cleaned and scaled when you buy it will save you some cleanup and make it easier to fillet the fish when you get home; the head and bones that remain after filleting are good for making stock.

SERVES 4

4 skin-on hybrid striped bass fillets, about 6 ounces each (yield from 2 fish of 1⅓ pounds each)

Salt and freshly ground pepper, to taste

1 sprig each fresh thyme and marjoram

1 teaspoon chopped chives

2 to 3 sprigs parsley

⅓ cup (approximately) dry bread crumbs

Olive oil

➤ Preheat the oven to 500°F. Set a 12-inch skillet with a heatproof handle over low heat to preheat thoroughly (or preheat the skillet in the oven). Score the skin side of each fillet with shallow cuts ½ inch or so apart, cutting about ⅛ inch into the meat. Lay them bone side up on a plate and season with salt and pepper. Chop the herbs together and spread evenly over the fish. Top with a generous layer of crumbs, pressing gently so they adhere.

➤ Turn the heat under the skillet to high and add oil to coat the surface. Carefully add the fillets, skin side down. Put the pan in the oven and cook until done by the skewer test, 6 to 8 minutes. Serve crusted side up.

Other Serving Suggestions: Hybrid Bass

In addition to the recipes here, hybrid bass fillets will work in most recipes for lean and white fish, especially Braised Fillets with Red Pepper and Sherry Sauce (page 117), "Unblackened" Seabass (page 126), Fish Fillets with Pasta and Summer Vegetables (page 129), and Fish Paillards with Tomato-Mint Sauce (page 132).

Serve simply sautéed, grilled, or broiled fillets with Romesco (page 321) or any of the sauces given for "summer fish" on pages 178 to 183.

Whole fish can stand in nicely for rockfish in any baked, steamed, or braised dish.

Six-Hour Baked Shad

Five to six hours (really!) of baking at a low temperature will render most of the small bones in a shad edible, and the larger ones easy to pick out. It may seem like this would produce an inedibly dry fish, and many of my food-writing colleagues scoff at the idea, but I love the result, which is rather like a giant canned sardine, served warm.

SERVES 4 TO 6

1 whole shad, about 3 pounds, cleaned and scaled

1 teaspoon oil

Salt and pepper

Juice of 1 lemon

1 large onion, thinly sliced

3 to 4 sprigs fresh thyme or marjoram

4 slices bacon

➤ Inspect the inside of the fish carefully; you will most likely have to remove the red kidney strip along the backbone, as fishmongers seldom remove it. Cut off the head and tail if necessary to fit your roasting pan. Rinse the fish thoroughly inside and out until no traces of blood remain.

➤ Preheat the oven to 200°F, or 225°F if that is the lowest setting it will hold. Lay out a large sheet of aluminum foil shiny side up and oil the middle of the sheet lightly. Season the fish inside and out with salt, pepper, and lemon juice. Spread half the onion in the middle of the foil, lay the fish on top, and stuff the cavity with the remaining onion and herbs. Lay the bacon strips on top of the fish and seal the foil tightly around the fish.

➤ Place the package in a roasting pan and bake 5 to 6 hours. Transfer the wrapped fish to a deep platter and slit open one side of the foil (it will release a lot of juices). Carefully slide out the fish and discard the foil. To serve, use a fork and spoon to pull pieces of meat away from the backbone and ribs, and spoon some of the juices over each portion.

Ukrainian Fish Soup

I learned to make this simple but delicately flavored fish soup several years ago from a Jewish immigrant family recently arrived from Odessa, a port on the Black Sea. It combines two traditions, the Eastern European love of freshwater fish and a general style of fish soup found all across the northern Mediterranean region (which in climate, geography, and cuisine can be extended to the shores of the Black Sea).

Our hostess explained that this soup had been cooked only once; to be really authentic, she said, it should be "thrice-cooked." Had she had the time and the fish, she would have made the broth once, throwing away the first fish, then a second time, again discarding the fish, and only on the third time around serve it with the fish. While that would certainly make a richer soup, it seems rather extravagant, and anyway this version had plenty of flavor. If you have some clear fish broth on hand, by all means use it.

In this, as in any clear fish soup, be especially careful not to let the broth boil after you add the fish or it will become cloudy. Cook it at the barest simmer for a sparkling-clear broth. If you want to make a smaller quantity, use a couple of fish steaks, but be sure to use a fish head for a rich broth.

SERVES 8

1 carp, preferably live, 3 to 4 pounds

3 quarts water

1 large onion, diced

1 large potato, peeled and diced

3 pale inner stalks celery, sliced

1 large carrot, peeled and thinly sliced

1 red or yellow pepper, cored and thinly sliced

2 small tomatoes, sliced

Handful of flat-leaved (Italian) parsley

1½ teaspoons salt, or to taste

Pepper, to taste

➤ Have the fish cleaned and scaled and cut into 1-inch steaks. Be sure all traces of gills and reddish organs are removed from the steaks and from the head.

➤ Bring the water to a simmer in a large pot; add the onion and simmer 10 minutes. Add the fish pieces, potato, and celery. Cover and simmer gently, never letting the liquid boil, until the fish is done and the vegetables are tender, about 30 minutes. Add the remaining vegetables and parsley and simmer 5 minutes more. Add salt and pepper to taste. Serve in large soup bowls and set each place with a smaller plate for bones; or serve the broth and vegetables as a first course and serve the fish on plates as a second course.

Real Sweet and Sour Fish

A good sweet and sour sauce is a delicious accompaniment to fried fish. This version is quite easy to make, and likely to be less sweet and less garishly colored than anything you can buy. If you miss the red color, add a tablespoon or so of ketchup. This is most authentically made with carp, but you might prefer rockfish, either a whole fish or a crosscut steak of a larger one.

SERVES 2 TO 4, WITH OTHER DISHES

1 whole fish, about 2 pounds, dressed
Cornstarch
Oil for deep-frying
Sweet and Sour Sauce I or II, below
Cilantro sprigs or green onion shreds,
   for garnish

➤ Inspect the fish inside and out for remaining scales, bits of organs, or blood, and rinse thoroughly. Cut 2 or 3 diagonal slashes almost to the bone on each side of the fish. Sprinkle cornstarch generously over both sides, rubbing it well into the skin and the slashes in the meat. Let stand 5 minutes, and repeat twice. Meanwhile, assemble the ingredients for your choice of sauce.

➤ Fill a wok or other deep, wide pan with oil at least 2 inches deep; allow at least 2 inches below the rim of the pan to prevent boilovers and spills when the fish is added. Heat to 375°F. Carefully lower the fish into the hot oil, and if some is sticking out above the oil, use a heatproof ladle to bathe the exposed part repeatedly in hot oil. Turn the fish after 4 to 5 minutes and continue cooking (no need to ladle the oil after turning) until the fish is golden brown on both sides and the meat in the thickest part is opaque.

➤ Lift the fish out with a large skimmer, let it drain briefly over the oil, and transfer it to a serving platter. Bring the sauce to a boil, blot away any oil that has accumulated on the platter, and pour the sauce over the fish. Garnish with cilantro or green onion.

Sweet and Sour Sauce I

Use this as a starting point; feel free to adjust the sweet and sour balance to your taste, or add more heat with bottled chile sauce.

SERVES 4 TO 6

½ cup water
¼ cup cider or rice vinegar
¼ cup sugar
2 teaspoons soy sauce
Pinch of white pepper
1 thick slice ginger, bruised
1½ teaspoons cornstarch dissolved in
   1 tablespoon water

➤ Combine all ingredients except the cornstarch mixture in a small saucepan. Bring to a boil, stirring to dissolve the sugar. Add the cornstarch mixture and simmer until glossy and lightly thickened. Discard the ginger slice and correct the seasoning.

Sweet and Sour Sauce II

The same basic flavor, but with some shredded vegetables added for color and texture.

SERVES 4 TO 6

Ingredients for Sweet and Sour Sauce I, above, minus the ginger slice

1 teaspoon oil

1 teaspoon minced garlic

1 tablespoon thin ginger shreds

½ red or green bell pepper, seeded and thinly sliced

2 green onions, cut into 2-inch lengths and shredded lengthwise

➤ Combine the sauce ingredients except the cornstarch mixture, using hot water to help dissolve the sugar. Heat the oil in a saucepan over medium heat and cook the garlic and ginger until fragrant, a few seconds. Add the bell pepper and onions and cook briefly, but do not let the garlic brown. Stir the liquid mixture and add it to the pan. Bring to a boil, reduce to a simmer, and stir in the cornstarch mixture. Cook until the sauce is glossy and lightly thickened.

Noodle Soup with Fish Balls

You don't have to make your own fish paste to enjoy this soup, vaguely Vietnamese in inspiration; you can buy ready-made fish paste in many Asian markets, or for that matter, already cooked fish balls.

SERVES 4

1 recipe Basic Fish Paste (page 218)

1 stalk lemongrass

2 green onions

2 thick slices fresh ginger

1 teaspoon oil

2 teaspoons sugar

6 cups water

2 tablespoons fish sauce

2 star anise pods

1 to 2 cups leftover shrimp shells (optional)

½ pound thin rice noodles

Mint or basil leaves

Lemon or lime wedges

Hot pepper sauce

➤ Have a pot of salted water at a simmer. Form the fish paste into small balls by hand or with 2 small spoons dipped in water. Poach until they float; remove and drain them. Refrigerate if not using immediately, up to 3 days.

➤ Cut the lemongrass and green onion bottoms into 1-inch sections; bruise them and the ginger slices with the side of a knife blade. Heat the oil in a saucepan over medium heat. Add the lemongrass, onions, and ginger and cook until fragrant. Sprinkle in the sugar and cook until it melts and begins to darken. Remove the pan from the heat and carefully pour in the water. Add the fish sauce and star anise and return to the heat. Simmer 15 minutes, add the shrimp shells, and simmer 10 minutes more. Meanwhile, drop the noodles into boiling water, turn off the heat, and let stand until soft; drain and rinse.

➤ Strain the broth, correct the seasoning, and keep warm. Divide the noodles among 4 large bowls; top with fish balls and sliced green onion tops. Pour the hot broth over all and serve, with mint, lemon, and hot sauce to add to taste.

Basic Fish Paste

1 pound carp, shad, or other white fish fillets

1 egg white

2 tablespoons minced green onion

1 tablespoon minced ginger

2 tablespoons rice wine or dry sherry

¼ teaspoon salt

1 teaspoon cornstarch

1 tablespoon bacon or ham fat or rendered chicken fat

➤ Skin the fillets and any bones with a knife, or by putting the meat through a food mill. Combine in a food processor with the remaining ingredients. Process to a smooth paste, scraping down the sides occasionally. Cover and chill until ready to use.

Not the Same Old Grind: Fish Paste and Fish Balls

One of the perennial challenges of seafood cookery is to turn the relatively inexpensive kinds of fish, which come in all different sizes and shapes and are often quite bony, into a form that is attractive and easy to cook and eat. One of the best ways is to make a Chinese-style minced fish paste, which can then be formed into balls, cakes, and other shapes to be to be poached, steamed, or fried with a variety of seasonings. And not just Chinese seasonings; see below for a dish that combines fried Chinese-style fish cakes with Moroccan couscous and an assortment of Mediterranean vegetables.

Fish paste can be made with anything from small, bony fish to chunks hacked off a large fish. Choose from white-fleshed saltwater fish like rockfish, lingcod, cabezon, and flounder, or carp and shad from fresh water. Shrimp and squid are also good choices, alone or mixed with fish.

The fish can be reduced to a paste several ways: by chopping fine with a knife, or in a food processor, or most traditionally, by scraping the meat off the skin and bones with a spoon or a dull knife. The last method is especially effective when the fish has lots of small bones, but it is time-consuming. The best tool of all is a food mill (see page 28), which quickly reduces the boniest fish to a smooth purée, straining out the bones in the process.

Most Chinese fish paste recipes include egg white and cornstarch as thickeners, ginger, and green onion for flavor, and some form of fat for lightness. I usually have rendered chicken fat on hand, but fresh pork fat, fatty bacon, or fat trimmed from ham will also work.

To make fish balls, dip your hands in cold water, then scoop up a fistful of the paste in one hand. Squeeze it out between the thumb and forefinger and use a spoon to scoop off small balls, which you drop into simmering water to poach 3 to 5 minutes.

Fish Cakes with Vegetable Couscous

Like fried tofu, fried fish paste doesn't get very crisp, but it takes on a firmer "skin" texture as well as a nicely browned color and flavor.

SERVES 3 TO 4

2 tablespoons olive oil

2 cloves garlic, sliced

¼ pound mushrooms, thickly sliced

½ onion, sliced

½ cup blanched and peeled fava beans

1 roasted and peeled sweet pepper, cut into 1-inch squares

8 marinated artichoke hearts

1 cup peeled, seeded, and roughly chopped tomato, with juices

½ teaspoon salt

Pepper, to taste

Oil for deep-frying

1 recipe Basic Fish Paste, above

3 cups cooked couscous

➤ Combine the olive oil and garlic in a large skillet over medium heat. When the garlic is fragrant, add the mushrooms and onion and cook until the mushrooms soften. Add the remaining vegetables, including any juices from the tomato and pepper, and seasonings. Simmer until well flavored.

➤ Meanwhile, heat 2 inches of oil to 375°F in a wok or deep skillet. With lightly oiled hands, form the fish mixture into 8 cakes, ½ inch thick. Fry 2 or 3 at a time in the hot oil until golden brown, about 3 minutes per side. (Cut one open to see if they are done, they can take longer than it appears to cook through.) Drain on paper towels and keep warm. To serve, make a bed of couscous, spoon the vegetable mixture over it, and top with fish cakes.

shellfish, part I:
crab, shrimp & lobster

The world of edible shellfish breaks down roughly into two groups, crustaceans and mollusks. We deal first with the former—shellfish with segmented bodies and paired, jointed limbs that give them plenty of mobility. The muscles that allow crabs and lobsters to scuttle around on the sea floor (and shrimp to both swim and walk) provide some of the sweetest, most tender meat that the sea has to offer.

American Lobster

Blue Crab

Box Crab

Dungeness Crab

Crayfish

Freshwater Prawn

King Crab

Northern Shrimp

Pink Shrimp

Ridgeback Shrimp

Rock Crab

Rock Lobster

Rock Shrimp

Snow Crab

Spiny Lobster

Spot Prawn

Tiger Prawn

White Shrimp

Crab

Dungeness crab, *Cancer magister*
King crab, *Paralithodes camtschaticus*
Snow crab, *Chionoecetes* spp.
Rock crabs, *Cancer* spp.
Box crab, *Lopolithodes foraminatus*
Blue crab, *Callinectes sapidus*

Nearly a dozen species of edible crabs occur in our part of the north Pacific, but three of them dominate the commercial market. Of these, king crab is the most valuable, and snow crab is in many years the most numerous. But for many West Coast seafood lovers, including me, the Dungeness crab is second to none in flavor.

Named after a town on Washington's Olympic Peninsula, which in turn was named after a point on the English coast, Dungeness crab is the main species caught south of Alaska, and is commercially important in nearly every fishing port north of Santa Barbara. Like lobster in New England, Dungeness crab is a symbol of many West Coast fishing ports, its distinctive shape showing up everywhere on signs, trucks, and buildings. And like lobster, it can be enjoyed as plain or as fancy as you like. Simple "cracked crab," the meat freshly picked from a cold boiled crab, served with sourdough bread and washed down with white wine, is probably the all-time favorite, but Dungeness crab is also excellent in salads, stuffings for other seafoods,

stir-fried dishes, and stews and gumbos, including the classic cioppino (page 237).

Fresh Dungeness crab is available all year from one part of the coast or another. In California, it's a winter fishery, beginning in November off the central coast and on the first of December off the northern counties; peak landings are usually in December and January. Oregon and Washington crabbers generally fish longer into the spring than their California counterparts, while the B.C. season doesn't even start until April. The southeast Alaska Dungeness fishery occurs mainly in summer. Supplies are tightest and prices highest in early fall, before the California season starts.

The minimum legal size for Dungeness crab (6¼ inches across the upper shell, or carapace) translates to a weight of about a pound and a third, and most crabs come in at 1½ to 2½ pounds. To protect the breeding population, only male crabs can be kept.

California shoppers, especially in the south, may also find smaller crabs similar in shape to Dungeness, but with larger, black-tipped claws. Three *Cancer* species, known collectively as rock crab, are found from Baja California to Oregon, and are fished commercially in some areas. Typical market size is 1 pound or less, though they may run as large as 1½ pounds. The large claws contain a much higher proportion of the meat than those of a Dungeness crab, and are sometimes sold separately like those of the Florida stone crab. Conversely, the legs are smaller, the largest ones corresponding in size to the second-smallest of a Dungeness.

Live or cooked, rock crab should sell for less than Dungeness; the meat cannot match the sweeter taste of its more expensive cousin, and may in fact have a trace of bitterness. However, if the crab will be combined with a strong sauce, as in gumbo, curry, or enchiladas, rock crab is just fine. Fishermen can keep female rock crabs as well as males, and the meat of the females has the sweeter taste. You can tell them apart by the shape of the triangular "apron" on the underside; the male's is slimmer and more pointed, the female's wider and rounder.

When Dungeness crab fishermen set their traps in deeper waters, they occasionally bring up another species, the box crab. This odd-looking relative of the king and snow crabs has a similar carapace shape to king crab (pointed at the front rather than rounded), but has much shorter and rounder legs and claws, which are usually tightly drawn in. Both the carapace and legs are covered with bumps, making the whole thing look like a small, warty catcher's mitt. It may not be the prettiest crab, but the meat is especially sweet and firm. As near as I can tell, most of the box crab catch is sold directly to the public by the few fishermen who catch them, but we may see more of this crab in the future.

Other than the Dungeness fishery in the southeast, most of Alaska's crab fishery is for two long-legged varieties, king and snow crabs. Because of the remoteness of the fishing grounds, most of these crabs are cooked before they get to market. The thick, meaty legs of king crab mostly go into the restaurant trade, but they sometimes show up in fish markets and supermarkets, and can simply be reheated in the oven, under the broiler, or on the grill. (If visiting southeast Alaska, you might try a local delicacy known as "crab tails," a fleshy flap from the underside of a king crab that is cut into bite-size pieces and marinated for salads and such.)

While king crab is associated with white-tablecloth dining, its smaller cousin the snow crab (actually several species, also known as spider or tanner crabs) has for many years been a staple of inexpensive "all you can eat" seafood restaurants. Now snow crab clusters, cooked body halves with the claws and legs attached, are becoming increasingly common in supermarkets as well, as a less expensive alternative to Dungeness. The meat is a little milder in flavor and a bit stringy in texture, but it works well in salads, soups, stuffings, and other dishes that call for cooked and flaked crabmeat.

SHOPPING, PREPARATION, AND COOKING

Purists insist on buying their own live crabs and cooking them at home. Once a crab dies, it begins to spoil rapidly unless promptly cooked. Many markets have saltwater tanks to keep crabs alive, but a tank is not in itself a guarantee of fresher crabs; tanks often have their share of dead or dying crabs. If a crab is alive and kicking, it really doesn't matter if it comes from a tank or from a box on the floor. Look for lively crabs and reject any that are listless or already dead.

Whole cooked crabs are often sold for the same price as live, and may be more convenient for many uses. Alive or cooked, choose a crab that seems heavy for its size and the shell will be more filled with meat. Legs that are tightly drawn in on a cooked crab are a sign that the crab was alive when cooked; splayed

223

legs are not a good sign.

Already picked crabmeat is certainly the most convenient, and if it is less than four times the price of whole crab, it's just as economical. Plus, you can buy just as much as you like.

To clean a live crab for cooking in pieces, you first need to kill it by one of two methods: heat or physical destruction of the nervous system (see below for a discussion of the humane issues involved). Having used both methods for years, I recommend boiling, especially if you want to keep the top shell (carapace) whole for presentation purposes. Either plunge the crab into boiling water until it stops moving, usually less than a minute, or (my preference) cover it with cold water and bring it to a simmer, then retrieve it. In either case, rinse the crab immediately with cold water to stop the cooking.

If you don't want to be bothered with boiling water and don't care about the top shell, you can kill a crab with a quick knife blow as follows: Place the crab on its back with the mouth toward you, and keeping your fingers clear of the claws, place the tip of a large chef's knife or Chinese cleaver against the underside about an inch behind the mouth. Rap the back of the blade sharply with a mallet or the heel of your other hand, cutting through between the eyes. Or, if it's easier, just chop the whole thing in half down the middle, cutting through the carapace.

Another variation, which is quick and effective though not for the squeamish, is known in the trade as "live-backing": Approaching the crab from behind, grasp the legs and claws on both sides and smack the underside smartly against a sharp corner of a table or the edge of a metal sink. The bottom shell should crack neatly down the middle, allowing you to draw the relaxed legs together in one hand and pull off the carapace with the other hand. This method also preserves the carapace.

With either of the physical methods, chilling the crab well first, or even freezing it briefly, will slow down its metabolism and render it a little more docile. Even so, it may continue to move its legs and claws for a few minutes after killing, especially if you touch any of the exposed muscle tissues with a knife or fingertip. If this bothers you, set it aside for a few minutes while you do some other cooking preparations. If the whole business seems too gruesome, some fishmongers will do it for you, but plan on buying your crab close to cooking time as possible to prevent spoilage.

To clean a crab, cooked or uncooked, look on the underside and lift the triangular shell flap or "apron," then carefully lift the spines hidden underneath. Twist off and discard these parts. Holding the crab body by the legs, pull off the carapace. Discard the feathery gills on both sides of the body, the jaw parts at the front, and the viscera (all the soft stuff in the middle of the back). Rinse until nothing shows but shell and meat. If you will be using the carapace, pull out the bits of spongy fat (olive green in a raw crab, pale yellow when fully cooked) from the corners and rinse the shell well.

Crab fat or "crab butter," which is concentrated in the viscera and also in the corners of the top shell, contains a lot of flavor, and is a traditional ingredient in many recipes. But it has come under suspicion in recent years. Dungeness crabs have been known to accumulate a

On Humane Killing of Live Crabs (and Lobsters)

A friend telephoned one day in a panic. She had bought a couple of live lobsters and her recipe called for killing them and cutting them up before cooking. But she wasn't sure how to do it, and meanwhile the lobsters were crawling around in the sink (recalling a scene in Woody Allen's *Annie Hall*).

When it is necessary to kill an animal, most of us want to do so in the most humane way possible. I don't know that anyone can tell exactly when and to what degree an invertebrate feels pain, but we can make some guess from the way it reacts. The standard way to cook crustaceans has long been to plunge them into already boiling water, which kills them quickly if not instantly. However, they do thrash about quite a bit during the first 15 seconds or so, and it is likely that they suffer pain in the process.

Nearly thirty years ago, a Texas biologist named Robert Gunter suggested that a more painless method is to place crustaceans in a pot of cold water and set it over low heat. As the temperature gradually rises to around 40°C (approximately human blood temperature), crabs and lobsters reach their "lethal limit of heat" and "die quickly and easily without showing distress." If removed at this stage, the meat remains uncooked, and the crab or lobster is ready for further cooking by whatever method. Or you can continue cooking until the water comes to a boil, by which time the meat is nearly or fully cooked.

Other experts are not so sure about Gunter's claim that slow warming is painless. Dustin Chivers of the California Academy of Sciences, for many years my guru on matters of invertebrate zoology, preferred to go to the other end of the temperature spectrum, putting lobsters or crabs in a freezer for one to two hours before cooking. The cold effectively shuts down their metabolism to the point that, in Dusty's words, "they die in their sleep." As long as you do not hold them too long in the freezer the meat will not freeze, although the lower temperature may require slightly longer cooking time.

The other way to minimize the suffering of crustaceans (or any animals, for that matter) is to physically destroy the nervous pathways that carry pain messages. In both crabs and lobsters, the brain is located very close to the mouth and eyes, and either splitting or live-backing presumably causes a quick death, involuntary muscle movements notwithstanding.

I frankly don't know which of the methods of killing crustaceans is most humane, but both experience and instinct make me favor slow warming. Based on the response of students in my cooking classes, this is the method most home cooks are likely to be comfortable with.

natural biotoxin called domoic acid (see page 35) in their fat, and although the risk of illness appears to be minimal, some health authorities continue to advise discarding the fat and viscera of Dungeness crabs. If you decide to use it, it's easiest to skip the part in the viscera and dig out the fat from the shell. If you want to avoid the fat and are using the shell for stock, clean the fat out of the corners first.

For stir-frying, soups, and stews, split the cleaned body in half if it is not already split, and cut each half between the legs toward the center to separate it into manageable pieces. If you prefer, you can separate the legs first and then cut up the body halves into sections.

Cracking crab legs and claws prior to cooking makes them a lot easier to eat, and it allows more of the sauce or seasonings to penetrate to

Crab vs. Krab

Crab is delicious, but it's also one of the more expensive items at the fish counter. For a less expensive alternative to real crab, many cooks turn to crab-style surimi (usually labeled "imitation crab" or sometimes "krab"), a fish-based product that provides some of the same flavor, texture, and appearance at a quarter to a third of the price of real crabmeat. I'm not saying you can't taste the difference, but for shoppers on a budget, surimi is a real alternative, especially for salads and other cold preparations.

Surimi is the Japanese name for a whole class of processed seafood protein. Starting with a base of lean white fish such as pollock or whiting, surimi processors (often right on the boats that catch the fish) fillet the fish, then mince, wash, and strain the meat to produce a concentrated, high-protein fish paste, which is stabilized with a small amount of salt or sugar. The bulk surimi, pure white and nearly tasteless, is then frozen in blocks for further processing into anything from seafood products to hot dogs.

Other than the Japanese-style fish cakes called *kamaboko,* the most popular form of surimi in North America is analogues of various shellfish, especially crab. By adding starch binders, color, and flavor, in some cases natural crab extract or even a small amount of crabmeat, and mechanically forming and extruding the mixture, surimi processors can produce something that looks a lot like crabmeat, in leg, stick, and claw shapes as well as flakes of various sizes.

Surimi products may be displayed anonymously at the fish counter, but you can bet they come into the store in brand-marked packages. Some brands are sweeter, some saltier, and the texture and the amount of shellfish flavor vary widely from one brand to the next. So if you don't like one brand or product form, try another. When you find one you like, find out the brand name and look for it next time. Better still, tell the person behind the fish counter which varieties you like and dislike and why.

the meat. Stand a leg up on its narrow edge and crack each section with one sharp blow of a mallet or sharpening steel, taking care not to mash the meat inside.

Even carefully cracked crab is a bit messy to eat. There is no better way than to roll up your sleeves and go at it with whatever tools are available—nutcrackers and picks, little shellfish forks, chopsticks, fingers, teeth, tips of crab claws—to get at every last morsel of meat. Provide plenty of napkins, or if you want to be fancy, warm moist hand towels for when the battle is over.

Whether you buy crabmeat already picked or pull it out of the crab yourself, be sure to pick it over carefully to remove any bits of shell. The small, soft inner shells are just a nuisance, but biting into a bit of the harder outer shell is no fun at all.

BASIC COOKING OF CRAB

COLD WATER METHOD Place live crabs in a deep pot with cold water to cover by several inches. Cover the pot and bring the water almost to a boil over high heat. For crab to be further cooked by another method, remove the crab just when the water reaches a simmer, before the shell turns red, and rinse with cold water to stop the cooking before cleaning. For fully cooked crab, turn off the heat when the water is just about to boil, and let the crab steep 10 minutes for a small crab (1½ pounds or less), 15 minutes for a 2½-pounder. Rinse with cold water before refrigerating.

HOT WATER METHOD Bring your largest pot of water to a rolling boil, add the live crabs, cover, and let the water return to a boil. Retrieve the crab after 1 minute if cooking by another method; for fully cooked crab, cook 15 minutes after the water boils for a small crab, 20 to 25 minutes for a large. Remove the crab from the pot, run a little cold water over it to cool the shell, then clean and crack to serve warm. If you plan to serve the crab cold, surrounding it with ice is the best way to cool it before cleaning and cracking.

Lobster

American lobster, *Homarus americanus*
Spiny or rock lobster, *Panulirus, Palinurus,*
and *Jasus* spp.

It's a bit of a stretch to include lobster in a West Coast cookbook, since the only lobster in our area is a very local and seasonal item in Southern California. However, live lobster from Maine and eastern Canada is shipped out here nearly every week of the year, so it's as much a part of our culinary resources as, say, Hawaiian tuna and Chilean sea bass.

To many, the sweet, firm meat of lobster is the ultimate in shellfish. Look at all the other seafoods, from rock shrimp to monkfish, that are said to be "lobster-like" in flavor or texture.

In the United States, Atlantic lobster is mainly identified with Maine, although it is found in other New England states as well, and considerably more comes out of the Atlantic provinces of Canada. While lobster can hardly be considered cheap, the gap in price between lobster and other seafoods narrowed in the 1980s and '90s. Large (and apparently sustainable) catches year after year, in the range of 60,000 to 80,000 tons, have meant a steady supply of lobsters, enough to ship across the country or around the world.

Although live Atlantic lobsters are available most of the year, the best availability and prices are in May, when nearly a third of the total annual Canadian catch is typically landed, and September, when fishing conditions are still fine in New England but the peak demand from tourists and summer residents has ended. After October, prices generally climb steeply, as winter weather limits the fishing effort.

October is also prime season for California's native spiny lobster (*Panulirus interruptus*). Found from Monterey southward but mainly around the Channel Islands, spiny lobster is part of a cosmopolitan family of warm-water lobsters also known as rock lobsters. The meat, a little coarser in texture than that of Maine lobster, is just as sweet and delicious. (Other members of the family found around the world supply the frozen lobster tails that are popular in "surf & turf" restaurants.)

Compared to Eastern lobster, the California spiny lobster fishery is infinitesimal, with average annual catches in the neighborhood of half a million pounds. While the season technically runs from October to spring, most of the catch is taken in the first few weeks of the season. Not surprisingly, these lobsters seldom get beyond the immediate Southern California market, where they sometimes end up in the local version of cioppino. The last time I saw some in the San Francisco area, they were more expensive than lobster flown in from Maine!

Like Dungeness crab, spiny lobster is usually sold in precooked form, but some are sold live. In either form, spiny lobster is easy to tell apart from the Atlantic variety by its lack of enlarged claws. Almost all of the meat is in the tail, except for a good-sized morsel of meat at the base of each of the long, thick antennae that arch backward above the body to beyond the tail.

Unless you are in Southern California in the fall, most of the following will apply only to Eastern lobster, However, if you get a chance to try California lobster, by all means do.

When buying live lobsters (and live is the best way to buy them, if you have a choice), look for those that are especially lively. Like crabs, lobsters do not feed in captivity, and while they can survive for several weeks, they gradually lose weight and shrink inside the shell. The most active are generally the freshest. Avoid any that are dead or extremely sluggish. Chinese markets are a good place to look for live lobsters at a competitive price, although not necessarily when local crabs are in good supply.

Lobster shells contain a lot of flavor, so don't discard them after picking out the meat; chop them up and freeze them for your next batch of fish stock. Even 15 minutes of simmering in the broth will add a subtle lobster flavor to a seafood risotto or paella.

Even when the price is at its lowest, lobster is a bit of a splurge. American tradition calls for a whole lobster per person, and a good-sized one at that. The Asian approach, in which several people share a whole lobster along with other dishes, is more sensible and economical. In the same spirit, I often combine lobster with pasta or rice to make it go farther.

BASIC COOKING OF LOBSTER

I use two methods for cooking live lobsters, and I'm still not sure which is better or more humane. (See page 225 for a discussion of the humane issue.)

COLD WATER METHOD Place the lobster in a deep pot with cold water to cover by several inches. Cover the pot and bring the water almost to a boil over high heat. When the water is just about to boil, turn off the heat. For meat to be cooked further in a sauce, let the lobster steep about 1 minute per pound, then remove it and rinse with cold water to stop the cooking (or surround it with ice cubes to chill even faster). For fully cooked lobster to be served cold, increase the steeping time to 10 minutes, and rinse with cold water to stop the cooking before refrigerating.

HOT WATER METHOD Bring a deep pot of water to a rolling boil, plunge the lobster in head first, and cover the pot. If just killing a lobster to be cooked by another method, retrieve it after 30 seconds and rinse it with cold water to stop the cooking. For fully cooked lobster, cook 8 minutes for a 1-pound lobster, 10 minutes for a 1¼-pounder, 12 minutes for a 1½-pounder.

Shrimp and Prawns

Northern shrimp, *Pandalus borealis* and *P. jordani*
Spot shrimp or spot prawn, *P. platyceros*
Coonstripe shrimp, *P. hypsinotus*
Sidestripe shrimp, *Pandalopsis dispar*
Rock shrimp, *Sicyonia brevirostris*
Ridgeback shrimp, *S. ingentis*
Pacific white shrimp, *Penaeus vannamei*
Chinese white shrimp, *P. chinensis*
Giant (black) tiger prawn, *P. monodon*
Gulf white shrimp, *P. setiferus*
Brown shrimp, *P. aztecus*
Pink or "hopper" shrimp, *P. duorarum*
Freshwater prawn, *Macrobrachium rosenbergii*

Shrimp is the most popular category of shellfish in America, and one of the most popular of all seafoods. But the name actually covers dozens of species, some from warm water and some from cold, some tiny and others surprisingly large. By far the majority of shrimp sold in the West is warmwater shrimp, imported from near (Mexico or the Gulf Coast) and far (farms in South America and Southeast Asia). However, we do have our own native shrimp on the West Coast, and they fall into three general types.

The largest shrimp fishery in our area is for small pink shrimp (*Pandalus borealis* and *P. jordani*), the kind usually called "bay shrimp" although they are caught by trawlers in the open ocean. Most of the fishery takes place off

229

Oregon and Northern California in spring and early summer, and the shrimp are sold cooked, peeled, and deveined. Outside the fresh season, they are widely available frozen.

Several larger species of *Pandalus* and the closely related *Pandalopsis* occur in our area, and they support small and local but very valuable commercial fisheries. The best known of these is the spot shrimp, a beautiful orange-pink shrimp with white markings found from Southern California to Alaska and caught commercially (mostly with traps) in several locations from the Channel Islands to British Columbia and southeast Alaska. In the California market, these are often identified by source, as Santa Barbara prawns or Monterey prawns; farther north they are just labeled spot prawns or spot shrimp. Spot shrimp can run quite large, sometimes fewer than 10 per pound, and females are sometimes caught bearing clusters of bright red roe under their abdomens. Closely related but generally smaller are the coonstripe and sidestripe shrimp, also caught on a limited scale in the Northwest. All three species are available fresh throughout the year, but rarely in large quantity. An increasing share of the catch is being delivered alive to the Chinese market, to be kept in live tanks like crab and lobster; a dish of prawns freshly plucked from a live tank in a Cantonese restaurant commands a premium price over the same dish made with ordinary shrimp. (A small amount is also being farmed in British Columbia, but mostly for export to Japan, where they can bring fantastic prices.)

The other local shrimp is the ridgeback prawn of Southern California. Related to the East Coast rock shrimp, ridgebacks have similarly heavy shells that make them less desirable to processors, so most of the (small) catch is sold whole, to be cooked in the shell and peeled at the table. Rock shrimp is caught in much larger quantities off Florida, and comes to our market as peeled, ready-to-cook tails sometimes sold as "stir-fry shrimp."

The total amount of all these coldwater shrimp is dwarfed by the shrimp we import from tropical and subtropical regions, mostly one species or another of *Penaeus*. Wild-caught penaeid shrimp come into our markets frozen from both coasts of Mexico, and both fresh and frozen from the southeastern United States. Most of these belong to several species known as "white" shrimp, although their shells vary in color through shades of gray to pink and are sometimes darker than other species known as "brown" shrimp.

However, the greatest growth in the warmwater shrimp supply has been in farmed shrimp, which are raised in ponds in coastal areas of the American and Asian tropics. Ecuador and Thailand are our leading sources of farmed shrimp, Ecuador producing mainly white shrimp (*Penaeus vannamei*) and Thailand the larger, distinctively marked tiger shrimp or black tiger prawns (*P. monodon*). China has also been a major supplier of mostly small farmed white shrimp of its native species *P. chinensis*. Given the choice, I'll always take a white shrimp over a tiger; the latter are pretty to look at, and cook to an especially rich color, but I've always found them a little lacking in flavor.

Most farmed shrimp are sold raw, in 2-kilo or 5-pound block packs, either headless or with heads on. Sizes are specified by the number of pieces per pound, usually expressed as a range like 16–20, 21–30, 31–40, etc. (the smaller the number, the larger the shrimp). Larger sizes command higher prices for various reasons—fewer pieces per pound to peel, a more impressive appearance on the plate, and usually a firmer texture. If you want to save time, use larger shrimp; to save money, use smaller.

Buying head-on shrimp won't save you any money over the equivalent size of headless; in fact, it will likely cost more. The reason is that many Asian cooks and diners prefer the eye appeal of shrimp cooked and served with the heads on. The heads do supply plenty of flavor, mostly from the pocket of reddish fat just forward of the abdomen (the muscular "tail" that contains the meat). If you do find a good price on head-on shrimp, by all means save the heads for your next seafood stock.

To peel any shrimp, start by raking along the inner curve with a thumbnail to pull off the small legs, then grab a section or two of the shell (it consists of several overlapping layers) and peel it away. Unless you need the last tail section of the shell for a handle, in shrimp to be dipped by hand, go ahead and remove all of the shell. To "devein," make a shallow slit down the outer (dorsal) surface of the peeled shrimp, exposing the "vein" (actually the intestinal tube). If it looks dark, remove it; sometimes a given batch of shrimp has nothing left in the veins and does not need deveining. There are various shrimp peeling tools on the market that accomplish both steps at once; designs vary, but when you insert the curved blade at the head end and push it toward the tail, it simultaneously pries off the shell and cuts open a channel to expose the vein, and often drags the vein out in the process.

If you want to cook shrimp in the shell—and they always taste better that way—but still want to devein them, use the deveining procedure in the Baked Red Curry Prawns on page 256. Try it with any size of shrimp to be grilled and see if you don't prefer the flavor over that of peeled shrimp.

To my taste, spot shrimp and the other large pandalids are better cooked by dry-heat methods, either in the shell or peeled, than by steaming or boiling, which can make the meat mushy.

Shrimp or Prawns?

"Shrimp" and "prawns" are used somewhat interchangeably in the English-speaking world for various related crustaceans. The British tend to call them all prawns, while in eastern North America they are all called shrimp. Here on the West Coast, the terms somehow developed into separate meanings: shrimp usually refers to the small cooked variety, while larger ones sold raw are often called prawns. But the distinction is not always observed; many a traditional restaurant menu offers both Shrimp Louis and Prawn Louis, the former topped with tiny "bay" shrimp, the latter with four or five large warmwater shrimp—but those same "prawns" hung on the edge of a glass are a Shrimp Cocktail.

In most of the recipes, you will find a salting and rinsing step, a Chinese technique for improving the flavor and texture of any shrimp, but especially the frozen varieties. As I understand it, salting the shrimp heavily but briefly, then rinsing off the salt removes a thin film of damaged protein on the surface of the shrimp which, while not spoiled, has begun to break down through freezing, thawing, and exposure to air. However it works, the result is shrimp with a cleaner taste and a slightly firmer texture, but not noticeably saltier than untreated shrimp.

Shrimp cook quickly, and are done as soon as the meat turns opaque and white; further cooking will only make the meat shrink and toughen.

Crayfish

Crayfish, *Pacifastacus* and *Procambarus* spp.

One other local crustacean needs to be mentioned. Crayfish, little freshwater cousins of lobster, are native to most of the rivers and creeks of the West, and in certain locations they support a commercial catch. It's nothing like the scale of "crawfish" production in Louisiana, but if you know where to shop you can find local crayfish, mostly in the summer months. (In my area they are sold in season at farmers' markets.) We also get a fair amount from Louisiana in its peak season, late winter through spring.

When it comes to cooking crayfish, I can't improve on the standard method: buy as big a batch as you can afford and boil them for 15 minutes (along with onions, new potatoes, and sweet corn) in a big pot of water flavored with Zatarain's Crab Boil. Drain and serve everything together on big platters, with the table spread with newspapers to receive the shells.

To eat boiled crayfish, grab the curled-under tail in one hand and the head in the other and twist them apart. The tail meat should come out with a good-sized dab of tasty orange fat on the exposed end; if not, or if you want to savor every bit of the crayfish flavor, the official method is to suck the juices out of the head. Crack open the underside of the tail, grasp the exposed meat in your teeth, give the tip of the tail a pinch, and the tail meat should come out in one piece. There is also meat in the two big claws, which in the largest crawfish is worth going after with a nutcracker.

Basic Steamed Crab

I've gone back and forth through the years on the best way to cook Dungeness crabs, boiling or steaming. Both produce good results, so the choice depends on the effect you want to achieve. If you want the plainest expression of crab taste, boil them whole, the way they do at the wharf, or steam them without any seasonings. If you prefer to flavor crab as it cooks, then add the ginger and soy sauce to the steaming plate (see variation).

SERVES 2

1 live crab, 1½ to 2 pounds
2 tablespoons soy sauce
1 teaspoon grated or minced fresh ginger
Rice vinegar
Hot pepper sauce

➤ Rinse the crab well under running water, especially the hairy parts on the underside. Kill the crab as directed on page 227; if your steaming pot is deep enough to hold at least 3 inches of boiling water, you can use it for the boiling step, then use the same hot water for steaming (although you may have to pour some out to fit the steaming rack).

➤ Clean the crab and set it right side up on a heatproof plate or glass pie pan that will fit inside your steamer; lay the shell loosely on top or alongside. Fit a rack in the steamer to hold the plate about 1 inch above the water and set the plate on top. Cover and steam 15 minutes, or until all the visible meat is opaque white. Meanwhile, put a small bowl of soy sauce with a little grated ginger at each table setting, and set out vinegar and hot sauce to be added to taste.

➤ When the crab is done, separate the legs from the body and divide the body into several sections, or cut the halves into leg and body sections as directed on page 224. Transfer the pieces to a platter or individual plates and serve immediately (see the note on page 243 for presentation).

NOTE As with all steamed dishes, you may need to modify the instructions here to fit your steaming pot. If there is not room for the whole crab in its natural position, either cut it up as in the following variation and pile the pieces together on the steaming plate, or split it in half and use two plates in two tiers.

VARIATION If you prefer to add flavor as the crab cooks, after killing, split the crab, divide it into individual sections, and crack the legs and claws. Toss the pieces—in a bowl

that will fit in your steamer—with soy sauce, a little rice wine or sherry, and plenty of shredded ginger and green onions. Marinate for a few minutes, then steam. Cooking time will be a little shorter due to the smaller pieces, which have more surface area exposed to the heat.

Fresh Rice-Paper Rolls with Crab

In Chinese and Southeast Asian restaurants, the ubiquitous appetizers known as spring rolls, egg rolls, or "imperial rolls" are usually fried. However, many home cooks and a few restaurants also serve them in a much more healthful "fresh" (not fried) form. Here is a simple version based on cooked crab and an assortment of other low-fat ingredients. The wrappers, known as rice papers, are not paper at all, but edible sheets of dried rice pasta. Look for them in Asian groceries, and pick up some rice sticks, wire-thin, dried rice noodles, at the same time.

For an informal meal, this can be a do-it-yourself-at-the-table affair: set out the bowls of crab and the other fillings and a tray of softened rice papers and let everyone assemble the rolls to his or her liking. The dipping sauce recommended here is only one possibility; for a simple alternative, try bottled sweet and sour sauce doctored to taste with hot pepper sauce.

SERVES 6 TO 8 AS AN APPETIZER

2 ounces rice sticks

1 medium cucumber

24 small rice paper rounds or quarter rounds, softened (see note)

⅓ to ½ pound cooked crabmeat (or a 1½- to 2-pound crab, cooked, chilled, and picked)

2 tablespoons finely shredded ginger

¼ cup finely shredded green onion or Chinese garlic chives

⅓ cup mint or cilantro leaves

Nuoc Cham (Vietnamese dipping sauce), page 326

➤ Cook the rice sticks in boiling water until soft. Drain and rinse with cold water. Cut enough into 1-inch lengths to make 1½ cups; save the rest for another use. Peel and seed the cucumber and cut 24 slender 2-inch spears.

➤ For each roll, lay out a sheet of rice paper and place a tablespoon of bean threads across the center. Add a piece of cucumber, a few pieces of crab, a few slivers of ginger and green onion, and a mint leaf or two. Fold in the two opposite sides and roll into a neat bundle. Place on a serving dish seam side down. Serve with dipping sauce, for eating with the fingers.

TECHNIQUE NOTE Rice papers must be softened with water before use. The traditional method is to dip them in a bowl of water, but an easier method I learned years ago from a Cambodian restaurant cook in San Francisco is to layer them between damp kitchen towels, where they will soften in 5 to 10 minutes. They will hold that way for an hour or more without becoming soggy or sticky.

Crab-Topped Cornmeal Blini with Guacamole

One of my favorite seafood and vegetable/grain combinations is crab and corn, especially corn in the form of savory pancakes. In summer, I like to add fresh kernels of sweet corn to crab cakes. In winter, the peak season for Dungeness crab, the corn comes in the form of ground yellow cornmeal, in this case made into dainty little two-bite pancakes inspired by Russian buckwheat blini. Topped with a dab of simple guacamole, these cakes make a perfect finger-food platform for flakes of Dungeness crabmeat. Try them as a stand-up appetizer at a cocktail party, or as a first course in an informal meal, or even as snacks for TV football games. They are equally at home with champagne, cocktails, or beer.

MAKES ABOUT 60 (8 TO 10 APPETIZER SERVINGS)

2 cups boiling water

1 cup fine yellow cornmeal

1 cup buttermilk

2 eggs

2 tablespoons corn or other mild vegetable oil

½ cup flour

½ teaspoon baking powder

½ teaspoon baking soda

½ teaspoon salt

Guacamole, below

½ pound crabmeat, large pieces broken up slightly, well drained

➤ Pour the boiling water over the cornmeal in a medium bowl. Stir to moisten evenly, then let cool. Stir in the buttermilk, eggs, and oil, then sift the dry ingredients together into the bowl. Stir until smooth. The batter should be the consistency of heavy cream.

➤ To cook the blini, heat a griddle or a

couple of large heavy skillets over medium heat until a few drops of water sizzle and dance on the surface before evaporating. Rub the surface lightly with a paper towel dipped in oil. Spoon the batter onto the griddle to make small cakes (a scant tablespoon makes about a 2½-inch cake, the ideal size) and cook until bubbles break on top and do not close again; turn and cook another 30 seconds. Transfer to a warm plate and keep warm in a low oven while preparing the rest.

➤ To serve buffet style, set out the plate of blini, with the guacamole and the crab in separate dishes with small serving spoons. For appetizers to be passed on trays, top each cake with a dab of guacamole and place a bite of crab on top.

Guacamole

➤ Combine 2 tablespoons minced green onion, 1 small chile, seeded and minced, and a large pinch of salt in a mixing bowl or mortar and mash until liquefied. Halve and pit 2 ripe medium avocados and scoop the flesh into the bowl. Mash with a pestle, spoon, or fork to a fairly smooth paste. Season to taste with lime juice, plus additional salt and hot pepper sauce if needed.

NOTE For easier service, the batter can be made several hours ahead and refrigerated, and the guacamole can be mixed and tightly covered (press plastic wrap right down against the surface to prevent oxidation). However, the cakes are best at least warm, if not fresh from the pan, so cook them as close to serving time as possible, and keep them warm in a very low oven if necessary.

Provençal Crab Soup with Vermicelli

Seafood soup finds one of its purest expressions in the Provençal soupe de pélous, in which whole crabs give their flavor to a simple saffron-scented tomato broth. The broth is then enriched with pasta or ladled over a slice of bread, and the crab is served as a separate course. In Provence, it would be made with one of several species of small Mediterranean crabs, with one or more crabs per serving. One blue crab per person can stand in for the Dungeness.

SERVES 2 AS A MAIN DISH, 4 AS A FIRST COURSE

1 live Dungeness crab, 1½ to 2 pounds

3 tablespoons olive oil

1 cup sliced leek (white and yellow part only)

2 cloves garlic, sliced

¾ cup peeled, seeded, and chopped tomato, fresh or canned

1 quart water

Bouquet garni of parsley, thyme, and bay leaf

Salt and pepper, to taste

Large pinch of saffron

3 ounces vermicelli or angel hair pasta, broken into short pieces

➤ Kill, clean, and crack the crab (see pages 224 to 227).

➤ Heat the oil in a heavy casserole or deep skillet. Add the leek and garlic and cook over medium heat until soft and slightly colored. Add the tomato, water, bouquet garni, and crab pieces; cover and simmer over low heat until the crabmeat is fully opaque, about 15 minutes.

➤ Remove the crab to a warm platter, cover loosely with foil, and set aside. Season the soup to taste, add the saffron and vermicelli, and cook until the pasta is tender, about 5 minutes. Serve the soup in shallow bowls, with the crab served separately.

NOTE Most of the time that Dungeness crab is in season, local tomatoes are not, so you will be better off with canned tomatoes in this and the following recipe. In summer, when tomatoes are in season but local crab is not, try either soup with Eastern blue crabs, commonly available in Asian markets.

Crab Soup with Chipotle Chiles

Here is another variation on tomato-flavored crab soup, based on one of the classic seafood dishes of Veracruz on Mexico's Gulf coast. The soup gets its particular punch from chipotle chile, the ripened and smoke-dried form of the familiar jalapeño chile. In Veracruz, the soup would be made with the local blue crab, the same species also found from Texas to New England (Callinectes sapidus). One of our local Dungeness crabs can stand in here for three or four of their smaller Eastern cousins.

SERVES 4 TO 6

1 live Dungeness crab, about 1½ pounds

1 can (16 ounces) whole peeled tomatoes

2 tablespoons oil

3 medium green onions, white parts sliced, tops reserved

2 cloves garlic, minced

2 dried or canned chipotle chiles (see note)

Salt, to taste

Lime or lemon wedges

Dried oregano leaves or fresh cilantro sprigs

➤ Boil the crab to the fully cooked stage according to one of the methods on page 227; remove and rinse with cold water until cool enough to handle, and reserve the cooking liquid. Clean and crack the crab and extract the meat, keeping the claw and leg sections as intact as possible. Save the shells for the broth.

➤ Drain and chop the tomatoes, reserving the juice. Heat 1 tablespoon of the oil in a large saucepan over medium heat. Add the green onion tops and cook 2 minutes. Add 1 quart of the crab cooking water, the tomato juice, and the crab shells. Bring to a boil, reduce the heat, and simmer 10 minutes.

➤ Strain the broth, wipe the pan dry, return it to the heat, and add 1 tablespoon of oil. Add the garlic and sliced green onions and cook until fragrant, about 15 seconds. Add the broth, chopped tomatoes, and chiles and simmer until the chile flavor permeates the broth, about 2 minutes. Taste for seasoning, then add the crabmeat to the broth to reheat. Serve with lime wedges and oregano for seasoning each bowl to taste.

TECHNIQUE NOTE Because the boiling liquid will become part of the finished soup, pay extra attention to rinsing the live crab well under cold running water. If the underside seems especially dirty, scrub it with a long-handled brush (but watch out for the claws).

NOTE Chipotle chiles are sometimes available dried, but they are much easier to find in small cans packed in a vinegar-based sauce (adobo). Use them with caution, as they are really hot. Unless you are a hero chile eater, one or two left whole is plenty to flavor the broth, and it's meant to be left behind in the pot.

Biting into a whole chipotle is not for the timid.

VARIATION If it's more convenient to start with a cooked crab, clean and crack the crab as usual, and make the soup base with the shells and plain water. You will lose a bit of flavor, but it will still make a good soup.

Cioppino

See Searching for Cioppino, page 238.

SERVES 4 TO 6

1 Dungeness crab, 1½ pounds or more, live or cooked

¼ cup olive oil

1 cup diced onion

1 medium green pepper, finely diced

½ cup finely diced celery

1 tablespoon minced garlic

Handful of parsley leaves, chopped

1 can (28 ounces) crushed or diced tomatoes, with juices

1½ cups dry white or rosé wine

½ teaspoon dried basil leaves, crumbled

Salt, to taste

1 dozen small clams or mussels

1 pound boneless white fish fillet or steak, cut into ¾-inch cubes

1 pound squid, cleaned and cut into rings

➤ If the crab is alive, kill it by one of the methods on page 227. Clean the crab, split the body in half, and cut the halves into sections, each attached to a leg or claw. Crack each leg and claw segment.

➤ Combine the oil, diced vegetables, garlic, and parsley in a large soup pot and cook over medium heat until the vegetables are soft but not browned. Add the tomatoes, wine, crab fat (if using—see note), and basil, bring to a simmer, and cook 10 to 15 minutes, or until the vegetables disappear into the sauce. Taste for seasoning. (Can be made to this point ahead of time.)

➤ If the crab is raw, add it to the simmering sauce 12 minutes before serving time. Add the clams 10 minutes before serving time, mussels and cooked crab at 5 or 6 minutes, fish cubes at 5 minutes, and squid for the last 2 minutes. The cioppino is done when the clams or mussels are fully open, the fish begins to flake apart, and the crabmeat and squid are opaque. Serve in soup bowls, with a side bowl or plate for the shells.

NOTE Traditionally, a cioppino would include some of the crab fat, an important source of flavor; see the caveat on page 224 and decide for yourself if you want to include it. If your fishmonger offers to clean and crack the crab for you, by all means take him up on it, but ask for the top shell as well; you should be able to dig out a tablespoon or two of fat from the corners of the shell.

Searching for Cioppino

A couple of times each winter, during the peak of Dungeness crab season in Northern California, I get in the mood to make a cioppino, the hearty tomato-based seafood stew that has been part of California cuisine since the arrival of the first Portuguese and Italian immigrant fishermen more than a century ago.

Of course, there is no one way to make cioppino, and the argument about what constitutes a good one has doubtless gone on since the first bowl was served. Fishermen's stews are by nature a "catch of the day" affair, made with whatever fish and shellfish are at hand. For a nineteenth-century fisherman on the central California coast, that would mean Dungeness crab; local fish such as rockfish, lingcod, flounder, halibut, or sole; squid (calamari) at certain times of the year; and perhaps some mussels gathered from the rocks at low tide, or clams dug on a beach or mudflat. I think it's safe to say that no two batches contained exactly the same mix of seafood, or the same amount of tomato; that one cook's cioppino was thinner, another's thicker; that some used red wine, some white; and so on for all the variables that go into any traditional dish.

So, when I set out to make a cioppino, it's both an attempt to stick as close as possible to how I imagine the "original" and an exercise in cooking locally and seasonally, although I'm not above using ingredients from farther away, if they fit the spirit of the dish. Shopping for cioppino ingredients raises a number of questions:

First of all, what kind of shellfish? Dungeness crab, of course, although south of Santa Barbara a case could be made for spiny lobster. And what form of Dungeness crab? If you're a purist, the only way to go is to buy a live crab and cook it yourself. However, I have made perfectly enjoyable cioppino with already cooked crab simply reheated in the stew.

Okay, what other shellfish? Most recipes call for clams or mussels, and sometimes shrimp and squid. Squid is cheap and tasty, so in it goes. Given my local bias, warmwater shrimp from Mexico, Ecuador, or Thailand doesn't make a whole lot of sense, so I usually skip the shrimp. But I wouldn't hesitate to include mussels from Maine or eastern Canada, or Manila clams from Puget Sound. So much for consistency.

How about fish? Some sort of fish is traditional in cioppino, and local rockfish ("snapper") seems the most traditional. But rockfish can be hard to come by when a lot of the local fleet is concentrating on crab or herring. This is where it is especially important to remember the "catch of the day" principle, and take whatever lean white fish looks best. More than once in mid-December, when the crab and swordfish seasons overlap, I have found chunks of swordfish trim selling for a dollar less per pound than rockfish fillets. Guess which wound up in the cioppino pot?

Cioppino demands tomatoes, but what kind of tomatoes? There is no advantage in fresh tomatoes this time of year, so I'm happy to use good canned tomatoes. If you like a thinner broth with identifiable chunks of tomato, use diced tomatoes; if you like it thicker and smoother, go for crushed. If they come packed with basil, so much the better.

White wine or red? Now it gets tough. Most traditional recipes say red wine, and I usually belong to the "all wine would be red if it could" school, and the old guys drank mostly red wine. But having tried it both ways lots of times, I have to admit I like it better with a white like sauvignon blanc. Maybe I'll try a dry rosé next time.

And for the rest of the ingredients? Onions and garlic, of course, and a good handful of parsley. Celery? Sometimes. Dried mushrooms? Traditional according to some sources, but I've never gotten around to trying them. Bell peppers? I've become such a red-pepper snob in recent years that I almost always walk right past the green bells, but I have to admit it—a cioppino made with green pepper tastes just right.

Crab Louis

Of the seafood dishes that could be called San Francisco classics—cioppino, charcoal-grilled sanddabs, and the fried oyster and scrambled egg concoction known as Hangtown fry—I would wager that none is more popular than Crab Louis (sometimes spelled Louie, and always pronounced that way). This substantial salad of cooked crabmeat on a bed of lettuce with a thick tomato-based dressing has spread from its apparent San Francisco origins throughout the West, and recipes are found in most American cookbooks.

Just exactly what constitutes a Louis dressing is a subject of some controversy, but most versions get their red color and much of their flavor from chili sauce, basically a spicier and chunkier version of ketchup. Any decent version also includes a fair amount of chopped fresh herbs, typically tarragon, parsley, and chives. Beyond these ingredients there is little agreement. Some versions contain heavy cream, some chopped bell pepper. But the ingredient that dominates most modern recipes, mayonnaise, may not be authentic at all. Several "authentic" recipes were published from the 1910s through the '30s, some without a speck of mayonnaise,

others where it makes up a third of the total dressing. Rather than take sides, I offer two versions of Louis dressing, one with mayonnaise and one without. Cooked shrimp, either the tiny cooked and peeled "bay shrimp" or larger "prawns," are often substituted for some or all of the crabmeat.

SERVES 2

½ head iceberg, romaine, or other crisp lettuce
½ cup Louis Dressing I or II, below
¼ pound cooked crabmeat
Optional garnishes:
    1 hard-cooked egg, quartered or sliced
    1 small jar artichoke hearts
    Cherry tomatoes
    Cooked asparagus spears

➤ Reserve some outer lettuce leaves for lining the plates or salad bowl if you like; tear the rest into bite-size pieces, wash, and spin dry.

➤ Toss the lettuce with a little of the dressing and arrange it on the plates, then top with crab and your choice of garnishes. Serve with additional dressing on the side.

Louis Dressing I

MAKES 1 CUP

2 tablespoons white wine vinegar or lemon juice

Pinch of salt and pepper

½ teaspoon dry mustard

¼ teaspoon paprika

½ teaspoon Worcestershire sauce

½ cup olive oil

¼ cup chili sauce

2 tablespoons chopped fresh herbs—parsley, chives, tarragon, or a blend

➤ Combine the vinegar, salt, pepper, mustard, paprika, and Worcestershire sauce and beat with a wire whisk until dissolved. Beat in the oil, then the chili sauce and herbs. Chill well and stir before serving.

Louis Dressing II

MAKES 1 CUP

¼ teaspoon dry mustard

1 tablespoon lemon juice

Dash of Worcestershire sauce

¼ cup olive oil

⅓ cup mayonnaise

⅓ cup chili sauce

1 tablespoon chopped fresh herbs—parsley, chives, tarragon, or a blend

➤ Combine the mustard, lemon juice, and Worcestershire sauce, beat to dissolve, and beat in the oil. Add the mayonnaise, chili sauce, and herbs and blend thoroughly. Chill before serving.

Crab and Leek Timbales

Crab season in central California traditionally opens a week or two before Thanksgiving, and crab dishes precede the turkey at many a holiday table in the Bay Area. Crab timbales, small individual savory custards, make a dainty first course for any holiday meal. Here, they are served with a simple tomato sauce using the last fresh tomatoes of the season.

SERVES 10

1 pound ripe tomatoes

Salt and sugar, to taste

2 medium leeks

1 tablespoon butter

1½ cups warm milk or half-and-half

4 eggs, at room temperature

¾ teaspoon salt

½ teaspoon paprika

Pinch of cayenne or white pepper

1 cup cooked crabmeat, shredded

➤ Quarter the tomatoes and place them in a heavy saucepan. Cover and cook over medium-low heat 15 minutes, or until they have rendered a lot of juice. Pass the tomatoes through a food mill, return the purée to the pan, and simmer until slightly thickened, about 30 minutes. Season to taste with salt and a pinch of sugar, if needed. Keep warm.

➤ Slice the white and pale green parts of the leeks crosswise and place them in a bowl of water. Pull apart and swirl to remove any dirt. Lift the leeks out of the water, drain in a colander, and cook gently in the butter until tender.

➤ Preheat the oven to 325°F. Combine the milk, eggs, salt, and seasonings and beat with a wire whisk until slightly foamy. Stir in the leeks and crabmeat. Pour into 10 buttered timbale molds or small ramekins or 10 cups of a muffin tin. Place in a baking pan and carefully add hot water to half the depth of the molds. Cover loosely with a sheet of oiled paper or foil and bake until a knife inserted in the center comes out clean, 20 to 25 minutes depending on the shape. Unmold the timbales and serve inverted on small plates, surrounded with a little tomato sauce.

Rock Crab, Okra, and Sausage Gumbo

Gumbo lends itself to endless variation. This version, loosely based on a Paul Prudhomme recipe, can also include shrimp or oysters. Of course, you can use Dungeness crab, as well as snow crab. Removing the crab from the shell is optional, but definitely makes the gumbo easier to eat.

SERVES 6 TO 8 AS A FIRST COURSE, 3 TO 4 AS A MAIN DISH

1 large or 2 small rock crabs, live or cooked

1 cup diced onion

1 cup diced celery

½ cup diced red bell pepper

2 or 3 large green chiles, seeds and ribs removed, diced

2 tablespoons minced garlic

½ teaspoon black pepper

½ teaspoon white pepper

½ teaspoon ground California or New Mexico chile

¼ teaspoon cayenne

¼ teaspoon dried thyme

¼ teaspoon dried oregano

1 teaspoon kosher salt (less if using table salt)

¼ cup plus 1 tablespoon peanut oil

¼ cup flour

½ pound sliced okra

1 quart chicken or fish stock

½ pound smoked sausage, in ¼-inch slices

2 cups cooked long-grain rice

➤ If using a live crab, boil it by either of the methods on page 227. While the crab is cooking, combine the onion, celery, bell pepper, chiles, and garlic and set aside. Combine the spices, herbs, and salt in another bowl.

➤ When the crab is fully cooked, rinse it in cold water to stop the cooking. Clean and crack it and extract the meat in as large pieces as possible.

➤ Heat ¼ cup of oil in a deep cast-iron skillet over medium heat until a pinch of flour sizzles on contact. Add the flour, reduce the heat to low, and cook, stirring with a wooden spoon or spatula, until the mixture (roux) is a deep reddish-brown color. (This may take up to 30 minutes, but vigilant stirring is necessary to prevent the roux from burning.) When the roux reaches the right color, turn off the heat and let cool slightly, stirring a few times more.

➤ Working carefully to avoid splattering the hot roux, add the onion mixture to the skillet and return it to medium heat. Cook, stirring, until the onions begin to soften. Add the seasoning mixture, cook 2 minutes, and remove from the heat. (This gumbo base may be prepared a day or two ahead of time and refrigerated, or frozen for longer storage.)

➤ In a large saucepan, heat the remaining oil over medium heat. Add the okra and cook until it begins to exude liquid. Add the stock and sausage and bring to a boil. Add the roux and vegetable mixture and cook 30 minutes. Taste for seasoning and adjust if necessary. Add the crabmeat and cook until just heated through. Serve in deep bowls over rice.

TECHNIQUE NOTE Cooking the roux requires attention, but not necessarily constant stirring. Once you are comfortable with the process, you can chop up the vegetables, cook and clean the crab, or do other preparations at the same time, so long as you stir the roux every minute or so to keep it from scorching.

Crab in Green Chile Sauce

In this recipe, I have taken the sauce and filling out of the classic green seafood enchiladas of Mexico, to be served on their own. Serve warm corn tortillas on the side.

SERVES 2

2 tablespoons mild olive oil or other vegetable oil

1 tablespoon minced garlic

4 small green chiles, seeds and ribs removed, minced

1 large can (26 to 28 ounces) tomatillos, drained and mashed

½ to ¾ pound crabmeat

¼ cup chopped cilantro

¼ cup sour cream or crème fraîche (see page 30), at room temperature (optional)

➤ Heat the oil in a medium skillet and cook the garlic and chiles until fragrant. Add the tomatillos and simmer until slightly thickened, about 20 minutes. Stir in the crabmeat and cilantro and cook until the crab is heated through. Serve immediately, with a dollop of sour cream on each serving.

NOTE If fresh tomatillos are available, start with 2 pounds and peel and cook as for Summer Vegetable and Tomatillo Sauce for Salmon, page 66.

Roasted or Grilled Marinated Crab

This technique of cooking crab and the chile-spiked marinade have been part of my crab repertoire since I worked for Jeremiah Tower at Santa Fe Bar & Grill in Berkeley in the early '80s. As I understand it, the dish went back a few years further at the restaurant, to the days of Mark Miller and Willie Bishop. Whoever invented it, it's a delicious way of cooking crab. We cooked the crab halves on the charcoal grill, which is fine when weather permits, but you can get much the same effect by roasting the crab in a hot oven.

SERVES 2

1 live crab, about 2 pounds

3 tablespoons olive oil

1 tablespoon shredded ginger

1 tablespoon chopped garlic

2 serrano or other small green chiles, chopped

Freshly ground black pepper

2 to 4 tablespoons butter

Salt, to taste

➤ Kill the crab, either by boiling or splitting (see page 224); if you are planning to use the upper shell in the presentation, boiling works better. Clean the crab and split the body into two halves with the legs and claws still attached. Carefully crack each leg and claw segment with a mallet. Place the crab in a large bowl with the oil, ginger, garlic, chiles, and a generous grinding of pepper. Marinate 1 to 4 hours in the refrigerator.

➤ Remove the crab from the marinade 15 minutes before cooking. Grill the halves and the shell over a hot fire until the outer shells are bright red and the meat in the largest sections is opaque (pry one open to check), 3 to 4 minutes per side. Or, place the crab halves and shell in a roasting pan lightly oiled with a bit of the marinade and roast in a 450°F oven until done as described above, 12 to 15 minutes.

➤ While the crab cooks, strain the vegetables out of the marinade and combine them with the butter in a small saucepan. Simmer 5 minutes and season to taste. Serve in small bowls as a dipping sauce for the crab.

Stir-Fried Crab with Chiles and Ginger

Marinating the crab pieces prior to stir-frying is not a classic Chinese restaurant technique, but it helps the flavors penetrate the meat. Taste the chiles and adjust the amount as necessary; some jalapeños are distressingly mild.

SERVES 3 TO 4 WITH OTHER DISHES

1 live Dungeness crab

2 tablespoons soy sauce

2 tablespoons Chinese rice wine or dry sherry

3 tablespoons shredded ginger

Oil for stir-frying

3 or 4 red or green jalapeño or Fresno chiles, seeds and ribs removed, cut into thin strips

1 tablespoon chopped garlic

½ cup water or unsalted chicken stock

1 teaspoon cornstarch dissolved in 2 tablespoons water

Shredded green onions or cilantro leaves for garnish

➤ Kill, clean, cut up, and crack the crab as directed on pages 224 to 227. Combine the soy sauce, wine, and 1 tablespoon of ginger shreds in a large bowl. Toss the crab pieces in this mixture and marinate 30 minutes.

➤ Drain the crab, reserving the marinade. Heat a wok over medium-high heat and add the oil in a thin stream around the edge of the pan. Add the chiles, garlic, and remaining ginger and stir-fry a few seconds. Add the crab pieces and stir-fry until the shells begin to turn red. Add the reserved marinade and stock or water. Cover and cook until the shells are entirely red and all the exposed meat is opaque white; lift the lid every minute or so and toss the mixture to ensure even cooking.

➤ Stir in the cornstarch mixture and cook until the sauce thickens and becomes glossy. Transfer to a serving platter and garnish with green onions or cilantro.

NOTE You can just pile the crab pieces in a tangle on the serving platter, but for a little fancier presentation, arrange them more or less in their original positions, with the redder sides of the legs and claws upward. For an optional finishing touch, include the top shell, laid back in place over the middle; in this case, return the shell to the boiling water after killing the crab and cook another 5 minutes or so until it has lost all traces of its raw color.

Dungeness Crab Cakes

Although the crab is from the Pacific, it's hard to improve on the basic Chesapeake Bay style of crab cakes. Two small Dungeness crabs or one very large one will yield a pound of meat, enough for eight crab cakes.

Most restaurant chefs would serve these over a bed of fancy greens as an appetizer, but a couple of them make a nice entree with potatoes and a side vegetable. Serve with your choice of tartar sauce, aioli, or one of the flavored mayonnaise sauces on page 323.

SERVES 4

1 pound crabmeat

1 egg

2 tablespoons mayonnaise

2 teaspoons Worcestershire sauce

1 teaspoon prepared mustard

1 teaspoon Chesapeake seafood seasoning (page 29)

½ teaspoon paprika

¼ teaspoon freshly ground pepper

¼ cup dry bread crumbs

1 tablespoon chopped parsley

Oil for pan-frying

➤ Look over the crabmeat and remove any bits of shell. Combine with the remaining ingredients except the oil and mix gently with a fork until everything is evenly moistened, but some good-sized chunks of crab remain. (A two-tined cook's fork makes a good tool for combining

the ingredients without breaking up the crab too much.) Refrigerate until ready to cook.

➤ Generously coat a 12-inch skillet with oil and set it over medium heat. For each cake, scoop up about ⅓ cup of the crab mixture and gently form it into a thick patty. Cook until nicely browned on both sides and heated through, 3 to 5 minutes per side depending on thickness.

NOTE Crab-style surimi (see page 226) can be used to make a less expensive version of crab cakes, if you like it. It's tempting to mix some surimi in with real crab as a less expensive stretcher, but in my opinion the real crab gets lost in the mix, and you would be better off using all surimi.

Fettuccine with Lobster Sauce Américaine

Homard à l'américaine is a classic French dish of lobster stewed with tomatoes and aromatic vegetables. Despite its name, its roots are more Provençal than American (see note). In the original version, the lobster (1 small per person, or half of a larger size) is cut up and cooked, then returned to the shells for serving in its sauce. This version uses a higher proportion of sauce to lobster, and the meat and sauce are served over fresh pasta.

SERVES 2 AS A MAIN DISH, 4 AS A FIRST COURSE

1 live lobster, 1 to 1½ pounds

3 tablespoons olive oil

1 carrot, finely diced

1 small onion, finely diced

1 stalk celery, finely diced

¼ cup minced shallots or green onions

1 clove garlic, minced

Pinch of cayenne

Salt and pepper

1½ ounces brandy (preferably Armagnac or Cognac)

¾ pound ripe tomatoes, peeled, seeded, and chopped (to yield a generous cup)

1 tablespoon tomato paste (optional, if the tomatoes need help in flavor)

2 or 3 sprigs parsley

1 sprig fresh tarragon, OR ½ teaspoon dried leaves

½ cup dry white wine

½ cup lobster stock, court-bouillon, or water

1 tablespoon softened butter

½ pound fettuccine or other fresh egg noodles

➤ Kill the lobster by either of the methods on page 229; rinse with cold water to stop the cooking. With a sturdy French knife or Chinese cleaver, cut off the claws where they join the body; crack each shell section with a mallet. Split the lobster lengthwise from head to tail. Discard the translucent stomach sac just behind the eyes and the white intestinal tube running the length of the tail; reserve the greenish liver (tomalley) and, if the lobster is a female, the roe. Separate the tail pieces from the body and cut the tail halves into 2 or 3 sections each.

➤ In a deep covered skillet or flameproof casserole, heat the oil to near smoking. Add the lobster pieces a few at a time and cook over medium-high heat until the shells turn red, removing them to a plate as they are done. Reduce the heat to medium, add the diced vegetables, shallots, garlic, and cayenne, and cook until the vegetables soften. Season

the lobster pieces lightly with salt and pepper and return them to the pan. Add the brandy, bring to a boil, and cook until nearly evaporated. Add the tomatoes, tomato paste, herbs, and liquids. Cover and simmer on top of the stove or in a 350°F oven for 20 minutes.

➤ While the lobster is cooking, mash the tomalley and roe and mix it with the butter. Have a pot of water ready for cooking the pasta.

➤ Remove the cooked lobster pieces from the pan and set aside. Over high heat, reduce the sauce by two-thirds. Meanwhile, remove the lobster meat from the shell and cut it into bite-size pieces. Discard the shells or save them for making stock or lobster butter.

➤ Check the sauce for seasoning and adjust if necessary. Stir in the butter mixture, return the lobster meat to the pan, and keep the sauce warm. Cook and drain the pasta and place it in a serving dish. Top with the sauce and toss lightly to combine.

NOTE Whenever I mention this dish in print, I can count on getting a letter or two insisting that it should be *à l'armoricaine*. Armorica is an old name for a coastal region of northwestern France, part of what is now Brittany and Normandy. It is certainly lobster country, so it's natural that a famous lobster dish would be associated with the region. But it's not exactly the part of France most famous for tomatoes and olive oil. In the second edition of *Larousse Gastronomique,* Prosper Montagné concludes that the dish was named by a chef who had worked in America, but was essentially Provençal. I like to think the name has something to do with the New World origin of tomatoes.

Spiny Lobster Salad

This works equally well with Atlantic lobster. If you buy your lobster already cooked, skip the first step.

SERVES 2

1 live spiny lobster, about 1½ pounds

3 tablespoons mayonnaise

½ teaspoon Dijon mustard

Dash of hot pepper sauce (optional)

½ cup diced celery

Large red or butter lettuce leaves

Cherry tomatoes, cucumber wedges, or
   cooked tiny new potatoes

➤ Several hours to two days before serving, cook the lobster by either method on page 229. Rinse with cold water to stop the cooking (or surround with ice cubes to chill even faster). Refrigerate until thoroughly chilled.

➤ Twist off and reserve the legs and large antennae. Split the lobster lengthwise and remove the tail meat from each half in one piece. Remove the intestinal tube running down the center of the tail. Reserve the tomalley (the pale greenish mass in the central part of the shell) for the dressing if desired. Discard the rest of the contents of the shell. Cut the tail meat into bite-size pieces and extract any good-sized chunks from the legs and antennae.

➤ Combine the mayonnaise and mustard in a medium bowl. Add hot pepper sauce and tomalley to taste. Remove half the dressing and set it aside; toss the lobster meat and celery in the rest of the dressing. Place the lobster shell halves on plates lined with lettuce leaves and spoon the salad into the

shells. Garnish with your choice of vegetables and serve the additional dressing on the side.

Lobster Sauté with Saffron Risotto

This is a dish for September, when lobster prices typically take a dip and the produce markets overflow with summer-ripe tomatoes.

Usually a shellfish risotto incorporates the meat into the rice dish, which is flavored with the essence extracted from the shells. But lobster is special enough that it deserves to stand more or less alone, so I prepare a flavorful risotto with lobster-flavored stock, and use it as a base for a simple sauté of lobster meat and ripe tomatoes. The recipe is easily doubled for entertaining, and makes a fine meal with a salad and some good bread.

SERVES 2

1 live lobster, 1 to 1½ pounds

4 tablespoons olive oil

3 to 4 cups unsalted chicken or fish stock

¼ cup thinly sliced green onion (white parts
   only—reserve tops for stock)

1 tablespoon minced garlic

¼ teaspoon saffron threads

1 cup arborio rice

¼ cup dry white wine

½ teaspoon salt (approximately)

Pepper, to taste

1½ to 2 tablespoons butter

1 cup peeled, seeded, and chopped tomatoes

¼ teaspoon vanilla extract

➤ Boil the lobster according to your favorite method (see page 229). Rinse with cold water or surround with ice to cool. Split lengthwise. Remove the stomach sac near the head and the intestinal tube running the length of the tail. Break off the claws, crack each section carefully, and extract the meat in as large pieces as possible (try especially to keep the mitten-shaped claw meat in one piece). Remove the tail meat from each half in one piece. If you want to use the tail shells for presentation, separate them carefully from the bodies and set aside. Ditto for the four pairs of small legs.

➤ Chop the shells (and the contents of the body) into small pieces with a heavy knife. Heat 2 tablespoons of the oil in a medium saucepan, add the shells and any juices from the cutting board, and sauté over medium-low heat until the liquid is gone, about 10 minutes. (If time permits, baking the shells in a 400°F oven for about 15 minutes does the job even better.) Add the stock, bring just to a boil, reduce the heat, and simmer 20 to 40 minutes. Strain and skim off the oil. Wash the pan and decant the strained stock back into to the pan, leaving behind the sediment. Keep the stock warm.

➤ Heat the remaining 2 tablespoons of oil in a deep skillet over medium heat. Add the onion and garlic and crumble in the saffron. Sauté until the onion and garlic are soft and fragrant. Stir in the rice, coating it well with the oil. Add the wine, ½ teaspoon salt, a pinch of pepper, and enough stock to cover the rice by about ⅛ inch. Cook, stirring occasionally, until the liquid drops below the level of the rice. Add stock to cover again and cook down again. Repeat with successive additions

of stock until a grain of rice has only a tiny trace of a raw center, then add one more addition of stock. The risotto will take 3 to 4 additions of stock in all and about 20 to 25 minutes of cooking time.

➤ While the risotto cooks, slice the lobster tail and miscellaneous pieces of meat into bite-size pieces; leave the claw meat intact. About the time you add the last addition of stock to the risotto, melt the butter in another skillet and add the lobster, tomatoes, and vanilla to reheat. Season to taste and serve over the finished risotto, heaped in and around the tail shell and garnished with the legs if desired.

NOTE Boiling the lobster and flavoring the stock can be done as much as a day ahead of time; the final dish can then be assembled in the 20 minutes or so it takes to cook the risotto. If you do the dish from start to finish in one session, figure about an hour and a half, much of it hands-off cooking time.

I don't know who first discovered this, but a trace of vanilla harmonizes nicely with the sweet flavor of lobster. You might try sneaking a little into the other lobster dishes in this chapter.

ALTERNATIVE SPECIES This risotto and sauce will complement just about any crustacean of the same general shape—spiny or slipper lobster tails, crayfish, langostinos, or large shrimp. Live crayfish should be boiled first and the meat picked out of the tails. With anything smaller than lobster, you won't have shell halves for presentation, so use all the shells in the stock.

Lobster Chow Fun

This is my own combination of two standard Chinese dishes, Cantonese-style lobster and the stir-fried rice noodle dish known as chow fun. If you are buying your lobster in a Chinese market, look for folded sheets of wide fresh rice noodles in plastic-wrapped trays, usually near the cash register. If you can't find them, you can substitute the fettuccine-like dried rice noodles, boiling them just until they soften and swell (about 3 minutes) and rinsing them with cold water to stop the cooking.

This sauce, which sometimes contains beaten eggs, is known as lobster sauce even when it's used on other shellfish. So if you see shrimp with lobster sauce on a Chinese menu, it doesn't mean there will be any lobster in the dish, just that the shrimp are served with the same sauce that would be used for lobster.

SERVES 4 WITH OTHER DISHES, 2 AS A MAIN DISH

1 live lobster, 1 to 1½ pounds

White parts of 2 green onions, sliced (reserve tops)

2 teaspoons minced ginger

1 teaspoon minced garlic

1 tablespoon Chinese fermented black beans, rinsed and coarsely chopped (optional)

2 tablespoons dry sherry or Chinese rice wine

½ cup chicken stock or water

1 tablespoon soy sauce

¼ teaspoon salt (omit if using salted stock)

1 pound fresh rice noodles

2 tablespoons peanut or other vegetable oil

2 ounces ground or minced lean pork

➤ Cook the lobster by one of the methods on page 229. While the lobster is cooking, prepare the remaining ingredients as follows Combine the green onions, ginger, and garlic in a small bowl. Combine the black beans and wine in another bowl. Combine the stock, soy sauce, and salt in a third bowl. Place the noodles in a large colander and pour boiling water over them to soften them slightly and rinse off the excess oil; drain.

➤ Remove the lobster from the pot with tongs and rinse it with cold water until cool enough to handle. Working over a bowl to catch the juices, twist off the tail. Split the tail lengthwise with a heavy knife, remove the intestinal tube running down the middle, and pull the meat out of each half in one piece, leaving the shell halves intact. Twist off the claws, crack them with a nutcracker, and remove the meat in as large pieces as possible. Chop the tail and claw meat into bite-size pieces. Split the body lengthwise; pull out and reserve the roe (if using a female lobster) and the creamy tomalley, plus any easily removable bits of meat. Set the tail and body shell halves aside.

➤ Heat the oil in a wok over high heat. Add the pork, stir-fry until it begins to lose its raw color, then stir in the minced ingredients and the lobster roe and tomalley. Cook 10 seconds, add the noodles, and stir-fry to break them up into smaller pieces. Add the liquids, the black bean mixture, and the lobster pieces and toss to combine everything and coat the noodles with the sauce. Serve immediately on an oval platter, garnished with the green onion tops and the empty tail shell and body halves arranged at either end.

Lobster Ragout with Black Beans and Tomatoes

Lobster and tomatoes meet again, this time medallions of tail meat simmered in a buttery East-West tomato sauce flavored with Chinese black beans. The sauce is inspired by a clam and mussel dish in Ken Hom's East Meets West Cuisine. *This dish makes an elegant first course or a not-too-filling main dish. In the latter case, you might precede it with a risotto or pasta made without tomatoes or basil.*

Use either spiny lobster or Atlantic (try to extract the mitten-shaped meat from Atlantic lobster claws in one piece). You can also use frozen rock lobster tails, but the result will not be as tender; eliminate the boiling step if using frozen tails.

SERVES 2 AS A MAIN DISH, 4 AS A FIRST COURSE

1 live Atlantic or spiny lobster, about 1½ pounds

1½ cups chicken or fish stock

2 cups peeled, seeded, and finely chopped tomatoes

2 tablespoons Chinese fermented black beans

½ cup fresh basil leaves

2 to 3 tablespoons butter, in small pieces

➤ Place the lobster in a deep pot with cold water to cover by several inches. Cover the pot and bring the water almost to a boil over high heat. When the water is just about to boil, turn off the heat and let the lobster steep about 1 minute per pound. Remove the lobster and immediately rinse with cold water to stop the cooking (or surround with ice cubes to chill even faster).

➤ Separate the lobster tail from the body. With poultry shears or a small knife, split open the underside of the tail, trying not to cut into the meat. Remove the tail meat in one piece and pull out the central vein. Reserve the shells for a shellfish stock (freeze if they will not be used the same day). Slice the tail meat crosswise into ¼-inch-thick medallions.

➤ In a deep skillet, combine the stock, tomatoes, and black beans. Bring to a boil and reduce by half. Reduce the heat, add the lobster medallions, and simmer just until the lobster is heated through. Transfer the medallions to warm shallow soup bowls with a slotted spoon. Return the heat to high, add the basil leaves, and add the butter pieces one or two at a time, stirring constantly as they melt. Pour the sauce over the lobster and serve immediately.

Grilled or Broiled Lobster

Grilling is ideal for both spiny and Atlantic lobsters. If the weather does not cooperate, they can be broiled indoors. Half a lobster is an adequate serving in terms of nutrition, but a whole one per person is traditional.

Live lobsters, about 1 pound per person
Melted butter

TO GRILL Prepare a very hot charcoal fire and spread it evenly in the grill. Kill, split, and clean the lobsters as directed on page 229. Grill the lobster halves cut side down 3 to 4 minutes. Turn and continue cooking shell side down until the meat is tender when probed with a thin skewer, about 12 minutes cooking time in all. Drizzle with melted butter and serve.

TO BROIL Kill, split, and clean the lobsters. Lightly oil the broiler pan, or line it with foil, and set the lobsters on it cut side down. Broil 2 to 3 inches from the heat for 4 minutes, turn, drizzle with a little butter, and continue cooking cut side up until done by the skewer test.

TECHNIQUE NOTE Sharp-eyed readers will notice that in the grilling method, the lobster halves begin cooking with the meat side toward the heat, and finish on the shell side, but cook in the opposite order under the broiler. Normally I recommend starting with the side that will be presented up on the plate against the heat first, because it gets the most browning. However, in this case it's more important to finish with the shell side down, to trap any juices that begin to seep out of the meat as it is done.

Other Serving Suggestions: Lobster

See Tagliarini with Shrimp in Lemon Cream Sauce, page 254.

Steamed Shrimp with Garlic

On a trip to Hong Kong a few years ago, a business associate took me to a little neighborhood restaurant I would never have found on my own. The setting was humble, but the food was excellent. The most memorable dish was also the simplest: a dozen or so shrimp, split lengthwise and steamed in the shell with a hefty topping of minced garlic. At first I thought the garlic taste would

be overwhelming, but it turned out to be fairly mild, the perfect complement to the sweet taste of the shrimp.

Because the whole dish cooks quickly, it's important to cut the garlic into even, very fine dice, rather than random-size chunks. Use the same technique as for dicing an onion, to produce cubes between ⅛ inch and 1/16 inch on a side. Even if your garlic is young, sweet, and fragrant, a preliminary blanching of the whole cloves tempers the taste and improves the texture. One minute is enough with fresh-crop garlic; if you have older, harsher-tasting garlic, cook it a minute or two longer.

Serve with a bowl of rice, a simple vegetable dish, and some fruit for dessert for a light but satisfying menu.

SERVES 3 TO 4

6 large unpeeled cloves garlic

¾ teaspoon kosher salt

½ pound raw headless white shrimp or spot prawns, medium or large (26–30 or 31–40 count)

2 tablespoons Chinese rice wine or dry sherry

1 tablespoon peanut oil

➤ Fill a wok or other large, wide steaming pot with water to just below the level of the steaming rack and bring to a boil. Drop the garlic into the boiling water and cook 2 minutes. Retrieve with a slotted spoon, rinse in cold water, peel, and cut into very fine dice. Combine with the salt in a small bowl.

➤ Split the shrimp lengthwise through the shell and devein if necessary. Arrange cut side up on a steaming plate in an attractive pattern. Drizzle the wine and oil over the shrimp, then carefully spread the garlic over the tops, with some on each shrimp. Place the plate on the rack, cover, and steam just until the shrimp is opaque, 2 to 3 minutes. Remove the plate from the steamer, spoon a little of the juices from the plate back over the shrimp, and serve immediately.

NOTE There is no dainty way to eat shrimp cooked in the shell, at least with chopsticks. You either have to take the whole piece in your mouth, work the meat out of the shell (watch out for that tail spine!), and spit out the shell, or else grab the tail of each piece and pull the meat out with your chopsticks. If you prefer a totally hands-off approach, serve with a knife and fork.

TECHNIQUE NOTE Splitting shrimp in the shell is always a bit tricky, and calls for your sharpest knife. Lay each shrimp on its side, with the fingers of your non-cutting had laid on top, fingertips up out of harm's way. Starting at the head end, hold the knife parallel to the cutting board and carefully cut through the shell and meat, neatly splitting the shrimp into equal halves. One long, smooth cut is better than a sawing motion, which tends to separate the meat and shell.

Vermicelli with Shrimp and Zucchini Ribbons

For quick meals, it's hard to beat the convenience of precooked shrimp. Small cooked and peeled pink shrimp from Oregon are often available fresh in late spring and early summer; the rest of the year I keep a bag on hand in the freezer for those times when I feel like a shrimp dish but don't have time to shop. And shrimp dishes don't get much easier than this uncooked sauce for pasta, part of a genre of summer pasta sauces where the freshly cooked pasta provides just enough heat to release the flavors of the olive oil, vegetables, and herbs.

The key to this dish is a chef's trick—using a vegetable peeler to reduce whole zucchini to a pile of thin green ribbons that need no cooking, just a sprinkling of salt to soften them. It's easier than it sounds; with repeated strokes of the peeler, the whole thing takes just a minute or two. If you work directly over the mixing bowl, so much the better, but if you find it easier, you can hold the zucchini down against a cutting board.

SERVES 4

3 medium zucchini

Scant teaspoon kosher salt

3 tablespoons lemon juice

1 large clove garlic, minced

¼ cup thinly sliced red onion (optional)

¼ teaspoon freshly ground black pepper

4 tablespoons olive oil

¾ pound cooked, peeled, and deveined shrimp

1 pound thin dried pasta such as vermicelli or spaghettini

¼ cup fresh basil or mint leaves, torn into pieces

➤ Trim off the flower ends of the zucchini, but leave the stems on as handles. With a vegetable peeler, peel off thin lengthwise strips, letting them fall into a large serving bowl. Try to include a little green skin with each strip, although this becomes impossible near the core. Discard the stubs at the stem ends. Scatter the salt over the slices and toss to distribute it evenly. Add the lemon juice, garlic, onion, pepper, and oil and let stand at room temperature for 15 to 30 minutes. Remove the shrimp from the refrigerator to let it come to room temperature.

➤ Bring a pot of lightly salted water to a boil. Add the pasta and cook according to package instructions. Meanwhile, toss the basil and shrimp in the zucchini bowl. Taste the mixture for seasoning and correct if necessary. Drain the cooked pasta and immediately add it to the bowl. Toss to combine evenly, stirring to break up the clumps of zucchini. Serve immediately.

VARIATION If you prefer, you can make this with larger warmwater shrimp that you have cooked yourself. The smaller sizes (41–50 and up per pound) offer the best bargain, as well as more bite-size pieces per pound.

Sautéed Shrimp with Vermouth

Here is a simple sauté for larger shrimp, more or less in the "scampi" style. Of course, it will work with smaller shrimp, but the cooking time will be a little less. The butter is optional, anywhere but in a restaurant kitchen.

SERVES 2

½ pound large raw shrimp (26–30 size or larger)

2 teaspoons kosher salt

1 tablespoon olive oil (approximately)

1 tablespoon chopped parsley

1 small clove garlic, minced

Freshly ground pepper, to taste

1½ ounces dry vermouth

1 to 2 tablespoons softened butter (optional)

➤ Peel the shrimp and devein if necessary; leave the final tail shells on or remove them, as you like. Put the peeled shrimp in a small bowl, sprinkle with 1 teaspoon salt, and toss quickly to distribute the salt. Let the shrimp stand for 1 minute (no longer, or it may become too salty), then rinse well and drain. Repeat.

➤ Heat a wok or large skillet over medium heat and add enough oil to coat the bottom. Add the shrimp, in a single layer if possible, and cook until the meat is turning opaque in the center, 3 to 4 minutes per side. If the shrimp are very large, turning them up on edge (tails up) may help them cook more evenly. Remove the shrimp from the pan to a warm plate as they are done.

➤ Add a bit more oil to the pan if it is dry and add the parsley, garlic, and pepper. Cook just until fragrant, about 10 seconds. Add the vermouth and cook until the liquid reduces by about half and the raw wine flavor disappears. Return the shrimp to the pan, add the butter if desired, and toss or stir to coat the shrimp with the sauce. Arrange the shrimp on plates and spoon the sauce over them.

Spring Shrimp Soup with Saffron Aioli

This soup is a bonus for those thrifty cooks who save shrimp shells. With the help of the reserved shells from a few other meals, it takes less than half a pound of small shrimp to make an elegant, colorful soup for four. Saffron lends both flavor and a warm yellow color to the aioli, which is beaten into the soup in a technique borrowed from the French fish soup bourride.

SERVES 4

6 to 8 ounces medium or small raw shrimp

Shells and heads from 1½ to 2 pounds shrimp (about 4 cups)

1 to 2 teaspoons olive oil

5 cups water

½ cup green onion tops

Saffron Aioli

2 large cloves garlic, peeled

Large pinch of saffron threads

¼ teaspoon salt

1 egg yolk

Pinch of white pepper

½ cup olive oil (approximately)

1 tablespoon lemon juice

🌿

Kosher salt

½ pound fresh asparagus, sliced diagonally into 1-inch pieces

1 cup peas, fresh or thawed

½ cup sliced green onions

➤ Peel and devein the shrimp, reserving the shells. Combine the shells and the extra shells in a large saucepan with 2 teaspoons oil (less oil if using shrimp heads). Cook over medium heat, stirring, until the shells turn red and become fragrant, about 2 minutes. Add the water and green onion tops, bring to a boil, reduce the heat, and simmer 45 minutes, periodically skimming any foam off the top. Strain the stock and let stand until the solids settle to the bottom; refrigerate if not proceeding to assemble the soup.

➤ While the stock simmers, prepare the aioli: Pound the garlic, saffron, and ¼ teaspoon salt together to a smooth paste in a mortar (or mash with the broad side of a knife on an impervious surface). Scrape the contents of the mortar into a mixing bowl, add the egg yolk and pepper, and beat with a whisk to a paler shade of yellow. Add a spoonful of oil and beat until it is absorbed. Continue adding oil in small quantities, beating constantly, until the sauce forms a smooth emulsion. After about half the oil has been added, alternate oil and lemon juice. Continue until the sauce is nice and thick; it should absorb about ½ cup of oil in all. Correct the seasoning. (Both the stock and the aioli can be prepared a day ahead and refrigerated.)

➤ If the shrimp are on the large side (31–35 or larger), split them lengthwise; otherwise leave them whole. Sprinkle with about a teaspoon of kosher salt, toss to coat evenly, and let stand 1 minute (no longer); rinse with cold water, drain, and repeat.

➤ Carefully decant the shrimp stock into a saucepan, leaving behind any heavy solids. Add salt to taste and bring to a simmer. Add the asparagus and peas, simmer 4 minutes, and add the shrimp and sliced green onions. Simmer until the vegetables are tender and the shrimp is just turning opaque, another 2 to 3 minutes.

➤ Place half the aioli in a mixing bowl and ladle in 1 cup of the hot shrimp broth. Whisk until thoroughly blended, then add the mixture back to the soup. Taste for seasoning and adjust if necessary. Serve immediately in shallow bowls, passing additional aioli at the table.

Shrimp and Vegetable Curry with Tamarind

This makes a simple, rather soupy curry to be served with rice as a one-dish meal. If you prefer, you can make it with just shrimp and serve a separate vegetable side dish. Look for jars of tamarind concentrate wherever Indian foods are sold. Cooked shrimp need only a minute or so to reheat once the curry is ready; raw shrimp take only slightly longer to cook.

SERVES 4

2 tablespoons oil

1½ cups diced onion

2 cloves garlic, minced

1 teaspoon minced or grated ginger

¾ teaspoon ground turmeric

⅛ to ¼ teaspoon cayenne

1 can (14 ounces) unsweetened coconut milk

1 teaspoon tamarind concentrate dissolved in 2 tablespoons warm water

2 or 3 small fresh chiles, sliced, loose seeds removed

1 to 2 cups assorted cut-up vegetables—diced new potatoes or sweet potatoes; sliced carrots; peas; sliced green beans; broccoli or cauliflower florets

½ teaspoon kosher salt

¾ pound small peeled and deveined cooked shrimp, thawed, OR 1 pound small raw shrimp, peeled, deveined, and salted (see page 231)

2 tablespoons cilantro

➤ Heat the oil in a wok or deep skillet over medium-low heat. Add the onion, garlic, ginger, turmeric, and cayenne and cook until the onion begins to brown. Discard some of the cream from the coconut milk, if desired, and add enough water to make 2 cups. Add

to the pan along with the tamarind liquid, chiles, vegetables, and salt. Heat to just short of boiling, reduce to a simmer, and cook until the vegetables are tender.

➤ If using cooked shrimp, add and simmer just until the shrimp are heated through, about 1 minute; with raw shrimp, simmer until opaque, about 5 minutes. Correct the seasoning, stir in the cilantro, and serve with rice.

Tagliarini with Shrimp in Lemon Cream Sauce

This is a rather fancy preparation for a special meal, or those times when the market turns up special crustaceans like spot prawns or other coldwater shrimp. Because it is so rich, serve it in small quantities as a first course and follow it with something leaner—a plain roast au jus, grilled chicken, or steamed fish—with plenty of accompanying vegetables.

If the shrimp are sold with the heads on, by all means freeze the heads and shells for stock. If the shrimp are females with roe attached, reserve the roe and add it to the sauce; it won't add any flavor, but it sure makes the dish look prettier.

SERVES 4 AS A FIRST COURSE

1 large or 2 small lemons

1 cup whipping cream

¾ pound headless spot shrimp

2 teaspoons chopped chives

½ pound tagliarini or other thin pasta

Salt and freshly ground black pepper, to taste

➤ Remove the zest from the lemon with a peeler, taking only the yellow part. Cut the zest into fine julienne shreds. Or, use a zester that cuts the zest into thin strips. Combine the cream and 1 tablespoon of the zest in a small saucepan. Bring almost to a boil, remove from the heat, and let stand 15 to 30 minutes.

➤ Peel the shrimp, reserving the roe if any. Unless the shrimp are especially small, split them lengthwise before deveining. Juice the lemon and toss the shrimp meat in 1 tablespoon of the juice.

➤ Have a large pot of boiling water ready to cook the pasta. In a large skillet, bring the cream and chives to a boil. Start cooking the pasta; meanwhile, drain the shrimp and add it to the cream, and cook until the cream is reduced by a third, adding the roe for the last minute or so. Season the sauce to taste, drain the pasta, add it to the sauce, and toss to coat. Serve immediately, on warmed plates.

NOTE The timing here is for fresh pasta, which will cook in about the same time as the shrimp. If using dried pasta, start cooking the shrimp in the sauce when the pasta is 2 to 3 minutes short of done.

VARIATION Substitute the meat of a 1- to 1½-pound lobster, boiled, cooled, and diced, for the shrimp, and add to the sauce just long enough to reheat. Very large wild shrimp or freshwater prawns should be peeled and diced while raw.

Basic Stir-Fried Shrimp

This dish can be varied almost endlessly, according to the vegetables available. The list of choices given here does not mean that they should all be combined. One to three vegetables, carefully chosen for their compatibility with the shrimp and one another, make a better dish than a jumble of colors and flavors.

SERVES 2 AS A MAIN DISH, 4 WITH OTHER DISHES

¾ **pound small or medium shrimp, peeled and deveined**

Kosher salt

¼ **cup Chinese rice wine or dry sherry**

2 **teaspoons minced ginger**

1 **tablespoon plus ½ teaspoon cornstarch**

½ **cup unsalted chicken stock**

2 **tablespoons oil**

Salt and white pepper

2 **to 3 cups diced or sliced vegetables—snow peas or sugar snap peas; sliced water chestnuts, celery, or bok choy; diced red or green pepper; blanched broccoli florets; diced bamboo shoots**

➤ Sprinkle the shrimp with 1 teaspoon kosher salt, toss to distribute the salt evenly, and let stand 1 minute. Rinse and drain. Repeat. Drain well and transfer to a small bowl. Add the wine, half the ginger, and 1 tablespoon cornstarch; stir to combine and let stand 15 minutes. Dissolve ½ teaspoon cornstarch in the stock and set aside.

➤ Drain the shrimp and discard the marinade. Place a wok or skillet over high heat and add 1 tablespoon oil and the remaining ginger plus a pinch of salt and pepper. When the ginger sizzles, add the drained shrimp and stir-fry just until they begin to stiffen and turn opaque. Remove. Add the remaining oil to the pan, add the vegetables, and stir-fry until heated through. Stir the stock mixture to dissolve the cornstarch and add it to the pan. Return the shrimp to the pan and cook until the sauce is thick and glossy. Serve immediately.

Baked Red Curry Prawns

In Thailand and other parts of Southeast Asia, where the shrimp get really big, a single one (usually cooked in the shell, often with a savory stuffing) makes a nice individual serving. When I come across really big shrimp, either farmed freshwater prawns (Macrobrachium) or the enormous wild tiger shrimp from Australia, I follow the same approach, serving just one or two per person, with other dishes including a soup, vegetables, and plenty of rice to round out the menu.

Here is one case where I use "whole" canned coconut milk, rather than discarding the cream; the extra body it gives helps carry the flavors of curry paste and lemongrass and bind them to the shrimp. Shake the can well to mix in the cream, then spoon out what you need for the recipe, and refrigerate or freeze the rest to use in a curry.

SERVES 4

2 tablespoons thick unsweetened
   coconut milk

2 teaspoons Thai red curry paste

2 teaspoons minced lemongrass

1 pound large shrimp (under-10 size or larger)

➤ Combine the coconut milk, curry paste, and lemongrass. Preheat the oven to 500°F. Split the shrimp shells down the back with scissors or by cutting outward with a knife. Remove the veins.

➤ Spread the shells slightly and rub the curry mixture over as much of the shrimp meat as you can reach. Arrange the shrimp in a single layer in a shallow pan and bake, uncovered, until the meat is opaque in the center, 7 to 10 minutes depending on size.

VARIATION The shrimp can also be broiled. Position the rack so they are at least 3 inches from the heat, and be prepared to lower it further if the shells start to blacken before the meat is done.

➤ These can also be served as an appetizer for a grilled meal; either cook them directly on the grill or enclose them in foil first. The latter is less messy to cook, but perhaps messier to serve and eat.

shellfish, part II:
oysters, mussels, clams, scallops, abalone & squid

The wonderful Italian name for shellfish, *frutti di mare*, seems to apply especially to the molluscan varieties. Sweet, rich in flavor but not in fat, and tender (so long as they are properly cooked), these shellfish are the true "fruits of the sea." Nearly every coastal marine and estuarine habitat on the West Coast is home to one sort or another of edible mollusk: squid swimming near the ocean surface, and scallops hovering near the ocean floor; mussels clinging to surf-splashed rocks and pier pilings, and oysters and clams resting on shallow bay bottoms and tidal flats.

American Oyster

Baltic Mussel

Bay Scallop

Blue Mussel

California Market Squid

Geoduck

Greenshell Mussel

Humboldt Squid

Japanese Scallop

Kumamoto Oyster

Manila Clam

Mediterranean Mussel

Olympia Oyster

Pacific Littleneck Clam

Pacific Oyster

Plate Oyster

Razor Clam

Red Abalone

Sea Scallop

Weathervane Scallop

Oysters

Pacific (Japanese) oyster, *Crassostrea gigas*
Kumamoto oyster, *C. sikamea*
American (Eastern) oyster, *C. virginica*
Olympia oyster, *Ostrea conchaphila*
European flat or plate oyster, *O. edulis*

Oysters have always been a favorite shellfish in the Northwest, but by the early twentieth century a combination of overharvesting and environmental damage had nearly wiped out the beds of native Olympia oysters. Occasional attempts to introduce oysters from the East Coast never produced self-sustaining populations, but finally another imported oyster introduced in the 1930s did take hold. Today the Pacific, or Japanese, oyster (*Crassostrea gigas*) is the foundation of a huge oyster culture industry from central California to southeast Alaska. Based almost entirely on this species, Washington has emerged as the top oyster-producing state in the United States, and British Columbia supplements the oyster production from Canada's Atlantic provinces.

Where oyster harvests in other parts of North America depend largely on natural oyster beds, virtually all of the West Coast harvest is cultured. In shallow and intertidal waters in bays, sloughs, and inlets, oyster farmers "grow out" seed oysters from hatcheries by various methods—directly on a bay bottom, on hanging ropes, or in wire cages or other structures—which determine in part whether the oyster will end up as a delicate, frilly-shelled morsel served raw at an oyster bar, or one of the shoe-size giants steamed with black bean sauce in a Chinese restaurant, or among those of assorted sizes shucked at a bayside processing plant and sold by the half-pint or by the gallon.

While *C. gigas* is by far the most common oyster in our area, it's not the only one. The native Olympia never quite disappeared, and it now makes up a small but treasured share of the oyster harvest in the waters near the city of the same name. Farms here and there raise another Japanese species, the Kumamoto oyster, as well as a flat-shelled oyster imported from Europe, and even Atlantic oysters.

Even within the same species, differences in water conditions (salinity, depth, temperature, tidal flow, nutrient supply) make every growing location potentially unique, and account for the fact that oysters grown just a few miles apart can taste different from one another. The distinctions among the various species and local varieties of oysters are best appreciated in their purest form, raw on the half shell. That's not to say you can't barbecue Kumamotos or garnish a spinach salad with fried Olympias; just that it is easier and more economical to prepare these dishes with the more standard Pacific oysters.

The oyster recipes in this chapter are organized according to which form of oysters you need to buy, live or shucked. For serving raw, live is the only way to go, for reasons discussed on page 4. Ditto for barbecued or baked oysters, where they cook in their own shells; see

The *R*-Month Myth

One of the oldest maxims in the seafood business is that oysters should be eaten only in the months with an R in them (September through April). Like most rules, this one has some validity, but it needs to be applied with judgment, especially when it comes to Pacific Coast oysters.

There are two main reasons behind the traditional shutdown of the oyster season in the summer, both with roots in the East Coast and Gulf Coast oyster fisheries. One has to do with safety (see page 262), while the other is more of an aesthetic issue, but the key factor in both is the temperature of the water.

All oysters require a certain minimum water temperature to spawn, and summer is the normal spawning season for Pacific oysters in their home waters on the coast of Japan. When an oyster prepares to spawn, it puts all its energies into eggs or milt, becoming what one California oyster grower described as "one big gonad." Unfortunately, while oysters are quite nutritious at this stage, they are not very palatable, tasting fat and milky rather than pleasantly plump and meaty.

Here on the West Coast, oyster growers can get touchy about the subject of spawning, pointing out that our growing waters are too cold for the oysters to spawn in most years. True enough, but that doesn't prevent them from trying. Even if the water never reaches the magic temperature point that triggers the release of eggs and sperm, the warming waters and longer days of summer cause the gonads of most oysters to swell in preparation for spawning. And that means an oyster that tastes and feels different from the same variety in cold weather.

Some growers try to avoid the spawning problem by growing "triploid" oysters, special genetic strains that have three sets of chromosomes instead of the usual two and are therefore sterile. As hatcheries continue to refine their breeding techniques to guarantee sterility, triploids may become the rule rather than the exception.

A summer oyster may not be that appealing for serving raw on the half shell, but it's fine for cooking, whether "barbecued" in the shell, baked à la Rockefeller, or in any of a number of dishes calling for shucked oysters (see recipes, pages 278 to 281).

Another traditional reason for shutting down oyster harvests in the summer is simple protection of the stocks. In the East, where oysters are often gathered from natural beds and the harvest depends on natural spawning for replenishment, leaving the oysters alone during their spawning season makes a lot of sense. However, almost all West Coast oyster culture is based on "seed" from hatcheries rather than wild spawning, so there is no disadvantage in terms of survival in harvesting all year.

page 8 for guidelines on buying and storing live oysters for these purposes. Otherwise, there is little reason for most cooks to buy live oysters in the shell for cooking. Leaving the shucking to the packing houses near the oyster beds will save you both money and trouble.

Some fish markets buy shucked oysters in bulk to sell by the pound, but the most common form in supermarkets is 10-ounce refrigerated jars. (For some reason, this size long ago became the standard "half pint" container for shucked Pacific oysters.) The number of oysters in a jar depends on the size. Since oysters are packed by hand and graded by eye, the exact count per jar will always vary, but Washington oysters graded small generally run 6 to 9 to a jar, and extra smalls 10 to 12. California oysters sometimes run a little smaller, but I have found them maddeningly inconsistent; a jar of smalls from one major brand had 16 on one occasion, and 6 another time!

The recipes in this chapter simply specify "small" oysters, which means the smallest you can find. Unfortunately, many supermarkets opt for the cheaper but enormous "medium" size, with as few as five pieces in a jar. (If that's a medium, I'd hate to see a large one!) These monsters are barely acceptable for chopping up in a stuffing, but for a pasta sauce, angels on horseback, or any other dish where you want bite-size morsels, an oyster this big is unappetizing at best, and borders on disgusting. If all you can find is the medium size, cut each one into two or three pieces for those uses—and complain to your grocer.

When buying shucked oysters, whether in jars or in bulk, look to see that the surrounding liquid ("liquor," in oyster parlance) is more clear than cloudy. The longer the oysters sit, the grayer and milkier the liquor becomes. Some jars carry a pull date, like dairy products. If you are at all suspicious about the freshness of the oysters, open the jar as soon as you get home (or right outside the store) and take a whiff; it should smell definitely oystery, but not fishy. Store the jar tightly sealed in the coldest part of the refrigerator and use it within a couple of days.

For those recipes that call for live oysters in the shell, a fish market is probably the most convenient source, but it's also likely to be the most expensive. If you live near an oyster farming area, driving to the farm for a sack of oysters can be a pleasant excursion; in my area, many of the shellfish farmers also sell directly to the public at city farmers' markets. If you don't have either resource available and want to have a good-sized oyster feed, check with your local seafood wholesalers and see if they will sell you oysters in quantity on a cash-and-carry basis. Local practice will dictate whether they are packed and priced by count (dozen, 50, 100, etc.) or by the bushel, and wholesalers will be most cooperative if you plan on buying in those units.

OYSTERS ON THE HALF SHELL

To many oyster aficionados, there is no better way to savor an oyster than to slurp it raw from the half shell. Assuming the oysters are of an appropriate size and season, I agree. From late fall through spring, West Coast oyster growers provide us with dozens of local varieties of oysters representing four or five different species, all delicious in their raw state at home or in an oyster bar or restaurant.

Even when the species are similar, each growing site is potentially unique in its water and nutrient conditions, giving its oysters a slightly different flavor, making oysters a fascinating ongoing study. Oyster traders have evolved some of the same kind of language as wine tasters, especially in describing the "finish" or aftertaste of each variety. Some tasters detect overtones of lettuce, cucumber, or melon (even specific melon varieties like watermelon and cantaloupe) in the finish of certain oysters. These are subtle and very subjective distinctions, so don't worry if your oyster simply tastes like an oyster. For most of us, the main thing to look for in a raw oyster is a balance of sweet and salty flavors, and a texture that is pleasantly plump and meaty rather than scrawny and tough or swollen and fatty.

Most of the oysters grown for the half-shell trade belong to the same species, the Pacific oyster, *Crassostrea gigas*. Where the oysters sold in shucked form are generally just grown on bay bottoms, often in clusters, the best half-shell oysters are grown by more labor-intensive methods. Hanging bags, pillow-shaped wire cages that rest on the bay bottom or on racks that raise them off the bottom, and stacking trays suspended in deeper water are just some of the ways growers keep each animal separate, allowing it to grow a shell of an ideal shape for shucking and serving raw.

Several West Coast growers also raise a smaller Japanese variety, the Kumamoto oyster (*C. sikamea*), native to the prefecture of the same name in Japan. The basic flavor is like that of *C. gigas*, but like serrano chiles, "Kumis" seem to pack as much flavor as their larger relatives into a smaller package. They are always among my favorites, even though they typically cost more.

In addition to Pacific oysters, several West Coast farms raise the European flat or plate oyster (*Ostrea edulis*). When these oysters first entered the West Coast market, they were almost always called "belons," although that name officially belongs to oysters from a particular location in France. Increasingly, they are identified as they should be, by geographic source and species, as "Pearl Point flat" oysters or "Wescott Bay flat" or whatever. This oyster, with its nearly round, shallow-cupped shape, looks like an oversized version of the Olympia oyster (*O. conchaphila*), and the two are in fact more closely related to each other than to other North American oysters. They also share a distinctly metallic aftertaste that is not necessarily for everyone, but is popular with their fans.

With all these variables, a well-stocked oyster bar can offer as many as two dozen named oyster varieties in the height of the season, and while few fish markets offer anywhere near that many, they should be able to stock several types. Sometimes oysters from several sources may be marketed together under a general geographic name like Hood Canal, or under a brand name like Royal Miyagi. (Miyagi, a word that shows up in several brand names, is not a separate variety or species, but simply refers to the prefecture in Japan that was the source of the original Pacific oyster seed.) However, an ever-increasing number of growers are trying to establish a brand identity for their own little stretch of beach or bay, the equivalent of a single vineyard designation on a wine label.

The R-Month Myth, Part 2: The Safety Issue

While oyster lovers may debate the culinary merits of winter versus summer oysters, a potentially more serious issue has to do with safety, especially when oysters are to be eaten raw. When water temperatures are at their seasonal high, typically in the months without an *R* in them, so are the populations of various bacteria that live in ocean and estuarine waters. One group, the genus *Vibrio,* includes various species found around the world that are responsible for cholera and other diseases. One of these, *V. vulnificus,* is endemic in the waters of the southeastern United States, and grows quite common when the water temperature exceeds 65°F. If ingested alive in sufficient quantity, or by persons with compromised immune systems, it can cause serious or even fatal illness. In the 1980s and early '90s, several outbreaks of vulnificus poisoning linked to Gulf Coast oysters gave rise to news stories with scary headlines like "Death on the Half Shell," and led California health authorities to require restaurants and oyster bars serving raw oysters from any source to post warning signs about the potential dangers of raw oysters.

Fortunately, *Vibrio vulnificus* has never been found in West Coast shellfish-growing areas, and presumably our water is too cold for it to grow if it were to appear. However, a related species, *V. parahaemolyticus,* is known to occur here when the water is warmer than normal. Parahaemolyticus can cause gastrointestinal illness that is certainly unpleasant, but rarely as dangerous as vulnificus. (And it's important to note that both of these forms of vibrio are a problem only when oysters are to be eaten raw, as the bacteria are killed by thorough cooking.)

In the summer of 1997, warmer than usual waters in the Pacific Northwest apparently caused major local blooms of *V. parahaemolyticus,* and more than a hundred cases of illness (none fatal) were traced to raw oysters from certain locations in Washington and British Columbia. This led members of the Pacific Coast Oyster Growers Association to voluntarily halt shipments of live oysters for almost a month in August and September, and to notify those already holding live oysters that they should be served only fully cooked. A similar pattern occurred in 1998, and the million-dollar question in the Northwest shellfish industry is whether these two summers were an anomaly (linked to El Niño) or a sign of the future (global warming, or at least long-term shifts in temperature patterns in the north Pacific). Time will tell, but in the meantime, it's probably best to save half-shell oysters for the colder months, and enjoy them only in cooked form in the summer.

Following are some of the oysters I have enjoyed on the half shell at one time or another.

CALIFORNIA Hog Island Oyster Company on Tomales Bay is one of my longtime favorites for its Hog Island Sweetwater, as well as Kumamotos, flats, and even some Atlantic oysters; Preston Point and Tomales Bay Oyster Company are other good producers on the same bay. Humboldt Bay is a major source of Kumamotos as well as *gigas*. Morro Bay is about the southern limit for half-shell oyster culture, producing good oysters in winter.

OREGON Not as many choices here, but the Pearl Point brand from Netarts Bay offers good flats and Pacifics.

WASHINGTON There are almost too many to count, but (in no particular order) my favorites include Dabob Bay, Eagle Creek, Quilcene, Hamma Hamma, and Sisters Point, all *gigas* oysters from various locations on or adjacent to Hood Canal; from the southern reaches of Puget Sound, Pacifics and flats from Little Skookum, Totten Inlet, and Steamboat Island, plus the incomparable little Olympias; and from farther north, Snow Creek, Dungeness Bay, and Samish Bay.

BRITISH COLUMBIA Fanny Bay, Royal Miyagi, and Malaspina are among the most common brands; I have also enjoyed oysters from Chef Creek, Evening Cove, and Buckley Bay. There is also at least one oyster farm operating in southeast Alaska, but I haven't tasted theirs.

HOW TO SHUCK AN OYSTER

As one oyster farmer told me years ago, "No one is born knowing how to open an oyster; it's a skill you learn, like tying shoelaces." Once you get the hang of it, it's really no more difficult. Here is a step-by-step guide that will also help you rate the presentation of oysters served at an oyster bar or in a restaurant.

First, a bit of anatomy. The shell of an oyster consists of two pieces, technically called valves but commonly referred to as the top and bottom shell. These halves are joined at one end by a hinge of ligament, and near the middle by the adductor muscle. Shucking is a matter of cutting these connections without damaging the rest of the oyster; how cleanly this is done separates the most skillful shuckers from the rest.

Two pieces of equipment are essential: an oyster knife and something to protect your hand. Oyster knives come in various designs, but they all have a thick, blunt-edged blade that is strong enough to pry the shells apart without breaking. An ordinary kitchen or table knife will not do, nor will a clam knife. Professional oyster shuckers generally use a relatively long knife with a straight tip. I use and recommend the Russell model S-120, with a white plastic handle and a stiff, 4-inch blade.

To protect your other hand, either wear a heavy-duty rubber glove or cradle the oyster in several thicknesses of folded kitchen towel. Some people prefer to hold the oyster down against the table with a hand on top, which is safer but slower.

Before shucking, inspect the oyster to make sure it is tightly closed, or closes quickly when handled; an unresponsive open oyster is a dead oyster, and possibly spoiled. Rinse or scrub the oyster to rid it of any mud or grit. With the deeper side of the oyster down, locate the hinge point of the shell. With whatever combination of swiveling and wiggling gets the job done, gently work the tip of the knife between the shell halves until you feel you have some leverage (¼ inch or so is plenty of penetration; any deeper and you risk cutting up the meat inside). Twist (do not push) the knife and pry upward to pop the shell open.

When you have popped the hinge, slide the knife in along the top valve to cut the shell free

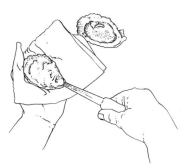

from the adductor muscle. Discard the top valve. Now slide the knife under the oyster to cut the other end of the muscle free from the bottom valve. Finally, remove any bits of grit, mud, or broken shell, rearrange the edges of the oyster if they have been disturbed, and the oyster is ready to serve.

If all this is done right, the shell will have remained upright all along, and a moist, glistening, perfectly shaped oyster sits there in a teaspoon or so of sea water, waiting to be enjoyed. If the oyster is dry or has a spoiled odor, discard it.

(If you are unsure of your skill at shucking oysters, you might want to ask for "beach cultured" oysters rather than one of the "rack and bag" or "tray cultured" varieties. The latter spend most of their lives in protective enclosures that keep them off the bay bottoms, and tend to have thinner shells with fine, frilly edges. In the hands of an experienced shucker, these light shells are easy to open, but they tend to shatter if you use excessive force. Some growers, especially in Washington and British Columbia, grow their oysters to near market size in bags or trays, then transfer them onto gravelly subtidal areas for six months to a year. This "hardening on the beach" makes for oysters with heavier, less brittle shells that are easier to open.)

Half-shell oysters are traditionally served on a bed of crushed ice, something you can forego at home if you serve them promptly. To my taste, a perfectly balanced oyster needs no sauce or other adornment, but most people like to season oysters with a squeeze of lemon or a bit of mignonette sauce (see page 328). Either adds a refreshing touch of acidity that goes well with the richness of almost any oyster, and can be just the thing to bring a bland or fatty oyster into balance. Hot pepper sauce and tomato cocktail sauce are also possibilities, but not for me, thanks. You can either spoon a little sauce into each oyster shell or spear the oyster with a fork and dunk it in the sauce. Either way, I like to slurp the oyster from the shell, nudging it out with a fingertip if necessary.

Mussels

Blue mussel, *Mytilus edulis*
Mediterranean mussel, *M. galloprovincialis*
Baltic mussel, *M. trossulus*
Greenshell mussel, *Perna canaliculus*

While many aquaculture products are on the expensive side, mussels are a dramatic exception to the rule. With proven farming technology, rapid growth rates, and still somewhat limited market demand, mussels are among the cheapest bivalves to produce, and with thinner, lighter shells than either clams or oysters, mussels provide the highest percentage of edible yield of any bivalve, up to 60 percent of live weight. They are ridiculously easy to cook, and have the sweet taste of all the bivalves and a texture that falls somewhere between the creamy plumpness of oysters and the chewy density of clams—a happy medium indeed. All in all, it's hard to think of another seafood, wild or farmed, that offers better eating at such a bargain price.

Although the center of mussel culture in North America remains in eastern Canada, particularly Prince Edward Island, mussels have become an increasingly important part of the shellfish industry in the Pacific Northwest in recent decades. By raising several distinct strains of mussels, Northwestern farmers have extended the season for fresh mussels to nearly year-round.

Other than the native *Mytilus californianus*, West Coast waters are home to a "Baltic" type and a "Mediterranean" type. Some authorities consider the last two to be subspecies of the Atlantic blue mussel, *M. edulis*, the variety grown in eastern Canada and New England, but I will follow the usual commercial practice and treat them as separate species.

Until recently, most mussel culture in the Northwest has been based on the native population, the Baltic type (*M. trossulus*). This is the mussel traditionally associated with Penn Cove on Whidbey Island, one of the most famous mussel farming areas in the region. These mussels are easy to farm, but suffer nearly total die-off of the adults each winter from a disease endemic to the region.

Looking for an alternative that would survive the year around, Washington farmers began to experiment in the 1980s with Mediterranean mussels. Mussels are notorious globetrotters, traveling either as larvae in the ballast water of ships or by attaching themselves to ship hulls when young and then spawning in waters far from their original home. Somewhere along the line, the mussel native to the Mediterranean (*M. galloprovincialis*) had established itself on the Pacific Coast from Southern California to central Oregon. Starting with broodstock gathered in Tomales Bay in California, researchers found that this species not only would grow in Puget Sound, but was immune to the disease that kills off the Baltic mussels every winter. Taylor United, the largest mussel farmer in southern Puget Sound, now grows exclusively "gallos."

Winter survival is only one of the advantages

of the Mediterranean mussel. It also spawns at a different time of year from other mussels, a point of key concern to cooks. Like other bivalves, mussels spend much of the year growing fatter and richer in preparation for their peak spawning period, then exhaust themselves in the spawning process. The best eating quality is in the six months or so prior to spawning time; for the month or two after spawning, the animals are at their poorest eating quality, thin and scrawny. The edible yield (weight of meat in a pound of mussels in the shell), can range from 60 percent at its peak to as low as 30 percent after spawning.

Both *edulis* and *trossulus* spawn in late spring, so they are not at their best for eating until the fall and winter months. *Galloprovincialis*, on the other hand, hits its spawning peak in winter, so the mussels are in prime condition in the summer. Even farmers in Penn Cove, once synonymous with the Baltic type, have added Mediterranean mussels to their product line, with a view to a year-round market. Eastern blue mussels are available most of the year, including late winter and early spring, when our local varieties both become scarce.

So which mussel should you buy, especially in fall when both types are available in good condition? That depends in part on the use. For risotto, paella, pasta, or a simple bowl of steamers, when a large number of mussels is an important part of the presentation, you might prefer the smaller Penn Coves or Eastern blues, which typically run 2 to 3 dozen per pound. At 12 to 20 per pound, Mediterraneans are a better choice for stuffing, or if you simply want

Wild Harvest

While there are relatively few places where you can pick oysters off the beach, and clams require a lot of digging, mussels are fairly easy to gather from the wild. Mussels grow mainly in the intertidal zone, making them easy to get to at low tides. Most states and provinces require a fishing license; check with local authorities for other regulations, including seasonal closures. (California, for example, does not allow wild harvest of mussels or other bivalves from May through October; see page 35.)

If you want to gather your own mussels, look for locations away from harbors and other sources of pollution. Try to go at the lowest possible tide to gather them from the lower part of the intertidal zone; mussels in the water more of the time can feed more often, and they don't have as heavy shells as those that spend more of their lives out of the water. A strong trowel or small prying bar is a good tool for getting them off the rocks. Choose mussels with shells no more than 3 inches long for the tenderest meat. And remember not to turn your back on the ocean, as unexpectedly large "sleeper" waves are a constant danger. Wild mussels will likely need more cleaning than the farmed variety; a plastic scrubbing sponge is handy for rubbing off bits of beard and grit from the outside of the shells.

a larger piece of meat (despite my prejudice toward smaller sizes of bivalves, I find even the largest of them not the least bit tough or over-grown in appearance and texture). More pieces also mean more cleaning time. Perhaps the most important test is to taste them side by side and decide which you prefer.

Until the Mediterranean type became common, summer was the prime season for greenshell or "greenlip" mussels from New Zealand. With the seasons reversed in the Southern Hemisphere, these large mussels with the striking green shell edges had the advantage of being shipped here in prime winter condition when our Eastern mussels were in their summer doldrums. These days, with more year-round availability of local mussels, green-shells seem to do best in niche markets, including frozen on the half shell. I must admit that I've never been a great fan of these mus-sels, as I find them too large for most uses other than baking with a stuffing (see page 292).

Unless frozen, mussels should be bought alive and kept alive until cooking time. If pos-sible, buy them the day you will cook them, and keep them refrigerated until ready to cook. If you have to store them for more then a few hours, be sure to perforate the plastic bag, or transfer them to a bowl covered with a damp towel. Do not cover them with water or leave them exposed to the drying air of the refriger-ator for long or they will die and spoil. Even under the best storage, expect to lose a few with overnight storage. In any case, wait until just before cooking to clean mussels.

To prepare mussels for cooking, first scrub the shells if they are at all gritty; this step may not be necessary with most farmed mussels, which come to market quite clean. Grasp the "beard" or bissus, the bundle of fibers extending from the shell on the flat side, and pull it off with a quick tug. Set aside any open mussels that do not close when handled; if they have not closed within a few minutes (it can take a while, espe-cially when they are cold), discard them.

The simplest way to cook mussels, or to open them for other uses, is by steaming. It's possible to cut them open with a clam knife, but I've never found an advantage in this method. If they will be baked or otherwise cooked further, you can shuck them as soon as the shells open a little bit; to eat as is, continue cooking until the shells are open wide and the meat has begun to shrink noticeably. Some of them always take longer to open than the others; if possible, watch over the pan and pluck the quicker ones out as soon as they are done so they will not get tough while waiting for the slower ones to finish. If a few mussels refuse to open, it could mean they are the healthiest and most tenacious or it could be that they are dead. Since there is no way to tell for sure, it's safest to discard them.

Scallops

Atlantic (sea) scallop, *Placopecten magellanicus*
Bay scallop, *Argopecten irradians*
Calico scallop, *A. gibbus*
Weathervane scallop, *Patinopecten caurinus*
Japanese scallop, *Patinopecten yessoensis*
Pink scallop, *Chlamys rubida*
Spiny scallop, *C. hastata*

My wife, who has no use for most bivalves, is crazy about scallops, and in talking to others I find she is not alone. Whatever it is about the flavor and texture of clams, mussels, and oysters that turns her and others off, she doesn't find it in the sweet, white meat of scallops.

Most likely, the reason is that we eat only a select part of the scallop. While the entire contents of a scallop shell are edible, Americans generally see only the white, cylindrical adductor muscle, the rest of the internal organs having been discarded when the scallop was shucked. All bivalves rely on this large central muscle to hold the two shell halves together (some, like clams, have a pair of them); but in the free-swimming scallop, the adductor muscle is especially large and well developed, making a sweet morsel that can run as large as a couple of ounces in the biggest species.

While we have some native scallops in our area, the most common scallop in North American markets is the sea scallop of the north Atlantic. These big scallops, caught by dredging the ocean floor off New England and eastern Canada, produce meats that run anywhere from 40 pieces per pound to fewer than 10. Sweet and flavorful, and meltingly tender despite their large size, these scallops set the standard for scallop flavor and texture, and are widely available both frozen and fresh.

New England's other native scallop, the smaller bay scallop, enjoys an even higher reputation among some scallop lovers, but it is usually in short supply. In the market, "bay scallop" is often used like "bay shrimp" as a term for any small variety, including a small Florida species properly known as the calico scallop. However, real bay scallops suddenly became plentiful in the mid-1990s as an import from China. Using a form of scallop farming pioneered by the Japanese, and broodstock originally imported from Nantucket, Chinese farmers began large-scale scallop farming off their northern coast in the 1980s, and by 1993 they were producing millions of pounds of bay scallops per year. A lot of those scallops came into the U.S. in frozen form at about half the price of New England bays. Other small scallops come in frozen from Argentina and other countries in South America.

One large scallop native to our area, the weathervane scallop, supports a small fishery in the Gulf of Alaska. Because of the remoteness of the fishing grounds, weathervane meats, which can run quite large, are all frozen at sea. The quality is very good, though the flavor is milder than that of an Eastern sea scallop.

Two nearly identical small scallops, the pink and spiny scallops, are caught on a small scale by divers in the Puget Sound and Strait of

Georgia. These scallops are usually sold alive, to be steamed or otherwise cooked in the shell (see page 295).

Aquaculturists in British Columbia have had some success growing a hybrid of the weathervane scallop and a Japanese species that has proven more successful than either species. So far, most of the production has gone into the restaurant trade, but as the supply grows, they could become a retail item as well.

Some scallops are sold fresh, but most (especially the imported varieties) are frozen, usually in IQF form. Sizes are specified in terms of the number of pieces per pound; large scallops are typically graded 20–30, 10–20, under-10, etc., while calicos and Chinese bays can run more than 100 per pound.

An increasing share of the scallops in the market carry descriptions like "chemical free," "dry pack," or "day boat." The last has to do with the length of time of the fishing trip, and mainly applies to Atlantic sea scallops; the former terms have to do with additives commonly used in processing frozen seafood. For years, most inexpensive frozen scallops (as well as many other frozen seafoods) have been treated with phosphates, particularly sodium tripolyphosphate (STP), to reduce so-called "drip loss." Used in moderation, phosphates are a legitimate way to preserve quality, by binding the natural moisture that would otherwise be lost in the freezing and thawing process. However, if used to excess, these same phosphates can cause scallops to soak up as much as 25 percent of their weight in additional water. The Food and Drug Administration has cracked down on phosphate abuse in recent years, with new standards based on analysis of the moisture content of the finished product. If the water content of a sample exceeds the maximum natural level of 80 percent, they fall into a separate product category which must be labeled "scallop product—water added."

Even if adding weight in the form of water were not an issue, phosphates can affect the naturally sweet flavor of scallops. Chefs and discerning consumers increasingly insist on "dry pack," or unsoaked, scallops.

When shopping for scallops, look for a creamy color rather than bleached white, and avoid scallops that are sitting in a lot of water. Dry-pack scallops may actually be slightly sticky, with a fairly strong sweet-briny aroma. Of course, reject any that smell sour or fishy.

At first glance, scallop meats appear to be 100 percent edible, and in fact many cooks prepare them that way. However, there is a small amount of meat attached to each scallop that has a different appearance and texture than the main muscle, especially when cooked. Look on the shorter side (scallop meats are not perfectly symmetrical cylinders; the top and bottom planes are not parallel) for a place where the grain of the muscle changes direction and density. This strip of meat is tougher than the main adductor muscle, and it gets tougher still as it cooks. The minute or two it takes to go through a batch of scallop meats and peel off these outer strips will be worth it in the tenderness of the finished dish.

The trimmings do contain flavor, so if you are preparing a large batch of scallops, you might want to save the trimmings in the freezer for your next batch of fish stock. In a dish like the risotto on page 296, you can add the trimmings to simmer with the stock, straining them out before adding the stock to the rice.

All scallops cook quickly, the smallest sizes in a matter of seconds. Sautéing, poaching, and stir-frying are all suitable cooking methods; you can also thread them on thin bamboo skewers for grilling or broiling. Really big scallops can be treated like little filets mignons, seared in a hot skillet for a minute or so on a side and given center stage on the plate. Whatever the method, cook scallops just until opaque; if you will be making a sauce in the skillet, remove the sautéed scallops first, and return them to the sauce just long enough to reheat.

Clams

Manila clam, *Tapes philippinarium*
Pacific littleneck clam, *Protothaca staminea*
Geoduck, *Panopea abrupta*
Pacific razor clam, *Siliqua patula*
Softshell or "steamer" clam, *Mya arenaria*

Like oysters and mussels, clams in the Pacific Northwest are a mixture of native and introduced species. While the natives have their unique charms, it's the imports that get most of the attention and pay the bills.

Two small hardshell clams are found in Northwestern bays and estuaries, the native Pacific littleneck and the Manila clam. The latter was introduced accidentally earlier in this century, probably as seed hitchhiking with

Pacific oyster seed, and it has established itself in most coastal bays and estuaries in Washington and British Columbia. To a practiced eye, the two species are not hard to tell apart: The littleneck has a smooth shell marked with concentric growth rings, like the typical clams of the East Coast, while in the Manila the same rings are intersected by ridges radiating from the hinge, like a cockle or scallop.

While some prefer the flavor of the native clam, the Manila has become the clam of choice for most of the region's shellfish farmers because of its faster growth rate, and also for its thinner shell, which means a higher proportion of the weight is edible meat than in other clam species.

If the distinction between littlenecks and Manilas is subtle, another native clam, the **GEODUCK** (pronounced "gooey-duck"), is not likely to be mistaken for any other seafood. At 2 to 5 pounds each, these giant soft-shell clams are bigger than any other clams except the giant deepwater varieties from the tropical Pacific. And much of that weight is in the protruding siphon, also known as the "neck" or "foot." Like other soft-shell clams—a slight misnomer since the shells are thin and brittle rather than soft—a geoduck cannot completely withdraw its siphon into the shell. On a good-sized specimen, the siphon may be a foot or more long. It's covered with a loose, wrinkled brown skin, which makes it look something like an elephant's trunk.

Until about a dozen years ago, geoduck was mostly thought of as chowder material, although a few cooks knew it as a low-price alternative to abalone, suitable for the same cooking methods and also delicious raw as sashimi. As abalone grew scarcer, the Asian market discovered geoduck in a big way, and the price has quadrupled. As late as 1987, live geoducks were cheaper than other clams, but by early 1999, they were commanding $8 to $9 per pound in Chinese markets in California. At these prices, and with the wild harvest already at or near its maximum, aquaculture looks to be the future of this species as well. At the time of this writing, at least one Puget Sound shellfish farmer, encouraged by early trials, was gearing up to plant some 2 million 1-centimeter geoduck seed in its clam beds, with a goal of producing hundreds of thousands of 1-kilogram clams in about five years.

Like abalone, geoduck has sweet, virtually fat-free meat that can be either butter-tender or tough as rubber bands, depending on how it is prepared. Slice it thin, pound it thinner, and stir-fry or sauté it, and you have a tender morsel full of sweet shellfish taste. The flavor won't fool anyone into thinking he's eating abalone; it's definitely stronger and more clamlike, but still delicious.

Two other soft-shell clams occasionally appear in our markets. Razor clams, named for their long rectangular shells, are a traditional favorite in the Northwest, but the already short supply has taken a major hit in recent years with the closure of many harvest areas due to domoic acid (see page 35). The only major commercial harvest areas unaffected are a few spots in Alaska. The typical cooking method is frying; Portland chef Cory Schreiber, of Wildwood Restaurant and Bar, first soaks the meat in buttermilk, then breads it with flour, bread crumbs, and cornmeal.

The Atlantic soft-shell clam or "steamer," an introduced species, is found in some bays in southwest Washington, and occasionally shows up in the market. It's best simply steamed, although you have to peel off a little bit of outer membrane that spans the shell and covers the neck.

Like other bivalves, clams should be alive up to the point of shucking or cooking. Stored in the refrigerator, covered with a damp cloth

The Hawaiian Connection

Every year Taylor United, the Northwest's biggest shellfish farmer, sends approximately 250 million clams and 50 million oysters on a Hawaiian vacation. If that sounds like a lot, consider that they go over to the islands as 400-micron larvae or "seed," so small that 10 million take up about as much space as a golf ball. Spread out to grow in a FLUPSY (floating upwelling system) with nutrient-rich water pumped up from below, the seed grow much more quickly than they could in their home waters. In three to four months, when they have reached a strapping 4 to 6 millimeters, they are packed a million or two to a box and flown back to Seattle, where they spend the rest of their days in Puget Sound and other nearby waters. Taylor vice president Jeff Pearson estimates that the Hawaiian sojourn cuts six months to a year from the growout cycle.

(not standing in water), clams can stay alive for up to a week. If an open clam does not close when handled, it is dead and should be discarded. Geoducks and other soft-shell varieties should react when prodded. Also, the longer and thinner the neck of a geoduck, the longer it has been out of the water.

A lot of older recipe books give instructions for soaking clams in water with cornmeal to "purge" them and rid them of grit. I've never found local clams that gritty, so I don't bother with this step. My guess is that farmed clams see so many changes of water after harvest that they rid themselves of any grit before they ever get to market. Some farmed clams go through a "depuration" stage during which they are held in cold sterilized water. This step eliminates the last food from their digestive system and slows down their metabolism, both of which extend their shelf life.

Squid

California market squid, *Loligo opalescens*
Humboldt squid or "giant calamari," *Dosidicus gigas*

Squid (calamari) is one of those love-it-or-hate-it foods. Some people are put off by its odd appearance, or dismiss it as fish bait, or perhaps harbor some deep fear of giant squid attacks. Or more likely, they have had bad experiences with improperly cooked squid, which bears a striking resemblance to thick rubber bands. But those who have had it properly prepared know

it as a delicious, tender, low-calorie, and still inexpensive seafood.

Not too many years ago, about the only squid eaters in this country were of Asian or Mediterranean descent. Adventurous diners may have tried "calamari" in Italian seafood restaurants, or perhaps encountered some in a Chinese "deluxe seafood chow mein," but squid was not part of American mainstream cooking. That has changed over the last two decades, and we now have squid festivals, restaurants specializing in squid, and squid showing up on more and more menus.

Squid may, in fact, be getting a little too popular. For decades, a seemingly endless supply, and modest demand outside of certain markets, put squid on nearly every list of underutilized seafood species. But as other fish stocks have declined, more and more effort has gone into catching squid. By the mid-1990s it was a fully exploited resource—50 million pounds harvested annually in California—and a coalition of squid fishermen and processors, remembering the boom and bust of the sardine fishery half a century earlier, were calling for a moratorium on new entry into the fishery.

Then came the El Niño of 1997–98, which disrupted the squid's food supply, and scattered them to who knows where. Fresh squid virtually disappeared from the market, and the frozen stocks were eventually depleted. Monterey, which normally handles tens of millions of pounds of squid in the summer and fall, had zero landings of squid in 1998. California squid packers were forced to buy larger Atlantic varieties just to have something to sell.

These changes have been reflected in the

price. For more than a dozen years, the price of fresh squid at my local fish market never budged from 99 cents per pound, but sometime in the mid-'90s the price went up to $1.25. That's still cheap, but something was clearly going on. During the squid drought of 1998, the occasional load of squid that showed up in the market commanded three or four times the price of past years. By midsummer 1999, water conditions and squid appeared to be back to normal, but I don't expect to see buck-a-pound squid anymore.

Except in coastal areas where it is caught, most squid is frozen in 3-pound or 5-pound boxes. Like other shellfish, it survives the freezing and thawing process well, although it never cooks up quite as tender as squid that has never been frozen. If your market goes to the trouble of getting fresh squid, by all means buy it. Fresh squid usually sells for only a few cents per pound more than frozen.

Fresh or frozen, whole squid is cheap in part because you have to clean it yourself, which is not difficult but does take some time. It is possible to find squid "tubes" that have already been cleaned, but that has always struck me as an extravagance, like paying extra for boned and skinned chicken breasts. Once you get the hang of it (see page 274), cleaning squid is no more time-consuming than many other kitchen tasks, such as peeling potatoes. The edible portion that remains after cleaning whole squid is almost two-thirds of the total weight, one of the best yields of any species.

You can tell a lot about the freshness of squid by the color. The thin outer skin of perfectly fresh squid is translucent gray, mottled with tiny black spots. By the second or third day out of the water (or the second day out of the freezer), those black spots begin to break down, releasing pigment that shows as pink to purple when diluted. (This pigment is not squid ink; that comes from inside—see page 311.) The more pink color showing, the older the squid and the staler the flavor will be. As with any seafood, reject any squid that smells unpleasantly fishy, regardless of appearance.

Squid can be fried, sautéed, grilled, boiled, or stewed; regardless of the cooking method, the most important thing is not to overcook it. As soon as the squid becomes firm and opaque, in anywhere from 30 seconds to about 3 minutes, depending on the cooking method, it is done. Cook it any longer and it will be tough. However, like pot roasts and old birds, it will become tender again with long, slow, moist cooking. Isaac Cronin, in *The International Squid Cookbook*, gives a simple rule: cook squid less than 3 minutes or more than 20, never in between.

There are various methods of cleaning squid, depending on how it will be cooked. All of them involve separating the edible parts—the tentacles and the outer sac or mantle, from the inedible—the head, beak, entrails, and transparent "quill." Like a lot of techniques, the process is harder to describe than it is to perform, so don't be put off by the length of the following instructions.

The first step in all methods is to cut off the tentacles as close as possible to the eyes, which keeps them together in a neat cluster. If you cut too far from the eyes, the tentacles will fall apart and you will be wasting some of the edible portion. Squeeze out and discard the

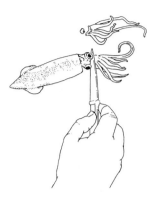

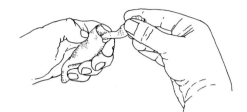

beak, a small hard piece about the size of a dried chick-pea in the middle of the tentacles.

For squid that will be cooked whole or cut into rings, grasp the mantle in one hand and squeeze gently while pulling the head with the other hand. Most of the entrails should come away with the head. Next, pull out the quill, which is attached to one side of the mantle.

Reach in with a finger to pull out any remaining bits of entrails, perhaps running in a little water to help loosen things. The mantle is now ready for cooking whole, for stuffing, or for cutting crosswise into rings of any thickness.

Whether or not you remove the outer skin is up to you. The dark spots in the skin release their color during cooking, giving a pinkish-purplish stain to the cooked dish. If the skin is removed, the squid come out pure white after cooking. Based on a survey of my colleagues

---

Giant Squid Invasion

One potential bright spot in the recent El Niño situation was a huge increase in the occurrence of another squid. The Humboldt squid, *Dosidicus gigas,* also known as giant or Chilean squid, is a very large variety (up to 5 feet and 10 pounds) typically found from Chile to northern Mexico. These giants have been known for years as an incidental catch in the Mexican shrimp industry, where shrimp packers process the thick mantles into frozen tenderized "steaks" sold under the brand name Grande Calamari (see page 310). Normally scarce north of Mexico, these squid were abundant in California and Oregon waters in 1998, showing up in good numbers in trawl fisheries (not to mention providing sport anglers with some exciting fishing).

At around 10 pounds each, one of these squid contains a lot of meat. The $\frac{1}{4}$-inch-thick mantle, after the tough outer skin and inside membrane are cut away, yields snow-white meat that can be sliced thin and sautéed or stir-fried; with a preliminary pounding, it is as tender as abalone. The octopus-size tentacles can be stewed like octopus or incorporated into a risotto or pasta sauce, although you have to scrape away a tiny toothy ring in the center of each sucker first. Unfortunately, I find the flavor of Humboldt squid is nothing to write home about.

and cookbooks, I have concluded that most cookbooks tell you to skin squid and most Asian cooks skin them, but most Western cooks don't, unless they have a particular reason to do so. To me, squid looks funny without the pink color, so I don't skin them. Also, the two triangular fins on the mantles usually come off when the squid is skinned, making it look less like squid.

There is an alternate way of cleaning the mantles, namely squeezing out the contents by scraping along the length of the mantle with the back of a knife blade. This method does keep your hands a bit cleaner, but I've never found it any easier or as reliable as the one above.

To clean the mantles Chinese style for stir-frying, cut off the tentacles as above. Slit the mantles open lengthwise, open them up flat, and scrape away all the entrails and the quill. Pull off the spotted outer skin and cut the mantles into pieces about 2 inches square; rinse and drain. For a decorative touch, score the outer side of each piece with shallow diagonal cuts every ½ inch or so in a diamond pattern; when cooked, the pieces will curl up like tiny pine cones.

Most instructions for cleaning squid say to do it under running water, which may seem like a socially irresponsible thing to do in the chronically water-short West. But it really doesn't take much water if you do it in an organized manner. Start by separating all the tentacles from the heads, then popping out the beaks, then rinsing the tentacles together. (Having a second colander in the sink to catch all the debris will make cleanup easier.) Now move on to the mantles; do the knife and hand work on all of them, and only then turn on the

water (remembering that a thin stream may be enough) for rinsing. Doing one task at a time on the whole batch saves not only water, but time as well.

Whichever cleaning method you use, if you can't cook the squid the same day you buy it, at least clean it the same day and plan on cooking and serving it the next day. A batch of cleaned and skinned squid will survive 24 hours in the refrigerator without much loss of quality, but whole squid usually begin to smell and taste a bit fishy by the second day.

Abalone

Red abalone, *Haliotis rufescens*

Everywhere you go on California's north coast, you will see fence posts, porches, trees, and just about every other available surface adorned with large, iridescent ovals 8 to 10 inches across. They are the shells of abalone, a large one-shelled marine mollusk that is one of the West Coast's greatest seafood delicacies. But in terms of relevance to today's seafood market, these shells might as well be fossils.

Treasured by generations of cooks and diners for their sweet, succulent meat, several species of abalone were once caught commercially all along the Pacific Coast. Overfishing, both legal and otherwise, sent one species after another into steep decline, and harvests became increasingly restricted. By the mid-1990s, the fishery was down to only one species and just a few locations, and the price of trimmed abalone meat had risen to $60 to $80 per pound, if you could find it at all. Facing declining catches and increasing difficulty in preventing poachers from mixing illegally caught abalone with the legal catch, California authorities finally closed the last stretch of coast to commercial abalone harvesting in 1998, and the fishery may never reopen. Some areas remain open to sport harvest, but sport-caught abalone cannot legally be bought or sold.

So why include abalone in a new cookbook? The answer is aquaculture. As the wild populations were declining, farmers in several locations on the California coast, as well as others in Asia, South America, and South Africa, were gradually perfecting the culture of abalone. California farmers now produce more than a million abalone per year, with the capacity to grow two or three times that many. Abalone is still a luxury item, but at least it is available.

While farming has made abalone more available than before, it hasn't necessarily made it cheaper. Ounce for ounce, the meat from farmed abalone sells for about the same as the wild version did, so most of the crop (what isn't exported to Asia) goes into restaurants that can charge plenty for a dish of abalone. For the rest of us, it's something to consider once in a while as a memorable appetizer.

Live abalone, which are mainly sold in Asian markets, will keep for up to three days in the refrigerator. Like other live shellfish, they survive best if covered with a damp cloth to protect them from the drying air of the refrigerator.

The edible part of an abalone is mainly the adductor muscle, the "foot" with which it clings to rocks by day and slithers out onto the kelp at night to feed. To remove the meat from an abalone, stand the shell on a cutting board with the thickest part down and the meat facing you. The breathing holes should be running down the right side of the shell. Starting a little to the left of the top (about 11 o'clock), slip the tip of an oyster or clam knife between the shell and the second of two flaps of meat. Jam the knife downward, staying a little to the left of center, to cut the adductor muscle free from the shell. When the muscle is completely free, the meat will flop out of the shell, exposing the soft, greenish entrails tucked into the heel of the shell. Cut the meat free from the entrails (a clam knife may be sharp enough to do this, but an oyster knife probably isn't). Discard the entrails.

Locate the end of the abalone that was closest to the heel of the shell. Dig with the tip of a knife near the base of the muscle to expose the pinkish parts (the gills and mouth) and cut them away. The rest is edible muscle, although the brownish outermost surface can be a bit leathery. The black edges of the muscle, a part scrubbed or cut away by many cooks, is perfectly edible.

The next step is to slice the meat across the grain (parallel to the outer surface). The easiest way to do this is on an electric meat slicer; if you don't have access to one, place the meat on a cutting board with coat-hanger wire or wooden skewers on either side. Holding the meat down with the heel of your hand, slice horizontally with a long, thin, stiff-bladed knife held parallel to the cutting board and riding along the top of the wire as a guide. Pull out the slice and repeat with the rest of the meat.

Traditional directions for wild abalone call for pounding the slices to tenderize them. Having tried it both ways, I think farmed abalone benefit from only the lightest pounding, if any. A far more critical variable in tenderness is cooking time. Forty-five seconds to a minute is just about right for tender meat; much more time over the heat and it will become tough. Too little cooking time, however, leaves a crunchy raw texture.

Cafe Beaujolais Oysters with Smoked Poultry Essence

Sometimes a single experience can shatter one's prejudices. I always thought raw oysters were best with as little adornment as possible, so I'm not quite sure what tempted me, at a dinner at Cafe Beaujolais in Mendocino some years ago, to try an appetizer of raw oysters with a warm cream sauce flavored with smoked duck essence. But I did, and wow! The dark, smoky flavors and silky richness of the sauce played beautifully against the briny-sweet oysters to make one of the most memorable dishes I have ever tasted. As soon as I got home, I called chef Christopher Kump, who gave me the recipe over the phone to share with my newspaper readers. His recipe, with a slightly different procedure, now appears in his book Evening Food.

Now I admit, smoked duck essence isn't something most of us keep around the house, but you can make a close equivalent with the bones and trimmings of easily available smoked chicken or turkey. An hour's simmering in unsalted chicken stock is all you need to extract the smoky flavor that permeates the skin, bones, and miscellaneous bits of meat. When the stock is greatly reduced, a spoonful or two can transform a simple sauce. With smoked chicken essence on hand, you can whip up the sauce in about the time it takes to shuck the oysters.

SERVES 4

Carcass from ½ a smoked chicken or duck, OR 2 cups smoked turkey bones
2 cups (approximately) unsalted chicken stock
½ cup whipping cream
16 to 24 live oysters

➤ Remove any remaining meat from the smoked chicken and reserve it for another use. Put everything else—skin, bones, miscellaneous trimmings, bits of gelatinous broth trapped under the skin—in a pot with the stock. Bring just to a boil, reduce the heat, cover, and simmer 1 hour. Let stand another 30 minutes, if time permits. Strain and let stand until the fat rises to the surface. Discard the fat, return the stock to the pan, and reduce to 1 cup. Taste for the level of saltiness; if the stock is not too salty, reduce it further to intensify the flavor. Refrigerate or freeze until ready to use.

➤ In a medium saucepan, bring the cream to a boil and reduce by a third. Turn the heat to a simmer, add 2 tablespoons of the smoked chicken essence, and reduce until the sauce coats a spoon. Meanwhile, shuck the oysters, pouring off most of the liquid in the shells (the sauce will provide enough salty flavor). Arrange 4 to 6 oysters per serving around a small ramekin of the warm sauce, with small forks for dipping the oysters in the sauce. Serve immediately.

NOTE The recipe makes enough essence for many servings of this sauce, because it's not really practical to make in smaller quantities.

Tightly sealed in the refrigerator, it will keep, like any concentrated stock, for at least a week, longer if you bring it to a boil every few days. It also freezes perfectly.

Warm Spinach Salad with Pan-Fried Oysters

The general idea for this salad, and the inspired touch of adding ground fennel to a cornmeal crust for frying oysters, comes from Bradley Levy, owner-chef of Firefly restaurant in San Francisco.

SERVES 2 AS A MAIN DISH, 4 AS A FIRST COURSE

⅓ cup fine cornmeal

1 tablespoon flour

1 teaspoon fennel seed, toasted and crushed

Salt and freshly ground pepper, to taste

10 to 12 small shucked oysters, drained

1 tablespoon balsamic vinegar

4 cups tender spinach leaves, washed well, drained, and spun dry

3 to 4 tablespoons olive oil

1 teaspoon minced shallot

1 teaspoon minced garlic

➤ Combine the cornmeal, flour, half the crushed fennel, and a pinch of salt and pepper in a shallow bowl. Toss the oysters to coat them well with the mixture and shake off the excess.

➤ Warm a stainless steel mixing bowl with hot water and wipe it dry. Add the vinegar and a pinch of salt and pepper and stir to dissolve the salt. Add the spinach leaves and toss to coat the leaves lightly with the seasoned vinegar.

➤ Heat half the oil in a skillet (preferably nonstick) over medium-high heat. Add the oysters and cook until they shrink noticeably and are golden brown, about 1 minute per side. Remove them with a slotted spoon and add them to the salad bowl. Add the remaining oil, the shallot, and garlic, and the remaining fennel to the pan and cook until fragrant. Pour the contents of the skillet over the spinach, toss to coat evenly, and serve on warm plates with the oysters arranged on top.

VARIATION For a more substantial salad, add strips of roasted and peeled sweet pepper, tiny tomatoes, or kernels cut from blanched sweet corn to the pan after the oysters are done to warm in the dressing.

Angels on Horseback

I never have figured out why these tidbits are supposed to resemble equestrian angels, but they are tasty nonetheless. Apparently of English origin, Angels on Horseback is found in most standard American cookbooks, with many variations. The only constants are oysters, bacon, and dry heat; other seasonings vary from nothing to elaborate marinades and sauces. Some authorities, including James Beard, reserve the name "angels" for oysters wrapped in thin slices of ham rather than bacon; if bacon is used, they become Devils on Horseback. (How many oysters can dance on the head of a pin?)

Cooking times also vary widely in recipes. I have seen published cooking times as long as 10 minutes, but about 3 minutes per side is more like it. The key is to cook them just until the bacon is crisp, but not so long that the oysters shrink and become tough.

SERVES 4 AS AN APPETIZER

1 (10-ounce) jar small oysters, OR 1 dozen live oysters, shucked

1 ounce dry white wine

1 green onion, minced

Freshly ground black pepper, to taste

Dash of hot pepper sauce (optional)

6 thin slices (approximately) fine-grained white bread

Butter

6 thin slices bacon, cut in half

Lemon wedges

➤ Empty the oysters (with their liquor) into a shallow bowl and add the wine, green onion, a generous grinding of pepper, and hot pepper sauce if desired. Set aside to marinate up to 30 minutes.

➤ Trim the crusts from the bread and cut the slices in half diagonally to make as many triangles as you have oysters. Place them on a dry sheet pan and toast them lightly under the broiler or in a 450°F oven. Butter them lightly and set aside.

➤ Drain the oysters well. Wrap each in a half slice of bacon, securing the ends with toothpicks. Place them in a baking pan (the same one used for the toasts is fine) and broil or bake, turning once, until the bacon is crisp, 5 to 6 minutes. Remove the toothpicks and serve immediately on the toast points, with lemon wedges.

Spaghetti with Oysters and Bacon

Oysters and bacon is too good a combination to feature only once, so here they are again in a simple pasta sauce. It's even better with pancetta, bacon cured in the Italian style with pepper but without smoke.

SERVES 2 AS A MAIN DISH, 4 AS A FIRST COURSE

1 (10-ounce) jar small oysters

½ teaspoon Worcestershire sauce

Large pinch cayenne or white pepper

2 slices smoked bacon, OR 4 thin slices pancetta

½ pound spaghetti, linguine, or other long thin pasta

¼ cup sliced green onions (white and green parts separate)

1 ounce dry white wine

1 tablespoon lemon juice, or to taste

1 teaspoon lemon zest

2 tablespoons butter

Salt and pepper or cayenne, to taste

➤ Drain the oysters, reserving the liquor. Sprinkle the oysters with Worcestershire and cayenne, toss to distribute the seasonings, and set aside. Bring a pot of salted water to a boil for the pasta. Cut the bacon crosswise into ¼-inch chunks. Cook the bacon over medium heat in a large skillet until crisp and brown. Remove the pan from the heat, push the bacon to one side of the pan, and swab out the fat with a paper towel.

➤ Start the pasta cooking, according to package directions. When the pasta is 5 minutes away from being done, return the skillet to medium heat, add the green onion bottoms and cook a few seconds. Add the wine, lemon juice, and oyster liquor and bring to a boil. Add the oysters and lemon zest and cook until the oysters have shrunk noticeably and the edges are curly, about 3 minutes. Stir in the butter and green onion tops; taste the sauce for seasoning and adjust if necessary. Drain the cooked pasta, add it to the skillet, and toss to coat. Serve in warm bowls with the oysters scattered on top.

Pasta with Oysters and Sorrel

This is pasta and seafood reduced to its essentials, with just enough sorrel to provide a touch of tart flavor and some spinach to maintain the green color.

SERVES 2

7 ounces spaghetti or spaghettini

1 tablespoon butter

1 cup shredded sorrel (about 18 leaves)

1 cup shredded spinach (about 18 leaves)

1 (10-ounce) jar small oysters, with their liquor

Salt and freshly ground pepper, to taste

➤ Start the pasta cooking in a pot of salted water. Melt the butter in a skillet over low heat. Add the sorrel and spinach and a ladleful of water from the pasta pot and cook, stirring frequently, until quite soft. The sorrel will turn dull green almost instantly, then become slightly brighter with cooking.

➤ When the pasta is nearly done, add the oysters and their liquor to the skillet and add salt and pepper to taste. Simmer until the oysters begin to shrink and curl. Drain the cooked pasta, add it to the skillet, and toss gently to coat with the sauce. Serve in warmed bowls with the oysters arranged on top.

Eggplant "Stuffed" with Oysters

In Creole cooking, lots of dishes are called "stuffed" even when the stuffing is heaped on top rather than actually stuffed inside. By the time it finishes cooking, the half eggplant in this dish is more of a platform for the oyster dressing than a shell. But no matter, it's still a delicious main dish or a substantial side dish.

SERVES 4

2 large eggplants, split lengthwise

2 jars (10 ounces each) oysters

3 tablespoons olive oil

1½ cups finely diced onion

2 large cloves garlic, minced

½ teaspoon mixed *herbes de Provence*

½ teaspoon Creole seafood seasoning (page 31) or Chesapeake seafood seasoning (page 29)

2 tablespoons dry white wine

1 cup fresh bread crumbs

1 tablespoon minced chives or green onion tops

¼ cup grated Parmesan cheese

➤ Bake the eggplant halves in a 400°F oven until just tender. Scrape out the pulp, leaving a shell about ½ inch thick attached to the skin. Discard any big clumps of seeds and chop the pulp coarsely.

➤ Drain the oysters, reserving the liquor. Chop the oysters into bite-size pieces. Heat the oil in a skillet and cook the onion and garlic until the onion softens. Add the herbs and seasoning, then stir in the oyster liquor and wine. Reduce slightly, then stir in the chopped eggplant, bread crumbs, oysters, and chives. Cook 1 minute, taste for seasoning, and adjust to taste. Spread the mixture evenly in the eggplant shells and top with cheese. Return to the oven and bake until nicely browned, about 15 minutes.

Oyster and Artichoke Pot Pies

One of the signature dishes at Commander's Palace in New Orleans, where the Brennan family serves updated versions of classic Creole cuisine, is Oysters Commander, an appetizer of artichoke bottoms filled with whole oysters and oyster stuffing. According to Dick and Ella Brennan's cookbook (see bibliography), oysters and artichokes appear together in several traditional Louisiana dishes, including casseroles and a classic Creole soup.

Oyster Pie is another traditional New Orleans dish, though one that is seldom found on restaurant menus. I don't know if there is any precedent for adding artichokes to an oyster pie, but it works just fine. You can use any unsweetened pie dough for the single (top) crust, but I like to use a biscuit dough, as if making a fruit cobbler. The pie itself is not the most colorful dish in the world, so use colorful baking dishes or serve it with other foods that add bright colors to the plate.

SERVES 4

4 medium or large artichokes
 (about 2 pounds)

Biscuit Topping

1⅔ cups all-purpose flour

2½ teaspoons baking powder

¾ teaspoon salt

Scant cup whipping cream

🌿

2 jars (10 ounces each) small oysters, drained, liquor reserved

3 tablespoons butter

1 cup finely diced yellow onion

½ cup finely diced green onion

¼ teaspoon Creole seafood seasoning (page 31)

3 tablespoons flour

¼ cup water or milk (approximately)

Salt and pepper, to taste

➤ Steam or boil the artichokes according to your favorite method until just done, about 45 minutes. Let cool, then pull off the outer leaves, leaving as much of the bases intact as possible. Discard the smallest inner leaves and chokes. Dice the bottoms. (Optional: Scrape off the pulp from the inside of each leaf and set aside; otherwise, reserve the leaves to serve as a separate course.)

➤ While the artichokes are cooking, combine the dry ingredients for the biscuit topping in a large mixing bowl and mix thoroughly. Stir in the cream with a fork, stirring just until the mixture is evenly moistened. Turn the mixture by hand in the bowl until most of the floury bits are absorbed. Cover the dough and let it rest for at least 15 minutes.

➤ Put the oysters in a sieve over a bowl to drain thoroughly. Meanwhile, melt the butter in a saucepan over medium heat; remove

1 tablespoon and set aside. Add both types of onion and the seasoning to the pan and cook until soft. Stir in the flour and cook, stirring, until lightly browned. Add the water or milk to the oyster liquor if necessary to make 1 cup; stir it into the saucepan along with the scraped artichoke pulp and cook until quite thick. Taste for seasoning and adjust if necessary; set aside to cool.

➤ Preheat the oven to 350°F. Divide the oysters and diced artichoke bottoms among 4 ovenproof individual casseroles (if the oysters are especially large, cut them into bite-size pieces). Spoon the sauce over all. Turn the dough out onto a lightly floured board and press it with your fingertips and the heels of your hands to between ⅛ and ¼ inch thick. Cut the dough in quarters and thin it out a little more with your fingertips, if necessary, to fit the casseroles. Top each casserole with dough, pressing it well against the edges to seal and trimming the excess with your hands. Brush the tops with melted butter and cut 3 or 4 small vents in the top of each pie. Bake until the crusts are golden brown, about 20 minutes. Serve hot or warm.

NOTE Several of the steps can be done ahead of time, including steaming and trimming the artichokes and preparing the sauce. If the sauce is thoroughly cooled, you can assemble the pies up to the point of adding the biscuit topping and refrigerate them overnight; add the topping just before baking.

Oysters Rockefeller

This most famous American baked oyster dish, invented at Antoine's in New Orleans around the turn of the century, probably derives from a French dish of oysters baked in the shell with spinach and Mornay sauce. Like so many dishes, Oysters Rockefeller has as many versions as there are cooks that prepare it, but most contain spinach and an anise-flavored liqueur. This version omits the cream sauce and has only a modest amount of butter, but the flavor is still "as rich as Rockefeller."

Tradition calls for a minimum of half a dozen oysters per serving, but four is really plenty for a first course. Clams or mussels can be prepared the same way after first steaming them open.

SERVES 4 TO 6 AS AN APPETIZER

24 small to medium oysters
¼ cup celery leaves
½ cup (loosely packed) parsley leaves
1 cup (loosely packed) spinach leaves
1 large bunch watercress, large stems removed (about 1 cup)
4 green onions
4 tablespoons butter
1½ ounces Pernod or other anise liqueur
¼ teaspoon white pepper
Dash of Tabasco or other hot pepper sauce
Salt, to taste
Rock salt, for lining the pan

➤ Shuck the oysters, reserving the deeper bottom shells. Wash the shells inside and out and set aside; discard the top shells. Drain the oysters and strain the oyster liquor. Keep both cold until ready to cook.

➤ Blanch the celery leaves, parsley, spinach, and watercress separately in boiling water

Oysters Cooked in the Shell

"On the half shell" doesn't necessarily imply raw; the deeper half of an oyster shell also provides a perfect bake-and-serve container for the oyster meat and its seasonings cooked in the oven, in a steamer, or on a charcoal grill. Oysters Rockefeller (see above) is the best known of a large repertoire of baked oyster dishes; they are also good steamed Chinese style (see page 286) or barbecued (see page 284).

The ideal way to prepare oysters for baking is to shuck them immediately before cooking (see page 263 for shucking instructions). If you are not skilled with an oyster knife, most fish markets that sell live oysters will shuck them for you at no extra charge except at their busiest hours. If you have an especially large order or cannot avoid shopping at a busy time, it's best to call in your order ahead of time. Plan to use store-shucked oysters the same day you buy them, ideally within a few hours so they do not dry out.

Another popular approach is to begin with whole oysters, bake them until the shells open, then remove the top shell and continue with the recipe. This avoids the most difficult part of shucking oysters, that is, getting the shells apart without breaking them; but you still have to remove the top shell and cut the oyster free from the bottom shell, and while the oyster is hot. In my opinion, it's not any easier than shucking them first.

I prefer the following method for all cooked-in-the-shell preparations, except for barbecued. First, shuck the oysters (or have your fishmonger do it for you), removing them entirely from the shell and storing them in their liquor. Second, wash the bottom shells (the deeper, more cuplike of the two) to get rid of any bits of shell or mud around the lip. Third, if the recipe calls for the oyster liquor, drain the oysters well and strain the liquor through a fine sieve. Finally, return an oyster to each shell, arranging it more or less in its natural position, and add the sauce or other topping. Lining the bottom of the baking dish with rock salt and embedding the shells slightly in the salt is a traditional way to keep them upright during cooking.

just until wilted; refresh with cold water and drain thoroughly. Chop the greens together with the green onions by hand or in a food processor. Melt the butter in a small skillet over low heat. Add the chopped greens and cook slowly until most of the liquid is gone. Add the Pernod, strained oyster liquor, pepper, and Tabasco and cook until reduced by half. Add salt to taste (the oyster liquor may provide enough). Allow to cool.

▶ Preheat the oven to 450°F. Line one or more shallow baking pans or pie pans with a ½-inch layer of rock salt. Press the oyster shells into the salt to keep them upright and place an oyster in each. Top with a scant tablespoon of sauce and bake until the sauce is bubbly, about 10 minutes. Serve on plates lined with additional rock salt, if necessary to keep the shells upright.

VARIATION Other Toppings for Baked Oysters

Another baked oyster classic from a century ago is Oysters Kirkpatrick, a San Francisco original intro-duced at the Palace Hotel, with crumbled bacon and ketchup among the ingredients. Somewhat similar, but with green pepper replacing the ketchup, is Oysters Casino. For Curried Oysters, the oysters are topped with a curry-flavored cream sauce. And the list goes on and on. Here are a few of my favorites.

➤ Taranto style: Combine 1½ cups fresh bread crumbs, 3 tablespoons chopped parsley, and a generous grinding of black pepper. Discard the oyster liquor or save it for another use. Pack the crumb mixture loosely into the shells, over and around the oysters, and drizzle with olive oil before baking.

➤ Use the topping from Coconut-Curry Baked Mussels, page 293.

➤ Bake Oysters with Black Bean Sauce (page 286) instead of steaming.

Barbecued Oysters

In Northern California, summer plus oysters equals barbe-cued oysters. Whether in a bayside restaurant, at a picnic ground, or in your own backyard, many people's favorite way to enjoy oysters in summer is hot off the grill, in their shells, with a dollop of sauce added to each shell as it cooks.

For years, I had always used the same method of barbecuing oysters: I'd set them on the grill right side up, that is, with the deeper cup-shaped valve (shell half) down. When the heat of the fire caused the shell to pop

open, I'd remove the oyster from the grill and use an oyster knife to pry off the upper valve. The problem was, there was often as much as a tablespoon of near-boiling water in each shell, which would have to be poured off or it would dilute the sauce (not to mention the danger of scalding the cook!). Eventually I started to keep a small bowl next to the grill, and would tip the shell and pour out the water before finishing the shucking step.

A couple of years ago, an oyster grower told me about a better way. Lisa Jang, who grows oysters at Preston Point on Tomales Bay north of San Francisco, used to sell hundreds of barbecued oysters every week at an evening farmers' market in Santa Rosa, where they cooked them upside down. "We had lots of people, including local chefs, stand there and tell us we were doing it all wrong," she says, "but we had lots of happy repeat customers who can vouch for our method."

Well, add me to the list of those who say that upside down is the way to go. When oysters cook with the flat valve down, a couple of good things happen. First, when the oyster begins to open, the excess water spills out onto the fire, so you don't have to deal with it. (To keep the water from damping down the fire too much, Jang suggests starting with a hotter than usual fire.) Also, the flat valve absorbs the brunt of the heat, so the cupped valve is a little cooler when you turn it over and add the sauce, and is less likely to overcook the oyster.

Serving barbecued oysters can be as formal or as informal as you like. If the oysters are small enough to be eaten in one bite, you can just pick up a shell and nudge the contents into your mouth with a free finger, oyster bar style. Medium or larger oysters are usually two- or three-bite affairs, which makes them knife and fork food.

The recipe here is enough for a sack of 50 to 60 oys-ters, about right for a single grill. How many people it will serve depends on the rest of the menu and the com-pany; I know some oyster lovers who can polish off

2 dozen of these. Half a dozen per person is a good average if there are other foods being served, closer to a dozen if this is the main dish. A few barbecued oysters can be a nice first course, but keep the number small so you don't use up all your fire on the oysters before you get around to cooking the rest of the meal.

Sauces for barbecued oysters run the gamut from standard bottled barbecue sauce or seafood cocktail sauce to upscale versions with sun-dried tomatoes and extra virgin olive oil. Garlic butter is a recurring theme, either alone or in combination with another sauce. Mexican-style red or green salsa, fruit-based salsas, Chinese black bean sauce, mignonette sauces with or without herbs, and Thai-style curry mixes with coconut milk are all possibilities. Look at baked oyster and mussel recipes for other inspirations.

SERVES 4 TO 12

5 dozen small or medium oysters in the shell

1 head garlic, loose skin removed

¼ pound butter

Juice of 1 lemon

2 cups Fresh Tomato Salsa (page 327), bottled red or green salsa, or cocktail sauce

➤ Scrub the oysters well with a stiff brush, especially around the hinge of the shell. Rinse. Discard any open oysters that do not close when handled. Lay the oysters in a bus tray or picnic cooler, flatter sides up, and cover with a damp towel or burlap. This can be done several hours ahead of serving time.

➤ Cut the root end off the garlic and slice the head in half crosswise, exposing all the cloves. Melt the butter slowly in a small saucepan and add the garlic, cut sides down. Simmer slowly for at least 15 minutes, or until the butter has a definite garlic flavor. Season to taste with lemon juice and set aside.

➤ Build a hot charcoal fire in an open or covered grill; if using briquets, count out enough to cover the fire grate in one layer and add about one-third more. When the coals start to cover over with gray ash, lay a batch of oysters on the grill, flat side down. Cook until the shells begin to open and steam hisses out between the shells, 3 to 5 minutes. Have the garlic butter and salsa handy.

➤ As each oyster begins to open, remove it from the grill with tongs, tipping it up to drain off excess water, and turn it right side up. Using an oven mitt or folded towel to protect your holding hand, pry off the top shell with an oyster knife and return the half-shell oyster to the grill, cup side down. Spoon a teaspoon to a tablespoon of salsa into the shell and drizzle with ½ teaspoon or so of the garlic butter. Cook the sauced oysters until the meat shrinks noticeably and the edges get wavy. As space become available on the grill, keep adding more oysters.

Steamed Oysters with Black Bean Sauce

Black bean sauce gets its name and its characteristic flavor from one of the fundamental ingredients of Cantonese cooking, fermented black beans (see page 29). It's often applied to stir-fried dishes, but here the sauce is spooned over oysters before they are steamed in the half shell. Because the beans are cooked only a short time in the shell, it's important to cook them briefly in oil before combining them with the other ingredients, according to Sacramento chef-restaurateur David SooHoo, who provided the proportions for this sauce.

The oysters typically sold in Chinatown and served in Chinese restaurants can run quite large, each good for several bites. Of course, you could use smaller oysters if you like, but you won't save any money; in terms of cost per ounce of meat, the larger sizes are a better bargain. Given the choice, however, I would still use no larger than medium size, to get one- or two-bite-size morsels.

SERVES 4 CHINESE STYLE, WITH OTHER DISHES

8 large or 12 medium oysters, in the shell

Black Bean Sauce

1 tablespoon oil

1 tablespoon Chinese fermented black beans, finely chopped

1 teaspoon minced ginger

1 teaspoon minced garlic

1 tablespoon Chinese oyster sauce

Heaping ½ teaspoon sugar

Pinch of salt

Pinch of white pepper

1 teaspoon sesame oil

Cilantro sprigs or diagonally sliced green onions, for garnish

➤ Open the oysters with an oyster knife, discard the top (flat) shells, and cut the oysters free from the bottom shells. Set the oysters in their shells in a deep plate that will fit inside a steaming pot. (You may need two plates on two levels, depending on the size of your steaming pot.)

➤ Heat the oil in a small skillet and cook the black beans for a minute or so, until they release their strong odor. Combine them in a bowl with the remaining sauce ingredients and any oyster juices. Mix well and spoon into the oyster shells.

➤ Bring the water in a steamer to a rolling boil, add the plate of oysters, cover tightly, and steam until the oysters have shrunk a bit and the edges begin to curl, about 3 minutes. Add a few sprigs of cilantro to each shell, replace the cover, and steam another minute or so. Transfer to a serving plate and serve immediately.

ALTERNATIVE SPECIES Greenshell or large Mediterranean mussels

VARIATION If you are not too confident in your ability to shuck raw oysters, you can steam them open, but the timing becomes trickier. When making the sauce, cook the ginger and garlic along with the beans, since the sauce will get less cooking time inside the steamer. Set the scrubbed oysters on the steaming plate and place it in the steamer over boiling water. Start checking after about 3 minutes, and remove the oysters as soon as the top shells have popped open. As soon as they are cool enough to handle, follow the same procedure as for shucking a raw oyster (see page 263), except that you can use an oyster knife, a clam knife, or a paring knife, since you don't need the strength of the knife to pry the shells apart. Set the oysters back on the plate, top with sauce and cilantro, and finish with just 1 minute of steaming.

Stir-Fried Oysters with Black Bean Sauce

If you prefer not to be bothered with the shells at all, stir-frying is another option. For that matter, if you order oysters in black bean sauce in a Chinese restaurant and don't specify that you want them steamed in the shell, you might get them stir-fried.

SERVES 4 CHINESE STYLE, WITH OTHER DISHES

⅓ cup unsalted chicken stock

1 tablespoon Chinese oyster sauce

Heaping ½ teaspoon sugar

Pinch of salt

Pinch of white pepper

½ cup plus ½ teaspoon cornstarch

1 tablespoon Chinese fermented black beans, finely chopped

1 tablespoon minced green onion

1 teaspoon minced ginger

1 teaspoon minced garlic

1 cup shucked oysters, drained

½ cup oil

Cilantro sprigs or diagonally sliced green onions, for garnish

➤ Combine the stock, oyster sauce, sugar, salt, pepper, and ½ teaspoon cornstarch; stir to dissolve. Combine the black beans and minced ingredients in a small bowl. Have a heatproof strainer set over a clean, dry heatproof container near the stove, to receive the hot oil.

➤ Set a wok over low heat to preheat thoroughly. Meanwhile, toss the drained oysters in ½ cup of cornstarch to coat them generously, then shake off the excess. Turn the heat under the wok to high and add the oil. When the oil around the edges begins to smoke, add half the oysters and fry until golden brown, about 1 minute per side. Transfer the oysters with a skimmer to the strainer, add the second batch to the wok, and fry until golden brown. Carefully pour the fried oysters and oil into the strainer. Return the wok to the heat, and in the bit of remaining oil stir-fry the minced ingredients until quite fragrant. Add the liquid mixture, bring to a boil, and cook until lightly thickened and glossy. Return the oysters to the wok to coat with the sauce. Garnish with cilantro or green onion.

Other Serving Suggestions: Oysters

Pan-fry drained oysters as in the spinach salad on page 278 and serve with tartar sauce, aioli or one of its variations, or one of the flavored mayonnaise sauces on page 323. Or to make a New Orleans-style po' boy sandwich, tuck them inside a hollowed-out sandwich roll with plenty of shredded lettuce.

Skewer several oysters together on thin wooden skewers and cook on a well-oiled grill or under the broiler.

Omit the crab in the gumbo on page 241 and add shucked oysters and their liquor to the finished soup, simmering just until the oysters have shrunk noticeably.

See Kurt's Salmon with Oyster Stuffing, page 72.

Basic Steamed Mussels

These mussels, known in France as moules marinière, *are delicious on their own, the wine and the mussel juices combining to form a delicious broth. There are also a number of variations: Add tomatoes, herbs, and garlic to the basic recipe, for example, and it becomes* moules provençale. *Or the mussels can be turned into various sauces and pasta dishes, or chilled and used in salads.*

SERVES 2

1 pound live mussels
¼ cup dry white wine
1 tablespoon chopped shallot or green onion
1 teaspoon minced parsley or chervil
Pinch of freshly ground pepper
2 tablespoons butter (optional)

➤ Scrub and debeard the mussels, discarding any open ones that do not close when handled. Place them in a skillet or saucepan with the remaining ingredients. Cover, bring to a boil, and steam until the shells are all open. Serve in bowls, with bread for dipping in the broth.

VARIATION Mussels in Lambic For a Belgian variation, replace the wine with the Flemish wheat beer called lambic (lam-BEEK). Like many other beers in which wheat replaces some of the barley malt, lambic has a tart flavor from lactic acid, which enhances seafood just like a squeeze of lemon juice or the acid in white wine. It's also less bitter than most beers, as the hops are specially aged to reduce the bitterness that brewers of other beer and ale styles demand. Lambic beers are not easy to find in this country, but with a rising interest in Belgian beers, many well-stocked liquor stores and wine shops have added some Belgian specialties to their beer selection. Ask for "straight" lambic, or the variety called Gueuze, rather than a fruit-flavored variety like Kriek or Framboise. And don't expect normal beer prices; ounce for ounce, this stuff sells for about the same price as a mid-priced Napa or Sonoma chardonnay.

If you can't find Belgian lambic, other wheat beers will give an interesting flavor to steamed mussels. The German Berliner Weisse is especially tart. Bavarian wheat beers, usually labeled Weizen, are typically less acid; in fact, they are often served with a wedge of lemon to balance the flavor in the glass. Many American microbreweries offer one sort of wheat beer or another; most I have tasted come closer to the Bavarian style than the Berliner or Belgian styles.

Coconut-Lime Mussels

Mussels in coconut milk broth has become almost as popular among West Coast chefs as the marinière *style. Everybody's version is a little different, but most include lemongrass in some form. The ingredients in this recipe, from Oakland restaurateur Geoff Deetz, should be available anywhere Southeast Asian foods are sold. Yes, I know coconut milk is full of saturated fat, but if you limit yourself to dunking the mussels in the broth as you pick them out of the shells, and resist the temptation to sop up all the broth with bread, a lot of those nasty calories will stay behind in the bowl. In any case, discarding the thick cream and using the thinner part of the milk will remove a lot of the fat with very little loss of flavor.*

SERVES 2

1 cup canned coconut milk

¼ cup chopped cilantro

1 teaspoon lemongrass powder, OR
   1 tablespoon minced fresh lemongrass

1 teaspoon galangal powder, OR 1 tablespoon
   minced fresh galangal

1 teaspoon garlic powder

1 teaspoon ground black pepper

Pinch of red pepper flakes

½ teaspoon salt

1 tablespoon olive oil

1 tablespoon minced garlic

2 dozen live mussels, cleaned

¼ cup lime juice

➤ Blend the coconut milk, cilantro, lemongrass, galangal, garlic powder, pepper, red pepper flakes, and salt. For the best flavor, cover and refrigerate at least 2 hours, or up to 4 days.

➤ Heat a large skillet to near smoking and add the oil and garlic. Add the mussels, stir quickly, and when they are all open, add the lime juice and coconut mixture. Cover and steam until the broth is heated through, 1 to 2 minutes. Serve in deep bowls.

Smoked Mussels

I was visiting some friends in Mendocino who were raving about the smoked mussels they had eaten in a restaurant, and were wondering if they would be easy to make at home. Consulting the tide charts, we headed for a rocky cove at low tide to gather a bucket of wild mussels. Back home, we fired up the charcoal grill, added a few sticks of apple wood, and cooked the mussels over the smoky fire until they popped open. They were absolutely delicious. In just the couple of minutes that the shells were open, the meat of the mussels had absorbed a delicate smoky flavor that married beautifully with their own sweet and briny flavor.

Fruitwoods, either commercial smoking chips or prunings from unsprayed apple, pear, or quince, make ideal smoking material for shellfish. I have used pruned wood from a flowering quince bush in my yard, and it worked fine. Red alder, a common hardwood along the Pacific coast, is another traditional favorite. Oak firewood split into thin sticks will also work.

SERVES 4 AS A FIRST COURSE, 2 AS A MAIN DISH

2 dozen mussels (about 1 pound)

½ cup hardwood smoking chips or sticks of
   fruitwood

3 tablespoons butter

1 clove garlic, crushed

Salt, pepper, and lemon juice, to taste

➤ Scrub and debeard the mussels. Prepare a moderate-size charcoal fire in a covered grill. Arrange the mussels (in a single layer if possible) in one or two disposable foil pans. When all the coals are lit but not yet covered with ash, add the fruitwood or smoking chips to the fire. Immediately put the grill in place, set the mussels in their pan directly over the fire, and cover the grill. Cook with the vents open until all the mussels open, 10 to 15 minutes depending on the heat of the fire.

➤ Meanwhile, melt the butter with the garlic and season to taste. Serve the mussels in the shells; add the mussel juices from the pan to the butter mixture as a dipping sauce.

VARIATION The same technique can also work with oysters or clams, but because they take longer to open over the fire, I suggest shucking them first and removing one shell half. Clams should go in a pan like the mussels, but oysters can be laid carefully on the grill itself in their deeper (bottom) shells. In this case, make the fire off center in the grill and place the oysters away from the fire. Cook just until the oysters shrink slightly and the edges curl.

Mussel Skillet Paella

Outside Spain, the best-known form of paella is an elaborate version with an assortment of shellfish and meats. However, there are many regional Spanish rice dishes that rely on a single fish or shellfish. Unlike the usual large-scale paella, which requires a special pan and serves eight or more people, this recipe cooks in an ordinary 12-inch skillet to serve four. If the very name paella makes it seem too complicated, just call it Baked Mussels with Saffron Rice.

SERVES 4

2½ to 3 cups mild chicken stock

2 tablespoons olive oil

1 small leek or onion, finely chopped

2 cloves garlic, minced

Large pinch of saffron

1⅓ cups Spanish paella rice or Italian arborio rice

1 large pimiento or red bell pepper, roasted, peeled, and diced

1 teaspoon salt

Freshly ground pepper, to taste

3 dozen small live mussels (about 1½ pounds), cleaned

➤ Preheat the oven to 350°F. Have the stock at a simmer. Combine the oil, leek, and garlic in a 12-inch skillet with a heatproof handle. Cook over medium heat until the leek is soft. Crumble in the saffron, then stir in the rice and red pepper. Cook until the rice is well coated with the oil, about 2 minutes, then add 2½ cups of stock. Sprinkle the salt and pepper evenly over the surface and simmer 10 minutes.

➤ Add the mussels in a ring around the outside of the pan, hinge side down. Transfer the pan to the oven and bake until the mussels are open, the liquid is nearly all absorbed, and the rice is tender, about 20 minutes. Check after 15 minutes; if the rice is in danger of cooking dry before it is tender, add another ½ cup or so of warm stock. Remove the paella from the oven and let it stand a few minutes before serving.

NOTE A 12-inch skillet is ideal for this quantity of rice, allowing it to cook in a thin layer. If the largest you have is 10 inches, either reduce the amount of rice to a cup or accept the somewhat softer texture that comes from rice cooked in a deeper layer.

Cold Curried Mussels in the Shell

Mussel shells make a convenient base for a mussel salad, especially for a buffet. If you prefer, you can serve the mussels out of the shell on a bed of tender lettuce or spinach leaves.

SERVES 4 TO 6 AS AN APPETIZER

1 pound mussels, cleaned

2 tablespoons chopped green onion or shallot

1 tablespoon fresh ginger slices and trimmings

2 tablespoons sake or dry white wine

2 teaspoons peanut or other vegetable oil

½ teaspoon curry powder

½ cup plain yogurt

1 teaspoon minced fresh ginger

Pinch of sugar

1 teaspoon chopped mint leaves

➤ Combine the mussels, onion, sliced ginger, and wine in a covered saucepan. Bring to a boil and steam until the mussels open, 1 to 3 minutes after the liquid comes to a boil. Transfer the contents of the pan to a large strainer set over a bowl.

➤ Wipe the pan dry and return it to very low heat. Add the oil and sprinkle in the curry powder. Cook until the oil is evenly stained yellow. Add 3 tablespoons of the strained mussel liquid, bring to a boil, and reduce by two-thirds. Let the mixture cool, then stir into the yogurt. Add the minced ginger and sugar.

➤ Shuck the mussels (half a mussel shell makes a good tool for scraping the meat free from the shell). Separate the mussel shell halves and save enough for serving. Stir the meats into the yogurt dressing, cover, and chill well before serving. Just before serving, stir in the mint and spoon a mussel into each half shell with a little of the dressing.

Tagliarini with Mussels in Saffron Cream

For easier eating, you can shuck the mussels after steaming, but the dish really looks better with the contrast of the blue-black mussel shells and the saffron-tinged sauce.

SERVES 2 AS A MAIN DISH, 4 AS A FIRST COURSE

1 cup whipping cream

Pinch of saffron threads

24 mussels, cleaned

1 shallot, minced

2 or 3 whole parsley sprigs

½ cup dry white wine

½ pound cooked tagliarini (preferably fresh) or linguine

Salt and pepper, to taste

➤ An hour or two ahead, combine the cream and saffron in a bowl and set aside in a warm place. The cream should stain yellow.

➤ In a deep skillet or wok with a tight-fitting cover, combine the mussels, shallot, parsley, and wine. Cover, bring to a boil, and steam until the shells open, 3 to 5 minutes. Remove the mussels and discard the parsley. (May be prepared to this point ahead of time.)

➤ Add the cream and a pinch of salt and pepper to the pan, bring the sauce to a boil, and reduce until slightly thickened. Return the mussels to the sauce to reheat, and toss the cooked pasta in the sauce. Serve in warm bowls, with the mussels arranged on top.

Fish Dieppoise

Sole Dieppoise is a classic French dish named after the city of Dieppe in Normandy. Dieppe is famous for its shellfish, so anything prepared à la dieppoise *implies the use of mussels and shrimp and their reduced cooking juices. The city also has a long history of ocean trade with the tropics, so dishes from the area are often highly seasoned with cayenne or curry powder.*

This recipe will work with fillets of any lean, mild-flavored fish (sole, flounder, orange roughy, tilapia), as well as whole pan-dressed rex sole or other small flatfish. It's on the rich side, with both cream and butter, so keep the rest of the menu simple. An assortment of julienne root vegetables, steamed or simmered in stock, makes a good side dish.

SERVES 4

1 tablespoon soft butter

1 heaping tablespoon flour

12 mussels, cleaned

1 tablespoon minced shallot

½ cup light, dry white wine

12 medium raw shrimp, peeled and deveined (reserve shells)

3 green onions, trimmed, or leek tops

4 sole or flounder fillets, about 3 ounces each

Salt

½ cup whipping cream

⅛ teaspoon cayenne pepper, or to taste

➤ Blend the butter and flour thoroughly; set aside at room temperature. Combine the mussels, shallot, and half the wine in a saucepan. Cover, bring to a boil, and steam until the mussel shells open, 3 to 5 minutes. Remove the mussels and set aside. Reduce the heat to a simmer, add the shrimp, and simmer just until they turn opaque. Remove the shrimp with a slotted spoon and set aside. Add the shrimp shells to the pan and leave at a simmer. Shuck the mussels, discard the shells, and add the mussels to the bowl with the shrimp.

➤ Combine the remaining wine and the green onions in a nonstick skillet just large enough to hold the fish. Add water to a depth equal to the thickness of the fillets, bring almost to a boil, reduce the heat, and simmer 5 minutes. Season the fish fillets lightly with salt, add them to the skillet, and poach until just done. Transfer to a warm platter or individual plates.

➤ Discard the green onions and strain the contents of the shellfish pan into the skillet. Bring to a boil, reduce by two-thirds, and add the cream, cayenne, and a large pinch of salt. Reduce until lightly thickened, whisk in the butter-flour mixture, and simmer another minute or so. Taste for seasoning and adjust to taste. Add the shellfish to the sauce to reheat briefly, then spoon the sauce and shellfish over the fish. Serve immediately.

Baked Stuffed Mussels, Tuscan Style

In La Grande Cucina Toscana, *Giovanni Righi Parenti gives a recipe for stuffed mussels from Grosseto in southern Tuscany. A sausage and bread crumb stuffing is packed into the steamed-open shells, which are then tied shut with thread before being baked in a tomato sauce. If this seems like a lot of trouble, the author also gives a simpler procedure for baking in the half shell. As in many traditional cookbooks, quantities of ingredients are inexact, but the proportions here provide a light stuffing to each shell. Doubling the amount of stuffing will emphasize its flavor over that of the mussels, but the result will still be delicious.*

SERVES 2 AS AN ENTREE, 4 TO 6
AS A FIRST COURSE

1 tablespoon olive oil

A few sprigs of parsley

2 dozen large mussels, cleaned

¼ cup white bread crumbs (no crust)

1 to 2 tablespoons milk

3 ounces sweet Italian sausage, removed from
its casing, or bulk pork sausage

2 tablespoons chopped parsley

1 clove garlic, minced

1 thin slice prosciutto

1 small onion, thinly sliced

2 cups peeled, seeded, and chopped tomatoes

12 basil leaves, shredded

➤ Heat the oil and parsley in a large skillet and add the mussels. Cook until they begin to sizzle, then cover and steam until most of the shells are open. Remove the open mussels, letting the stubborn ones cook another minute or so until they open. Set aside to cool.

➤ Soak the bread crumbs briefly in the milk, then squeeze out the excess. Combine with the sausage, chopped parsley, garlic, and prosciutto and chop together (on a cutting board or in a food processor) as finely as possible.

➤ Preheat the oven to 350°F. Remove one of the shell halves from each mussel (for the best presentation, try to serve them all facing the same way, i.e., all right or left shell halves).

Pack a little of the sausage mixture in around each mussel, spreading it evenly; it's okay if the mussel meat peeks out through the stuffing.

➤ Choose a bake-and-serve dish just large enough to hold the mussels in a single layer. Cover the bottom of the dish with sliced onion and top with the tomatoes and basil. Carefully place the mussels in the dish and bake uncovered until the stuffing is nicely browned, about 20 minutes. Serve from the casserole.

Coconut-Curry Baked Mussels

A crunchy bit of coconut and a touch of fiery Thai curry paste go nicely with the sweetness of mussels. Smaller mussels make bite-size tidbits suitable for eating with the fingers; the larger greenshells are more knife-and-fork fare. Bake or broil them, whichever is more convenient.

SERVES 4 TO 6 AS AN APPETIZER

⅓ cup minced onion or shallot

2 tablespoons minced ginger

1 large clove garlic, minced

3 or 4 sprigs cilantro

2 teaspoons Thai red or green curry paste

1 teaspoon oil

2 tablespoons shredded unsweetened coconut

1 dozen greenshell mussels, OR 18 blue
mussels, cleaned and steamed open

➤ Mince the onion, ginger, garlic, and cilantro together as finely as possible, or better still, pound to a paste in a mortar. Stir in the curry paste and oil, then the coconut.

293

➤ Preheat the oven to 450°F, or set up the oven for broiling. Steam the mussels open with a little water as described on page 267. Remove and discard half of each shell and cut the adductor muscle holding the meat to the other half. Spoon a little of the coconut mixture into each mussel and lay them in a baking dish or on the rack of the broiler pan. Bake or broil until the coconut mixture is nicely browned, 10 to 12 minutes in the oven or 8 minutes under the broiler.

NOTE If you buy cilantro in a Southeast Asian market, you may find it with the roots attached; by all means mince the roots along with the leaves and stems for an authentic Thai flavor.

Iron Skillet Roasted Mussels

Skillet-roasted mussels have been a popular item at Restaurant LuLu in San Francisco since its opening in 1992. Roasting is actually a bit of a misnomer; these mussels are cooked in an open skillet on top of the stove, not in an oven. But, as founding chef Reed Hearon, who later went on to North Beach to open Rose Pistola, explains, the mussel juices evaporating on the hot skillet give a bit of smoky, roasted flavor and aroma to the dish.

SERVES 2 AS AN APPETIZER

2 dozen live mussels, cleaned

¼ teaspoon salt

¼ teaspoon pepper

2 tablespoons warm clarified butter

➤ Heat a heavy cast-iron skillet over high heat for several minutes. Add the mussels in a single layer. Turn off the heat and let stand until the mussels open, 1 to 2 minutes; add heat only if the mussels are slow to open. Arrange the mussels with the open sides up and sprinkle with salt and pepper. Drizzle butter over all and serve in the skillet, with small forks for spearing the mussel meats.

Other Serving Suggestions: Mussels

Substitute mussels for the squid in Spaghetti with Spicy Calamari Sauce, page 304. Either steam the mussels open and add them to the sauce at the end or, even easier, add the live mussels to the skillet in the second step along with the oil and garlic, and cover the pan when you add the tomatoes. By the time the sauce is ready, the mussels should be too.

Use large mussels in place of baked oysters (pages 282 to 284) or clams (page 300).

Sautéed Scallops and Leeks

I have always liked the combination of leeks and scallops; both have subtle flavors and interesting textures, and just seem to make a meal a little special. The pale green of the leeks also makes a nice color contrast to the scallops.

SERVES 2 AS A MAIN DISH, 4 AS A FIRST COURSE

2 medium leeks (about 1¼ inches diameter)

½ pound scallops, trimmed

¼ cup flour

1 teaspoon paprika

½ teaspoon salt

¼ teaspoon white pepper

3 tablespoons oil

¾ cup chicken or fish stock

¼ cup dry white wine

Juice of ½ lemon

4 tablespoons butter, softened

Salt and white pepper, to taste

➤ Wash and trim the leeks. Starting at the bottom, cut into 2-inch lengths. Cut each section lengthwise almost in half, open like a book, and slice lengthwise into thin ribbons. As you work your way up the leek, remove the outer dark green leaves of the upper sections, but use the yellow and pale green hearts. Save the outer leaves for the stockpot. You should have a generous 2 cups of julienne. Wash well in a bowl of water, lift out of the water, and drain.

➤ Drain the scallops thoroughly (if wet) and pat dry. Warm the serving plates and a small bowl in a low oven.

➤ Combine the flour, paprika, salt, and pepper. Dredge the scallops in the seasoned flour, transfer to a strainer, and shake off the excess flour. Heat the oil in a nonstick skillet over high heat. Add the scallops and sauté, stirring or shaking, until they begin to brown, about 1 minute. Transfer to the warm bowl. Wipe the oil out of the skillet with a paper towel.

➤ Add the leeks to the skillet, stir or toss for a few seconds, and add the stock. Cook over medium-high heat until the leeks are tender. Remove the leeks with a slotted spoon to the plates, making a ring about 6 inches across in each plate.

➤ Add the wine and lemon juice to the skillet and bring to a boil. Reduce by half,

then swirl in the butter and season to taste. Return the scallops to the pan to reheat slightly. Spoon the scallops into the middle of the plates and spoon the sauce over all.

Steamed Singing Scallops

"Singing scallops" is a diver's name for the small pink and spiny scallops found in Northwestern waters—not because of any sound they make, but for the way they can quickly open and close their shells for propulsion when disturbed. Unlike most other scallops, they are delivered to the market alive in the shell, like mussels and clams, and like those other bivalves, they are delicious simply steamed open in wine. If you prefer a richer broth, add a little butter or cream to the steaming liquid. Singing scallops are noticeably less salty than clams and mussels, so they may require a bit of salt added to the steaming liquid.

SERVES 2 AS A MAIN DISH, 4 TO 6 AS A FIRST COURSE

½ cup light, dry white wine

¼ cup water

1 tablespoon minced shallot or green onion

1 clove garlic, minced

Pinch of salt

Freshly ground black pepper

2 dozen live pink scallops (about 1 pound), well rinsed

1 tablespoon butter, OR ¼ cup cream (optional)

➤ In a covered nonreactive saucepan, combine the wine, water, shallot, garlic, salt, and pepper. Bring to a boil. Add the scallops, cover, and cook at a boil until the scallop meat has shrunk slightly, about 2 minutes.

➤ Remove the scallops with a slotted spoon to shallow bowls. Add the butter or cream to the broth if desired, taste for seasoning, and pour over the scallops. Serve with crusty bread.

NOTE To match the delicacy of the scallops, use a wine without too fruity or oaky a flavor. Sparkling wine is ideal, or a modest sauvignon blanc; barrel-aged chardonnay is definitely not in order, nor is a sweeter wine like a chenin blanc.

Stir-Fried Scallops and Broccoli with Black Bean Sauce

Stir-frying is typically fast cooking, but with scallops the time is especially short, just enough to heat them through. The broccoli, on the other hand, takes a while to cook, so it benefits from some preliminary cooking before it goes into the wok.

SERVES 2 AS A MAIN DISH, 3 TO 4
WITH OTHER DISHES

1½ tablespoons Chinese fermented black beans

2 tablespoons Chinese rice wine or dry sherry

½ pound broccoli

1 tablespoon oil

½ pound bay or sea scallops, trimmed

2 teaspoons minced ginger

1 green onion, minced

¼ cup unsalted chicken stock

1 teaspoon soy sauce

➤ Roughly chop the black beans and combine them with the wine. Trim the broccoli, separate the florets, and cut the stems crosswise into thick slices. Blanch or steam until just tender.

➤ Heat a wok or deep skillet over high heat and add the oil. Add the scallops and stir-fry for a few seconds, just until heated through; remove from the pan with a slotted spoon and set aside.

➤ Add the ginger, green onion, and broccoli and stir-fry until the broccoli is heated through. Add the bean mixture, stock, and soy sauce and cook until the raw wine flavor disappears and the liquid is reduced slightly. Return the scallops to the pan to reheat, and serve immediately.

Easy Scallop and Shrimp Risotto

I have always made risotto by the traditional method, adding the liquid in several stages and cooking until it is nearly gone before adding the next batch. This certainly works, but it takes close attention to keep it from cooking too dry and scorching. A growing number of cooks have asked whether there isn't a simpler way. Instead of adding the liquid gradually, why not just put it in all at once?

Well, I tried it, and it works. After adding all the liquid at the beginning, all you have to remember is to stir the rice several times while it cooks. This leaves you free to prepare other dishes, even to sit down to a first course if the table isn't too far from the stove.

When making risotto by the taste-and-add method, the cook naturally adjusts for older rice by adding a little more liquid and cooking a little longer. (Fresher rice cooks faster, with less liquid.) In the all-at-once method, you have to guess how much liquid will be needed. The only danger is in using too much liquid, which will make the rice mushy rather than al dente. If your rice is fresh, use the amount of liquid called for in the recipe; if it is older, use ¼ to ½ cup more. To be on the safe side, use slightly less than you think you need, and have additional stock or water simmering at the end of the cooking time, to be added if needed.

SERVES 2 AS A MAIN DISH, 4 AS A FIRST COURSE

⅓ pound small or medium scallops

⅓ pound small raw shrimp

1 cup chicken stock

3 cups water

½ cup dry white wine

½ cup chopped green onion tops

1½ teaspoons kosher salt

2 tablespoons olive oil

¼ cup thinly sliced green onion (white parts only)

1 cup arborio rice

Pinch of white pepper or cayenne

1 teaspoon grated lemon zest

1 tablespoon chopped fresh chervil,
   OR 1 teaspoon chopped fennel leaves

➤ Trim the scallops (see page 269); place the trimmings in a saucepan. Peel and devein the shrimp; add the shells to the saucepan. Add the stock, water, half the wine, and the green onion tops, bring to a boil, reduce the heat, and simmer 10 minutes.

➤ While the stock simmers, sprinkle the peeled shrimp with 1 teaspoon of the salt, toss to coat evenly, and let stand 1 minute (no longer); rinse with cold water and drain. If the scallops are on the large size, slice them in half horizontally. Refrigerate the scallops and shrimp until ready to cook.

➤ Strain the stock and return it to a clean saucepan; there should be at least 2½ cups. Heat the oil in a 10-inch nonstick skillet or shallow flameproof casserole. Add the sliced green onion and cook until fragrant. Stir in the rice and cook until well coated with the oil. Add the remaining wine and 2¼ cups of stock, ½ teaspoon salt, and pepper. Bring to a boil and reduce the heat to maintain a lively simmer. Cook 25 minutes, stirring several times.

➤ When the level of the liquid drops to the top of the rice, taste a grain for doneness. If it still tastes raw in the center, add another ½ cup of warm stock (use water if you are out of stock). When the rice has lost the raw center and the liquid is nearly absorbed, stir in the scallops, shrimp, and lemon zest. Cook until the shellfish is done and the liquid is reduced to a thick, gravy-like consistency. Adjust the seasoning, stir in the chervil, and serve immediately in warm pasta bowls.

VARIATIONS You can use just about any combination of shellfish in this dish: skip the shrimp and use all scallops; steam open small clams or mussels and add them to the risotto at the end, or add them in their shells halfway through cooking to steam open; chop some cleaned squid finely and add it to the pan at the beginning, or stir sliced squid in for the last couple of minutes.

➤ For a saffron risotto, crumble a large pinch of saffron threads into the reserved wine while you simmer the stock; setting the bowl or measuring cup of wine in a warm place will help extract the flavor faster.

➤ If you have really large scallops, you can make a plain risotto (especially the saffron version) based on seafood stock, and serve it as a side dish with scallops simply seared for a minute or two per side in a hot skillet.

Potato Crepes with Scallops, Salmon, and Asparagus

Potato crepes are not at all Chinese, but I like the way they provide an absorbent base for this luxurious seafood stir-fry. Note that the pancakes require the potato to be cooked and cooled ahead of time, which can be done earlier in the day or the night before.

SERVES 4 AS A FIRST COURSE

½ pound fresh asparagus

½ teaspoon cornstarch

1 tablespoon dry white wine

1 egg white

⅛ teaspoon white pepper

¼ pound scallops

¼ pound salmon fillet (or a 5-ounce steak, skinned and boned)

½ cup chicken stock

2 teaspoons soy sauce

½ teaspoon rice vinegar

¼ teaspoon sugar

Potato Crepes, below

2 tablespoons peanut or other vegetable oil

1 teaspoon minced fresh ginger

1 tablespoon minced green onion

½ teaspoon cornstarch dissolved in 1 teaspoon water

➤ Starting at the tip end, cut the asparagus into 1½-inch lengths with a diagonal rolling cut: slice off the tip at an angle, roll the asparagus about a quarter turn and cut again, and repeat on down the stalk until you reach the tougher base. Discard the bases.

➤ In a medium bowl, dissolve the cornstarch in the wine; add the egg white and pepper and beat lightly. Trim the scallops; if they're on the large size, cut them crosswise into ¼-inch-thick discs. Remove any pin bones from the salmon and slice across the width of the slice (parallel to the backbone) into ¼-inch-thick rectangles. Add the salmon and scallops to the egg mixture and toss gently to coat. Combine the stock, soy sauce, vinegar, and sugar in a bowl and set aside.

➤ Preheat the oven to 175°F and set 4 small plates in it to warm. Prepare the Potato Crepes and place one on each plate. Keep warm in the oven.

➤ Bring about a quart of water and 1 tablespoon of the oil to a simmer in a medium saucepan; have a colander waiting in the sink. Set a wok or deep skillet over very low heat to preheat thoroughly.

➤ Drain off any excess marinade from the scallops and salmon and slide them into the simmering water, stirring to separate them. Simmer just until the seafood begins to lose its raw color, 20 to 30 seconds, then drain through the colander.

➤ Turn the heat under the wok to high and add the remaining oil. Add the ginger and green onion and stir-fry until fragrant. Add the asparagus and stir-fry until it begins to brown. Add the stock mixture, cover, and cook until the asparagus is crisp-tender, 2 to 3 minutes depending on size. Remove the cover, add the seafood, and stir in the cornstarch mixture. Cook until the sauce is slightly thickened. Taste for seasoning and adjust if necessary, then divide the seafood, asparagus, and sauce over the potato crepes. Serve immediately.

Potato Crepes

1 medium russet potato (about ½ pound), boiled in its skin until tender, cooled

¼ teaspoon salt, or to taste

Freshly ground pepper, to taste

2 tablespoons all-purpose flour

1 egg

⅓ cup milk

2 tablespoons oil (approximately)

➤ Peel the potato and mash it, or put it through a food mill or ricer. Season to taste with salt and pepper. Stir in the flour. Beat the egg and milk together, add them to the potato mixture, and stir until smooth. Heat a little oil in a small nonstick skillet over medium heat. Pour in a quarter of the potato mixture, shaping it into a thick pancake 4 to 5 inches in diameter. Cook until well browned, 2 to 3 minutes, turn, and cook on the other side. Transfer to a plate and keep warm in the oven. Repeat with the remaining oil and batter. You can also cook the crepes on a well-seasoned griddle.

TECHNIQUE NOTE The preliminary cooking of salmon and scallops in water is a Chinese method known as "velveting," for the tender texture it gives to the seafood. If you prefer, you

can use the warm-oil method in the Salmon with Three Beans recipe on page 63, cooking the seafood in a generous amount of still-warming oil just until the salmon loses its raw color, then pouring the contents of the wok through a sieve over a heatproof container. Return the wok to the heat and continue the stir-fry with the bit of oil that remains.

Beer-Steamed Clams

Clams steamed in beer is a standard dish wherever clams can be found, and for good reason. The aroma of the hops in a good beer perfumes the steaming shellfish, and the slight malty flavor of the beer adds an extra richness and roundness to the flavor of the broth. However, a highly hopped beer (which includes a lot of West Coast microbrews) can make the broth too bitter. A standard American pale lager works fine for my taste, but you might prefer the maltier flavor of a dark lager. Another option is wheat beer, which is usually not highly hopped (see Mussels in Lambic, page 288).

SERVES 2

2 dozen live Manila clams

½ bottle beer

6 to 8 slices fresh ginger

2 green onions or shallots, sliced

1½ tablespoons butter, at room temperature (optional)

French bread

➤ Scrub the clams well, discarding any open ones that do not close when handled. Place them in a saucepan with the beer, ginger, and green onions. Cover, bring to a boil, and cook until most of the shells are open, 3 to 5 minutes depending on the variety. Transfer the open ones to a serving bowl and cook the rest another minute or two. If they do not eventually open, discard them. Swirl the butter into the broth and pour it over the clams, leaving the last bit behind in the pan to trap any grit. Serve with crusty bread for dunking in the broth.

Lemon-Scented Pasta with Manila Clams

A generous amount of lemon zest gives an additional lift to a simple clam sauce. The wine should provide enough acidity, so you can save the rest of the lemon for another purpose.

SERVES 4

1 lemon, preferably unsprayed

4 tablespoons extra virgin olive oil

1 tablespoon chopped garlic

2 green onions, white and green parts separated, thinly sliced

Large pinch of red pepper flakes or coarsely ground black pepper

3 dozen small Manila clams (about 1½ pounds), well rinsed

⅓ cup dry white wine

⅓ cup fish stock or diluted clam broth

12 to 14 ounces spaghettini, fedelini, or other thin dried pasta

➤ Bring a pot of salted water to a boil for the pasta. Remove the outer zest of the lemon with a peeler, taking as little as possible of the white pith. Stack the slices and cut them into thin 1-inch shreds.

➤ Heat half the oil in a large skillet or wok and sauté the garlic, green onion bottoms, and pepper flakes until fragrant; do not brown. Add the clams, wine, and stock, cover, and bring to a boil. Meanwhile, start cooking the pasta. When the clams begin to open, add the lemon zest and green onion tops. When all the clams are open wide, reduce the heat and uncover to let the sauce reduce a little. Taste for seasoning; often the clams provide enough salt.

➤ Drain the cooked pasta and add it to the skillet. Drizzle in the remaining oil and toss to coat the pasta with the sauce. Transfer to warm plates or shallow bowls, with the clams arranged on top.

Clams with Sausage, Portuguese Style

While I can enjoy the most simply steamed mussels until I am full, or eat unadorned oysters until I run out of money, I always find clams a little boring with such minimal treatment. More than that of any other bivalve, the sweet but slightly bland flavor of clams seems to me one-dimensional without some more assertive ingredients to complement it.

One ingredient that shows up in one form or another in a lot of traditional clam recipes is cured pork. Think of the bacon or salt pork in New England clam chowder, or the bacon stuffing of clams casino. A Portuguese variation on this theme, both at home and in Portuguese fishing communities in this country, is to cook clams with spicy sausage in a special clamp-lidded pot called a cataplana. A slightly simplified version appears here, to be served either on its own as a simple stew or combined with pasta. In addition to Portuguese-style linguica or chourico, possible sausages include Spanish chorizo (preferable to the more crumbly Mexican version), Cajun andouille, and kielbasa. Lacking any of these, use a fine-textured smoked sausage and add some minced garlic and as large a pinch of red pepper flakes as suits your taste.

SERVES 2

3 dozen Manila clams (about 1½ pounds), OR 2 dozen littlenecks (2 pounds)

2 ounces hot sausage, finely diced

2 tablespoons olive oil

½ cup sliced green onions

⅔ cup diced tomatoes, with juice

➤ Rinse the clams well and drain. If using uncooked sausage, brown the pieces in a wok or deep skillet, and if it renders an excessive amount of fat, wipe out the excess with a paper towel. Add the olive oil and onions and cook over medium heat until fragrant. If your sausage is fully cooked, add it together with the onions to cook just until fragrant.

➤ Add the clams and tomatoes and bring to a boil, stirring. Cover tightly and steam until the clams are open, 2 to 4 minutes for Manila clams, 4 to 8 minutes for littlenecks. Open the pan and transfer the fully open clams to shallow soup bowls; return any closed clams to the pan to cook a few more minutes, but discard any that do not open in twice the time it takes the others to open. Spoon the tomato mixture over the clams and serve immediately.

VARIATION Boil ½ pound of thin dried pasta such as angel hair, spaghettini, or vermicelli in salted water, timing the pasta to be done just after the clams are all open. Drain the pasta, reserving some of the cooking water, and add to the clam mixture, moistening with a little pasta water as needed to extend the sauce.

Geoduck and Asparagus with Oyster Sauce

While this looks like a stir-fry, the clam meat actually doesn't go into the wok until the very end, just to cook for a few seconds in the sauce.

About a half pound of geoduck meat is the most you can cook in a typical wok, and the smallest geoduck you can buy will likely yield more meat than that. If you want to double the recipe, it's probably best to cook it in two batches, either side by side or one after the other.

SERVES 2 TO 3 CHINESE STYLE, WITH OTHER DISHES

6 to 8 dried shiitake mushrooms

1 small live geoduck

2 tablespoons Chinese rice wine or dry sherry

1 tablespoon oyster sauce

1 tablespoon soy sauce

½ teaspoon sugar

¼ teaspoon salt

¼ teaspoon white pepper, OR a dash of hot pepper sauce

½ pound fresh asparagus

1 tablespoon oil

1 tablespoon minced ginger

1 tablespoon minced green onion

½ cup chicken stock

2 teaspoons cornstarch dissolved in 2 tablespoons cold water

➤ Put the mushrooms in hot water to soak until soft. Shuck and clean the geoduck (see note). Slice crosswise a little more than ⅛ inch thick, and give each slice a whack with the side of a cleaver or a mallet to flatten it slightly. Combine the wine, oyster sauce, soy sauce, sugar, salt, and pepper and stir to dissolve. Marinate the geoduck slices in 1 tablespoon of the sauce mixture.

➤ Starting at the tip end, cut the asparagus diagonally into bite-size pieces; stop when the stems become pale and tough. Drain the mushrooms, remove the stems, and cut the caps into strips.

➤ Heat a wok or large skillet over high heat and add the oil. Add the ginger and onion, let them sizzle a few seconds, and add the asparagus and mushrooms. Stir-fry 30 seconds, then add the stock and sauce mixture and cover the pan. Cook over high heat until the asparagus is just tender, 2 to 3 minutes depending on size. Uncover the pan, add the cornstarch mixture, and simmer until the sauce is glossy and slightly thickened. Stir in the geoduck, cook 1 minute, and serve immediately.

NOTE Most Chinese markets will clean geoduck for you, but to do it yourself, first scrub the shell to remove any sand or mud, then drop the whole clam into boiling water for 30 seconds. Retrieve it and run it under cold water to stop the cooking. With a paring knife, cut the meat away from the shells. Peel away the dark mantle (the membrane spanning the shell opening) and the brownish skin covering the neck; these are edible but tough, and may be used for stock or ground finely for chowder. Remove and discard the entrails,

the darker tissues in the main body of the clam. The remaining cream-colored meat, about 50 percent of the live weight, is edible.

VARIATION Substitute the meat of a 4- to 5-ounce farmed abalone, cleaned and sliced ⅛ inch thick (no pounding is necessary).

Other Serving Suggestions: Clams

Small clams can be substituted in any recipe for mussels; figure more per person because of the heavier shells, or accept less edible portion per dozen.

Steam larger clams just until they begin to open, remove one shell half, and bake with the Taranto-style bread crumb stuffing for oysters on page 284; cooked and crumbled bacon makes a nice addition.

See Stir-Fried Oysters with Black Bean Sauce (page 287). Stir-fry clams in the shell in a little oil flavored with ginger and garlic, then add the remaining sauce ingredients, cover, and cook until the shells are all open.

Calamari and Fennel Salad

This recipe is just one seasonal snapshot of a salad I make in various forms throughout the year, with lightly cooked squid and a vegetable or two in a garlicky vinaigrette. This fall and winter version features fresh fennel; see below for ideas for other seasons.

If you have a large enough pot, you can cook the squid all at once. Otherwise, use a medium saucepan and cook about a third of the batch at a time.

SERVES 4 TO 6 AS A FIRST COURSE

1 pound squid, cleaned, mantles cut into rings or strips

1 medium bulb fresh fennel

1 medium sweet onion, peeled

1 clove garlic, minced

¼ teaspoon salt

¼ teaspoon freshly ground pepper

2 teaspoons sherry vinegar

3 tablespoons mild olive oil

¼ teaspoon red pepper flakes (optional)

Lettuce leaves

➤ Bring a pot of lightly salted water to a boil and have a large bowl of ice water nearby. Add a few handfuls of squid to the boiling water and cook until it becomes opaque and the tentacles begin to curl, 15 to 30 seconds. Retrieve the squid with a skimmer and plunge it into the cold water. Repeat with the remaining squid, letting the water return to the boil before adding the next batch. When the cooked squid is cold, drain well.

➤ Slice the fennel and onion crosswise as thinly as possible. If the onion is too hot to use raw, cover it with a little boiling water, then drain.

➤ Combine the garlic, salt, and pepper in a medium mixing bowl and mash the garlic with the back of a spoon. Stir in the vinegar, then the oil and red pepper flakes. Taste for seasoning and adjust to taste. Add the squid, fennel, and onion and toss to coat evenly with dressing. Serve immediately, or cover and refrigerate up to 4 hours. Serve on large lettuce leaves.

VARIATION Vary your salad according to what vegetables are in season. In spring, try diagonally cut asparagus spears or sugar snap peas. Later in the year, use summer vegetables like green beans (again, cut very thin on the diagonal), fresh tomatoes, or sweet peppers. Produce staples like celery and hothouse cucumbers are a year-round option. Onion in some form is a constant, whether it's pickled rings of red onion (see page 176), the immature bulb onions that appear in early spring, blanched julienne leeks, Chinese chives, or slivers of green onion. Or try Vidalia, Walla Walla, Maui, or other sweet onions raw.

➤ The dressing can also be varied with slivered or minced fresh chiles in place of the chile flakes, or salty accents like capers or olives, or distinctive herb like fresh basil or tarragon or dried oregano. For an oil-free dressing, try Nuoc Cham, page 326.

Grilled Calamari

Grilled squid cooks quickly but takes a lot of surface area on the grill, so plan to use the same fire to cook other foods as well. Try it as part of a mixed grill with other seafoods and vegetables, or serve it as a first course while a slower-cooking main course cooks on the grill. Aioli, tartar sauce, lemon butter, sauce verte, and soy sauce dips are all good choices for a dipping sauce. Leftovers make a great salad (see page 303).

SERVES 4 AS AN APPETIZER, 2 AS AN ENTREE

1½ **pounds squid**

➤ Clean the squid, leaving the mantles whole; don't remove the spotted skin and fins unless you prefer it that way. Thread the tentacle clusters together on thin skewers.

➤ Prepare a hot fire in a charcoal or gas grill and preheat the grill thoroughly. Lay the skewered tentacles near the edge of the fire. If your grill bars are close enough together, you can grill the mantles individually; if you are afraid they will fall through the grill, skewer several together near the open end. In either case, lay them on the grill so their length goes across the bars. Start them on the hottest part of the fire and cook until they shrink noticeably, usually less than a minute. Turn and finish cooking on a slightly cooler part of the fire, next to the skewered tentacles, until the meat is opaque white. Spill out any liquid that has accumulated inside the tubes and serve immediately, with your choice of dipping sauce.

Spaghetti with Spicy Calamari Sauce

Not only is squid cheap food, it is also potentially fast food. If you have a market that sells fresh or thawed squid, you can pick up the ingredients for this dish on the way home from work and have dinner on the table less than a half hour after you walk in the door. Once you've got the hang of cleaning squid, it's easy to prepare the sauce in the time it takes to boil water and cook the pasta. The sauce is simply squid added to the southern Italian pasta alla puttanesca, a quickly cooked tomato sauce studded with garlic, hot pepper, olives, anchovies, and capers.

SERVES 2 TO 4

1 **pound squid, fresh or thawed**
1 **can (16 ounces) peeled tomatoes**
½ **pound spaghetti or other long, thin pasta**
2 **tablespoons olive oil**
1 **large clove garlic, minced**
¼ **teaspoon red pepper flakes, or to taste**
2 **anchovy fillets, chopped**
2 **tablespoons chopped green olives**
1 **tablespoon capers**

➤ Put a large pot of salted water on the stove for the pasta. Meanwhile, clean the squid and cut the mantles into rings or strips. Drain the tomatoes, reserving the juice; place the tomatoes in a bowl and chop them roughly with the edge of a spoon.

➤ When the water boils, start cooking the pasta. Meanwhile, heat the oil in a large skillet over medium heat and cook the garlic, red pepper, and anchovy until fragrant. Add the tomatoes, olives, and capers and cook, stirring, until the sauce is slightly reduced.

Add the squid and cook just until opaque, about 30 seconds. If you prefer a slightly wetter sauce, add a little of the reserved tomato juice along with the squid. Taste the sauce for seasoning and adjust if necessary. When the pasta is cooked, drain it and toss it in the sauce, either in the skillet or in a serving bowl. Serve immediately.

Noodle "Paella" with Squid

We don't usually associate pasta with Spain, but the regions of Valencia and Catalunya have a unique and delicious pasta specialty: very thin noodles (fideos or fideus in Spanish and Catalán respectively) that are first browned in oil and then simmered in a tomato-flavored fish stock. Like the rice in paella or risotto, which the finished dish resembles, the noodles absorb nearly all the liquid. (The same technique, but with chicken rather than seafood stock, is also found in Mexican cooking as sopa seca de fideos, a "dry soup" that undoubtedly came from Spain. Nest-like coils of fideos can be found in the Mexican food section of supermarkets.)

Some Catalán and Valencian versions of this dish include shrimp, lobster, or fish cubes cooked with the noodles; others use only the fish stock, to make a simple first course to precede a substantial entree. Here is a version relying mainly on the economical squid. Feel free to use more shrimp or even lobster if your budget permits; don't forget to add their shells to the stock to bolster the flavor.

SERVES 4 TO 6

⅓ cup olive oil

½ pound dry, uncooked angel hair pasta (the thinnest you can find)

2 cloves garlic, minced

½ teaspoon hot paprika

½ cup finely diced onion

1 cup peeled, seeded, and diced tomatoes, with juices

Scant teaspoon salt

½ teaspoon saffron threads

¼ pound medium raw shrimp, peeled and deveined

1 pound squid, cleaned and sliced

4 cups hot fish stock (page 329)

➤ Preheat the oven to 400°F. Heat the oil in a large skillet or paella pan over medium-low heat. Break the pasta into about 3-inch pieces, and cook slowly until it begins to turn golden brown, 8 to 10 minutes. Push the pasta aside and add the garlic to the middle of the pan; cook until fragrant.

➤ Add the paprika, onion, tomatoes, salt, and saffron and cook 2 minutes. Stir in the shrimp and squid, then add the stock. Bring to a boil, stirring frequently. Transfer to the oven. Bake uncovered until the pasta has absorbed the liquid and is drying out and sizzling around the edges, 25 to 30 minutes.

VARIATION To turn this into a multicourse meal, use the fish stock first to poach a good-sized piece of cod or other firm white fish before adding the stock to the pasta. Cover the poached fish loosely with foil while the noodles bake. Serve as a first course, followed by the fish (which will be lukewarm by then, but that's fine) with Aioli (page 320). It's common to stir some aioli into the noodle dish as well.

Thandua Moli

*Squid has always appealed to the more adventurous
eaters. The kind of people who seek out the newest ethnic
restaurants and are always ready to dabble in cooking
new cuisines also tend to be more open to unusual foods
like squid. Conversely, those who shy away from anything that looks as weird as a bunch of squid tentacles
are also likely to avoid more exotic and spicy cuisines.*

*This fiery southern Indian squid curry is not for the
faint of heart. It comes from India Joze restaurant in
Santa Cruz, California, which has featured squid promi-
nently on its menu for the last two decades.*

SERVES 3 TO 4

1 can (14 ounces) coconut milk

1½ pounds squid

3 tablespoons minced garlic

1 tablespoon minced fresh chile, or more or
less to taste

3 tablespoons peanut oil

½ teaspoon black mustard seed (optional)

1 medium onion, grated or finely chopped

1 tablespoon slivered fresh ginger (slice across
the grain, then cut slices into shreds)

1 teaspoon turmeric

1 teaspoon ground cumin

2 or 3 green onions, white parts only,
in ½-inch lengths

1 tablespoon dried mango powder (*amchoor*,
available in Indian stores), or substitute
tamarind water or lemon juice

Salt, to taste

Chopped cilantro, for garnish

➤ Shake the can of coconut milk well,
measure out ½ cup, and set aside. Add water
to the remainder to make 2 cups. Clean the
squid and cut the mantles into rings. Pound
the garlic and chile together to a paste with a
mortar and pestle, or against a cutting board
with the side of a knife blade.

➤ Heat the oil and mustard seed in a
large skillet over medium heat until the seeds
sizzle and pop. Quickly add the onion to keep
the seeds from burning, then add the ginger,
turmeric, and cumin. Sauté until the onion is
lightly browned, adding a little water if necessary to keep the onion from scorching.

➤ Add the garlic-chile mixture and cook
briefly. Add the 2 cups thinned coconut milk,
green onions, and mango powder. Bring to a
boil over high heat, stirring constantly, until
reduced to about ⅔ cup. Add salt to taste.
Stir in the squid and the reserved thick
coconut milk and simmer over low heat until
the squid is done, about 1 minute. Garnish
with cilantro.

Stuffed Squid

There is something about the tubular
shape of squid that makes it irresistible to
cooks who like to stuff things. From southern
Europe to Southeast Asia, wherever there is
squid and there are cooks, there is stuffed
squid. Stuffings range from the squid's own
chopped tentacles to ground mixtures of
shrimp, fish, and other seafood, fresh pork,
and even ham and cheese.

For less work in stuffing, look for squid on
the larger side (8 to 10 pieces per pound,
round weight). But smaller ones will work fine
if that's all you can find. A small spoon, a
large funnel, or a pastry bag (preferably the

disposable kind, not the same one you use for pastry work) are all handy ways of getting the stuffing into the tubes. Remember in any stuffed squid preparation to pack the stuffing in very loosely, as the stuffing tends to expand and the squid shrinks in cooking. As a rule of thumb, fill the cavities no more than one-third full to keep the stuffing light in texture.

Spinach-Stuffed Squid in Tomato Sauce

This is my favorite Mediterranean-style squid stuffing, based on spinach and bread crumbs. Although it tastes best with a simple homemade tomato sauce, canned or bottled marinara sauce will also do. If you prefer something more elaborate, you can add chopped olives, capers, or shreds of prosciutto to the sauce.

SERVES 4

2 cloves garlic, minced

½ cup minced onion

3 to 4 tablespoons olive oil

½ pound spinach, washed, stems removed, leaves finely chopped

2 pounds squid, cleaned with mantles left whole, tentacles finely chopped

¼ cup bread crumbs

Salt and pepper, to taste

Pinch of hot pepper flakes (optional)

¼ cup dry white wine

1 cup tomato sauce

➤ Sauté the garlic and onion over medium heat in 2 tablespoons of oil until soft. Add the spinach and cook 2 minutes or until wilted. Add the chopped tentacles to the pan, turn the heat to high, and cook until opaque. Stir in the bread crumbs, cook until the liquid is all absorbed, and season to taste. Let cool.

➤ Stuff the squid loosely (see above), and secure each opening with a toothpick.

➤ Heat the remaining oil in a skillet until almost smoking. Add the stuffed squid and sauté until opaque. Remove from the pan. Add the red pepper flakes if used, plus any capers, olives, or other garnishes. Deglaze the pan with the wine, reduce by two-thirds, and add the tomato sauce. Meanwhile, remove the toothpicks from the squid. Bring the sauce to a boil and return the squid to the pan to reheat briefly.

Squid Stuffed with Thai Fish Mousse

This Thai-inspired version of stuffed squid was described to me by jazz saxophonist George Brooks, an avid cook and a devotee of all sorts of spicy Asian cuisines. He and I frequent the same markets, and when we meet we often share recipe ideas. One time, he described a baked version of this dish. It sounded so good, I tried it, and came up with this recipe.

The fish mousse stuffing is related to the otak-otak of Malaysia and Indonesia, which is steamed in banana leaf packets. It can be made with any lean white fish, such as rockfish, lingcod, tilefish, or catfish. For a little more luxurious version, add some peeled raw shrimp.

SERVES 4

2 teaspoons oil

1 heaping teaspoon Thai red curry paste (see page 31)

1 pound lean white fish fillets

2 tablespoons minced green onion

12 leaves fresh Thai basil or other sweet basil

1 egg

2 teaspoons Thai fish sauce

2 pounds medium to large squid, OR ½ pound cleaned squid tubes

½ medium cucumber, sliced

1 recipe Nuoc Cham (page 326)

➤ In a small skillet, combine the oil and curry paste and cook over low heat until quite fragrant. Remove from the heat and let cool slightly. Remove any bones from the fish fillets and cut them into 1-inch chunks. Combine the fish in a food processor with the green onion, basil, egg, fish sauce, and the contents of the skillet. Process to a paste.

➤ Clean the squid, setting aside the tentacles for another use. Stuff the mantles loosely with the fish paste (see page 306), and close the ends with toothpicks. If you have any leftover stuffing, form it with moistened hands into 1-inch balls to cook along with the stuffed squid.

➤ Place the squid on two heatproof plates that will fit inside a steamer and steam 20 minutes. Or place them in a single layer in a lightly oiled baking pan, cover with foil, and bake 20 minutes at 350°F.

➤ Divide the cucumber slices among 4 shallow bowls and pour Nuoc Cham over each portion. Serve as a dipping sauce for the squid.

VARIATION If you want to include the squid tentacles, try the method suggested by San Francisco restaurateur Carlo Middione in his book *The Food of Southern Italy*: After stuffing, fit a cluster of tentacles back into the opening of each squid and secure it with the same toothpick used to enclose the stuffing. The squid come out looking remarkably like they have been cooked whole, although it does mean serving them with the toothpicks in place, not exactly a formal presentation.

Calamari Fritti

To many people, "calamari" is synonymous with "fried." While that's not true linguistically, it is the first way many people taste squid, and it remains the favorite. Frying squid couldn't be simpler. There are no complicated batters; you just dredge the rings and tentacles in plain, unseasoned flour, shake off the excess, and cook the squid in hot oil for about a minute. Of course, you have to be somewhat comfortable with deep-frying; see page 25.

Most restaurants use large commercial deep-fryers for calamari, but the best fried-calamari cook I have ever known used a simple stovetop setup. At Augusta's in Berkeley, where I worked for a while in the early 1980s, there was no deep-fryer, so cook Judy Matluck (who later went on to Squid's restaurant in San Francisco) turned out great fried squid in a deep pot of oil on top of the stove. Of course, you can deep-fry in any large pan; all you need is some way of retrieving the cooked food quickly from the oil. A 16-inch wok and a Chinese-style wire skimmer do the job quite well.

Sauces for fried calamari can range from a squeeze of lemon juice to tartar sauce and other mayonnaise-based sauces. Garlic lovers will want to try it dipped in aioli, the pungent garlic and olive oil paste of Provence. Clear Asian-style dipping sauces, especially those spiked with chiles or garlic, are also delicious.

SERVES 2 AS A MAIN DISH, 4 AS AN APPETIZER

Peanut or other vegetable oil (at least 4 cups)

1 pound squid (preferably fresh), cleaned and cut into rings, well drained

1½ cups (approximately) flour

➤ Fill a wok or other frying pan with oil to a depth of at least 2 inches, but allow at least 2 inches from the top of the pan to prevent the oil from boiling over. Fix a frying thermometer on the edge of the pan. Heat the oil to 400°F.

➤ Dredge a third to half of the squid in the flour and transfer it to a frying basket or coarse strainer; shake off the excess flour. If using a frying basket, lower it into the oil; otherwise, carefully drop the squid into the oil. Fry to a light golden brown and remove. Drain for a few seconds over the oil, then transfer to

a tray lined with paper towels. Wait for the oil to return to 400° before frying the remaining squid. Serve immediately.

Gung Bao Squid

Squid, one of the quickest-cooking seafoods, and stir-frying, one of the quickest methods of cooking, were made for each other. A minute or two is all it takes to cook squid to a tender texture; longer cooking will just make it tough.

The authentic flavor of gung bao (also spelled kung pao) dishes comes from dried chiles that have been cooked almost to the point of burning before adding the other ingredients. The chiles will release acrid fumes that can irritate eyes and noses, so use your kitchen's hood fan (if you have one) at its maximum setting. Otherwise, you might want to stop short of fully charring the chiles.

SERVES 2 TO 4 WITH OTHER DISHES

2 tablespoons soy sauce

2 tablespoons water or chicken stock

1 tablespoon vinegar (preferably Chinese black rice vinegar)

½ teaspoon sugar

2 tablespoons minced ginger

2 tablespoons minced garlic

2 tablespoons minced green onion bottoms

3 tablespoons peanut or corn oil

8 small dried chiles

1 pound squid, cleaned and scored Chinese style (see page 273)

½ cup sliced bamboo shoots

¼ cup thickly sliced green onion tops

➤ Combine the liquid ingredients and sugar in one small bowl and the minced ingredients in another bowl; set aside.

➤ Heat a wok or deep skillet over high heat and add the oil. Add the chiles and cook until they are well browned. Push the chiles aside, add the squid, and stir-fry until it begins to stiffen and turn opaque, about 30 seconds. Remove the squid to a plate.

➤ Add the minced ingredients and cook a few seconds until fragrant. Add the sliced vegetables and stir-fry until heated through. Stir the liquid mixture to dissolve the sugar and add it to the pan. Return the squid to the pan and stir-fry until the liquid is reduced by half. Taste for seasoning and correct if necessary. Serve immediately, removing the charred chiles or leaving them in the dish as you like (in either case, they are not to be eaten).

NOTE To be really authentic, you can combine fresh and dried squid. Dried squid is available in well-stocked Chinese markets, and must be soaked overnight in cold water to soften it, then cleaned, cut up, and parboiled for 30 minutes. Don't be put off by the powerful aroma of dried squid; it tastes better than it smells.

Calamari, Abalone Style

One of the traditional glories of West Coast seafood cookery is sautéed abalone. But as fishermen and cooks in Monterey and other California ports have known for years, their locally caught squid, as abundant and cheap as abalone is scarce and expensive, can stand in quite nicely as the "poor man's abalone." One popular restaurant on Monterey's Fishermen's Wharf even took its name, Abalonetti's, from its signature dish of flattened squid mantles prepared in the manner of abalone.

A newer option for mock abalone is the mechanically tenderized "steaks" cut from the mantles of a giant Mexican squid (Dosidicus gigas). Sometimes sold under such fanciful names as "cabalone" and "squid abalone," these frozen quarter-pound steaks sell for quite a bit more per pound than ordinary squid, but as there is no waste, they still come out cheaper than most seafoods in cost per serving.

Here are two methods, one for small squid and the other for steaks. Both give a result remarkably close to abalone in texture, if not quite in taste. True abalone has a distinct sweetness a little like that of clams; squid, while also on the sweet side, is milder in overall flavor.

The high heat required for this dish is not good for most nonstick skillets, so use a plain cast-iron or rolled steel pan. It will also work in a flat-bottomed wok, although you may have to cook the steaks one at a time. To serve more than two, it is best to use two pans to avoid a long delay from the pan to the table. If you like, you can use the bread crumb coating with flattened small squid, but don't try the flour-and-egg version with giant squid steaks; the flour gets in the holes left by the tenderizing machine and comes out raw and gummy.

Method 1

SERVES 2

1 pound good-sized squid (about 8)

1 egg, beaten

⅛ teaspoon dried thyme leaves, crumbled

⅛ teaspoon each salt and freshly ground pepper

2 to 3 tablespoons peanut or corn oil

½ cup flour (approximately)

Lemon wedges

➤ With the tip of a sharp knife, split the squid mantles open along the side where the transparent internal skeleton or "quill" is attached. Open each mantle out flat and scrape away the quill and entrails with the knife. Turn the flattened mantle over and remove the spotted skin and triangular fins. (Separate the tentacles from the rest and save them for another dish, such as a pasta sauce or salad.)

➤ Combine the egg and seasonings in a shallow bowl. Heat a large skillet to near smoking and add enough oil to coat the skillet well. Dredge the flattened squid pieces in flour, shake off the excess, and dip each piece in the egg to coat it. Lay the squid pieces in the skillet and cook until golden brown, 30 to 45 seconds per side. They tend to curl up in the pan after turning, so use tongs to unroll them and hold them flat against the pan. Transfer to warm plates and serve immediately with lemon wedges.

Method II

SERVES 2

1 egg, beaten

⅓ cup unseasoned dry bread crumbs

⅛ teaspoon dried thyme leaves, crumbled

⅛ teaspoon each salt and freshly ground pepper

2 to 3 tablespoons peanut or corn oil

2 (4-ounce) squid steaks

Lemon wedges

➤ Place the egg in a shallow bowl. Sift the bread crumbs through a medium sieve into another bowl and combine them with the seasonings. Heat a large skillet to near smoking and add enough oil to coat the

skillet well. Dip the steaks first in egg, then in bread crumbs, and add them to the skillet. Cook until golden brown, 30 to 45 seconds per side. Transfer to warm plates and serve immediately with lemon wedges.

Risotto with Squid Ink

Like other cephalopods (octopus and cuttlefish), squid sometimes escape predators by releasing a jet of purplish-black ink, clouding the water around them and confusing predators. This ink, contained in a small gland inside the animal, has been extracted and used for centuries as a pigment. Somewhere along the line, someone discovered that it also has a distinctive taste—briny, a bit metallic—and that, together with the distinctive color, has made it a traditional ingredient in many squid dishes around the Mediterranean. Rice cooked with squid ink is known in Italy as risotto nero *("black rice"), and in Spain as* arroz negro, *and I'm sure there is also a Portuguese version, a Yugoslavian version, and several others. This Tuscan version, like most, is not really black, but it has a definite stain from both the squid ink and the chopped beet tops.*

SERVES 4 TO 6

1 pound squid, fresh or thawed

6 tablespoons olive oil

½ cup finely diced onion

2 cloves garlic, minced

1 bunch (about ¾ pound) beet tops or red chard, finely chopped

Salt and pepper

2 to 3 cups mild chicken stock or meat broth (dilute canned broth or strong stock with an equal part water)

2 cups arborio rice

1 to 2 tablespoons butter

➤ Clean the squid by cutting the mantles open lengthwise and pulling away the entrails and quill. Reserve the ink sacs (a silvery piece about ¾ inch long attached to the entrails). Cut the mantles into strips, then chop them fine together with the tentacles.

➤ Heat the oil in a large heavy saucepan and cook the onion and garlic until lightly colored ("blond"). Add the chopped squid and cook until the mixture is lightly browned. Add the beet tops and a little salt and pepper, cover, and cook 30 minutes, adding a little broth if necessary to keep the mixture from sticking to the pan.

➤ Bring the broth to a simmer in another pan. Stir the rice into the squid mixture. In a small bowl, mash about half the ink sacs with a spoon to release the ink, and add it to the rice. Cook, stirring, until the rice is well coated with the sauce. Add broth to cover, bring to a boil, reduce the heat to medium, and cook uncovered until the rice has absorbed most of the liquid. Add broth again to cover and repeat. Continue adding broth in stages and cooking it down until the rice grains are tender outside but *al dente* in the center. If you run out of broth, use warm water. Adjust the seasoning with the last addition of broth, if necessary. Stir in the butter and serve promptly.

TECHNIQUE NOTE Adding the squid at the beginning of the cooking rather than the end is a typical Italian technique for pasta and rice dishes. Like the *soffritto* of minced vegetables, herbs, and pancetta in many an Italian soup or stew, the minced squid more or less disappears as it provides a flavor base, and the remaining bits are tenderized by the long cooking time.

Squid Adobo with Ink

Most Philippine dishes called adobo are long-simmered stews, but this quick-cooking dish also qualifies for the name because it features the same basic seasonings of garlic, black pepper, and vinegar.

SERVES 4 IN AN ASIAN-STYLE MEAL, WITH OTHER DISHES

1 pound fresh or thawed squid

⅓ cup palm vinegar or rice vinegar (available in Asian markets)

2 tablespoons oil

2 tablespoons minced garlic

Salt and black pepper, to taste

➤ Clean the squid, reserving the entrails. Separate the ink sacs, the small silvery organs about ¾ inch long, and place them in a fine sieve set over a bowl. Crush the sacs with a spoon to release the ink. Pour the vinegar through the sieve to extract additional ink. Discard the empty ink sacs and entrails. Cut the mantles into rings, strips, or stir-fry squares and combine them with the tentacles.

➤ Heat a wok or skillet over medium-low heat and add the oil. Add the garlic and cook slowly until it begins to brown. Turn the heat to medium-high, add the squid, and stir-fry just until it begins to turn opaque, about 30 seconds. Add the ink-stained vinegar and a pinch of salt and pepper. Turn the heat to high and reduce the sauce by half. Correct the seasoning and serve with rice.

Abalone en Papillote

This and the following recipe come from Luc Chamberland, of the Abalone Acres farm on Tomales Bay. This dish uses a classic Chinese-restaurant trio of abalone, asparagus, and shiitake mushrooms, but the cooking technique and butter take it in a Western direction.

SERVES 2

3 tablespoons butter, softened

1 teaspoon minced shallot

1 teaspoon grated lemon zest

1 tablespoon lemon juice

Salt and freshly ground pepper, to taste

½ pound fresh asparagus

6 dried shiitake mushrooms, soaked in hot
    water until soft, drained

1 live abalone, 4 to 5 ounces

➤ Preheat the oven to 450°F. Beat the butter until light. Beat in the shallot, lemon zest, and juice. Season to taste with salt and pepper.

➤ Blanch the asparagus in lightly salted boiling water for 1 minute. Drain, rinse with cold water, and slice into bite-size pieces. Stem the mushrooms and cut the caps in half. Shuck and clean the abalone and slice it ⅛ inch thick.

➤ Cut two 12-inch squares of baking parchment, fold each in half diagonally, and crease the corners. Arrange half the abalone slices, half the asparagus, and half the mushrooms on one side of a square and dot with half the lemon butter. Fold the other side of the paper over the fish and seal with a series of creases, starting with one corner and finishing with a twist at the opposite end. (See illustra-

tion, page 22.) Repeat with the other portion. Bake on a sheet pan until the packets are puffy and beginning to brown, about 6 minutes. Serve in the paper or transfer to plates.

Abalone and Chanterelle Salad

This is a general formula; the proportions can be adjusted according to your budget, or your luck in finding mushrooms.

SERVES 2 TO 4

¼ pound chanterelles or oyster mushrooms

1 tablespoon olive oil

1 clove garlic, lightly crushed

Salt and freshly ground pepper, to taste

1 teaspoon minced shallot

1 tablespoon balsamic vinegar

2 tablespoons extra virgin olive oil

Chicken or fish stock or court-bouillon

1 live abalone, 4 to 5 ounces, shucked,
    cleaned, and sliced

1 cup cherry tomatoes

➤ Clean the mushrooms and slice them thick if large, halve if small. Toss them in a bowl with the olive oil, garlic, and a bit of salt and pepper. Spread them on a sheet pan and roast in a hot oven until tender. Let cool.

➤ Combine the shallot in a medium bowl with a pinch of salt and pepper and mash with the back of a spoon. Stir in the vinegar and oil, and blend thoroughly with a fork or whisk. Adjust the seasoning.

➤ Bring about ½ inch of stock or court-bouillon to a simmer in a skillet and poach

313

the abalone slices until just tender, 30 to 45 seconds. Remove and let cool slightly. Whisk the dressing in the bowl again if it has separated. Add the abalone, mushrooms, and tomatoes and toss to coat with the dressing.

Poached Abalone with Lemongrass and Ginger

This recipe is from Manka's restaurant in Inverness, California. If you have Japanese-style pickled ginger on hand, a bit of the pickling juice makes a nice addition, but don't go out and buy it just for this purpose.

SERVES 2

2 tablespoons extra virgin olive oil

1 small stalk lemongrass, chopped

1-inch chunk fresh ginger, coarsely chopped

1 cup dry white wine

1 live abalone, 4 to 5 ounces

½ cup cream

1 teaspoon juice from a jar of pickled ginger (optional)

Salt and freshly ground pepper, to taste

➤ Combine the oil, lemongrass, and ginger in a small saucepan over low heat. Simmer for 20 minutes, keeping the heat very low so the ginger barely starts to brown. Add the wine, bring the mixture to a boil, and reduce by two-thirds. Meanwhile, shuck, clean, and slice the abalone.

➤ Strain the oil and wine mixture into a skillet and add the cream. Bring the mixture just to a boil and reduce it slightly, enough to coat a spoon. Season to taste, adding the ginger juice if desired, then slip in the abalone slices and poach until just tender, 30 to 45 seconds. Serve the abalone slices in the creamy broth.

Other Serving Suggestions: Abalone

Sautéed Abalone with Lemon Butter: Use the sliced meat of 2 farmed abalone in the first method of Calamari, Abalone Style (page 310). After transferring the sautéed slices to warm plates, remove the skillet from the heat, wipe out any remaining oil with a paper towel, then melt 2 tablespoons of butter with 1 tablespoon of lemon juice, or to taste. Pour over the abalone and serve immediately.

Substitute sliced abalone in Geoduck and Asparagus with Oyster Sauce, page 301.

sauces

After the basic skill of cooking fish and shellfish to the proper stage, sauces are probably the most important part of a seafood cook's repertoire. Whether it's a thin liquid for dipping bites of shellfish, a velvety sauce spooned over poached fish, or simply a bit of flavored butter melting over a grilled fish steak, a good sauce adds flavor and moisture that complements the flavor and texture of the seafood. In some cases a sauce can tone down or counterbalance strong flavors; in blander fish, it can add extra layers of flavor to make the whole dish more interesting.

The Vinaigrette Family

Vinaigrette sauce, a mixture of oil, vinegar, and seasonings, is so tied to the idea of salad dressing that it is easy to overlook its other uses. But vinaigrettes offer an endless variety of possibilities for the fish cook as well. A vinaigrette can be flavored with chopped or puréed herbs, vegetables, or fruits, which also add volume. With several varieties of each component on hand, making sauces becomes a fascinating game of mix and match.

The first choice to make is the oil. Both the examples given here use olive oil, but they call for two different types. In the tomato version, a dark green, peppery Tuscan or California olive oil contributes the major flavor, with the tomatoes acting as an accent. The same flavor might be too much in the roasted pepper version, so I use a milder oil, such as a yellow French extra virgin or an everyday blended Italian oil.

Other possibilities for oils include flavorful nut and seed oils, especially good with trout. Hazelnut and walnut oils from France are delicious, but expensive. Some of the cold-pressed nut oils sold in health food stores have a strong enough nut aroma and flavor to carry a sauce, and the Lion and Globe brand of peanut oil from Hong Kong, sold in gallon cans in Chinese markets, has the most peanut aroma this side of a peanut butter jar. Most distinctive of all is Chinese or Japanese sesame oil, expressed from toasted sesame seeds.

Spanish sherry vinegar, which retains some of the smooth, round flavor of the wine from which it was made, is my favorite vinegar for fish vinaigrettes as well as for salad dressings. It's not terribly expensive, though you may have to go to a wine shop to find it. A well-aged red wine vinegar is another good choice. Japanese rice vinegar (be sure to get the unseasoned kind) is especially delicate in flavor, and goes well with sesame oil. Balsamic vinegar adds a sweet note, and can be used in a higher ratio to oil than other vinegars. And while a sauce isn't strictly a vinaigrette unless it is made with vinegar, using lemon, lime, or other citrus juices opens another whole range of flavors (see Salmoriglio, page 318, or Cold Steelhead and Asparagus Citronette, page 85).

I use coarse kosher salt for vinaigrettes, in large part because it's easier to manage the quantity by pinches. Remember to decrease the salt if using other salty ingredients such as olives, anchovies, or soy sauce.

Chopped or puréed vegetables, herbs, or fruits add both flavor and body to a vinaigrette. The simplest variation is to stir a compatible herb such as basil, dill, or tarragon into a plain oil and lemon dressing. The tomato and pepper in the following recipes also provide some bulk to sit on top of the fish. Other possibilities include tomatillo purée or finely diced cucumber, citrus fruits, or papaya, to name just a few.

The basic procedure for making a vinaigrette

is simple. Measure the acid ingredient into a bowl, add salt and pepper, and stir until the salt dissolves, then whisk in the oil until the mixture is emulsified. Stir in other ingredients at this point. The oil and vinegar will separate as it stands, so give it a good stir or shake before serving. I like to spoon a little of the sauce over the fish at first and pass the rest separately at the table, to be added to taste.

In addition to the following recipes, see Trout with Walnut or Hazelnut Vinaigrette (page 84).

Tomato Vinaigrette

This is not meant to be blended; rather, it's a basic vinaigrette with discrete little chunks of tomato that look nice against white fish like halibut or sea bass. The finer you can dice the tomato without losing its identity, the better. Add a little chopped fresh basil or marjoram if you like.

MAKES ABOUT ⅓ CUP (4 SERVINGS)

½ medium tomato
Pinch of sugar
1 teaspoon sherry or red wine vinegar
Pinch of salt and pepper
3 tablespoons extra virgin olive oil

➤ Carefully cut out the core and seeds from the tomato, leaving the outer shell of meat attached to the skin. Cut the meat into fine dice. Sprinkle with sugar. In a small bowl, stir the salt and pepper into the vinegar until the salt dissolves. Stir in the oil and tomatoes.

Red Pepper Vinaigrette

In addition to white fish, this is good on darker fish such as mackerel, tuna, and yellowtail. Use red bell peppers, pimientos, or one of the longer sweet roasting peppers such as Corno di Toro.

MAKES ABOUT ⅓ CUP (4 SERVINGS)

1 medium sweet red pepper, roasted and peeled
3 tablespoons mild olive oil
1 teaspoon sherry or red wine vinegar
⅛ teaspoon salt
Pinch of black or white pepper

➤ Slit the pepper open over a bowl to catch the juices from inside. Remove the seeds and ribs and cut or tear the pepper into strips. Combine it in a blender or food processor with the remaining ingredients, including any pepper juices and blend until almost smooth. A few bits of pepper should remain to give the sauce texture.

Salsa Verde (Italian-Style Green Herb Sauce)

This exuberant, bright green sauce, which in texture falls somewhere between mayonnaise and vinaigrette, is an ideal match for the slightly smoky flavor of grilled fish. It's equally good on fish cooked by other methods— poached, baked, steamed, or broiled. The amount here gives four ample servings, so there will be plenty to spoon over the fish as well as for dunking bread and vegetables.

MAKES ABOUT ½ CUP (4 TO 6 SERVINGS)

2 unpeeled cloves garlic

1 cup loosely packed Italian parsley leaves

1 tablespoon fresh tarragon leaves,
   OR 1 teaspoon dried

2 anchovy fillets

1½ teaspoons sherry vinegar or white wine
   vinegar

¼ cup olive oil

Salt and pepper, to taste

1½ tablespoons mayonnaise (optional)

➤ Drop the garlic cloves into boiling water and cook 1 minute. Retrieve them with a slotted spoon and set aside until cool enough to handle. Blanch the herbs in the same water.

➤ Peel the garlic and combine it in a blender or food processor with the herbs, anchovies, vinegar, and oil. Blend until smooth and season to taste with salt, pepper, and more vinegar if you like. If you prefer a thicker, clingier sauce, blend in the mayonnaise.

TECHNIQUE NOTE The easiest way to blanch small quantities of herbs is in a long-handled sieve. Just put a handful in the sieve and lower it into the boiling water until the herbs are wilted, then pull it out and rinse them under cold water to stop the cooking. Repeat with the remaining batches.

Charmoula (Moroccan Marinade and Sauce for Fish)

To use charmoula, spread it on whole fish, fillets, or steaks and let stand an hour or so before cooking. If you want to use it as a sauce, either cook it along with the fish (especially appropriate for baking), or heat it up in a separate pan while the fish cooks, or use half as a marinade and keep some back to add to the finished fish. Any marinade used on raw fish should be cooked before serving to prevent possible spoilage by bacteria on the surface of the fish.

MAKES ABOUT 1 CUP, ENOUGH FOR 1½ TO 2 POUNDS FISH FILLETS OR 3 TO 4 POUNDS WHOLE FISH

½ cup fresh cilantro leaves

½ cup fresh parsley leaves

4 cloves garlic

Juice of 1 lemon

1 tablespoon sweet paprika

1 teaspoon ground cumin

Pinch of cayenne

1 teaspoon salt

½ cup olive oil

➤ Combine the cilantro, parsley, and garlic in a food processor or blender and chop fine. Add the lemon juice, seasonings, and oil and process until thoroughly blended.

Salmoriglio

Serve this garlicky Italian sauce on simple grilled, baked, or poached fish.

MAKES ABOUT ½ CUP (4 TO 6 SERVINGS)

2 cloves garlic, peeled

½ cup Italian parsley leaves, loosely packed

2 tablespoons fresh oregano or marjoram
   leaves

6 tablespoons extra virgin olive oil

3 tablespoons lemon juice

Salt and freshly ground pepper, to taste

➤ Chop the garlic and herbs together finely. Transfer to a bowl, add the oil and lemon juice, and whisk together. Season to taste.

Emulsion Sauces

Olive oil and garlic, two of the indispensable ingredients of nearly every Mediterranean cuisine, are the basis for a family of sauces found all across the region, from Spain to the Middle East. The details vary from one cuisine to another, but the common thread is a mayonnaise-like emulsion of oil and garlic, bound with another ingredient that absorbs and holds the oil—egg yolks, bread crumbs, potato, or nuts.

Since garlic is the essence of all of these sauces, make sure you use good garlic. The cloves should be firm, without a trace of yellowing, brown spots, or green sprouts. On the other hand, you might not want to use your best extra virgin olive oil, as its delicacy could be lost under all the garlic; just use a good everyday brand.

Homemade Mayonnaise

Good mayonnaise is simple to make at home, and understanding the technique is fundamental to other emulsion sauces as well. Making your own allows you to have as much or as little olive oil flavor as you like. With all the scare stories about salmonella in raw eggs—a greatly exaggerated risk in my view—I wonder how many people make their own these days. If you want to, here's how.

MAKES ABOUT 1¼ CUPS

2 egg yolks, at room temperature

½ teaspoon salt

Pinch of white pepper or cayenne

Pinch of dry mustard, OR ¼ teaspoon prepared mustard

1 cup oil (mild olive oil, neutral vegetable oil, or a blend)

3 tablespoons vinegar or lemon juice

➤ Combine the egg yolks and seasonings in a large stainless steel mixing bowl; set the bowl in a ring of twisted kitchen towel to hold it steady. Beat with a wire whisk until the mixture is pale yellow and foamy and increases noticeably in volume.

➤ Add a tablespoon of oil and whisk until it disappears into the egg. Repeat, and once the emulsion holds (when no oil seeps out if you stop whisking), drizzle in the oil in a slow stream as you beat. When about half the oil is beaten in, start alternating oil and vinegar. Taste the finished sauce for seasoning and refrigerate until ready to use.

VARIATION A food processor makes the job even easier, and many models are designed with an insert in the feed tube that dribbles in the oil at the right rate. Process the egg mixture with the steel blade until foamy, then add the oil in a thin stream with the motor running. You can also make aioli and various other emulsion sauces this way, although some claim they never taste the same as when blended by hand or in a mortar.

Aioli I (Provençal Garlic Sauce)

Sometimes called "the butter of Provence," aioli is the most direct expression of the oil and garlic genre. This version is bound with potato in place of the more common egg yolks, so it will not form as smooth or stable an emulsion as some. It is best made in a traditional mortar, but lacking a mortar, you can mash the garlic with the side of a knife. I don't recommend a food processor or blender for this sauce because the potato can turn gummy.

MAKES 2 CUPS

10 to 12 large cloves garlic, peeled

1 teaspoon salt

1 small potato (about 4 ounces), cooked, peeled, and mashed

Pinch of white pepper

1 to 1½ cups olive oil

Juice of 1 lemon

➤ Pound the garlic and salt together to a smooth paste in a mortar (or with the broad side of a knife on an impervious surface). Combine the garlic paste, potato, and pepper in the mortar or in a bowl and stir until thoroughly mixed.

➤ Add a spoonful of oil and beat until it is absorbed. Continue adding oil in small quantities, beating constantly, until the sauce forms a smooth emulsion. After about half the oil has been added, alternate oil and lemon juice. Continue until the sauce is nice and thick (not all the oil may be necessary). Taste and correct the seasoning.

Aioli II

This version uses egg yolks for the smoothest, most mayonnaise-like emulsion.

MAKES ABOUT 1 CUP

5 large cloves garlic, peeled

½ teaspoon salt

2 egg yolks

Pinch of white pepper

¾ to 1 cup olive oil

2 tablespoons lemon juice

➤ Pound the garlic and salt together to a smooth paste in a mortar (or mash with the broad side of a knife on an impervious surface). Scrape the contents of the mortar into a mixing bowl, add the egg yolks and pepper, and beat with a whisk to a paler shade of yellow.

➤ Add a spoonful of oil and beat until it is absorbed. Continue adding oil in small quantities, beating constantly, until the sauce forms a smooth emulsion. After about half the oil has been added, alternate oil and lemon juice. Continue until the sauce is nice and thick; taste and correct the seasoning.

VARIATIONS

Saffron Aioli Crumble saffron threads (a hefty pinch per cup of sauce) over the garlic and salt when pounding.

Basil Aioli Shred a small handful of basil leaves and pound with the garlic and salt.

Rouille (a variation with hot red pepper): see page 121.

Romesco I

This delicious orange-red sauce is the Catalán representative of the aioli family; it is one of my favorites for all kinds of hot and cold seafood. In this case, the binding agent is ground almonds, and the identifying flavor comes from dried sweet or slightly hot red pepper.

MAKES ABOUT ¾ CUP (8 TO 10 SERVINGS)

1 dried California or New Mexico chile, OR 2 *ñoras* (see note)

½ cup plus 2 tablespoons olive oil

1 medium onion, chopped

4 cloves garlic, 3 of them chopped

1 medium tomato, quartered

1 small red pepper or pimiento, seeded and sliced

½ cup blanched whole almonds

1 tablespoon vinegar

Salt and pepper, to taste

➤ Slit open the dried chile and remove the stem, seeds, and ribs. Cut or tear the chile into 4 or 5 pieces. Place it in a small saucepan with ¼ cup water, bring to a boil, and simmer until soft. Drain.

➤ Heat 2 tablespoons of the oil in a skillet and sauté the onion, chopped garlic, tomato, sweet pepper, and chile until fragrant. Cover and cook over low heat until the sweet pepper is quite soft. Uncover, turn up the heat, and cook until nearly dry. Purée the sauce through a food mill to remove the tomato and pepper skins.

➤ In a food processor, finely chop the almonds and the remaining clove of garlic. Add the vinegar and puréed sauce, and with the motor running, slowly drizzle in the remaining oil, as if making mayonnaise. Stop once or twice to scrape the corners of the bowl. Season the sauce to taste. If possible, let stand a few hours before serving. Refrigerate for longer storage.

NOTE In Spain, romesco would be made with a dried sweet pepper called *ñora*. I know of only one source of these peppers around here, The Spanish Table in Seattle (206-682-2827). Real aficionados can tell the difference between a sauce made with *ñoras* and one made with the slightly hotter California or New Mexico dried chiles, but to me they taste awfully close.

TECHNIQUE NOTE Although this recipe uses a food processor for the final blending, a food mill is still the best tool for making the red pepper purée. If you don't have one, force the mixture through a sieve, mashing well with the back of a spoon to get all the pulp through and leave the skins and any seeds behind.

Romesco II

This is a simpler version of romesco. The technique is unorthodox, but I like the results.

MAKES ½ CUP (4 TO 6 SERVINGS)

1 dried California or New Mexico chile, OR 2 *ñoras* (see note above)

⅓ cup olive oil

4 small cloves garlic, peeled

1½ ounces blanched whole or slivered almonds

¼ teaspoon salt

1 teaspoon vinegar

➤ Slit open the chile and remove the stem, seeds, and ribs. Cut or tear the chile into 4 or 5 pieces. Place it in a small bowl and barely cover with boiling water. Let steep at least 1 hour.

➤ Meanwhile, combine the oil and garlic in a small saucepan and simmer over the lowest possible heat until the garlic is soft and beginning to color, about 20 minutes. Remove from the heat and let cool.

➤ Lift the chile pieces out of the soaking water and place them on a plate, skin side down. With a teaspoon or the edge of a dull knife, carefully scrape all the soft pulp off the skin. Discard the skin.

➤ Combine the almonds, cooked garlic, pepper purée, salt, and vinegar in a food processor or blender (if using a blender, chop the almonds as finely as you can with a knife first). Blend, stopping to scrape down the sides, until the mixture is an even color. With the motor running, add the garlic-flavored oil in a slow trickle, as if making mayonnaise. Thin at the end with a teaspoon or so of the chile soaking water.

Pesto for Seafood

Without the usual cheese and pine nuts to thicken it, this is really closer to a vinaigrette than an emulsion sauce, and the oil separates rather quickly as it stands. It makes a tasty marinade and sauce for "summer fish" like white seabass or striped bass, and it's particularly good on salmon. You could also use a standard store-bought pesto, although most include cheese, and fish and cheese is a combination I don't much care for.

MAKES 4 SERVINGS

1 clove garlic

Salt

1 cup (loosely packed) basil leaves

3 tablespoons olive oil

Pepper

➤ Pound the garlic and a pinch of salt to a paste in a mortar. Tear the basil leaves into small pieces and pound them in until well blended. Stir in the oil and let the mixture stand a few minutes. The oil will separate; that's okay.

➤ Use half the pesto to marinate fish fillets to be grilled, broiled, or sautéed; season the fish first with pepper and a little more salt, if desired. Brush on more pesto just before serving.

NOTE A food processor or blender is not a very efficient tool for making a small amount of pesto. If you don't have a mortar and pestle, combine the garlic and salt on a nonporous surface and mash them together with the side of a knife blade until liquefied. Transfer them to a bowl, add the basil, chopped as finely as possible, and add the oil as above.

Mayonnaise-Plus Dipping Sauces

Here are three of my favorite ways of doctoring bottled mayonnaise as a dip for cold shellfish. Feel free to use a low-calorie version if you like. Each serves two. See also the wasabi mayonnaise in Seared Tuna Salad with Wasabi Mayonnaise, page 150.

Mustard and Horseradish Sauce

2 tablespoons mayonnaise

1 teaspoon Dijon-style mustard

½ teaspoon prepared horseradish

Lemon juice, to taste

Red Chile Sauce

2 tablespoons mayonnaise

¼ to ½ teaspoon Sriracha sauce, or a smaller amount of Chinese chile paste or Indonesian-style *sambal oelek*

Lemon juice or rice vinegar, to taste

Soy and Ginger Sauce

2 tablespoons mayonnaise

1 teaspoon soy sauce

2 teaspoons grated fresh ginger, with juice

1 teaspoon balsamic vinegar or Chinese black rice vinegar

Red Pepper and Garlic Mayonnaise

I like this sauce with tuna and other meaty, medium- to full-flavored fish. Red-ripe Anaheim chiles would be my first choice, followed by other long, sweet peppers such as Gypsy and Corno di Toro, but red bell peppers or pimientos work fine. If possible, roast and peel the peppers a day or two before making the sauce. As they sit in the refrigerator, they exude a thick, flavorful juice that is a crucial part of the sauce.

SERVES 4

½ pound sweet or mildly hot red peppers, roasted and peeled

2 tablespoons fine dry bread crumbs

3 cloves garlic, blanched until just tender, peeled

¼ teaspoon salt

2 tablespoons extra virgin olive oil

2 tablespoons mayonnaise

Hot pepper sauce, to taste (optional)

➤ Working over a bowl to catch the juices, slit open the peppers and remove the stems and seeds. Measure 2 tablespoons of the juice and combine it with the bread crumbs. (If there is not enough juice, reduce the amount of crumbs proportionally.) Let stand 5 minutes.

➤ Cut the peppers into manageable pieces. Combine with the garlic and salt in a large mortar and pound to a paste. Stir in the bread crumbs, then whisk in the oil. When the sauce is smooth, stir in the mayonnaise and correct the seasoning. Serve at room temperature.

TECHNIQUE NOTE The sauce can also be made in a food processor. Combine all the ingredients except the oil and process to a smooth paste, then add the oil gradually as if making mayonnaise.

Tartar Sauce

Everyone has a slightly different idea of tartar sauce, and most are far too sweet for my taste. I simply add a tablespoon or two of capers and an equal amount of dill pickle, both finely chopped, to a cup of mayonnaise. Add some minced onion if you like; rinsing the onion in a fine sieve after chopping will minimize the raw-onion bite, especially if the sauce is kept overnight.

Sauce Verte (Green Mayonnaise)

This and Salsa Verde (page 317) are really just two extremes of the same basic sauce. This milder version, made without the anchovy and garlic, is perhaps better suited to cold fish dishes. It's also a fine dip for cooked shrimp. Feel free to create anything in between the two to suit your taste.

MAKES A GENEROUS ½ CUP (4 TO 6 SERVINGS)

8 sprigs watercress

8 sprigs parsley

1 tablespoon chervil or tarragon leaves (optional)

4 spinach leaves

½ cup mayonnaise

Salt, pepper, and lemon juice, to taste

➤ Blanch the herbs and spinach separately in lightly salted boiling water; transfer to a strainer as soon as they wilt, and cool under running water. Drain thoroughly and purée together. Stir the purée into the mayonnaise and season to taste. Serve with cold or warm poached fish.

Basil Oil

Streaks of bright green basil oil drizzled over the food and onto the rim of the plate have become something of a cliché in restaurant cooking, and may even be hopelessly out of date by the time this book sees print. But it's still a great way for home cooks to finish a dish with the flavor and aroma of fresh basil. It's called for specifically in the Fish Fillets with Pasta and Summer Vegetables on page 129, but you may find yourself reaching for it for other dishes (try it on simply grilled salmon).

MAKES 1 CUP

Leaves from 1 bunch fresh basil

¾ cup mild olive oil

➤ Have a bowl of ice water handy; drop the basil leaves into boiling water for 30 seconds, then retrieve them and transfer them to the ice water to stop the cooking. Drain well, pat dry, and place in a blender with the oil. Blend to as fine a purée as possible (give it several minutes).

➤ Transfer the mixture to a covered jar and refrigerate overnight, then strain through several layers of cheesecloth. Return to the refrigerator overnight. If a lot of green sediment settles out of the oil, decant the clear portion into a new container. Store in the refrigerator and use within a month; the flavor is best in the first two weeks.

Butter Sauces

Despite the preponderance of olive oil sauces in the preceding pages, butter still has a place in my kitchen. A little butter can go a long way in carrying the flavors of herbs, citrus, and other seasonings to seafood, especially the leaner varieties of fish.

Beurre Blanc

This tart, creamy "white" butter sauce is at home with any lean to moderately rich fish. Melting butter in a highly acid reduction of wine and shallots keeps the butterfat and milk solids in a creamy suspension, and while it will not last as long as a true emulsified sauce like hollandaise, it will hold for several hours at a warm temperature. If it "breaks" (the clear butterfat separates), start another small batch with some of the reserved reduction and a little more cold butter and you should be able to rescue the broken sauce by slowly whisking it into the new one.

MAKES 1 CUP

¼ cup minced shallots
¼ cup dry white wine or vermouth
¼ cup fresh lemon juice or white wine vinegar
¼ pound cold butter

➤ Combine the shallots, wine, and lemon juice in a nonaluminum saucepan. Bring the mixture to a boil and reduce until the liquid is nearly gone and the mixture begins to darken. Do not let the reduction scorch. Meanwhile, cut the butter into small pieces.

➤ When the shallot mixture is fully reduced, remove the pan from the heat and let it cool slightly. Remove half of the reduction and reserve it for another batch of sauce. Add a piece or two of butter to the pan and stir steadily with a spoon or whisk until it melts. Return the pan to very gentle heat, add another piece of butter, stir, and continue adding the butter a bit at a time as the previous piece melts. (If the butter begins to separate, the heat is too high; remove the pan from the heat and beat until the butterfat is absorbed.)

➤ Continue adding butter until it is all incorporated and the sauce is a creamy yellow. Season to taste with a little salt and pepper if desired, although none is really necessary. Keep the sauce in the saucepan if using promptly, or in a water bath or an insulated container for longer keeping.

VARIATIONS

➤ Add a tablespoon of chopped herbs, especially herbs with an anise flavor like dill, fennel, tarragon, or chervil, to the finished sauce. Chives are also good.

➤ Add 2 tablespoons chopped ginger to the reduction; if the ginger is especially fibrous, you might want to strain the finished sauce.

Flavored Butters

Also known as compound butters, the following sauces are simply softened butter with other flavorings worked into it, ready to melt over a hot piece of fish. You can make these butters just before serving, but the flavor is usually better after several hours. For longer storage, make the butter in quantity, roll it into a cylinder, and store it tightly wrapped in the freezer, ready for you to cut off single-serving discs as needed.

The following proportions are for 4 ounces (1 stick) of butter, enough for 8 servings. The procedure is the same in all cases: Let the butter come to room temperature and beat it with a wooden spoon or electric mixer to a light consistency. Add the flavoring ingredients, chopped finely, and salt to taste, and beat until well blended. Set aside for 30 minutes to several hours to let the flavors develop; taste for seasoning before serving and adjust if necessary.

Maître d'Hôtel Butter

1 tablespoon shallots
2 tablespoons parsley
Zest of ½ lemon
Lemon juice to taste

➤ Good on just about any fish.

Ginger-Lime Butter

1 tablespoon grated fresh ginger, with its juice
Grated zest of ½ lime
Lime juice, to taste

➤ Serve with tuna, opah, yellowtail, and other flavorful fish.

Anchovy Butter

2 anchovy fillets, rinsed
1 blanched clove garlic
Generous pinch of pepper
Lemon juice, to taste

➤ My favorite butter sauce for swordfish.

Chile-Orange Butter

1 teaspoon ancho or New Mexico chile powder
2 teaspoons grated orange zest
Orange juice, to taste

➤ Good on rockfish, California halibut, and other fish with good texture but in need of a little flavor boost.

Dipping Sauces and Salsas

Not all sauces for fish contain oil or butter; here are a few of my favorites, to be spooned over fish and shellfish or set out in individual bowls for dipping.

Nuoc Cham

Clear, flavorful dips based on fish sauce are found all over Southeast Asia. This is the version from Vietnam, used with fresh spring rolls, lettuce-wrapped tidbits, and cold noodle dishes. It's equally good as a dip for grilled or broiled shrimp, or with simply cooked fish.

SERVES 2 TO 4

1 clove garlic

1 small red or green chile

3 tablespoons best-quality fish sauce

1 teaspoon lime or lemon juice or rice vinegar

1 teaspoon sugar

2 tablespoons hot water, or to taste

¼ teaspoon red chile paste or Sriracha sauce, or to taste

➤ Finely mince the garlic and chile, or pound them together in a mortar. In a small bowl or right in the mortar, combine with the fish sauce, lime juice, sugar, and hot water (the hot water both helps dissolve the sugar and releases some of the strong aroma of the fish sauce). Stir in chile paste or Sriracha to taste. Divide among individual dipping bowls.

Fresh Tomato Salsa

Salsa simply means sauce in Spanish (and Italian), but these days it usually implies a Mexican-style mixture of diced tomato and other ingredients, served raw or cooked as a dip or topping for other foods. Fish tacos are an obvious use for this kind of salsa, but it's equally at home on any grilled fish.

SERVES 2 TO 4

1 large or 2 small ripe tomatoes, OR ½ pound oval Roma tomatoes

Salt, to taste

1 small green chile (jalapeño or serrano)

1 good-sized green onion, minced

2 or 3 sprigs cilantro, chopped not too fine

Lime or lemon juice, to taste

➤ Split the tomato crosswise (lengthwise if using Romas). Holding a half in your palm, gently squeeze and shake out the seeds; discard the seeds. Cut the tomato into medium-fine dice and place it in a mixing bowl with a pinch of salt.

➤ Remove the stem end of the chile and split the chile lengthwise. For a milder salsa, carefully cut out the seeds and most of the white ribs; for a hotter flavor, leave them in. Mince the chile fine and add it to the tomato with the onion and cilantro. Toss to mix well, season to taste with lime juice and more salt if needed, and let stand a half hour or so before serving.

NOTE For this and the following recipe, you can peel the tomatoes as described on page 34, but I usually don't bother for a raw tomato salsa.

Herbed Tomato Salsa

Adding fresh herbs to a simple, chile-less tomato salsa opens up endless possibilities. While some blends can work, I prefer to choose a single herb and let it make a solo statement. Tarragon, with its slightly bitter, anise-tinged flavor, is a classic partner to fish in butter-based sauces, but it also goes quite well with uncooked tomatoes. Go ahead and use it in quantity, a couple of good sprigs for each tomato. Chervil, a delicate parsley-like herb with a touch of anise flavor, is not easy to find in the market, but if you grow your own or know someone who does, you can use it generously in place of tarragon.

Another obvious choice is basil; the combination of ripe tomatoes and fresh basil practically defines the taste of summer. In addition to the familiar large-leafed basil, try other varieties such as the purple-stemmed, anisey Thai basil or the appropriately named lemon basil. Or try basil's close cousin, spearmint. Again, if you want the herb to be the primary flavor in the sauce, use it in abundance, a couple of tablespoons of chopped leaves per tomato.

Some other herbs call for a lighter touch. A tablespoon or less of marjoram or oregano per tomato is sufficient to carry the sauce. Ditto for rosemary, which even in small quantities may be too much for fish. Peppermint also goes farther than other mints, to my taste.

With any of these herbs, you can include some chile if you want, or just a dash of hot pepper sauce. Grated or minced ginger takes it in an Asian direction. Don't add too many flavors, however, or they can lose their identity. You can also use yellow tomatoes in place of some or all of the tomato.

SERVES 2 TO 4

1 medium tomato, seeded and diced
Pinch of salt
1 to 2 tablespoons chopped fresh herbs

1 teaspoon fresh lemon or lime juice, or to taste
1 tablespoon minced green or yellow onion (optional)

➤ Combine the ingredients in a small bowl and set aside at least 15 minutes and up to 2 hours. Taste for seasoning and adjust if necessary.

Mignonette Sauce

Mignonette sauce is the ideal accompaniment to raw oysters, but it also makes a zero-fat dipping sauce for other seafoods. You can vary it with chopped herbs (see Steamed Salmon with Tarragon Mignonette, page 56), finely chopped tomato, or chile.

To make a mignonette for a dozen oysters, combine 1 tablespoon each of minced shallot and good wine vinegar (sherry vinegar is my favorite) and season to taste with freshly ground black pepper. If the mixture seems too tart, cut it with a tiny bit of water. A quarter to a half teaspoon of the mixture is about right for spooning on top of each oyster.

Stocks

A few basic stocks are the building blocks of many of the sauces in this book. It is possible to buy good canned or frozen stocks, but they are expensive, and none is hard to make at home. Only one takes more than a few hours, most of which is unattended simmering time.

These stocks will keep for several weeks in the refrigerator if brought to a boil every fourth or fifth day, but it's probably more convenient to freeze them. If freezer space is a problem, you can boil the strained stocks down to reduce their volume, and reconstitute them with water if you want to restore them to their original concentration (though you may find you prefer the more concentrated form).

Court-Bouillon for Fish

A court-bouillon is a flavored liquid for poaching fish, meats, or vegetables. Those used for fish typically contain some anise flavor; if you prefer, you can also use a small sprig of fresh tarragon in place of the anise seed. After poaching fish, strain and freeze the court-bouillon for future use; it picks up more body and flavor each time it is used.

MAKES ABOUT 1 QUART

1 quart water

1 cup dry white wine, OR ¼ cup white wine vinegar

½ onion, OR 2 green onions, sliced

2 or 3 sprigs fresh parsley

1 bay leaf

12 peppercorns, cracked

¼ teaspoon anise or fennel seed (optional)

➤ Combine all the ingredients in a saucepan (preferably not uncoated aluminum) and bring to a boil. Simmer 15 to 20 minutes and strain.

Fish Stock

Fish stock provides a more flavorful poaching liquid than court-bouillon, and when reduced and enriched with a little butter or cream, it makes a simple sauce. Flatfish,

especially larger ones like halibut, are ideal for fish stock. Other good candidates are lingcod or rockfish heads and frames (commonly sold in Chinese fish markets) and monkfish bones. Avoid darker-fleshed, oily fish like mackerel, which give too strong a flavor to stock. You can make a good stock out of salmon, but use it just for salmon.

MAKES 2 QUARTS

5 pounds heads, bones, and trimmings from lean fish

2 tablespoons butter or oil

1 cup diced onion

1 cup diced carrot

8 sprigs parsley

½ bay leaf

½ cup mushroom stems and trimmings (optional)

1 teaspoon white peppercorns

1½ cups inexpensive but drinkable dry white wine

➤ Wash the fish parts well, removing the gills and any trace of blood or organs. Chop them into manageable pieces and soak them in cold water to cover.

➤ Melt the butter in a large stockpot over low heat. Add the onion and carrot and cook, covered, until soft but not browned. Drain the fish parts and add them to the pot. Add the parsley, bay leaf, mushrooms, peppercorns, and wine and add water to cover (about 2 quarts).

➤ Bring just to a boil, reduce the heat to low, and simmer uncovered 30 minutes, skimming occasionally and not letting the stock boil. Strain through a fine sieve and refrigerate or freeze.

NOTE With most stocks, longer cooking with the bones produces a more flavorful stock, but with fish stock, 30 to 45 minutes is all it takes to extract the optimum flavor. Longer cooking may give the stock a bitter taste. If you want a more concentrated fish stock, strain it and then simmer it until it has reduced in volume.

Shrimp or Lobster Stock

The shells of shrimp and lobster contain a lot of flavor, and I always think twice before throwing them in the trash. More often, I save my shrimp shells in the freezer for the next time I am making a fish stock, gumbo, or jambalaya. However, if you have the carcasses of a couple of lobsters or a good-sized batch of shrimp shells and heads, you can to make a straight shellfish stock. (For some reason, crab doesn't really make much of a stock.)

MAKES ABOUT 1 QUART

Shells from 2 pounds lobster, OR shells and heads from 2 to 3 pounds shrimp

2 tablespoons oil

Water, or equal parts water and unsalted chicken or fish stock

➤ If using lobster, chop the shells, legs, and any contents of the bodies into small pieces with a heavy knife. Heat the oil in a medium saucepan, add the shells as well as any juices from the cutting board, and sauté over medium-low heat until the liquid is gone, about 10 minutes. Or combine the shells and oil in a shallow pan and bake in a 400°F oven for about 15 minutes.

➤ Add enough water and stock to the saucepan just to cover the shells, bring just to a boil, reduce the heat, and simmer 20 to 40 minutes. Strain and let settle for a few minutes, then skim off the oil and decant the strained stock off the cloudy sediment. Use or freeze within a day or so.

Chicken Stock

A good chicken stock is the basis of many seafood soups, pastas, and rice dishes, and if unsalted it can be reduced as necessary to give extra body and flavor to sauces. There are some good unsalted, canned stocks, sold mainly in health-food stores, but none of them can compare with a good homemade stock. Buying whole chickens and cutting them up yourself is by far the most economical way to buy chicken, and by using the backs, necks, wing tips, and other trimmings, you can make stock for a few pennies per cup. Save the spare parts in the freezer until you have enough to make a batch of stock.

MAKES ABOUT 2 QUARTS

2 to 4 pounds chicken parts—backs, necks, wings, giblets (but not livers), heads, feet

1 large onion, peeled and sliced, OR a large handful of leek or green onion tops

1 carrot, sliced

1 stalk celery, sliced

3 or 4 sprigs parsley

1 bay leaf

1 sprig thyme (optional)

1 teaspoon peppercorns

➤ Rinse the chicken parts well under cold water. If using backs, remove and discard the kidneys, the reddish organs along the backbone near the tail. Place the parts in a large pot with cold water to cover. Bring just to a boil and reduce to a simmer. Cook 10 minutes, skimming off the foam from the surface.

➤ Add the remaining ingredients and simmer uncovered for 1 to 3 hours. Do not let the stock boil or it will become cloudy. Strain the finished stock and refrigerate it until the fat solidifies on top, or for immediate use, skim off the fat with a ladle.

Brown Veal or Poultry Stock

A good brown stock based on beef, or preferably veal, bones is like money in the bank to a chef, and equally valuable to the home cook in search of concentrated flavor. Alone, or in combination with red wine, mushrooms, or other robust, earthy flavors more typically associated with meats and game, a brown veal stock can be a surprisingly harmonious addition to the sometimes delicate flavors of fish and shellfish. Sufficiently reduced, it also provides enough gelatin to give both richness and body to a sauce without the use of thickeners or added fats.

Making a batch of brown veal stock takes relatively little work, but many hours of simmering time, making it a good project for a rainy weekend. The modest investment of time to produce a gallon of stock can pay off many times over in the weeks or months that follow. Keep an eye out for specials on veal bones, especially breast of veal, a cut that provides some tasty meat in addition to the bones and cartilage that give richness to the stock. You can always freeze the bones until you are ready to make the stock.

If you don't feel like making it yourself, you can buy frozen veal stock in some well-stocked delis. The price

may seem steep at first, but it represents a fair amount of material and work, and it can be kept in the freezer and doled out in small portions as needed. A dish like Pan-Seared Halibut with Dried Mushroom Crust (page 100) uses 1 cup for four servings, a little over a dollar's worth at my neighborhood deli's price. Considering what it brings to the dish, it seems worth it to me.

Those who avoid red meat in general, or veal in particular, can make a good brown stock entirely from poultry bones. The initial browning stage may not take as long as with veal bones, and the total simmering time will be more like 4 hours, after which you should plan to reduce the strained stock by at least a third. In a pinch, a standard "white" chicken stock, reduced to a nearly syrupy thickness, can stand in for brown veal stock.

MAKES ABOUT 4 QUARTS

5 pounds veal bones (include some breast of veal if possible)

3 large onions, peeled and quartered

3 carrots, peeled and cut into 2-inch chunks

3 ribs celery, cut into 2-inch pieces

½ bottle dry red wine

2 bay leaves

1 sprig thyme

1 teaspoon whole peppercorns

➤ Have the butcher saw the bones crosswise into manageable pieces. If using breast of veal, have the ribs cut crosswise in half, then cut between the bones into roughly square sections.

➤ Place the bones and vegetables in a roasting pan and roast at 400° to 450°F, turning occasionally, until everything is nicely browned, about 30 to 40 minutes. Transfer the bones and vegetables to a large stockpot.

➤ Pour out any excess fat in the roasting pan and add the wine. Return the pan to the oven for a few minutes, then scrape up the browned drippings from the pan and add the wine and drippings to the stockpot. Add cold water to cover, bring to a boil, and skim off the foam that rises to the surface. Add the bay, thyme, and peppercorns, reduce the heat, and simmer, uncovered, adjusting the heat so the stock never boils, for 6 to 8 hours.

If you are using veal breast or another meaty cut, and you want to reserve the meat for another use, pull out those pieces after the first 2 or 3 hours, remove the meat, and return the bones and gristle to the pot.

➤ Strain the finished stock into containers of 2 quarts or less and refrigerate or freeze. Discard the fat from the top of the stock before using.

appendixes

Epilogue:

The Future of Fishing

Cod disappearing from Georges Bank. Pacific salmon on the endangered species list. Rockfish and lingcod quotas getting tighter. One might get the idea that we are running out of fish to catch, or will run out soon. Clearly aquaculture (see page 00) will become more important in years to come, but it is far from the whole story. Much of our seafood supply into the future will continue to come from the wild, and while some wild fisheries are in dire straits, there is some cause for optimism.

Much of the history of commercial fishing in the twentieth century has been characterized by too many boats chasing a diminishing number of fish—a prime example of what biologist Garrett Hardin, in a famous 1968 essay, called "the tragedy of the commons." Hardin's model is a pasture that belongs to no one, used by several herders to graze their cattle. Up to a point, more cattle can be added without overwhelming the pasture's ability to grow more grass. Once the carrying capacity is reached, each additional cow hurts everyone marginally, as their cattle find a little less food than they need. However, the herder who adds one more cow gets all the benefit from that cow. If everyone pursues his individual interest, the common is soon over-grazed and everyone suffers.

Until very recently, the oceans have been viewed as a commons, and an inexhaustible one

at that. An explosion of ocean fishing effort in the post–World War II era, with ever larger, wider-ranging, and more efficient fishing fleets, often subsidized by governments, led to declining catches of many species by the late 1960s. The early 1970s saw a major shift in international maritime law, as most nations acted to "fence in" their share of the commons, exerting exclusive economic rights extending 200 miles off their coasts. (The old standard had been 3 miles; not coincidentally, the 200-mile zones cover almost all of the continental shelves that constitute the world's productive fishing habitat.) But the fundamental problem remains. Locally or globally, when a valuable fishery is viewed as a common resource, it attracts more fishing effort until the amount of fish each boat can catch diminishes. Boat captains are then forced to fish harder (to catch a large enough share of the fish to pay for their own fuel, labor, and capital costs) or give up fishing and increase the unemployment rolls. The most dramatic recent example of this is the collapse of the New England cod and haddock fishery in the 1990s.

The New England cod crisis came about despite the efforts of government regulators to prevent it. Regulatory agencies have various tools at their disposal: fishing time restrictions, including seasonal closures, open and closed days and hours within seasons (e.g., daylight hours or weekdays only); geographic restrictions, designed to move the fishing effort around and in some cases to create no-fishing refuge zones; overall numeric quotas on the catch, sometimes linked to time periods designed to spread the catch out over the

335

season; limited entry (requiring specific permits to participate in a given fishery, and limiting the number of those permits); and gear limitations, such as minimum mesh size for nets to allow smaller fish to escape. Most management plans combine several of these methods.

One of the newer forms of management, individual quotas, takes the total quota and divides it among the permitted boats, and allows each boat owner to decide when and where to fish (within the season and other rules of the fishery) to catch his quota. If the quotas are transferable, boat owners who choose not to or are unable to catch their full quota can sell all or part of it to more active permit holders. Some have criticized limited-entry and individual quota systems as "privatizing" a "public" resource; on the other hand, when fishermen own the resource, they are perhaps more likely to be good stewards. The north Pacific halibut fishery, formerly a series of very short "fishing derby" seasons, switched to individual quotas beginning in 1991, and the new system seems to be working at least as well as the old.

All the best efforts and intentions of regulators are limited by one basic fact: we simply don't know how many fish are out there, and how much fishing they can stand. Regulators use sophisticated mathematical models to estimate the size of fish populations and calculate the maximum sustainable yield (the rate at which caught fish can be replaced by the reproductive capacity of the remaining population), but the basic population numbers on which these calculations depend are inferred from a limited amount of hard data. The most concrete indicator of population trends is catch data, which tend to show up problems after the population has already declined.

What can the individual consumer do? First, become familiar with more varieties of fish, and be open to trying new ones as they appear. This both reduces pressure on the familiar species and reduces the amount of non-target fish or "bycatch" that is wasted. If consumers always insist on the same half dozen varieties, fishermen will continue to target those fish because that's where the money is. The same goes for retailers; if your fishmonger goes to the trouble to obtain oddball fish like skate wings, fresh anchovies, or wolffish and then can't sell them, who can blame him if he goes back to the same old varieties tomorrow?

Second, become a more informed consumer; look beyond the headlines for the whole story. Yes, many stocks of salmon are in steep decline, but others are in robust health. When a group of chefs announced a "give swordfish a break" boycott in 1998, designed to take pressure off certain overfished Atlantic stocks, the fact that Pacific swordfish were in good supply was buried deep in most stories, if mentioned at all. The next time an environmental group announces a "save the tribbles—don't eat owl-fish" campaign, find out just which varieties or methods of catching owlfish are involved and which are not, so you don't punish those who are catching owlfish in environmentally responsible ways.

Third, support scientifically sound, sustainable fisheries management. Fishery management is ultimately a political process, balancing the often competing interests of commercial and sport fishermen, processors, scientists, environmentalists, and the general public. Fishermen will always try to maximize their profit, and recreational anglers their share of the resource. Government has a major role in authorizing and funding basic research on fish populations, evaluating available information, setting harvest guidelines, and allocating limited resources. I believe we all have a stake in more and better research and catch quotas that err on the conservative side. If you agree, let your elected representatives know how you feel.

Finally, realize that fish and shellfish do not exist in isolation. Support vigorous clean-water and clean-air legislation and enforcement, not just for the sake of the oceans, but for the health of the rivers and estuaries on which most marine life depends for at least part of its life cycle.

Appendix:

Down on the Fish Farm

Aquaculture, or farming of fish and shellfish, has been touted for decades as the food source of the future. But aquaculture is not just fish pie in the sky; it's here and now, and it has already transformed the national and global seafood market. Roughly half of the recipes in this book are for fish and shellfish that are available as cultured products, many exclusively so.

Aquaculture is essential to our future supply of seafood because most "capture fisheries" are already operating at or beyond their sustainable capacity. Most of the growth in global supply of fish and shellfish will have to come from aquaculture rather than from fishing. Some observers, like chef Elka Gilmore, see a "moral imperative" in producing more of our own food supply rather than gathering it all from the wild: "It's simply more appropriate to farm our food than it is to hunt for it."

Global issues aside, the biggest advantage of aquaculture can be summed up in one word: consistency. As much as is possible in agriculture, aquaculture promises a predictable supply of product at a predictable quality level. How that quality relates to the wild product remains debatable. Some buyers don't like the flavor of farmed fish as much as wild; others prefer it. There is also some perception of wild seafood as a more "natural" product. However, for chefs, retailers, food-service managers, and a growing number of home cooks, being able to count on finding a given fish or shellfish in a given size on any given day counts for at least as much as flavor.

THE AQUACULTURE PROCESS

Details of aquaculture processes vary from one species to the next, but overall they follow a basic pattern. The first step in the aquaculture process is to choose the species of fish or shellfish to farm. It must be one that grows rapidly; has a market value that will allow the return to the farmer to exceed the cost of production; and is able to withstand confinement without cannibalism, physical stress, or disease.

Next, the farmer must provide a manageable environment, to contain the livestock. The obvious requirement is clean water, of the appropriate temperature and salinity required by each species. The containment structure depends on the species. Oysters and clams may simply be spread on the bottom of a bay, or enclosed in wire-mesh bags to keep out predators. Shrimp are mainly raised in diked ponds in coastal areas. Catfish farmers use diked fields flooded with well water, and trout farmers use concrete raceways with water diverted from a nearby river. Other forms of farming use enclosures suspended in the water, from the net pens used to raise salmon to strings of lantern-shaped cages for scallops and nylon mesh bags suspended from rafts for mussels. The most intensive form of aquaculture creates a totally artificial environment, such as the solar-heated tank farms in the Southern California desert that grow tilapia under tented domes, filtering and reusing their water in a closed system that grows supplemental feed from the fishes' waste.

Finding a site for a farm is not just a matter of finding land and water. Tidelands in some areas are leased from the state, and farms must be balanced with other uses of waterways. Would-be salmon farmers in a Northwestern bay may find themselves opposed by environmentalists, fishermen, pleasure boaters, and shoreside residents who don't want to look across at another pier or a raft of net pens.

The next step is stocking the farm. A few forms of aquaculture rely on capturing wild larvae or juvenile animals; one way to grow mussels is simply to provide a suitable place for free-swimming larvae to attach themselves, and some coastal shrimp farms are flooded with seawater when naturally occurring shrimp larvae

are at their most abundant. However, more intensive aquaculture requires stocking a farm with young fish or larvae ("seed" in shellfish farming) from hatcheries. The breeding stock may be adults captured from the wild, especially at first, but captive-born stock provides more predictable results. Hatchery operations are often as complicated and difficult as the growout phase, or more so, and may require large-scale cultivation of algae or other feed organisms.

Feeding requirements depend on the species grown. Bivalves (clams, oysters, mussels) filter food out of the water, and require nothing more than being situated where there is food available. Herbivores like carp and certain shrimp can live on the algae in the water, the growth of which can be stimulated by adding plant nutrients. Most of the more valuable species, however, require substantial inputs of feed. Catfish, most shrimp, trout, and tilapia can get by on a diet mainly based on grains and soybeans, but grow better and faster with higher protein and higher fat (especially in the form of high-fat fish meal). Predatory fish like salmon require a high-protein, high-fat diet, and fish meal and oil make up the bulk of processed salmon feed. Much of the dramatic progress in the efficiency of fish farming, especially of salmon, has come from fine-tuning the feed formulas so the fish digest as close as possible to 100 percent of the nutrients in the feed.

In open-water systems, feces and other waste products are borne away by currents, where they add nutrients to the food chain. Tank farms and other intensive systems rely on filters, especially biofilters containing bacteria that break down wastes into relatively benign compounds. A few farms combine fish farming and hydroponics, using the nitrates and other components of fish waste to nourish vegetables and herbs grown on top of the tanks.

Diseases are a major concern in aquaculture, as animals are typically grown in high density, and water provides an ideal medium through which bacteria and viruses can spread. The history of aquaculture is full of examples of large-scale failures due to disease, especially in Asian shrimp farming. Despite a popular perception that farmed fish are full of antibiotics added to the feed, actual antibiotic use is rare and highly regulated. (In fish as in people, antibiotics work only on bacteria, and are useless against the viruses that cause most disease problems. Vaccinating individual fish at a young age is much more effective with viruses.)

Predator control is another problem. Double nets and other physical barriers are sometimes necessary to keep sea lions out of salmon cages and diving ducks from stripping mussel ropes. The pillow-shaped wire bags favored by oyster farmers not only keep track of the oysters, they keep them safe from starfish and other predators. Catfish farmers use various methods to deter cormorants, herons, and other fish-eating birds, from noisemakers and reflectors to scare the birds to wires strung across the ponds to make diving difficult.

When fish or shellfish reach an appropriate size, they may be harvested by various methods, from dipping out salmon one at a time to dragging a net through a fish pond to draining a whole shrimp pond. For many species, withholding feed for a period of time before harvest, or transferring the fish to a food-free "finishing" tank, allows them to be shipped with their digestive systems empty, which can improve shelf life and flavor.

Processing ranges from doing nothing (delivering the fish alive to a retailer's or wholesaler's tank) to killing the fish (sometimes by rapid chilling) and shipping them round to on-site dressing, pan-dressing, filleting, packaging, and freezing operations. Marketing may be directly from the farm, or through usual wholesale and retail channels.

Economically, aquaculture is at least as risky as any other form of food production. Startup costs can be high, especially for intensive aquaculture operations (those that involve a lot of inputs in facilities, energy, and feed). Lots of species that looked promising in the laboratory have never proven economically viable to farm, even high-value species like lobster.

As the technology for established species matures, it usually grows more efficient; witness the steady drop in the price of farmed salmon relative to wild. However, there is usually a floor below which the cost of farmed fish cannot go, and it's often higher than that of similar wild fish. There is also a maximum price that consumers will pay for a given fish, and sometimes the two curves get dangerously close. Catfish farmers felt the squeeze several times in the 1980s and '90s when supply got ahead of demand and prices didn't cover the cost of feed and harvesting. In the early 1990s, we saw a lot of small Canadian salmon in the market because in the face of competition from cheap farmed Chilean salmon, it didn't pay the farmers to grow them any bigger.

Many forms of aquaculture have been criticized on environmental grounds. Of course, one cannot grow any crop or raise any livestock without altering the environment, whether it's turning prairies into wheat fields or grazing sheep in the hills. A typical salmon farm with its array of net pens has been compared to a cattle feedlot, and it certainly deposits additional wastes in the water. Farmers say these wastes are dispersed by currents and simply become part of the food chain, and that if you pulled out the pens or towed them to a new site, there would soon be no evidence that the farm ever existed. Other forms of aquaculture make more lasting changes; much of the early history of tropical shrimp aquaculture involved conversion of mangrove forests to shrimp ponds, but most shrimp-producing countries have stopped new destruction of mangrove habitat and are attempting to restore at least some of the damage.

What does the future hold for aquaculture and our seafood supply? Undoubtedly more species will be added to the selection. Not every fish and shellfish can be cultured (but name an edible species and there's probably a commercial or academic laboratory somewhere working on its culture). Some, like salmon and clams, have already reached commodity status, though individual producers will continue to try to establish brand-name loyalty. Luxury varieties like abalone will likely remain luxuries, but some glamour species like European turbot could become much more affordable. Even West Coast sablefish, a slow-growing fish in nature, has shown surprisingly fast growth in experimental farming in Canada.

A major question for the future of aquaculture is where the feed will come from. Fish meal, and particularly fish oil, is the critical ingredient in feed for many of the most valuable farmed fish varieties. The main source of fish meal and oil is "industrial" fisheries for low-value fish like anchoveta and menhaden, but most of these are already being fished at their maximum sustainable rates. Some meal and oil can be recovered from byproducts of wild fish processing, but the total supply will always be limited, and fish farmers must compete with poultry farmers and other users of fish oil.

In the long run, the growth of aquaculture may require moving down the food chain a notch, relying more on legume-based proteins and oils to supply the necessary nutrients in fish feed. No doubt the genetic engineers will get involved, grafting omega-3-producing genes from marine plankton into soybean or lentil DNA. These transgenic experiments will bring up their own concerns, keeping aquaculture one of the more interesting subjects to watch into the twenty-first century.

Bibliography

Bayless, Rick, and Deann Groen Bayless. *Authentic Mexican.* New York: Morrow, 1987.

Beard, James. *James Beard's New Fish Cookery.* Boston: Little, Brown, 1976.

Bell, Frederic W. *Food from the Sea: The Ecnomics and Politics of Ocean Fisheries.* Boulder, CO: Westview Press, 1978.

Boni, Ada. *Italian Regional Cooking.* New York: Dutton, 1969.

Brennan, Dick and Ella. *The Commander's Palace New Orleans Cookbook.* New York: Clarkson N. Potter, 1984.

Brown, Helen Evans. *Helen Brown's West Coast Cookbook.* Boston: Little, Brown, 1952.

Bugialli, Giuliano. *Bugialli on Pasta.* New York: Simon and Schuster, 1988.

Cone, Joseph. *A Common Fate: Endangered Salmon and the People of the Pacific Northwest.* New York: Henry Holt, 1995.

Cronin, Isaac. *The International Squid Cookbook.* Berkeley: Aris Books, 1981.

_____, Jay Harlow, and Paul Johnson. *The California Seafood Cookbook.* Berkeley: Aris Books, 1983.

Davidson, Alan. *Mediterranean Seafood,* 2nd ed. Baton Rouge: Louisiana State University Press, 1981.

_____. *North Atlantic Seafood.* New York: Viking, 1980.

_____. *Seafood: A Connoisseur's Guide and Cookbook.* New York: Simon and Schuster, 1989.

Del Conte, Anna. *Gastronomy of Italy.* New York: Prentice Hall, 1987.

Dore, Ian, and Claus Frimodt. *An Illustrated Guide to Shrimp of the World.* Huntington, NY: Osprey Books, 1987.

Eschmeyer, William N., and Earl S. Herald. *A Field Guide to Pacific Coast Fishes of North America* (Peterson Field Guide Series, vol. 28). Boston: Houghton Mifflin, 1983.

Exler, Jacob, and John L. Weihrauch. *Provisional Table on the Content of Omega-3 Fatty Acids and Other Fat Components of Selected Foods.* Human Nutrition Information Service, U.S. Department of Agriculture, 1985.

Foulke, Judith E. "Mercury in Fish: Cause for Concern?" *FDA Consumer,* September 1994.

Goldstein, Joyce. *The Mediterranean Kitchen.* New York: Morrow, 1989.

Gunter, Gordon. "Painless Killing of Crabs and Other Large Crustaceans." *Science* 131, 327 (1961).

Hardin, Garrett. "The Tragedy of the Commons." *Science* 162, 123–142 (1968).

Hom, Ken. *Ken Hom's East Meets West Cuisine.* New York: Simon and Schuster, 1987.

Kasper, Lynne Rossetto. *The Splendid Table.* New York: Morrow, 1992.

Kump, Christopher, and Margaret Fox with Marina Bear. *Evening Food: Cafe Beaujolais.* Berkeley: Ten Speed Press, 1998.

McClane, A. J. *The Encyclopedia of Fish Cookery.* New York: Holt, Reinhart and Winston, 1977.

McGee, Harold. *On Food and Cooking.* New York: Scribner's, 1984.

Middione, Carlo. *The Food of Southern Italy.* New York: Morrow, 1987.

Montagné, Prosper (Marion Hunter, trans.). *The New Larousse Gastronomique.* New York: Crown, 1977.

Nehlsen, Willa, Jack E. Williams, and James A. Lichatowich. "Pacific Salmon at the Crossroads: Stocks at Risk from California, Oregon, Idaho, and Washington." *Fisheries* 16:2, 4–21 (Mar.–Apr. 1991).

Page, Lawrence M., and Brooks M. Burr. *A Field Guide to Freshwater Fishes of North America North of Mexico* (Peterson Field Guide Series, vol. 42). Boston: Houghton Mifflin, 1991.

Parenti, Giovanni Righi. *La Grande Cucina Toscana.* 2 vols. Milan: SugarCo, 1976.

Prudhomme, Paul. *Chef Paul Prudhomme's Louisiana Kitchen*. New York: Morrow, 1984.

Radovich, John. *How to Catch, Bone and Cook a Shad*. Sacramento: California Department of Fish and Game, n.d.

Robins, C. Richard, et al. *A List of Common and Scientific Names of Fishes from the United States and Canada*, 4th ed. Bethesda, MD: American Fisheries Society, 1980.

———, and G. Carleton May. *A Field Guide to Atlantic Coast Fishes of North America* (Peterson Field Guide Series, vol. 32). Boston: Houghton Mifflin, 1986.

Smith, Gerald R., and Ralph F. Stearley. "The Classification and Scientific Names of Rainbow and Cutthroat Trouts." *Fisheries* 14:1, 4–10 (Jan.–Feb. 1989).

Tower, Jeremiah. *New American Classics*. New York: Harper & Row, 1986.

Tropp, Barbara. *China Moon Cookbook*. New York: Workman, 1992.

———. *The Modern Art of Chinese Cooking*. New York: Morrow, 1982.

Tsuji, Shizuo. *Japanese Cooking: A Simple Art*. Tokyo and New York: Kodansha International, 1980.

Turgeon, Donna S., et al. *Common and Scientific Names of Aquatic Invertebrates from the United States and Canada: Mollusks* (Special Publication 26), 2nd ed. Bethesda, MD: American Fisheries Society, 1998.

Wieland, Robert. *Why People Catch Too Many Fish: A Discussion of Fishing and Economic Incentives*. Washington: Center for Marine Conservation, 1992.

Williams, A. B., et al. *Common and Scientific Names of Aquatic Invertebrates from the United States and Canada: Decapod Crustaceans* (Special Publication 17). Bethesda, MD: American Fisheries Society, 1988.

Williams, Lawrence, and Karen Warner. *Oysters: A Connoisseur's Guide and Cookbook*. San Francisco: 101 Productions, 1987.

Wolfert, Paula. *Couscous and Other Good Food from Morocco*. New York: Harper & Row, 1973.

———. *Paula Wolfert's World of Food*. New York: Harper & Row, 1988.

index

Index

N–O

Q–R

X–Z